Asian Americans in Michigan

GREAT LAKES BOOKS

A complete listing of the books in this series
can be found online at wsupress.wayne.edu

Editor

Charles K. Hyde, Wayne State University

Advisory Editors

Jeffrey Abt, Wayne State University

Fredric C. Bohm, Michigan State University

Sandra Sageser Clark, Michigan Historical Center

Brian Leigh Dunnigan, Clements Library

De Witt Dykes, Oakland University

Joe Grimm, Michigan State University

Richard H. Harms, Calvin College

Laurie Harris, Pleasant Ridge, Michigan

Thomas Klug, Marygrove College

Susan Higman Larsen, Detroit Institute of Arts

Philip P. Mason, Prescott, Arizona and Eagle Harbor, Michigan

Dennis Moore, Consulate General of Canada

Erik C. Nordberg, Michigan Humanities Council

Deborah Smith Pollard, University of Michigan–Dearborn

Michael O. Smith, Wayne State University

Joseph M. Turrini, Wayne State University

Arthur M. Woodford, Harsens Island, Michigan

ASIAN AMERICANS IN MICHIGAN

Voices from the Midwest

Edited by Sook Wilkinson and Victor Jew

With a Foreword by Frank H. Wu and an Afterword by Bich Minh Nguyen

WAYNE STATE UNIVERSITY PRESS

DETROIT

19 18 17 16 15   5 4 3 2 1

Library of Congress Control Number: 2014947713

ISBN 978-0-8143-3281-8 (paperback)
ISBN 978-0-8143-3974-9 (ebook)

Grateful acknowledgment is made to Wilkinson Foundation
for generously supporting the publication of this volume.

Designed and typeset by Bryce Schimanski
Composed in Chapparal Pro and Trade Gothic

CONTENTS

FOREWORD

I wish I could have read this book when I was growing up in the Detroit metropolitan area in the 1970s. I had no idea that other Asian Americans even existed, never mind having any conception of what it meant to be a member of such a community. Ironically, the very term *Asian American* probably would have seemed alien to my family and paradoxical to everyone else around us.

I recognized well enough that our family was different from the other families on the street. We were expected to be the same, just as the houses in our subdivision repeated three floor plans over and over with but a few minor differences in the facades. From the cruelties of children, the teasing and the taunting, I realized that there was something wrong with straight black hair, almond-shaped eyes, and yellow skin. I was always vaguely embarrassed—by myself, my parents, our ancestors, Bruce Lee, Charlie Chan, Suzie Wong, and those others who, like us, were not appropriately all-American and accordingly assaulted by the random ching-chong chanting of strangers.

We were comically in the wrong place and the wrong time. You would expect to see us if you journeyed as a tourist to the other side of the globe or if you read an exotic account of an ancient civilization.

My parents were immigrants from Asia. Like so many others before them of all backgrounds, they had decided to stay in this land of freedom and opportunity. My father could scarcely have imagined anything better professionally than to land a job in Detroit, a place that represented progress based on industry, where the moving assembly line was invented and modern manufacturing was perfected. The state of Michigan as a whole offered culture of all types, sports in the major leagues, and outdoor recreation of every form.

Then the events in Detroit of 1967, variously called a "riot" or a "rebellion," permanently altered the landscape as businesses and homes burned, four dozen people were killed, a curfew was imposed, and tanks rolled down the city's major thoroughfares. The damage done, it took Detroit's baseball team, the Tigers, to restore calm and generate hope by winning the hard-fought 1968 World Series. The mythology of the region has since harkened back to 1967 as the crucial moment of the city's racial history. Although the violence of those days ostensibly began when police broke up an after-hours celebration for African American veterans returning from the Vietnam War, the flight from the city core had begun as soon as highways crossed Eight Mile Road.

The area would shortly become the toughest in the United States to be an Asian American because of its dependence on a single industry—automobiles—that was vital to the sense of national identity yet challenged as no other by global competitors. With the oil embargo and energy crisis of the 1970s that highlighted the vulnerability of a superpower, imported Japanese cars were no longer deemed inferior because of their origin and instead came to be regarded as superior because of their efficiency. They may have had names that were difficult to pronounce, but it was no longer embarrassing to park one in the driveway. But as the American V-8 ceased to be an icon of upward mobility and became a symbol of gas-guzzling excess, to have an "Oriental" face gave one the look of the enemy in the economic war. The theme of Yellow Peril was revived: Asian Americans symbolized the rise of the East and the decline of the West. Others demanded to know which "side" we were on, unaware that we suffered the same anxieties they did about the course of our country. No distinction was made between Asians and Asian Americans or between products and people. "Jap" was used casually to refer both to "Jap" crap and to Asian Americans, with people dismissing objections with "Remember Pearl Harbor!" and the claim that the slur was only an abbreviation.

Our neighbors were almost all of European extraction. They had assimilated so thoroughly that they had no discernible ethnicity, or so we supposed. They identified themselves as Americans, not by the nationalities their forebears claimed. Unlike my family, they simply seemed to belong. They were comfortable with the unwritten rules of social interaction, and they were casual in their encounters with each other. It seemed to us that they were all friends. Of course I, having grown up among them, could relax in their company, and I did make new friends here and there—but I could not help but be aware that my friends' parents were not and would never be my parents' friends.

For my parents, who recalled a different homeland than the one their children were born into, it could not have been easy to leave everything familiar behind, however necessary it may have been to their attainment of the American dream. Their children could insist that all they wanted was to be "Americans," but to no avail. My parents called native-born white Americans "foreigners." They called black people "black people" in a matter-of-fact manner. Both Jews and stereotypes of Jews were unknown to us. We were largely ignorant of Arab immigrants, Christian or Muslim, other than as the proprietors of small businesses, and of the Mexican migrant workers who had long ensured that Michigan was as productive in agriculture as in manufacturing, working the fields of corn, soybeans, and cherries.

My brothers and I were both the same as and different from our classmates. Even to a child who wanted to be like every other child, without the need to assimilate, it seemed somehow an impossible task, the constant demand to imitate our social betters. We wanted to be just like them, wearing popular sneakers, eating meatloaf, hanging out after dark, and watching cartoons on Saturday morning. We could not help being always conscious that we were different from them, wearing home-sewn clothes and hand-me-downs, using chopsticks to eat meals that looked disgusting to our peers, doing extra homework instead of playing outside, and attending Chinese school on the weekends.

We could be just as angry at the strangers who mocked our parents for their accents as we were angry with our parents for possessing those accents. It mattered not that our parents wrote with textbook grammar in an elegant script, nor that they had earned advanced degrees with honors. They could not control their circumstances, as we expected adults to do. Neither our parents nor we knew the language of civil rights, for our parents literally spoke another language and we had no teachers in the art of protest.

Books such as this volume did not exist. Studies of race omitted Asian Americans no matter how learned or progressive the authors purported to be. The absence suggested that Asian Americans did not exist. And, in a sense, "Asian Americans" did not. Certainly, there were people of Asian ancestry in Michigan, some whose forebears had arrived in the United States during the nineteenth century. There were, for instance, Chinese sojourners (as there were European sojourners), men who worked jobs in America and sent money home to their families in China. They were independent and transnational in an age before mass air travel made it easy to imagine repeated oceanic crossings and modern communications allowed intimacy to flourish over such distances. Their children came to these shores, departed, and came again.

Yet they likely would not have identified themselves as "Asian Americans," implying any sense of unity among Asians of different nationality. Their ancestors had hated one another. The only pan-Asian movements overseas embodied the extremes of idealism or imperialism. Nor would non-Asians have applied such a respectful term. No, the immigrant generation as a whole was distinctly Chinese, Korean, Japanese, Filipino, Indian, and so on. Or, with a finer gradation of ethnicity and no less pride, immigrants were from Canton, Toisan, Fukien. They identified themselves by province, village, and clan, and they were no less suspicious of the stranger from the nearby county than the one from afar.

"You all look alike," they would be told by observers who claimed to be confused. "You speak English so well," they would be complimented in sincerity.

Unlike New York, Los Angeles, and San Francisco, Detroit had no physical center for a shared daily life—no Chinatown, Japantown, or Little Manila. There was a Chinatown in Detroit, but it was destroyed to build a freeway. Its successor, an area consisting primarily of restaurants catering to a non-Asian trade, was overwhelmed by the urban decay for which the Motor City became the paradigmatic example.

Japanese Americans, by and large, arrived after World War II. Leaving the internment camps where they had been locked up because of unfounded suspicions about their loyalty, they were forced to disperse into the heartland. But even after 1965, when legal reforms opened America's borders to people from across the Pacific as the nation had earlier to those from across the Atlantic, relatively few Asian Americans came to the Great Lakes State. There were a few South Asian and Filipino professionals, including doctors and nurses; a few Southeast Asian refugees, some sponsored by churches; and a few adoptees, girls and boys from orphanages. They were no more than a few.

Consequently, Asian American families were physically distant, cousins socially isolated. Their alienated situation meant that each person was alone in his or her familiarity with prejudice. There was no community awareness of the phenomenon. Non-Asian Americans may have been surprised to encounter us; Asian Americans were no more accustomed to the sight of others who looked like themselves.

Thus, Asian Americans have been figures in the background of Michigan history. Perhaps their role is personified by the anonymous Ford engineer depicted in the Diego Rivera mural *Detroit Industry* at the Detroit Institute of Arts. He is nameless, identified only by employer and occupation. His features are discernibly Asian, and it is fair to infer he is an archetype. In this painting, unveiled amid controversy during the Great Depression but subsequently recognized as a masterpiece, Rivera intended to depict racial representatives. According to the oral history of the Japanese American community, the engineer is based on a man named James Hirata. This is likely true, for other people Rivera depicted are real, and many have been identified. In fact, company archives do contain photographs of one Mr. Hirata from the appropriate era. Ford also recruited Chinese workers from Hawaii, with the notion that they would eventually help the company expand into China.

Michigan's Asian Americans have often been overlooked because of the tendency to categorize by black and white. There are many divisions in the state of Michigan, and the separation of blacks and whites is only the most visible. There also are the indelible differences between the Lower and Upper peninsulas, the state's eastern and the western halves, the urban centers and the rural counties, and labor and management. These dichotomies make it more difficult to identify the figurative in-between spaces. Asian immigrants and their American-born descendants, Asian children with white parents, and Asians of mixed bloodlines are ambiguous. Their diversity defies established categories.

We are compelled, then, to write this book. We learn ourselves, even as we teach others, in doing so. It is not surprising that Asian Americans turn into Asian Americans through a course of study. After all, Asian Americans have valued education as the means of advancement—that much is not doubted. But we study more than business, medicine, science, or engineering. We educate ourselves about our history and our future as Asian Americans. We meet others who, it turns out, have plagiarized our story. We read about episodes that are dismissed as trivial by those who have not had similar experiences, even though these stories explain so much about our condition.

In this book we record the multiple means of becoming Asian American, participating in the great democratic experiment. Now we reveal that each of us has our own unique set of experiences, but we have universal memories as well. Communities depend on shared stories. Individuals are assured they have not imagined everything. We are not alone as Asian Americans, any more than we are all the same. We are able to attach a face to an abstract theme: here is our friend, who exemplifies chain migration; there is our other friend, who personifies entrepreneurial success.

It is important to emphasize the optimism of the endeavor. This project is positive, a list of ambitions and accomplishments, not negative, a catalogue of wrongs and slights. The opportunity is offered to us to declare who we are and who we wish to become on our own terms rather than through stereotypes. It is an American yearning for self-invention, consistent with our national mythology and belief in our own exceptionalism. Others before us and alongside us have had the same aspiration, whether they were Irish, Polish, Italian, or German. In the New World, we are allowed to declare our destinies. Race does not control any of us, and neither does gender. Nor do the traditions that forced our forebears to depart for a better future, such as primogeniture, the division of the family wealth on the basis of birth order. A woman can be educated, a third son may make his fortune, and their children will dream further.

Thus we claim a birthright of equality. It has become possible, finally, to explain what it means to be Asian and American in Middle America because it has become necessary to map out the profound transformation in our common conception of what it means to be a citizen.

Frank H. Wu

PREFACE

Sook Wilkinson

This book is dedicated to the memory of Vincent Chin.

The year 2012 marked the thirtieth anniversary of the racially motivated killing of Chin, which occurred during a time of economic recession in the Detroit automobile industry. Chin, a Chinese American, was mistaken for Japanese by two autoworkers who brutally clubbed him to death as retribution for their economic misfortunes. They served not one day of jail. This case prompted outrage from many Asian Americans in and outside Michigan and sparked awareness of the dangers of nationalism. It united many Asian Americans who learned the importance of speaking up, becoming better known in their communities.

This book tells the story of Asian Americans in Michigan—our cultures, our hopes, and our life journeys. An intimate glimpse into our communities, schools, workplaces, homes, and our lives helps you discover our most cherished moments as Asian Americans. The stories are told from a range of perspectives, including first-generation immigrants, those born in the United States, and third- and fourth-generation Americans of Asian heritage. The Asian Americans featured in the book trace their ancestries back to East Asia (China, Japan, Korea, Taiwan), South Asia (Bangladesh, India, Pakistan), and Southeast Asia (Cambodia, Laos, Philippines, Thailand, Vietnam, and the Hmong).

The significant contributions made by many Asian Americans in Michigan are palpable in various fields—the arts, education, science, engineering, business, religion, journalism, medicine, politics, sports, and others. In addition, nonprofit organizations in the community play tremendous roles in bringing different ethnic groups and their heritage together. For example, American Citizens for Justice (ACJ), created in 1983 after the killing of Vincent Chin, fights for the civil rights of all Americans to prevent similar injustices. The Council of Asian Pacific Americans (CAPA), created in 2000, was the first grassroots pan-Asian organization. Its primary goal is to celebrate the Asian Pacific American Heritage Month of May with dazzling cultural performances showcasing the diverse heritage and history of so many talented Asian Americans. CAPA's mission is "to unite Asian Pacific Americans and the community at large through culture, education, and community service." The Asian Pacific American Chamber of Commerce (APACC), also created in 2000, dedicates itself to the economic advancement of Asian Pacific American businesses and professionals. Its membership spans Fortune 500 corporations, multiethnic private business enterprises, corporate professionals, and small businesses. Another pan-Asian nonprofit group, Asian Pacific Islander American (APIA)—Vote Michigan, was created in 2007 to serve the community through civic participation, advocacy, and education. Its main focus is voter registration, voter education, and mobilizing Asian Americans to serve as Election Day volunteers. In 2005, Governor Jennifer M. Granholm of Michigan created the Governor's Advisory Council on Asian Pacific American Affairs (ACAPAA) in recognition of the significant contribution of Asian Pacific Americans to Michigan's culture and economy. She wanted to ensure that "Asian Pacific Americans are equal participants in our community and our economy."

The Census Bureau projects that by 2050 the racial and ethnic makeup of the United States will have changed dramatically. Asian Pacific Americans are predicted to be the fastest-growing group in the next fifty years. While the Asian Americans in Michigan join the rest of America in pursuing the "American dream," this book will show that there is no singularly authentic Asian American experience. By increasing our knowledge and understanding of Asian Americans in Michigan, Michiganders can take one step closer to join the ranks of culturally competent global citizens.

ACKNOWLEDGMENTS

This book was created to celebrate Asian Americans in Michigan. Joe Grimm, a journalism professor at Michigan State University, saw the need to create a book dedicated to raising awareness of the rich spectrum of ethnicity in Michigan. I am honored to help tell the stories of the struggles, strengths, and successes of Asian Americans in Michigan.

I'd like to thank my coeditor, Dr. Victor Jew, who teaches at the University of Wisconsin and whose expertise in Asian American studies provided a broader and deeper perspective for the book.

Kathryn Wildfong at Wayne State University Press was instrumental in bringing this book to life. Her knowledgeable guidance was invaluable every step of the way.

For their inspiration, brainstorming, creativity, and editorial support, I thank Wayne State University Press director Jane Hoehner, former *Detroit Free Press* photographer Amy Leang, and *Metro Parent* publisher Alyssa Martina.

Abundant appreciation goes to the contributors, whose stories reveal intimate portraits of the lives of Asian Americans in Michigan.

Frank Wu, chancellor and dean of the University of California Hastings College of the Law, previously dean of the Wayne State University Law School, deserves special recognition for writing the foreword to the book. Through his brilliance, leadership, and compassion for the community, he makes all Asian Americans proud.

Last but not least, I acknowledge the precious support, encouragement, and help my family members provided, whether it was to edit, read, critique or just to be there for me. Thank you, Gina, TJ, and Todd, for sustaining me with your love and faith in me.

S.W.

If coeditors can second acknowledgments, then I'm happy to echo the sentiments Sook Wilkinson expressed. She did the key work of collecting the first batch of essays, and both she and Kathy Wildfong graciously invited me to join their efforts to make this book. My own thanks go to the following persons who helped me think about Asian America and Michigan. Professor Susan E. Gray of Arizona State University wrote her first book on Yankee Michigan in the nineteenth century and she read the earliest of rough drafts that eventually became chapter 2. Dan Veroff (Detroit Tigers fan and die-hard Wolverine) of the University of Wisconsin–Madison's Extension and Applied Population Laboratory returned to his home state (at least virtually) when he compiled demographic data about Asian Americans in Michigan outside of Detroit. The two anonymous reviewers at the press provided insightful and keen remarks that helped the manuscript in no small way.

Former and current Michiganders always gave encouragement whenever I saw them at annual meetings of the Association for Asian American Studies. These persons include Andrea Louie, who teaches at Michigan State University, Jaideep Singh, who grew up in Kalamazoo, and Daniel Y. Kim, Shilpa Dave, Daryl Koji Maeda, K.Scott Wong, Larry Hashima, and Barbara Kim (all graduates of the University of Michigan). Colleagues with the Asian American Studies Program at the University of Wisconsin–Madison were generous about long-distance calls to Michigan.

Another daughter of Michigan whom I knew only from her words (and then by Skype connections that she agreed to hold with my students in Wisconsin) is Bich Minh Nguyen. A true "pioneer girl" from Grand Rapids, she agreed to write the afterword and give the voices in this volume the perspective of someone who has traveled the state speaking on what it meant to grow up as a 1.5 Vietnamese American immigrant in Michigan.

Finally, I would like to thank my sister, Katherine Jew, who always had a place in Pasadena, California, for me to get away (especially in December and January) to write, think, and reflect about Asian Americans in a state so marked by stretches of land and large bodies of water.

V.J.

INTRODUCTION

Victor Jew

Asian Americans in Michigan guides readers through some uncharted territory, a landscape that possesses some familiar landmarks but has remained mostly obscured. This terrain is not topographical but social: the world of Asian Americans living in Michigan in the early twenty-first century. The volume's contributors aim to make this obscured side of Michigan visible by sharing with readers the observations and memories of Michiganders who have reflected on what it means to be Asian American in the middle of the country. *Asian Americans in Michigan* gives voice to everyday Asian American Michiganders.

This is the first book to collect a large number of contemporary Asian American voices in the Midwest. While other Asian American projects have preserved the words of Chinatown residents, Filipino Americans, Hmong refugees, and Vietnamese young people, those oral histories and first-person narratives recorded West Coast situations, specifically in San Francisco, San Mateo, California's Central Valley, and Southern California.[1]

The Asian American Midwest is rarely explored, certainly not in book-length projects, and Michigan's Asian American voices have never been recorded to the extent published in this collection. The project arose from the interest of someone who is a Michigander but not a member of the communities represented in these essays: Joe Grimm, a journalism professor at Michigan State University. Involved already in Michigan history projects, Grimm asked whether a reference existed on Asian-derived communities and individuals in the state. The answer in 2006 was no, but his query sparked the impetus for this project. Requests went out for contributions, and more than fifty people responded with reflections, short histories, poetry, reports, and images.

The result is this volume. Along with additional essays that set the personal recollections within larger historical and social contexts, these contributions enable other voices, ones that might be faint to fellow citizens at the moment, to be audible and another kind of Michigan experience to be known. The Michigan presented here is both familiar and yet different, the difference due to the special historical legacies that have shaped the identity called Asian America. Many of the essays make reference to the 1970s, and a few to the Japanese American incarceration of the 1940s. All are written in the shadow of 9/11, highlighting how that recent watershed in U.S. history makes for an uncertain future. As our lives move forward into that future, we will find guidance and wisdom from the contributors to *Asian Americans in Michigan*, all of whom agree on the need to remember historical events such as the Japanese American experience of 1942-46, an episode especially relevant in a world so often trip-wired by anxiety, insecurity, and the need to assign "blame" by ethnic association.

A volume of essays about Asian Americans in Michigan begs a number of questions. What is Asian America? Who are Asian Americans? What is their relationship to the U.S. Midwest? And how does Michigan fit into this story? Asian America and all its variations (Asian Americans, Asian America(s), Asian/America and Asian Pacific Islander America) are terms that have come to name the deliberately embraced umbrella category that covers an expanding list of communities and identities. All of these communities are related to the ways Asian- and Pacific-derived migration flows have traveled to the United States and led to diverse individuals and subcultures claiming both their Asian legacies and their American experiences. History and diversity are the strong cords that bind Asian America as a category, and they intersect to make what is distinctive about the Asian American experience.

Diversity among different Asian origins has marked Asian American history throughout its course. For example, prior to the Second World War, there were five large Asian-derived communities across the country: Chinese America, Japanese America, Korean America, South Asian (Indian) America, and Filipinos. The last-named occupied a shadow land, classified as "U.S. Nationals," a category marking them as not quite aliens but ineligible for U.S. citizenship. These separate groups were often classified as one. Considered in hindsight, they were the precursors to contemporary Asian America. Their differences notwithstanding, the five groups (along with smaller communities such as those that came from Pacific Islander origins) all experienced the blunt force of the racializing and racist meanings stirred by the word *Oriental*.

After the Second World War, these communities grew and further diversified, the entire range of Asian America expanding dramatically, particularly after the watershed markers of 1965 and 1975. Those years saw, respectively, massive reforms in U.S. immigration law and a reversal of U.S. geopolitical fortunes in Southeast Asia. The Immigration and Nationality Act of 1965 was a key congressional decision that overturned the restrictive features of the xenophobic Immigration Act of 1924. In particular, the family reunification provisions of the 1965 law and the immigration opportunities for persons trained in the sciences and engineering initiated new flows of Asians to the United States. Developments from 1975 to the 1980s changed the face of Asian America by adding Vietnamese, Cambodian, Lao, and Hmong communities from the refugee resettlement flows after the Vietnam War. As events have proved since the 1980s, many individuals and groups within these communities found a shared new American identity under the capacious and dynamic term *Asian American*.

Asian America and *Asian American* have come to operate in a variety of ways, reflecting the history of both self-definition and being defined by others. For those in the 1960s and 1970s who self-consciously forged the hybrid name *Asian American,* the term was an improvement on *Oriental* and a way to name the historically similar formative experiences that different communities of Asian descent have undergone as they came to the United States. At roughly the same time, the classification became useful in a practical sense to expedite local delivery of social services or to fulfill national requirements such as U.S. Census data collection and differentiation. From its inception, then, the term has operated at different registers of claiming and naming: as adopted self-understanding and communal empowerment and as a means of institutional ascription.

Recognizing that the name has worked and works both ways does not cancel out its most far-going possibilities. Well beyond being a census category or a self-identifying box that can either be checked or not, the promise of "Asian America" lies in its ability to tell a different kind of American history. It is a history that largely remains outside mainstream textbooks except for a few sentences about Chinese exclusion or the Japanese American incarceration, and even those few sentences often appear without larger contexts that can impart a more informed understanding. Asian America tells a Pacific-facing story and it also narrates a deeper alternative history, one that captures the tangled and deeply woven weave of connections between Asian and Pacific sites and what formed as the United States. Deeply implicated in that story were and are long-running cultural, political, social, and economic ways of how America operated in the world. Deeper still in Asian American history are the dynamics of that stubborn social conundrum called "race" in the United States. Asian American history can teach the history of race in the United States from the position of having been neither black nor white yet nevertheless racialized within the white-over-black hierarchy. These are the history lessons that the concept of "Asian America" has always been available to teach and can impart in the twenty-first century.

"Asian America" is like an umbrella, but knowing what kind of cover it gives is important, certainly to those who hold it over their Asian *and* American selves, but also to non-Asian Americans who are curious about the term and its users. As terminology, *Asian America* groups together a remarkable range of individuals and communities because it puts into action the ideal of a panethnic formation. That is a significant idea for this volume: *panethnicity*. It is important to state what this is not since the idea and its relation to Asian America are often misconstrued. It is *not* an attempt to invent a Frankensteinian new "race," as one reporter in the 1990s got it so hilariously wrong. Rather, forging Asian American panethnicity is the deliberate practice of acting in common on the basis of claiming a commonality. What is being claimed is the social history and the ongoing social process of negotiating the lived circumstance of being able to trace two histories and experiencing the interconnection between those two. The two histories are Asian origins and their American settings and how these interacted in the past and continue to do so today. As an overall covering, "Asian America" enables persons from a wide and expanding variety of communities to see beyond the immediate national origins of themselves, their parents, or grandparents and grasp the common historical circumstances of negotiating public spheres, everyday lives, and social worlds where *Asian* and *American* are related.

Does Asian American panethnicity mean forgetting one's parents? Does embracing an Asian American identity mean disassociating from the legacies and lineages passed down through the generations? Does it mean foreswearing interest in transpacific familial connections in Taiwan or Hong Kong or China or Vietnam or the Philippines or Pakistan or Bangladesh or India or Korea or Japan? No, it does not. Putting panethnicity into practice does not mean erasure. It does mean relating these inherited elements to another long chain of history—in the Asian American case, it is the chain of long connections that made Asian America through the back-and-forth of numerous interactions across the Pacific. Practicing Asian American panethnicity means taking different Asian legacies and seeing how they were and are related to the long history of how any group or individual from an Asian background became (and continues to become) enmeshed in an ongoing larger process that struggled (and continues to wrestle) with the hybridic self-fashioning of being both Asian and American.

Responding to this, one might say this is informative, but what does it have to do with Michigan? The old bugbears that accompany all efforts to recover Asian America in the Midwest (as well as the heartland experiences of other communities such as the Chicano and Latino Midwest and African Americans in the region) still exist. Isn't the Asian American story a West Coast story, specifically a California history? What is Asian American about the Midwest? What is midwestern about Asian America?[2]

Asian Americans in Michigan addresses these questions and provides some surprising answers. Not only do the voices and contributions in this volume reveal an Asian American legacy in the U.S. Midwest, they also point to its remarkable extent. Unbeknownst to many, Asian America has a long history in the Midwest, much longer than many midwesterners suspect, to the extent that Asian America can claim more than a century's worth of settlement, homemaking, and community building in such midwestern sites as Chicago, Milwaukee, and Detroit. While this may be surprising, the important place of Michigan in Asian American midwestern history is even more astounding. Indeed, events in Michigan (starting in Detroit but building across the state) initiated changes that affected Asian Americans not only in the Great Lakes region but throughout the nation. It is no exaggeration to say that Michigan's Asian American experience helped to reenergize Asian American politics, activism, and discourse from the 1980s onward. Its effects are felt to this day as events in 1982-87 made the name of Vincent Chin forever linked with Asian American civil rights.

Many essayists in *Asian Americans in Michigan* mention the Vincent Chin case. All of the contributors stand affected by it. As many of them recount, this 1980s hate crime transformed them into Asian Americans. That the incidents happened in Michigan settings—on a street in Highland Park, in the court-rooms of Detroit—makes the legacy especially dear and crucial to preserve. The contributors actually pay homage to two legacies from that watershed moment. The first, of course, is the memory of Vincent Chin, the murdered Chinese American. The second is the rise of the Asian American community, which began to mobilize after the crime and continued to do so thereafter.

A key insight into that mobilization is preserved in the memory of Helen Zia, one of the participants in that Detroit-based struggle. Originally from

New Jersey, she had moved to Detroit to be a labor organizer and became a worker on the line at a Chrysler stamping plant. The community outrage at the judicial leniency shown to Chin's killers reignited Zia's activism for Asian American causes, dormant since college. She participated as middle-aged Detroiters engaged with activism for the first time, making rough-hewn moves toward panethnic cooperation and coalition building. She recalled that prior to one of the early meetings of Detroit's small Asian American community in March 1983, the Chinese speakers had to make sure they correctly pronounced the name of Minoru Togasaki, the Japanese American activist who worked with them. "A practice session was held," and a room full of Chinese Americans "gingerly repeated the name 'To-ga-sa-ki' until they got it right."[3]

That practice session represents the ongoing legacy of the Vincent Chin episode. Without anyone telling these nascent activists how to "do" panethnicity, they did it. When those same Michigander Asian Americans started their cooperative civil rights organization, American Citizens for Justice (ACJ), they continued making Asian American panethnicity. Building on the Vincent Chin case, they moved into civil rights advocacy in general. Focusing on Asian American community building throughout the state, the members of ACJ expanded the panethnic umbrella to include ever-growing numbers of Asian Americans in Michigan. ACJ filled in where the state of Michigan fell short. In 1991 the group produced a report on the public health needs of Hmong Michiganders, the latest large group of Asians to settle in the state. The activism of ACJ and its panethnic inclusiveness continues to this day. One can say that the spirit and practice of Asian American panethnicity moved beyond ACJ itself. More than thirty years after the Vincent Chin incident, *Asian Americans in Michigan* continues to enact that commitment to community, as shown by the following roll call. Within these pages are the contributions of Chinese Americans, Filipino Americans, Korean Americans, Indo-Americans, a Bangladeshi from outside Detroit, Vietnamese Americans, Hmong Americans, a mixed-heritage female who grew up in Ann Arbor, a white person who adopted two children (one Chinese, one Korean), and two young Korean Americans who were adoptees themselves. Of course there are differences, but the spirit of the enterprise is not unlike that first tentative effort that took place on a cold evening in March of 1983 when everyone in the room agreed that something had to be done.

Asian Americans in Michigan is organized into five parts, each covering an overarching theme that encompasses the experiences of Asian American lives in the Great Lakes State. Most of the contributions are personal. Writers report experiences of growing up and growing older in Michigan and how the Asian American side to their lives made a difference. Other contributors reflect on the larger currents of social, political, economic, and institutional trends that made the conditions for those Asian American differences. The five parts of *Asian Americans in Michigan* steer this combination of the personal and the public into the following themes: recent scholarship (part 1), memory keeping (part 2), culture and heritage (part 3), autobiographical reflections (part 4), and the concerns and hopes of the next generation of Asian American Michiganders (part 5).

In addition to giving form to the contributions, the five thematic parts also supply momentum. Overall, the book's thematic parts move in a "from . . . to" manner. From a historical and sociological overview in part 1, the book progresses to the local keeping of memories and stories in part 2, the keeping of which is indispensable to maintaining a sense of continuity and identity for communities. Building on this foundation of academic overview and communal knowledge, *Asian Americans in Michigan* listens closely to anecdotal and personal recollections in the parts 3 and 4 to show how culture and heritage are inescapable lifelong negotiations for Asian Americans and that life journeys are often perplexing yet rewarding further negotiations of the public and the private, the Asian and the American in Michigan settings. Public and private are explored in other ways in the final part, part 5. Two essays survey contemporary sites of Asian American public involvement: Leslie E. Wong (at the time the president of Northern Michigan University and now the president of San Francisco State University) examines the circumstances of Asian America in higher education while Sook Wilkinson explores the shape of Asian American political engagement in the state. Youth is represented in the final five essays in part 5 as the voices of college-aged Asian Americans (and one high school student) are aired, thus completing a longer "from . . . to" that binds the entire volume. From the historical to the contemporary, from the sightings of "John Chinaman" in Detroit in the 1870s to the wise comments of a seventeen-year-old Chinese American girl in twenty-first-century Ann Arbor, from old to new, the flow of the five thematic parts aims to capture some of the dynamism that marks Asian America in the Midwest and Asian Americans in Michigan.

So *Asian Americans in Michigan* gives readers a new vantage and lets them hear new voices. The two work together. As a vantage, the essays in part 1 provide a place from which to see Michigan in new and different ways. That new horizon of a deeper and longer Asian American legacy should motivate forays into archives, microfilm rolls, government documents holdings, and local histories to find more instances of early Asian America in Michigan. Doing so will enrich the narrative Michigan has always told of itself. And then there are the voices. Young and old, recent immigrant and third-generation American, student and professional, specialist and everyday local citizen, they all have their stories to tell.

The essays are placed in further perspective by an afterword written by another daughter of Michigan, Bich Minh Nguyen, who came to the United States with her family from Vietnam in 1975. Both a novelist and a professor in the Master of Fine Arts in Writing Program at the University of San Francisco, Professor Nguyen reflects upon her growing up as a Vietnamese American in Grand Rapids during what she calls the "long 1980s." *Asian Americans in Michigan* invited her to present her perspectives on being an Asian American Michigander from the viewpoint of someone who has traveled the length of the state speaking to the issue after the Michigan Humanities Council selected her memoir, *Stealing Buddha's Dinner,* as the Great Michigan Read in 2009.

Finally, the last essay in part 5 features a voice of the next generation, that of Emily Hsiao, who submitted her essay while she was in high school. She writes, "We have a right and responsibility" to a new Michigan future, and she asks her generation of Michiganders to work toward this goal. She envisions that future as a place where the casual harmful racializing of oversights, slights, misunderstandings, and slurs will be de-privileged from their usual unexamined positions, their safe places from which they so easily inflict harms. In that spirit, let this book of essays by Asian American Michiganders go forth to bring us closer to that promise.

PART I

Taking Soundings of Asian America in Michigan

Victor Jew

They say there is a complicated and unseen landscape underneath Lake Michigan. Since the nineteenth century, scientists have measured that invisible world by producing bathygrams, the technical term for a graph of underwater soundings. With those, they have been able to tell us that beneath the waters of Lake Michigan there is a world of channels, basins, ridges, and valleys. The same can be said of Lake Superior and Lake Huron.

What do soundings have to do with *Asian Americans in Michigan*? I use that metaphor because it not only refers to lakes dear to Michiganders; it also captures the status of knowledge about Asian Americans in the state and the need to take historical and sociological "soundings" of Michigan's Asian American communities and their historical legacies. Both are largely uncharted. Indeed, we know more about the bottom of Lake Michigan than we do of the Asian American communities in the state surrounded by Lakes Michigan, Huron, and Superior.

The essays in part 1 measure the extent, depth, and contours of Asian America in Michigan and in doing so, they give the big picture against which to view the body of particulars, anecdotes, and personal information that follows. Going beyond personal reflections, the authors in part 1 ground their observations in sources and discourses that supply a context for their assessment of Asian American communities in the state. The contributors to part

1 have sounded out the past by listening to interviewees (Zuzindlak) or by inventorying what has been written by other scholars (Jew and Song) or by counting the numbers from the U.S. Census (Metzger) or researching little-known facts in archives and manuscript depositories (Jew) or conducting a sociological ethnography in a Michigan college town with Asian Americans from a range of Asian-derived backgrounds (Kim).

We start with Kurt R. Metzger's demographic profile, which draws upon the enumerations in the U.S. Census for 2000 and 2010. Taken together, these numbers reflect change and the diversity of Asian America in Michigan. Victor Jew then supplies another kind of big picture. His is historical and transnational as he charts the long history of connections between Michigan's public figures and institutions and sites in Asia. All had some effect on Asian migration and the subsequent formation of Asian American communities in the United States. Drawing upon archival sources in the Bentley Historical Library at the University of Michigan, the archives at Michigan State University, and other depositories in the Midwest, he has sounded out a ridge of historical linkage made by public institutions and individuals associated with Michigan that connected with Asia from 1880 to the 1970s. Chelsea Zuzindlak also probes historical channels, but her findings are local. She reconstructs the history of the Chinese American community in Detroit by weaving oral history interviews, newspaper archives from the *Detroit Free Press*, and other primary sources to build a mosaic about a Chinese American presence that has persisted since 1870. Barbara W. Kim, a sociologist, did fieldwork in Ann Arbor and listened carefully to Asian Americans as they talked about living in Michigan and the Midwest. Finally, Min Hyoung Song, a professor of Asian American literature at Boston College and a specialist in urban race relations, locates his own coming-of-age in Detroit within the urban cultural studies scholarship about the city and its deindustrialized fate during the 1970s and 1980s. In the process, he reveals aspects of Korean American Detroit seen only when the personal is placed within a scholarly context that dissects how globalizing economic change manifests itself in local circumstances and individual lives.

As early soundings, these essays give us data, insights, and details that can guide future scholarship. They are new soundings because they produce information that goes beyond anything that has been published heretofore about Asian America in the state. Part 1 tells us that much has happened in the Asian America of this Great Lakes domain. Not unlike the ridges, channels, and valleys lying beneath the lakes that border Michigan, these features of the social topography have long existed. They simply await discovery by penetrating the depths that obscure them.

Notes

1. Victor G. Nee and Brett de Bary Nee, *Longtime Californ': A Documentary Study of an American Chinatown* (Palo Alto: Stanford University Press, 1972); Yen Le Espiritu, *Filipino American Lives* (Philadelphia: Temple University Press, 1995); Sucheng Chan, ed., *Hmong Means Free: Life in Laos and America* (Philadelphia: Temple University Press, 1994); and Sucheng Chan, ed., *The Vietnamese American 1.5 Generation: Stories of War, Revolution, Flight, and New Beginnings* (Philadelphia: Temple University Press, 2006).

2. As of 2010, scholarship on Asian Americans in Michigan is discrete and particular. Needless to say, there is neither a large-scale overview nor a "synthesis" of this research topic. The former requires an overarching narrative yet to be written, and the latter entails many more close-up studies yet to be done. The latest ethnographic overview of many Asian American communities in Michigan is Barbara Kim's PhD dissertation, "Race, Space, and Identity: Examining Asian American Racial and Ethnic Formations in the Midwest" (University of Michigan, 2001). Preceding Kim by three decades is Emiko Ohnuki, "The Detroit Chinese—A Study of Socio-cultural Changes in the Detroit Chinese Community from 1872 through 1963 (master's thesis, University of Wisconsin, 1964). A promising new direction is Vibha Bhalla's "Detroit and Windsor as Transnational Spaces: A Case Study of Asian Indian Migrants" which appeared in the 2008 special issue of the *Michigan Historical Review* on transnational borders. Chelsea Zuzindlak has been excavating a historical recovery of Detroit's lost Chinatown by conducting oral history interviews and studying archived newspaper articles. She has posted her findings and commentary on her website, DetroitChinatown.org. A fascinating artifact of Chinese American Ann Arbor and Detroit can be found in Katherine Anne Porter's *Mae Franking's "My Chinese Marriage": An Annotated Edition* (Austin: University of Texas Press, 1991). For Asian Americanists, the call went out in 1998 to study Asian American instances outside of California and the West Coast. Steve Sumida argued that case in "East of California: Points of Origin in Asian American Studies," *Journal of Asian American Studies* 1, no. 1 (1998): 83-100. Not insignificantly for this volume, Sumida included Michigan references to demonstrate the viability of studying Asian American communities and individuals outside the typical California context. A wave of new studies about the Midwest as a distinctive region started to appear in the late 1980s. Key examples of this work include James H. Madison, ed., *Heartland: Comparative Histories of the Midwestern States* (Bloomington: Indiana University Press, 1988); and Andrew R. L. Cayton and Susan E. Gray, eds., *The Identity of the American Midwest: Essays on Regional History* (Bloomington: Indiana University Press, 2001.)

3. Helen Zia, *Asian American Dreams: The Emergence of an American People* (New York: Farrar, Straus, and Giroux, 2000), 77.

1

A DEMOGRAPHIC PORTRAIT
OF ASIAN AMERICANS IN MICHIGAN

Kurt R. Metzger

National Asian Population Developments

From 2000 to 2010, the total Asian population in the United States increased from 11.9 million to 17.3 million.[1] This 45.6 percent increase in population resulted in the Asian share of the country's total population rising from 4.2 percent to 5.6 percent.

The number of persons indicating just one Asian category as their race (referred to as Asian alone) increased by 43.3 percent over the decade, from 10,242,998 to 14,674,252. The number listing an Asian category with another race, or another Asian category, increased by 59.8 percent, to 2,646,604 in 2010.

Change in Total U.S. Population, 2000–2010

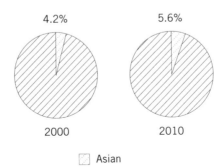

4.2%   5.6%

2000   2010

Asian

Source: U.S. Census Bureau

Asian Population in the Midwest by State

The number of people with Asian ancestry in the 12 states that the Census Bureau defines as being in the Midwest topped 2 million in 2010. The national total was 13.2 million.

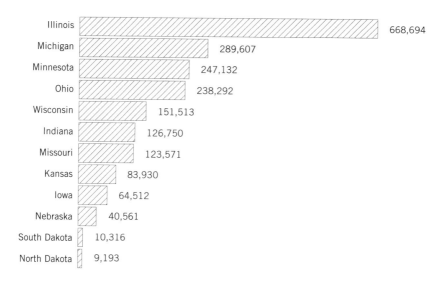

Illinois	668,694
Michigan	289,607
Minnesota	247,132
Ohio	238,292
Wisconsin	151,513
Indiana	126,750
Missouri	123,571
Kansas	83,930
Iowa	64,512
Nebraska	40,561
South Dakota	10,316
North Dakota	9,193

Source: U.S. Census Bureau

While still much smaller than the African American or Hispanic minorities, Asian Americans have considerably more presence today than in the past, and are very prominent in some states and metro areas.

Michigan's Asian American Population Trends

Michigan experienced a 39 percent increase in its Asian population, rising from 208,329 in 2000 to 289,607 in 2010.[2] This increase occurred at the same time that the overall population of the state was decreasing.

Asian Indians were by far the largest of the national-origin groups in Michigan, accounting for 28.7 percent of the total, after growing by 41 percent over the decade. The Chinese (not including Taiwanese) came in a distant second with 16.4 percent of the total, and Filipinos passed Koreans to move into third place at 10.9 percent. Koreans were followed by Vietnamese, Japanese, and Pakistani. The Bangladeshi population, concentrated in Hamtramck, Detroit, and southern Macomb County, experienced the greatest percentage increase (224 percent) and increased its share of the Asian American total from 1.3 to 3 percent.

Top Countries of Origin for Immigrants to Metro Detroit, 2003–2010

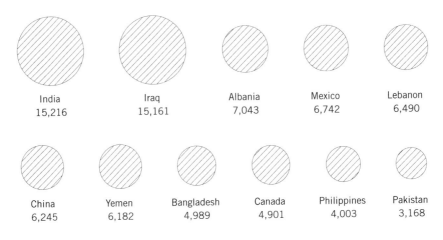

| India | Iraq | Albania | Mexico | Lebanon |
| 15,216 | 15,161 | 7,043 | 6,742 | 6,490 |

| China | Yemen | Bangladesh | Canada | Philippines | Pakistan |
| 6,245 | 6,182 | 4,989 | 4,901 | 4,003 | 3,168 |

Source: U.S. Department of Homeland Security | Meagan Choi

Asians outside Ann Arbor and the Detroit Metro Area

The top ten counties outside the areas of Ann Arbor and the Detroit metro region that had sizeable Asian-derived populations were Ingham County, Kent County, Ottawa County, Kalamazoo County, Berrien County, Calhoun County, Saginaw County, Eaton County, Midland County, and Isabella County.

Of these top ten counties, Ingham County had the most persons who self-identified with one of the following thirteen Asian-origin categories: Asian Indian, Bhutanese, Chinese (not Taiwanese), Hmong, Indonesian, Japanese, Korean, Malaysian, Nepalese, Pakistani, Sri Lankan, Taiwanese, and Thai.

Asians in Southeast Michigan

The six-county Detroit metropolitan area contained 140,558 Asians, concentrated in Detroit's tri-county area of Wayne, Oakland, and Macomb counties, and accounting for 59.4 percent of the state's total of Asian Americans (see table 1). That area is home to 43.5 percent of the state's total population in general. Ann Arbor, dominated by the University of Michigan and high-technology industries, contains a larger share of Asian Americans relative to the total population, 11.4 percent versus 3.5 percent, while Flint has the reverse situation. When you add in Ann Arbor's home county of Washtenaw and Flint's home county of Genesee, southeast Michigan's share of the state's Asian population rises to 72.4 percent.

Table 1. The Racial/Ethnic Distribution in the State and Southeast Michigan

	Michigan	Ann Arbor metropolitan statistical area	Detroit-Warren-Livonia metropolitan statistical area	Flint metropolitan statistical area	Tri-county area
Total population	9,883,640	344,791	4,296,250	425,790	3,863,924
Population of one race	9,256,886	320,772	4,047,540	403,294	3,632,674
White	7,569,939	248,675	2,916,144	309,683	2,511,271
Black	1,383,756	43,152	972,689	87,352	967,157
Hispanic or Latino	436,358	13,860	168,065	12,983	156,275
Asian	236,490	27,005	140,558	3,834	138,075
American Indian or Alaska native	54,665	976	12,501	1,961	10,858
Native Hawaiian or other Pacific Islander	2,170	118	793	74	684
Other	9,866	846	4,855	390	4,629
Two or more races	190,396	10,159	80,645	9,513	74,975
Share of state's Asian population (by percent)		11.4	59	1.6	58.4

Source: 2010 U.S. Census.

Asians are the fastest-growing racial/ethnic group in Detroit's tri-county area. Between 2000 and 2010, Asians increased their number by 37,283, or 37 percent. While growth occurred in all three counties, most occurred in Oakland County, where 49 percent of the area's Asian population lives. Oakland County added 18,365 Asians (37.3 percent), while Macomb County experienced the greatest percentage growth at 49 percent. Wayne County, which had the largest population loss of any county in the country during the decade, registered a 31 percent increase in its Asian population. Growth did not occur evenly across all cities, nor did all Asian groups grow at the same rate.

Spatial Distribution in the Tri-County Area

The distribution of Asians in the tri-county area resembles a crescent stretching from western Sterling Heights on the east to Canton Township on the west, with pockets in Detroit, Hamtramck, Warren, and Inkster. If you extended that crescent beyond Canton, it would reach into Washtenaw County and the city of Ann Arbor. Most of the crescent lies in Oakland County. As stated, 49 percent of the tri-county's Asian population lives in Oakland County, particularly Troy, Rochester Hills, Farmington Hills, Bloomfield Hills, Bloomfield and West Bloomfield townships, and Novi. Other areas with large Asian populations include Detroit, Canton Township, Sterling Heights, and Warren.

Population losses experienced by Detroit resulted in a reduction in its Asian population and a fall in tri-county rankings for cities with Asian populations from second to seventh. In addition, the cities of Livonia and Pontiac fell out of the top twenty. The trend for Asians in the tri-county area is to live in predominantly white, newer, more affluent suburbs. This is in sharp contrast to other minority groups, who are more likely to live in Detroit and the older suburbs. However, not all Asian groups follow this trend. Smaller groups, such as Laotian, Hmong, and Bangladeshi Asians have different settlement patterns than those of Indian, Japanese, and Chinese Asians.

The Bangladeshi community is one of the smallest and most concentrated of the Asian groups. Seventy-two percent of the tri-county's Bangladeshi population lives in Hamtramck and surrounding Detroit neighborhoods. This marks a dilution from 2000's 84 percent share, as the community has continued to move north into the southern Macomb County cities of Warren and Sterling Heights. The Hmong and Laotian populations are concentrated in southern Warren, northeast Detroit, and central Pontiac. Movement of the Hmong out of Detroit occurred to a greater degree than that of the Bangladeshi in the decade, as the population in Detroit dropped by two-thirds and further concentrated in Warren. Larger groups, such as Asian Indians, Japanese, Filipinos, Koreans, and Chinese, continue to concentrate in the crescent. Reasons for variations in settlement patterns are discussed below.

Detroit

Unlike in suburban cities, the Asian population in Detroit is in clusters. There are four.

Asians on the northeast side are predominantly Hmong, with a small number of Laotians. Both groups experienced significant migration out of

Table 2. Top Twenty Tri-County Communities for Asian Population

Rank	Community	Total population	Asian population (Asian alone)	Percentage Asian
1	Troy	80,980	15,439	19.1
2	Canton Township	90,173	12,720	14.1
3	Novi	55,224	8,756	15.9
4	Sterling Heights	129,699	8,713	6.7
5	Farmington Hills	79,740	8,063	10.1
6	Rochester	70,955	7,447	10.5
7	Detroit	713,777	7,436	1.0
8	Warren	134,056	6,170	4.6
9	West Bloomfield Township	64,690	5,412	8.4
10	Hamtramck	22,423	4,806	21.4
11	Northville Township	28,497	3,205	11.2
12	Bloomfield Township	41,070	2,968	7.2
13	Westland	84,094	2,526	3.0
14	Macomb Township	79,580	2,446	3.1
15	Livonia	96,942	2,441	2.5
16	Shelby Township	73,804	2,403	3.3
17	Auburn Hills	21,412	1,888	8.8
18	Clinton Township	96,796	1,723	1.8
19	Madison Heights	29,694	1,711	5.8
20	Dearborn	98,153	1,696	1.7

Source: 2010 U.S. Census.

Detroit over the decade. The Hmong population fell by 68 percent, while the Laotian population experienced an 81 percent decrease.

The area of Detroit next to eastern Hamtramck contains a large and growing Bangladeshi community, with a smaller, and decreasing, Asian-Indian population. Combined with the growth that has occurred in Hamtramck, this area represents one of the most concentrated and fastest-growing Asian areas in the region. Nearly three of every four of the region's Bangladeshi population live here. The Asian population in this area is largely Muslim, living side by side with Muslim Serbs, Croats, Yemeni, and African Americans. Many either hold blue-collar jobs or own small businesses, catering to their growing community as well as to a general interest in Asian foods and culture.

Detroit also has a large Asian population residing just north of downtown, in the area that includes Wayne State University, the Detroit Medical Center, and Henry Ford Hospital. Here we find individuals from a number of Asian national-origin groups, most of whom are either students at Wayne State University or employees of the hospitals. The largest groups are Chinese and Asian Indian, but there are also Filipinos, Koreans, and Pakistanis. In contrast to the first two areas mentioned, the university/hospital community tends to be quite transient. Few Asians set up permanent residences in the area once their schooling is completed. Because they are attending school or working in hospitals, Asians in this area also tend to have higher educational levels and incomes compared to those in other parts of the city.

There are several small Asian enclaves on Detroit's west and southwest sides, though these are much smaller and more dispersed than those already described. Detroit's western border with Redford and Dearborn contains a few small neighborhoods, populated mostly by Asian Indians. In southwest Detroit, there is a relatively small Vietnamese/Laotian community, very similar to the Hmong and Laotian community in northeast Detroit.

In summary, the Asian community followed the general population out of Detroit over the decade, though at a slightly lower rate. As a result of the 18.6 percent decline in the Asian population (the city's total population fell by 25 percent), Detroit's ranking among cities in the tri-county area for total number of Asian residents fell to seventh, but its 1 percent Asian representation was by far the lowest among the top twenty communities. Current trends point to a growing Bangladeshi population that will continue to disperse from its concentrated area in Hamtramck and adjoining neighborhoods in Detroit. In addition, the midtown area of Detroit will continue to attract a rather transient Asian community connected to Wayne State University and the medical community centered in the areas around Henry Ford Hospital and the Detroit Medical Center. It is difficult to predict whether the trend toward increasing employment in the downtown area, particularly tied to information technology–related firms, coupled with the desire for young, educated adults to move back to the city, will translate to much growth in Detroit's Asian community. These trends are just beginning and will be very interesting to track.

Conclusion

From 2000 to 2010, the total Asian population in the United States increased from 11.9 million to 17.3 million. The 2010 U.S. Census reveals that there are now as many as six distinct Asian national-origin groups (Asian Indian, Chinese, Filipino, Japanese, Korean, and Vietnamese) with more than a million residents—each with unique characteristics. The Asian community in Michigan, particularly in southeast Michigan, where 72.4 percent of the state's total resides, while still relatively small, made great strides. Michigan experienced a 39 percent increase in its Asian population, rising from 208,329 in 2000 to 289,607 in 2010. Southeast Michigan's Asian population grew by 34 percent. Asians are the fastest-growing minority population in the tri-county area.

Notes

1. The 2010 census allowed, for the second time, respondents to list more than one race on their questionnaires. Analyzing census results on the Asian population, one finds that 14,674,252 persons listed a single-race Asian response. This is sometimes viewed as the equivalent of past census enumerations. The total is obtained by combining the single-race responses with multiple-race responses in which one or more race given indicates an Asian group.
2. When single-race responses alone are tracked, Michigan is found to have experienced a 34.9 percent increase, from 176,510 to 238,199.

2

ASIAN AMERICANS AND MICHIGAN

A Long Transnational Legacy

Victor Jew

Michigan has never lacked for histories or historians. As I walk past the shelves of Michigan history and Michigania in a neighboring Great Lakes historical society library, I cannot help but be impressed by how the state has preserved its past and told its stories. By my reckoning, as I count eight shelving cases with six full shelves apiece, there are more than a thousand volumes on Michigan history packed into this dark library space. I happen to be walking through the holdings of the State Historical Society of Wisconsin and this wealth of material on Michigan is probably welcome news to Wisconsinites who regularly come to the society on Saturdays to trace their genealogies, a rewarding task for those surnamed VandenHeuvel or Wiersma, curious about family lines across Lake Michigan.

Those volumes are one way to gain access to Michigan's past, but Michiganders can also travel through their state and get a direct sense of their history. Landmarks established by the Michigan Historical Marker Program dot the state from Alcona County to Wexford County and everywhere in between.[1] More than sixteen hundred of these aluminum markers tell passersby that they are standing at the Chrysler Corporation building at 12000 Oakland Avenue, or the Highland Park Plant at 14100 Woodward Avenue, or the Temple Beth El synagogue at 7400 Telegraph Road in Oakland County.[2]

In addition to books and landmarks, Michigan's history is conveyed through photographs. Among the volumes I see are numerous books with sepia-tinted covers that reproduce images of the Michigan of long ago. There is a volume on Ann Arbor showing pictures of State Street in the 1890s. In the pages of a volume on Detroit, Woodward Avenue in the 1950s comes alive through black-and-white images. A photograph of Highland Park in the 1960s is also at hand.[3]

But amid this wealth of print about all things Michigan, there is a missing history. That untold story is the history of Asians and Asian Americans in the state. At first glance, this gap seems understandable because the number of Asians in Michigan was small for a good portion of the state's history. One standard volume about Michigan's past said there were only 12,388 Asians who migrated to the state from the late nineteenth century to 1940.[4] One might conclude that such small totals justify the lack of attention.

That is the conventional view, but one can argue that the neglect actually stems from an unexamined prejudice. After all, what is the threshold number that makes a community suddenly worthy to be included in a state's historical narrative? Who sets that magic number and how do its arbiters justify setting a bar that declares a population's history inconsequential? These questions carry special force in the twenty-first century because of demographic and historiographical changes in the times.

Demographically, a variety of Asian-derived communities have settled in Michigan and their numbers have grown. Historiographically (the ways historians think about and write history), scholarly developments since the 1960s have shown how to recover the lost histories of communities forgotten in traditional narratives. Due to such changes in historical research, the histories of communities that had long been untaught have been researched and published to a greater extent. The histories of women, racial and ethnic minorities, and marginalized communities enrich the national narrative, benefiting those communities and society as a whole. The same could be said for recovering the histories of Michigan's Asian American individuals and communities.

Both demographic and historiographical developments combine to make a new history of Asian Americans in Michigan both possible and necessary. At least one historian of Michigan's past realized that the growth of the state's Asian-derived populations signaled a demographic change that could not be ignored. In 1995, Professor George S. May of Eastern Michigan University updated and revised the third edition of a standard history, written by Professor Willis Frederick Dunbar of Western Michigan University, that was first published in 1965. At that time Dunbar had nothing to say about Asians in the state, but in 1995 May could not dismiss what the U.S. Census recorded in 1990, that there were 105,000 Michiganders who self-identified as Asian or Pacific Islander.[5] Moreover, those 105,000 individuals identified themselves as belonging to distinct Asian communities, a diversity within the Asian and Pacific Islander categories that was evident twenty years earlier. In 1970, the census counted persons who specified the following attachments: to India (17,000 persons), to China (6,500), to Japan (5,000), and to the Philippines (3,600). The 1990 census would add 6,500 people in Michigan who claimed a Korean affiliation, and refugees from Vietnam added 6,000 to the Asian American Michigan totals. In addition, an increasing number of Cambodians, Lao, and Hmong became new neighbors in places as "traditionally Dutch" as Holland, Michigan.

This chapter seeks to enhance what George May found irresistible in 1995 when he included Asians in his revised Michigan history. That first step is worth continuing, but in our day the next step should go beyond merely updating census totals. Updating the growing numbers is important, but Michigan's history of interactions with Asia is much more complex, long lasting, and intersectional than many Michiganders have ever known or learned in school. A few contributors to this collection, *Asian Americans in Michigan*, have spotted some of these connections, specifically as they concerned the Philippines in the nineteenth century. In chapter 11, Emily Lawsin and Joseph Galura mention professors at the University of Michigan (naturalists and botanists) who collected plants and fauna from the Philippines as early as 1876.

Such sightings suggest a long history of Michiganders undertaking various activities in Asian settings. The fact of these activities has never been disputed; they just seem buried in specialized histories, such as those narrating the past of the University of Michigan or that of the Ford Motor Company. Nevertheless, when these details are recounted within larger settings, they stand out. In his third revised edition of the standard history, May called the University of Michigan's involvement in the Philippines "remarkable," noting that it remained unbroken from 1899 through the cold war.[6] That a number of Michiganders exerted influence in Asia in the nineteenth and twentieth centuries is surprising and significant, but it was never entirely unknown. But because their activities took place offshore, thousands of miles across the Pacific Ocean, they were out of sight and out of mind for most Americans and Michiganders. Told as remarkable singular instances, these Michigan moments in Asia seem doubly disconnected: first as separate examples without any larger connection or consequence, and second as unrelated to developments in U.S. history and society. Seen this way, these incidents would most likely remain buried as mere curiosities, but that need not be the case. One way to connect these separate instances is to follow what they had in common, namely, each of these events came to affect Asian migrations to the United States. From that influence, however delayed or roundabout, came the results that stemmed from those migrations: the formation of Asian American communities within the United States. If this history is studied with an Asian Americanist perspective, an outlook that specializes in tracing long transnational and transpacific connections, then Michigan's past with Asia and Asian America is less unusual (or even freakish) and more continuous and connected.

Telling this story calls for a framework that can trace connections whose deep roots are compelling when one considers the histories of both Michigan and Asian America. At the very least, a new framework needs to avoid merely listing occurrences. The effect of such lists is to make them nothing more than separate events. A more perceptive framework captures these events as a series. The intersections between Asian sites and Michigan happened time and again over nearly one hundred years from 1880 to the 1970s. The repeated instances formed continuities that undergird a sense of history revisiting itself, an uncanny feature that can be told only if its long stretch is adequately imagined. In other words, a new framework needs to be systematic as it places these rarely studied moments in a long, "change-over-time" narrative structure and chronology.

Broadly put, the history of Asian America and Michigan tells the story of two streams of developments that ran parallel to each other. One stream made the familiar history of Michigan: the story of its prominent citizens and institutions, the history of its enterprises and industries. The other stream recounts the history of Asian-derived communities arriving in Michigan and sinking roots in places such as Detroit, Ann Arbor, and Kalamazoo. These two streams ran parallel to each other and Michigan's public sphere seemed comfortable keeping them separate, often leaving its Asian denizens and local citizens unnoticed. Nevertheless, intersections between the two occurred. Before the Second World War and into the cold war era, at the same time that Chinese, Japanese, Filipinos, Koreans, and South Asians formed communities inside the state, the state's high-profile citizens and institutions made forays across the nation and across the Pacific to Asian settings. Their activities ranged from scientific exploration to staffing the new U.S. political presence in Southeast Asia as well as recruiting labor and establishing commercial outposts in Asian markets for American products. Henry Ford was prominent in this regard. These intersections between Michiganders and Asia would not only produce particular outcomes for the United States in Asia, they would affect Asian migrations and thereby influence the making of Asian American communities in the United States, Michigan being one of the sites that would experience this roundabout effect.

To explore these connections and provide historical context for the essays in *Asian Americans in Michigan*, this chapter will sketch this interpretive possibility in an essay divided into six sections. Each section corresponds to a time period and focuses on a particular theme. As the story moves through the twentieth century, there is overlap in the histories of various Asian-derived communities, but this six-part scheme helps to isolate major sequential developments and marks particularly important moments that contributed to other, subsequent formations. The first section, "Michigan's Early Asian Arrivals: Toward the Exclusion Era, 1870s-90s," is primarily a Chinese story that recognizes that the first Asian arrivals were Chinese who most likely came to Michigan as part of the 1870s traverse to the Midwest from California. This first section also discusses Michigan's singular contribution to the national legal regime that limited Chinese migration from 1882 to 1943. The second part, "Michigan in the Philippines," summarizes the history of institutional connections between the state's premier university and the administration of the Philippines as a U.S. territory, a set of intersections that were indeed "remarkable," as George S. May wrote.

The third part, "Michigan's Changing and Diversifying Asian American Communities, 1920s–40s" highlights demographics of the time period, showing that Chinese, Japanese, Koreans, Filipina/os and South Asian East Indians began to call this midwestern state their home. The 1940s also saw Asian America in Michigan receiving a large influx of new residents whose arrival was voluntary but not entirely free. This paradoxical contribution to Michigan's Asian American history was made by the Japanese Americans who resettled in Michigan after having been forcibly removed from their homes on the West Coast during the Second World War.

After the war, Michigan's growing and changing Asian population began to consolidate its stakes even as another of Michigan's higher-education institutions began a new interconnection between the state and a site in Asia. During the cold war, Michigan State University became involved in U.S. policies in Southeast Asia and the regime politics within South Vietnam. This story, which would have consequences for both United States–Asia relations and Asian American history, is recounted in the fourth section, "Michigan's Cold War–Era Asian and Asian American Histories."

While the interconnections between Michigan, Michiganders, and Asia had varying degrees of direct relation to Asian American history, Michigan in the 1980s became the unlikely epicenter for direct developments in Asian American history and contemporary Asian American cultural, political, and civic dynamics. "Michigan as the Site of the New Asian American Panethnicity, 1982-87 to the Present" covers this as it considers the consequences of the Vincent Chin case. The last section, "Michigan and Asian America: Toward a New Past and a New Future," completes this theme as it analyzes the ways the parallel histories of Michigan and its Asian American communities have further entwined in the years since the Chin episode.

Michigan's Early Asian Arrivals: Toward the Exclusion Era, 1870s-90s

The earliest Chinese in Michigan, as reported in the English-language newspapers, showed up in 1872. The *Detroit Free Press* stated "John Chinaman" was seen in the city. The next year the paper reported an additional sighting, duly noting the fact under the brief heading "Another John." However extraordinarily announced, the Detroit Chinese population grew on the foundation of these early Chinese settlers. The *Free Press* kept track of these sightings, its paper trail pointing to the following modest yet rising numbers: one Chinese in 1872, two the following year, a jump to twenty-seven in 1886. The number hit the one hundred mark in 1911, moving from there to thousands: fifteen hundred in 1929, and by 1942 there were between twelve hundred to two thousand Chinese in Detroit. In 1963 *the Detroit News* enumerated a total of thirty-six hundred Chinese residents. These bare figures can be supplemented by other details that convey a sense of place. We learn from newspaper reports that a Chinese lived on Gratiot Street in 1872; ten years later, Gratiot and Michigan Avenue both had Chinese businesses fronting their pavements. By 1905, the number of street locations with Chinese laundries, restaurants, and residences included Larned, Randolph, Grand River, and Lafayette Boulevard.[7]

Those early Chinese Detroiters did not come out of a social or political vacuum. "John Chinaman" and "Another John" most likely made their way to Michigan in the 1870s by way of California, but a larger set of political circumstances had set the stage for Chinese migration during the years after the U.S. Civil War. These Chinese Detroiters did not emerge mysteriously from China without historical precondition making their arrival possible. Rather, many Chinese came to the United States drawn by work and what were construed as promises seemingly vouchsafed by a treaty between the United States and China. Ratified in 1868, the Burlingame Treaty aimed to increase the commercial and cultural exchange between the two countries. One such exchange was immigration, and the treaty grandly announced that it was to the mutual benefit of both countries that free migration be permitted between the two.[8]

In retrospect, the treaty was a mixture of grand sentiment and withheld fulfillment that led to an eventual sense of broken promises. On the one hand, the Burlingame Treaty seemed to welcome Chinese migrants and protect them with a vague evocation of rights expressed as "privileges and immunities." On the other hand, the treaty fell short of fulfilling those rights when it refused to permit naturalization and citizenship to those same Chinese immigrants. Despite this contradiction, the treaty achieved its aim. It pulled thousands of Chinese laborers to the United States, and its spectacular result was the completion of the Transcontinental Railroad in 1869, a feat that saw Chinese laborers carving a throughway across the Sierra Nevada Mountains, a seemingly impossible task.

Unfortunately for Chinese laborers and immigrants, after the line's completion they were no longer wanted as workers or as residents. They became the focus of anti-immigrant and anti-Chinese anxieties and ultimately the scapegoats for the economic downturns that occurred in 1873 and the 1880s. Increasingly depicted as the cause of the nation's economic woes because of their alleged willingness to work for near-starvation wages, the Chinese were blamed for the social effects of the larger economic convulsions that transformed the United States in the late nineteenth century.[9]

Chinese Detroiters in the 1870s may have felt insulated from the din of anti-Chinese political agitation because so much of it seemed to emanate from California and the West Coast, but it was a Michigander in nearby Ann Arbor who would play a pivotal role in affecting Chinese immigration not only in Michigan but throughout the nation and at the source across the Pacific Ocean. James Burrill Angell, the president of the University of Michigan, had been summoned to Washington, DC, by the secretary of state and offered the post of member of a diplomatic team to renegotiate the Burlingame Treaty. Angell accepted, and in 1880 went to China, where the treaty he signed on November 24 acquired his name, the Angell Treaty. Although its language seemed to iterate the notion of protection and rights for Chinese immigrants, Angell negotiated a key concession from his Chinese counterparts: henceforth China recognized Congress's power to suspend Chinese laborer migration. While this proviso appeared to be limited by conditions and safeguards meant to prevent xenophobia, it nevertheless opened the door to what would become the sixty-one-year regime of Chinese exclusion.[10]

Angell finished his diplomatic task and spent the next two years traveling through Asia and Europe before returning to Ann Arbor on February 24, 1882.[11] During those intervening years, political events within the United States moved quickly and Congress acted upon the concession Angell had wrested during his mission. On May 6, 1882, Congress passed the Chinese laborer suspension bill, a law that eagerly seized the concession and declared that the migration of Chinese laborers was "suspended" for ten years. The long-term ramifications of this bill were not immediately apparent to all observers in 1882 (the same could be said of the Angell Treaty in 1880), but seen in the long view, the treaty and the resulting legislation set in motion the momentum that would lead to Congress passing fifteen laws between 1882 to 1913 that cemented the Chinese exclusion system. The change that Chinese exclusion made in U.S. laws and immigration policy has been recognized by all historians of U.S. immigration history. The Chinese Exclusion Act was the first time that Congress set a racially discriminatory bar to govern immigration and migration policy, a discrimination directed against entrants based on "race," ethnicity, and national origin.

Angell probably thought his treaty in 1880 was a reasonable way to deal with the concerns that animated the increasing anti-Chinese agitation on the West Coast. Nevertheless, whatever mitigating provisions Angell may have believed his treaty had, they proved inadequate to offset or deflect the anti-immigrant movement. Even some white American commentators in the late nineteenth and early twentieth centuries shuddered at the "exceedingly harsh" aspects of the anti-Chinese laws.

Resuming his duties at the University of Michigan in Ann Arbor, Angell most likely did not know "John Chinaman" in Detroit, but the aftereffects of his treaty eventually affected all Chinese Michiganders, and indeed all Chinese who had some transnational relation with the United States from 1882 to 1943. This effect was most immediately felt in February of 1882 when the Detroit Trade Assembly passed an anti-Chinese resolution. A little more than a week earlier, the *Detroit Free Press* had published yet another story about John Chinaman in Detroit, but the tone seemed changed since that first sighting in 1872. While newspapers throughout the nation always seemed to gild their coverage of local Chinatowns with some exoticism, the 1880s became a decade that licensed racial slurring. Instead of curiosity and subdued Orientalizing, there seemed to be open denigration. The *Detroit Free Press* story of February 8, 1883, made sport of the city's Chinese residents with painful mimicry of what passed for Chinese talk: "Flebuary Sleventh; John China-man's New Year" was a time when the paper reported Detroit's "Chinamen All Good Flends Floor Days Allee Time."[12]

The regime of Chinese exclusion did more than create a poisoned social environment that produced the local cultural effects seen in this *Detroit Free Press* story. Due to the exclusion laws and their enforcement, Chinese throughout the nation had to run a gauntlet of checks, interrogations, and documentation that the exclusion system set. It was through this system that Chinese Michiganders of the exclusion era had their names, movements, pho-tographs—their very lives—processed and kept on record for never-ending exclusion-enforced discipline.

Michigan in the Philippines

At the same time that Congress hardened and solidified the Chinese Exclu-sion Act through amendments that renewed its provisions, the United States ventured across the Pacific in a new direction—south to the Philippine Archi-pelago, where in 1899 it waged a war against Filipino independence. The war technically lasted four years, but extended in the southern Philippines for another ten years.[13] As a part of the determined attempt to pacify the coun-tryside and transform the Philippines into a ward, U.S. institutions actively encouraged Americans to go to the Philippines. Michigan sent soldiers, administrators, teachers, missionaries, businessmen, lawyers, doctors, min-ers, and planters. Some Michiganders attained high rank and helped to create a structure of American-administered governance.

Dean Conant Worcester, an 1889 alumnus of the University of Michigan, became active in U.S. governance of the Philippines, first as a member of the Philippine Commission (1899 to 1901) and then as secretary of the interior for the Philippine Insular Government (1901 to 1913.) The University of Michigan saw one of its government professors, Joseph Ralston Hayden, become the vice governor of the Philippines in the 1930s, and the university's law school saw one of its own, George A. Malcolm, become a justice on the Philippine Supreme Court in 1917. Another prominent Michigan citizen who had a con-nection to the Philippines was Detroit's Frank Murphy. He was the mayor of Detroit from 1930 to 1933 and Michigan's governor in 1937 and 1938. In Washington, DC, he was Franklin Roosevelt's attorney general for three years before being appointed to the U.S. Supreme Court, where he served from 1940 to 1949. Less well known is that in between those career points Murphy served in the Philippines as governor-general and high commissioner. His time administering the Philippines coincided with the tail end of large-scale Filipino migrations to the United States.[14]

This thirty-year involvement in the Philippines was more than the sum of individual Michiganders spending a part of their lives in the archipelago. Michiganders helped create the governance infrastructure of the Philippines and the cultural infrastructure of immigration to the United States. A key part of that infrastructure of immigration, what could be called the cultural-social facilitation of transpacific movement, was the way the United States was depicted in classrooms in the Philippines. During the years of U.S. tutelage, American teachers in those classrooms conveyed to Filipino and Filipina students an image of the United States as democratic and desirable, an ideal place to work, study, and live. One such student was Carlos Bulosan, a Filipino immigrant who came to the United States in the 1930s and wrote of his experiences traveling along the West Coast. The title of his memoir, *America Is in the Heart*, captured the range of idealism, disappointment, and hope that animated many Filipinos. American teachers did much to plant an idealized image of America in immigrants' hearts, and the educational infrastructure that made that planting possible was part of the larger Americanizing that many Michiganders oversaw and nurtured.

In a circuitous way, Filipinos who migrated to the United States in the 1920s and the 1930s and then moved from the West Coast to Michigan were "coming home"—or at least coming to places that American educators had made familiar. Those who found their way to Michigan eventually formed a small but growing community. By 1930, when Filipino migration to the mainland United States had reached 45,208, the Filipino population in Michigan was 787. This was small compared to California's 30,470, but within the midwestern setting, Michigan's Filipinas and Filipinos occupied a demographic niche common to the region. Before the Second World War, no midwestern community of Filipinas and Filipinos had significantly more than 2,000 members; the largest in the 1920s and 1930s was Illinois' Filipino population of 2,011.[15] While not large, Michigan's community of "Pinoys," or Filipinos, reflected changes in the state's composition of Asian-derived settlers, a composition that increased and diversified during the period between the First and Second World Wars.

Michigan's Changing and Diversifying Asian American Communities, 1920s-40s

During the 1920s to the 1940s, large-scale events transformed Michigan. The state underwent massive and centralizing industrialization in the 1920s; it endured the Great Depression, during which labor resistance took a distinctive Michigan cast in the sit-down strike at Flint; and it became the "arsenal of democracy" during the Second World War, producing tanks, bombers, and military vehicles in factories that had once made cars for American roads. During this time significant but largely unnoticed events also transformed the demographic profile of Michigan's Asian America, making it both bigger and increasingly diversified as more and different Asian communities took root.

Michigan's Chinese population, the state's first Asian residents, showed its own diversification in terms of gender as the number of female residents increased. This took time, most likely because historically sex ratios had been unbalanced in Chinese American communities in the nineteenth century and because U.S. immigration laws continued to operate in gendered ways to discourage Asian female migration. Despite these odds, Chinese American Detroit grew. In 1910, the first Chinese female in Detroit's community was Mrs. Rose Fong. By 1934, there were fifty women among the five hundred Chinese counted in Detroit.[16]

A growing and maturing society is also measured by its deaths, and the Forest Lawn Mortuary at 11851 Van Dyke Street began to hold the remains of Chinese Detroiters. The first burials were in 1918, after the Chinese American community negotiated to have a Chinese plot set aside at Forest Lawn. By 1963, 583 Chinese American Detroiters had been buried in the cemetery. According to one study, the "burial of infants started to appear" in cemetery records in the early 1920s, thus "indicating the beginning of a second generation."[17] For these small graves, no names seem to have been recorded, only the bare facts of a brief life span. In 1923, there was one female infant. In 1928 there were three children (two males, one female), ranging from less than one year to seven years. In 1930, three males (one to four years old) and one baby girl found permanent rest in the Chinese plot, the girl having spent so little time on this earth her age could not be recorded even in days.[18]

The growth and diversification of Asian American communities in the 1920s were due in no small part to the automobile industry. In between the words and pages of the oft-recounted histories of Chrysler, Ford, and General Motors lie forgotten Asian stories. For example, in the 1920s, Henry Ford sought Chinese students for his school in automobile manufacturing,

bringing Chinese to Detroit to forge links to what he hoped would be a growing automobile market in Asia. According to one local historian, Ford also
sought workers, and in 1922 the company recruited Asian laborers from
Hawaii to work assembly lines in the Midwest.[19]

The 1920s also saw the arrival of East Indians to Michigan. One recent
account brings to light the largely untold detail that Bengali Muslim males
came to Detroit during the 1920s. There they married African American
Detroiters and established lines of descendants who continue to live in the
city, describing themselves as Afro Indians.[20] Other groups of East Indian pioneers came from California, their first home in the United States after migrating from northern India. Michigan beckoned them in the 1920s with the lures
of higher education and industrial jobs. The former was often associated with
the University of Michigan, the latter with Henry Ford's 1914 wage offer of
$5 a day. One old-timer from this migration in the 1920s recalled, "I started
working for Mr. Ford in 1924 and remained with the company for forty-two
years . . . retiring in 1966. I did everything . . . welding, painting, and tooling.
. . . Some [other Punjabi Indians] worked and studied at the University of
Michigan. They learned agriculture so they could use their knowledge upon
returning to Punjab."[21]

A good pair of words to describe the qualities of Asian Americans in
Michigan history during the 1920s to the 1940s would be *resilience* and *commitment*. Each Asian-derived community showed the intention to sink roots
in the state and make homes and livelihoods in the Midwest, all the while
being active transnational participants in the back-and-forth relationship circuit that bound Asians in the United States with events happening in their
original homelands. The resilience and commitment of Chinese, Japanese,
Korean, Filipino, and South Asian Michiganders showed in the willingness to
stay put and develop livelihoods through good times (the 1920s) and bad (the
Depression 1930s.) It also showed in the willingness to protest discriminatory
laws that affected all Asian communities in the United States before the Second World War. It is noteworthy that two challenges to such discrimination
took the form of Asians confronting hostility through litigation pursued in
the federal courthouse in Detroit.

In 1925, John Mohammad Ali, an immigrant from Punjab in northern
India, discovered that what he had gained in 1921 had suddenly been taken
away. He had become a U.S. citizen on May 26, 1921, a testament to having
lived in the United States for twenty-one years, the last eleven in Michigan.
Unfortunately, events in Washington, DC, would change Ali's standing, a fate

he shared with other immigrants of Japanese and Asian Indian descent. In the nation's capital, the U.S. Supreme Court reinterpreted the long-standing racial qualification for citizenship, which could be granted to "free white persons," according to the first naturalization law passed in 1790. The law was now interpreted as disqualifying Japanese and South Asian immigrants. Thus, in 1925, the U.S. district attorney for the Eastern District of Michigan instituted proceedings to cancel Ali's certificate of citizenship. The U.S. District Court, Eastern District of Michigan, agreed. Ali reverted to alien status on August 3, 1925.

Although Ali lost both his citizenship and his case, his courtroom struggle should be remembered as one in a sequence of acts of legal resistance pursued by Asians as they challenged various discriminatory laws. Ali's fight against the whiteness bar to U.S. naturalization continued what began in 1872 when a Chinese Californian first asked whether persons from Asia could be naturalized. More relevant to Michigan's Asian American history, Ali's 1925 case carried forward the torch of legal resistance that four Chinese Detroiters brandished in 1896 when they pushed back against certain harsh features of the Chinese exclusion system. Those four were Wong Wing, Lee Poy, Lee Yon Tong, and Chan Wah Dong. They challenged exclusion's mean and punitive provisions, and when they lost in the federal courthouse in Detroit, they appealed to the U.S. Supreme Court. The 1896 and 1925 cases were small events in constitutional history, but taken together they contributed to the long line of Asian American legal and constitutional history. In pursuing their rights, these Asian Americans also claimed spaces of public inclusion within Michigan, a testament to their own willingness to live in the state and fight for their civic standing.[22]

The Depression decade of the 1930s tested the resilience of Asians in Michigan, as it did that of everyone in the state and nation, but resilience for those Asian Michiganders meant persisting while being largely ignored or invisible. As the 1930s gave way to the first years of the 1940s, one Depression-era study assessed the state's prospects and proclaimed Michigan's diversity as the key to its present and future. In 1942, the New Deal's Federal Writers' Project published a state guide to Michigan, one of many such guides that provided employment to writers during the downturn. The volume for Michigan observed that "Michigan's cultural heritage and current trends can be understood only in relation to the diversity of its 47 percent of foreign racial stock." A vivid example of that "foreign racial stock" could be seen and heard in the "immigrant ante room" at the corner of St. Antoine and Lafayette in

Detroit. There, amid the many languages spoken in the neighborhood, were utterances in "Hindustani." For the writers in 1942, it was one sound in an immigrant cacophony, but for us, it is another historical trace that South Asians (and, by implication, other Asians) were speaking, working, and living in Detroit.

The Federal Writers' Project volume on Michigan was published the year the United States entered the Second World War. The war did much to change the social fabric of the nation at home, and it affected the Asian American communities in Michigan. It could be said that the Second World War was a high-water mark for both Detroit and Asian Americans throughout the nation. By producing tons of military matériel that won the war, Detroit garnered its worldwide reputation as the "arsenal of democracy." For four of the five major Asian American communities in the United States before 1945, the war was not only a high-water mark, it was a positive watershed. Events on the home front gave Chinese, Filipinos, Koreans, and South Asians a new lease on the American dream. These communities made several gains: the congressional repeal of the Chinese Exclusion Act in 1943, the entry of Asian Americans into the U.S. armed services and home front war industries, and the eventual granting of U.S. naturalization to Filipinos and South Asians in 1947. Those were the positives. But the most spectacular wartime effect on Asian Americans was not a gain, it was a catastrophe. For Japanese Americans, the home front was a whirlwind of disruption and displacement.[23]

Within ninety days of the U.S. entry into the Second World War, the U.S. government began the process of forcibly removing some 120,000 Americans of Japanese descent from their homes on the West Coast.[24] The action was officially sanctioned as a wartime measure to protect the West Coast from sabotage and espionage, but this justification would have been exposed as empty had anyone bothered to examine the actual demographic facts of Japanese America. More than 70 percent of the population consisted of school-aged, American-born children. But in the fervor of wartime mobilization, realistic assessments of Japanese Americans on the West Coast were few and far between. The end result of this climate of fear was brutally efficient and fast. From March to September 1942, more than 100,000 persons were removed from their homes and livelihoods, packed off to assembly centers under jurisdiction of the U.S. Army, and then shipped to ten "relocation centers," or camps, administered by the civilian entity known as the War Relocation Authority (WRA).

The WRA thought something good could be "salvaged" from these events—the long-term resettlement of Japanese Americans, who would be dispersed across the nation. According to the officials in the WRA, the best candidates for this dispersal would be the internees who had the most potential to reject their alleged "old Japanese" ways and transform themselves into conforming Americans. Japanese Americans who passed a "loyalty" test that supposedly demonstrated their trustworthiness on the home front could leave the camps under "leave of absence" authorizations. For the WRA, the Midwest beckoned as territory wherein this replanting and rebirth could happen most effectively. Michigan stood out as a promising destination; the state could serve as an experimental station to fulfill the WRA prescription that it "would be good for the United States generally and [it] . . . would be good from the standpoint of the Japanese-Americans themselves, to be scattered over a much wider area and not to be bunched up in groups along the Coast."[25]

To that end, the War Relocation Authority produced a seventeen-page typescript pamphlet titled *Farming in Michigan*.[26] The cover featured a black-and-white photograph of a smiling Japanese American man harvesting Michigan apples. Working from a stepladder, contented in his manner as he reached for one more fruit, emblematic of the state's bounty, he seemed to embody what the pamphlet announced in its text. "Farming in Michigan has been a successful enterprise for more than a hundred years. Several of Michigan's newest successful farmers in 1944 were issei and nisei who previously had farmed on the West Coast." The WRA drove its point hard, contending that these resettled "Japanese American farmers who came into the area early have established a very fine reputation for themselves and for those to follow."[27]

The tone in *Farming in Michigan* was upbeat. "Michigan ranks high among the 48 states in its agriculture." Showcasing that claim, *Farming in Michigan* cited the state's leadership in dry beans, potatoes, sour cherries, celery, and apples. For each commodity, the state could claim it was "at or near the top" as the nation's leading producer. *Farming in Michigan* had to reassure former internees that the soil was good, the future was bright and, most important, the neighbors were friendly. Its author was eager to dispel anxiety about the racial reception that might await internees. The work quoted a Farm Security agent from Lapeer who said he had been able "to determine little, if any, racial discrimination" against resettlers; indeed, one family's success story showed itself in the small details of the two children who attended a "rural school near the farm." The Farm Security agent reported, "The children like their schoolwork very much and are getting along better than they did in California." Not satisfied with simply reporting these details, whoever wrote *Farming in Michigan* unmistakably emphasized Michigan's difference from California in capital letters centered on the page: "OUR NEIGHBORS ARE FRIENDLY." A number of Michigan neighbors were indeed friendly and supportive. Royal Kaji, a new transplant to Wayland who worked as a sharecropper, related, "The employer's attitude toward evacuees was excellent and very understanding." When his neighbors discovered that the Kaji family had a one-month-old baby girl (Shirley Ann), they gave her a "stork shower" in which twenty-five ladies showered her with "66 gifts, [a] bassinet and every clothing our baby needed."[28]

Royal had a positive experience in Wayland, and four other new Japanese American Michiganders echoed his upbeat message. Nevertheless, even these positive testimonials had to be tempered. For example, Jack Y. Matsumoto said that from the start his employer was sympathetic and understanding but he added that "the present shortage of farm workers facilitated his decision to employ us." Likewise, James Ouye and Paul Shimida, two former internees from the Rohwer camp in Arkansas, came to Lansing as "employees in the agricultural department of Michigan State College" in early 1943. A positive outcome resulted but only after a rocky start. Looked upon "with suspicion at first," they later found work in Davison and Clarksville. The War Relocation Authority probably knew that an unleavened broadcast of optimism would not be entirely convincing. Japanese Americans who had been forcibly removed from their homes and incarcerated in assembly centers and WRA camps had firsthand experience with the rough side of the American racial dilemma and its realities could not be smoothed away.[29]

Japanese American resettlers increased the numbers of Asian Americans in Michigan and added to the populations of cities such as Detroit and Ann Arbor. The former saw an increase of 1,649 Americans of Japanese ancestry, while Ann Arbor received 534, and 864 went to other cities.[30] Smaller towns also received new Japanese Americans. *Farming in Michigan* put out the call—from Niles, Eau Claire, Northville, Lapeer, St. Johns, Hartford, and Benton Harbor—that many Michigan farms and countryside factories could use entire families of Japanese American farm operators and farm workers.

In resettling, these Japanese Americans proved as resilient as their forebears had been in establishing new roots. Events during the postwar era and during the cold war would continue the Asian American story within Michigan and begin a new generation of Michiganders with ties to Asia.

Michigan's Cold War–Era Asian and Asian American Histories

The pattern that made Asian America in Michigan accelerated and magnified after the Second World War. Due to cold war pressures and opportunities, that pattern produced two notable phenomena: a continuation of the Michigan institutional presence in Asia but under a new guise, and policies undertaken by notable Michigan public figures that significantly increased and diversified Asian populations in the United States to an extent and at a rate unseen in Asian American history.

Japanese Americans knew the early form of that diversification and growth firsthand. Indeed, they both experienced and helped create it. Those who resettled in Michigan found not just the soil but the atmosphere good for replanting their lives. One measure of this was the establishment of a Detroit branch of the Japanese American Citizens League (JACL), which helped members of the resettler community maintain links with each other, monitor discrimination, and adjust to life in the Midwest. The JACL's national organization pursued an active civil rights agenda. In the postwar years the Detroit chapter participated by monitoring instances of housing discrimination and offering legal aid to persons who sought court remedies for employment discrimination.[31] With that civil rights outlook, Japanese Americans in Michigan carved a public presence for themselves and a space for civic engagement. For issei and nisei who became Michiganders, their efforts showed they were in Michigan to stay. Little did they know that Michigan was about to undergo wrenching economic and social change.

Japanese Americans and all Asian Americans who lived in postwar Michigan were inextricably mixed together with the long-term economic changes that churned the state. Asian American communities, like other ethnic communities tossed into this turmoil, were roiled as Michigan saw the beginnings of what would afflict the state for the next seventy years. According to urban historian Thomas Sugrue,[32] the deindustrialization of Detroit's industrial core began in the 1950s when automobile manufacturers started moving production away from the city to rural areas. The effects of deindustrializing's far-reaching woes were communicated nationally on February 25, 1961, when the *Saturday Evening Post* featured Michigan in its cover story, "The Plight of Michigan." The theme was grim: plateaued population growth, rising unemployment, and "old industries . . . moving out or merging, and new businesses . . . not coming in numbers great enough to keep the work force busy."[33]

While this observation was prophetic, few could anticipate the extent to which deindustrialization would hammer the state ceaselessly. Another type of wrenching change that accompanied Michigan's industrial shift was the wholesale denigrating of urban neighborhoods suddenly deemed expendable. That happened to Detroit's Chinese American community, specifically Chinatown on Third Avenue. It bore the brunt of this new turmoil when officials in Detroit condemned the neighborhood and tore it down in the name of "slum clearance." Chinatown got the notice in 1959 and the bulldozing did not stop until two years later. When it ended, the old Chinatown had been obliterated. Although a new Chinatown was supposed to replace the old at another location, many felt their community had been leveled. Ben K. Yee told the *Detroit News*, "People think of Chinatown as just a bunch of restaurants. But it really is a people, Chinese people, living together." For Yee, the Chinese American district was more than businesses and buildings. It meant home and a sense of community so distinctive that the longtime residents were nicknamed "the Chinatown crowd." Left to fend for themselves, members of that "crowd" had to help those unable to adjust. Left especially vulnerable were the old-timers, the ones who had settled in Detroit in the 1900s but sixty years later had neither families nor means of support. The city left those human costs uncalculated when it cleared room for its new urban tomorrow in the 1960s.[34]

Disruptive urban change dislocated Americans such as Detroit's Chinese Americans, but dislocation was not restricted to cities in the United States. The 1960s witnessed numerous large-scale upheavals that unsettled people and sent them moving to tumultuous circumstances far away from their original homes. Much of that upheaval happened in Southeast Asia, and America's involvement in Vietnam witnessed yet another twisting together of Michigan and Asia and then Asian America. Much like the University of Michigan's experience in the Philippines, one of Michigan's public institutions became directly involved in an Asian setting, unintentionally laying the groundwork for the large Southeast Asian migrations that happened twenty years later. Roundabout, delayed, yet connected due to the way the history of U.S. involvement in Southeast Asia eventually transpired, this Michigan–Asian–Asian American link was no less loaded with aspirations shared by earlier Michiganders who desired to reach across the Pacific and leave the state's mark on the broader stage of U.S. foreign relations in Asia. The vehicle for those hopes was the Michigan State University Vietnam Advisory Group (MSUVAG).[35]

MSUVAG was a technical assistance program implemented by Michigan's land-grant agricultural university from 1955 to 1962. Under a U.S. government contract, MSUVAG pursued a number of institution-building activities to benefit the government of South Vietnam. In its heyday, it spearheaded a four-point program to modernize and "stabilize" South Vietnam: (1) to manage refugee resettlement; (2) to create a program of police administration; (3) to build an infrastructure of state bureaucracy though the National Institute of Administration and Civil Servant Training School; and (4) to supervise the training and education of select South Vietnamese in colleges and universities within the United States.[36]

The reach of these many activities reflected the broad sense of mission that MSUVAG had, but this was not without controversy. Historians have characterized MSUVAG as an international aid program whose ambition matched that of the institution that quickly grew from Michigan Agricultural College to Michigan State College to Michigan State University. One historian of the Vietnam War noted that MSUVAG was the brainchild of "an ambitious land-grant institution, which may have thought to balance its considerable reputation in agricultural science and extension services with more contemporary governmental good works, such as international consulting." While its mission could have been classified under the rubric of "nation building," it wound up being too tied to a particular political figure in South Vietnam (its controversial first president, Ngo Dinh Diem) and too involved with policies that would unduly benefit his regime.[37]

The activities of the MSUVAG were never limited to events in Saigon or Vietnam. Its far-flung aims often led to sponsoring Vietnamese visits to the United States for the purpose of educating a Vietnamese bureaucracy to administer an anti-Communist and Americanized form of public administration, one that differed from both Communist and French colonial policies and structures. Michigan became a showcase for these cold war emulations. For example, one South Vietnamese official, Nguyen Van Dai, saw the Detroit City Planning Commission at work and made similar observational trips to the Michigan Economic Development Commission and the Lansing City Planning Commission. Another Vietnamese official examined the Detroit Public Schools as part of his study of "the financial features of educational administration." For some Vietnamese, the visits turned into extended stays, especially for students who entered graduate programs at U.S. universities and colleges through the "Participant Training Program" of the MSUVAG.[38]

This Michigan tie was more than a fortuitous by-product of a chance connection between the nation's first land-grant university and an Asian-derived population. The MSUVAG became involved in Vietnam as part of its larger land-grant university vision, and the program invested the reputation of MSU in its effort. Comment to that effect appeared in the *Congressional Record* for April 21, 1955, wherein the state's congressman from the Sixth District, Donald Hayworth, a former speech professor at Michigan State, entered his remarks about the "Michigan State University Mission to Vietnam." For Hayworth, the MSUVAG was more than a government contract with the U.S. Foreign Operations Administration. It was a technical assistance program shot through with the values of the land-grant college system and its manifestation in Michigan. The MSUVAG was "a practical approach" that got its strength from "the great down-to-earth tradition of our land-grant colleges." According to Hayworth, the MSUVAG was the chance for one of Michigan's "great educational institutions" to "apply our educational and technical skills on an international scale."[39]

Michigan State University's Vietnam Project ended in 1960 when its contract with the U.S. government expired; however, the United States would continue to pursue its foreign policy aims in Southeast Asia for the next fifteen years. During that time, two major events reshaped the demographic face of Asian America to create contemporary Asian America. The first was the congressional reform known as the Immigration and Nationality Act of 1965; the second was the collapse of allied forces and governments in Southeast Asia in 1975 that in turn set in motion Southeast Asian refugee flows that later became Southeast Asian American communities. By coincidence, two national political figures from Michigan played key roles in inaugurating both events. Philip Hart, who served as U.S. senator from 1959 to 1976, cosponsored the Immigration and Nationality Act. Ten years later, Gerald R. Ford, the thirty-eighth president of the United States, urged Americans to welcome Southeast Asian refugees into the country, thus providing crucial moral leadership at a divisive moment. While in many ways coincidental, especially when contrasted with the direct activities of earlier Michiganders in Asia, the individual political acts of Philip Hart and Gerald Ford can nevertheless be included in the complicated history of Michiganders who happened to have shaped Asian migration flows that reformed into Asian American communities in the United States.

A brief look at the Immigration Act of 1965 and the Southeast Asian refugee episode of 1975 shows that both Philip Hart and Gerald Ford were more than place markers who happened to have come from Detroit (Hart) and Grand Rapids (Ford). In 1965 and 1975 they proved to be national figures who used their political capital to endorse new kinds of Asian entrance into the United States.

Taking the Immigration Act of 1965 first, it was during the early to mid-1960s that the presidential administrations of John F. Kennedy and Lyndon B. Johnson pursued immigration reform. The result of their efforts was the Immigration and Nationality Act of 1965. Dubbed "the conscience of the Senate," Senator Hart endorsed the legislation and advocated on its behalf. He spoke of removing the "national origins" formula that had discriminated against southern and eastern European immigration and shut down Asian immigration. Ruling immigration policy since 1924, the "national origins" system fell especially hard on Asian immigrants because it closed off large channels of migration to those deemed "ineligible for citizenship," a euphemism that lawmakers in 1924 knew referred to Asians. Hart understood this history and how congressional restrictions had affected Asian communities in the United States. He wrote that his "bi-partisan bill . . . would abolish the national origins system of quota allocation [that] discriminated against Asians and Southern and Eastern Europeans." He also noted that his cosponsored bill would "make permanent provision for the admission of refugees" who up until 1964 had "been admitted only under temporary, emergency legislation."[40]

The overall effect of the Immigration and Nationality Act of 1965 on Asian America was profound. With the removal of the national origins quotas and the inclusion of the act's statutory provisions for family reunification along with an official preference category for refugee entry status as well as a preference for highly skilled employees, the immigration reform of 1965 made possible new and diversified flows of migration from many more regions of Asia. These new migrations affected the Asian American demographic profile in Michigan as more diverse Asian communities made the heartland their home. A notable result was the emergence of new South Asian communities in Ann Arbor and East Lansing composed of East Indians who contributed to the civic spheres of those university cities.

Ten years later, another political initiative produced results as far reaching as the 1965 Immigration and Nationality Act. Gerald R. Ford of Grand Rapids was six months into his improbable term as the unelected thirty-eighth president of the United States when his administration midwifed the largest and latest Asian American diversification in the cold war era. With the rapid demise of the U.S.-backed government of South Vietnam in April 1975, the Ford White House and the U.S. Congress worked to admit South Vietnamese into the United States as refugees. Faced with an emergency, the Ford administration convened an Interagency Task Force that established the channels for transpacific migration and U.S. resettlement for 150,000

Southeast Asians. Refugees included Cambodians, Lao, and Hmong. The efforts started in 1975 laid the groundwork for what became in 2010 Vietnamese America (1,548,449 persons), Cambodian America (231,616), Laotian America (209,646), and Hmong America (247,595).

Michigan as the Site of the New Asian American Panethnicity, 1982–87 to the Present

Philip Hart's legislative efforts in 1965 and the implementation of refugee resettlement by the Ford White House in 1975 continued the historical interaction between Michiganders and Asian American history. The interactions of 1965 and 1975 reshaped the demographic profile of Asian America by significantly diversifying the origins of Asian American communities in the United States and increasing the overall numbers of Asian derived individuals and communities.

Before the 1980s, when non-Asian Michiganders did things in Asia, they contributed to a larger process whereby Asian migrations stirred at one end of the Pacific and later manifested as Asian American communities in the United States. It can be said that Michiganders participated in a larger demographic current that saw Asians travel the world over in numerous diasporic flows. Those non-Asian Michiganders therefore participated in a larger historical unfolding that did not originate in Michigan, much less aim to make Asian American history. Nevertheless, some of the state's major institutions and a number of its prominent public persons played roles in this history, whether directly or indirectly in Asia, planned or unplanned, fully cognizant or not of what their acts could do to either discourage or encourage Asian migrations to the United States. Before the 1980s, this story of Michigan and Asian America was a series of delayed results or a number of roundabout outcomes that nevertheless added to the making of Asian American communities. That linked history would continue in the 1980s, but a key shift occurred in the years 1982 to 1987. During that break and as a result of its rupture, Asian Americans in Michigan acted for themselves to deal with conditions that marginalized them. Acting consciously as Asian Americans, they unleashed a burst of activism that mobilized Asian American communities in Michigan and across the nation. It was a seismic shift and it started in Detroit.

Few had any inkling that this would happen. None expected it on the West Coast, where most of the nation's Asian American reformers and professionals lived. On the eve of 1980, the national headquarters of the Japanese American Citizens League sent a special mailing to its Detroit chapter announcing plans for a new civil rights initiative. Given the banner name of

"Operation 80s," the JACL initiative attempted to move national civil rights efforts forward.[41] Those who envisioned Operation 80s probably saw two geographical sites as primary for an Asian American civil rights push in the 1980s; it would have emanated from California and climaxed in Washington, DC. It is a safe bet that no one in 1979 thought Michigan or Detroit would be the venue for a nationwide revitalization of Asian American political and social activism. The last person in the world who would have seen himself as its catalyst was a Chinese American Detroiter, twenty-seven years old in 1979, who had no notion of what was to come. His name was Vincent Chin.

The catalyst started in Highland Park and seemed to have ended bloodily outside a McDonald's restaurant. On the evening of June 19, 1982, a confrontation occurred between Vincent Chin, celebrating his upcoming marriage, and two unemployed white Detroiters, Ronald Ebens and his stepson, Michael Nitz. Enough aggressive words were said that revealed the underlying tensions behind the exchange. Ebens thought he knew what Chin was. To an autoworker whose stepson had recently been laid off, Vincent Chin wore the face of the Oriental threat behind the flood of Japanese-made automobiles. Addressing that face, Ebens said it was because of "you motherfuckers" that Americans were out of work. The deeper implications of that mis-signifying meant any Asian-looking person, including the Chinese American Vincent Chin, could be roped into the blame category of Japanese car manufacturers. What happened next showed that something more was at work than a typical male brawl.

The belligerent exchange continued in the parking lot of the club. Ebens opened the trunk of his car and took out a baseball bat. Seeing that the trouble was ratcheting up, Chin and his companions left, but Ebens and Nitz were not willing to let it go. Instead, for the next twenty-five minutes, they cruised five blocks of Highland Park looking for Chin and his friends. The hunting even acquired a bounty: Ebens and Nitz paid $20 to another Detroiter to help them "find the Chinaman." At a McDonald's restaurant, the two white Detroiters found their quarry. Nitz held Chin from behind and Ebens proceeded to deliver blows with his baseball bat to Chin's head. Only when two off-duty Detroit policemen confronted Ebens did the beating stop. Comatose, Chin was taken to Henry Ford Hospital. Eight hours of surgery could do no good. He died four days later of brain injuries.

That was the physical killing of Vincent Chin, but what ensued in the courts amounted to a dismissal of his civic being. Both Ebens and Nitz had been caught red-handed—and by police officers at that. There was no getting around their act of assault, but the sentence pronounced by Judge Charles S.

Kaufman seemed to classify their violence as nothing more than hotheaded-ness gone too far. Kaufman sentenced Ebens and Nitz to three years' proba-tion and a fine of $3,000. For Asian Americans in Detroit, Kaufman's sentence turned the perpetrators into objects of public sympathy and his judicial act erased the person who was actually killed. Looking back thirty years later, one can say that privileging mercy for Ebens and Nitz while de-privileging the loss of Chin's life had much larger implications. Construing the killing as merely a brawl gone bad meant being deaf to the ways Ebens wielded not only his baseball bat but his hateful slurs and hired someone for $20 to hunt "a China-man." Even more, it meant turning a blind eye to how two entities ceased to exist: first was the physical end of a Chinese American man; second was the legal dismissal of his standing as a human being. The implication was that similarly situated people could likewise be cheapened in such circumstances. The Vincent Chin case made Asian Americans realize they faced that peril just by looking as they did.

The Vincent Chin incident revitalized Asian American communities across the nation. As one observer put it, before the crime and its aftermath, the Asian American movement had been student oriented and centered on university and college campuses. Simultaneously during the mid-1970s, the notion of "Asian America" was increasingly professionalized as social workers, lawyers, and government agencies adopted the term to efficiently distribute social services. The mobilization of "Asian America" in the wake of the Vin-cent Chin episode led to new locations and a new embrace. The new locations were communities outside classroom settings and away from the West Coast orientation of Asian American professionals in California: places such as the East Coast, the South, and the Midwest. The new embrace was made by a range of communities and individuals who had heretofore identified solely with places of national origin, but who now began to think about the collec-tive category of Asian American.

Nowhere was this truer than in the city where it started. Detroit efforts assumed an organizational form that not only cemented the coalition of dif-ferent Asian communities, it consolidated into a new panethnic community organization that saw its mission as advocating for the unaddressed needs of all Asian-derived persons and communities in the state. In March 1983, this support network adopted a name: American Citizens for Justice (ACJ). At first agitating to educate more people about the Chin incident, it soon trans-formed into a larger effort for Asian Americans in general, both in Michigan and the nation.

This change can be measured by the way American Citizens for Justice broadened its mission. It added employment discrimination to its agenda and supplied legal aid to Asian American Michiganders who had experienced racial discrimination and who now had a voice in ACJ. The group also provided a new public face to the changing facets of Asian America in the state. In the late 1980s, a South Asian served as its executive director. In the 1990s, ACJ proactively sought to provide for the health needs of the most recent Asian-derived community to take root in Michigan. Hmong, who had resettled in Michigan after their refugee arrival in the mid-1970s through the 1980s, found their public health issues inadequately addressed by the existing social service structure. To fill that gap, ACJ completed an exhaustive and original study that became the publication *Research Survey of the Hmong Health Needs Assessment,* which contributed to the well-being of Hmong in Michigan and cemented the panethnic commitment of the state's active Asian Americans.[42]

Michigan and Asian America: Toward a New Past and a New Future

Michigan and Asian America. An unlikely pairing at first glance, but their union is considered improbable only because their shared histories have remained untold. Their histories ran alongside each other within Michigan's borders, but sealing their intimate relationship is the fact that at key points their pasts intersected outside the United States, an intersection that shaped Asian migrations and later manifested as Asian American resettlements in the United States. Operating through prominent Michigan institutions, the activities of Michiganders such as James Burrill Angell, representatives of the Ford Motor Company, faculty at the University of Michigan, and faculty at Michigan State University shaped the flows of Asian migrations, whether directly or indirectly, immediately or delayed. To capture this neglected history I have proposed a way to catch its irregular shape and comprehend its strange twists. I suggest that the best way to tell this story is to envision the histories of Michigan and Asian America as a *series* of interactions that created an unintended continuity that linked Michigan and Asia and thus created Asian American Michiganders. Understood this way, the presences of Michiganders in Asia and Asians in Michigan no longer seem like disconnected instances or isolated moments, but rather form a deeply resonating history. As repeated occurrences in a series of connections that spanned a long stretch of time, this history tells the relationship between Asia, Asian America, and Michigan in all its richness, contradictions, and eerie repetitions.

Both streams of this history merged when Governor Jennifer Granholm signed Executive Order 2005-10 on May 4, 2005. The order established the Advisory Council on Asian Pacific American Affairs, a body developed to assess the needs and ongoing concerns of Michigan's Asian Pacific American communities and report those needs to the governor. Four years later, the Michigan legislature created the Michigan Asian Pacific American Affairs Commission, a body with a fourteen-point mandate to improve conditions for Asian Americans in Michigan. These enactments signal Michigan's new commitment to its Asian Pacific American denizens and citizens. Yes, these recent advances are significant, but Michigan has long been invested in Asia, as this chapter has shown. The difference in the twenty-first century is parity: today Asian Pacific Americans are officially recognized as active contributors to the public citizenship of Michigan and its future.

This chapter began with a walking tour through the shelves of Michigan history. The volumes on those shelves tell the state's history in terms familiar to anyone who might consume that past, whether in an elementary school, at a Michigan college or university, or at the public institutions that preserve and display Michigan's history of statehood. The familiar names (Angell, Ford, Frank Murphy) are invoked and the well-known events are paraded, but now a new beat is added to the music of Michigan's history. Readers of this chapter can point to names, persons, and details that made a history that ran parallel to the mainstream story, but one that had always been shrouded in ignorance and neglect. To appreciate the long interconnected relationship between Michigan, Asia, and Asian America, one need only connect.

To leave you with such a connection, consider Chinese exclusion in the early twentieth century and see how that far-flung system took tangible form in Detroit. Here is a Chinese Michigander in 1917 named M. K. Suey. Due to the surveillance structure of Chinese exclusion, he one day found himself having to account for his whereabouts to inspectors of the U.S. Immigration Service. A migrant to Detroit after leaving Chicago in 1917, he gave the itinerary of his Michigan life. A series of local journeys had him going to *"2429 Jefferson Avenue East, Detroit, Mich., for eight or nine months, helping in the laundry. I was at Moy Wing's laundry, 134 Brooklyn Avenue, for four or five months. I lived upstairs, but did not work. The laundry moved to 401 Michigan Avenue, and I went with it and stayed there off and on, and at 2429 Jefferson Avenue until I found the place at 1754 Michigan Avenue, Detroit, about two weeks ago."*[43]

This testimony evokes the way one Chinese Detroiter lived, worked, and walked the streets of the city alongside other Michiganders, but the key difference separating him from his fellow Detroiters was the shadow of Chinese exclusion. For readers of *Asian Americans in Michigan*, his remembrances of Jefferson Avenue, Brooklyn Avenue, and Michigan Avenue bring the historical fact of Chinese exclusion intimately into Michigan's early twentieth-century past. The precise mention of particular streets and addresses weaves a thick sense of local Detroit, a sense as thick and recognizably "Michigan" as when the War Relocation Authority urged Japanese Americans to venture to Niles, Eau Claire, Northville, Lapeer, St. Johns, Hartford, and Benton Harbor in the 1940s.

One more connection. I mentioned at the start of this essay the landmarks that the Michigan Historical Marker Program recognizes throughout the state. I noted Temple Beth El synagogue at 7400 Telegraph Road in Oakland County, State Register Number 673 in the Historical Marker Program. That notable building has an Asian American connection: its architect was Minoru Yamasaki, a Japanese American who grew up in the state of Washington. Because he had moved to New York before the Second World War, he escaped the fate of those who had been moved off the West Coast and sent to WRA camps. After the war, he moved to Detroit, but in the 1980s he faced his own need to address the stakes of being Asian American. At a key moment in the mobilization that stemmed from the Vincent Chin episode, Yamasaki addressed Detroiters who came from Chinese American, Japanese American, Filipino American, and Korean American backgrounds. At the time, he was seventy-three years old, "dignified but frail," and that evening he rose up slowly from his seat with the assistance of a companion. In a strong, clear voice he told the assembled group, *"If Asian people in America don't learn to stand up for themselves, these injustices will never cease."*[44]

With those words, Yamasaki encapsulated his sense of the past, the urgency of the present, and the consequences of both for the future. By the time those Detroiters had assembled that evening and heard his words, much history relating Asian America and Michigan had happened, but it remained unknown even as they were starting a new chapter in its progression. Perhaps greater awareness of the long run of Michigan's deep connections to Asian American history and Asian Americans' long commitment to the state could further Yamasaki's call and deepen the self-understanding of everyone in Michigan, the state that is dotted with history from Alcona to Wexford and so much more in between.

Notes

1. Alcona to Wexford is the alphabetical list of Michigan's eighty-three counties. Geographically, the list could read as Keewanaw to Monroe in a northwest to southeast direction.
2. Laura Rose Ashlee, ed., *Traveling through Time: A Guide to Michigan's Historical Markers*, rev. ed. (Ann Arbor: University of Michigan Press, 2005), 504-5, 321-22.
3. The volumes I perused are in the Images of America series published by Arcadia, an imprint of Tempus Publishing. The Detroit volumes include *Detroit, 1930-1969* by David Lee Poremba, *20th Century Retailing in Downtown Detroit* by Michael Hauser and Marianne Weldon, *Cruisin' the Original: Woodward Avenue* by Anthony Ambrogio and Sharon Luckerman, *Detroit's Woodlawn Cemetery* by A. Dale Northup, *Detroit's Polonia* by Cecile Wendt Jensen, and *Italians in Detroit* by Armando Delicato. Ann Arbor is represented by *Lost Ann Arbor* by Susan Cee Wineberg.
4. George S. May, *A History of the Wolverine State*, 3rd rev. ed. (Grand Rapids: Eerdmans, 1995), 591.
5. Ibid., 591-92; Willis Frederick Dunbar, *Michigan: A History of the Wolverine State* (Grand Rapids: Eerdmans, 1965). Another standard history of Michigan that can be contrasted with May's inclusion of Asian Michiganders is F. Clever Bald, *Michigan in Four Centuries*, rev. ed. (New York: Harper, 1954, 1961).
6. May, *History of the Wolverine State*, 390-91. May described Dean Conant Worcester's time in the Philippines as "beginning a remarkable connection between Michigan and the Philippines that would continue for many decades."
7. Emiko Ohnuki, "The Detroit Chinese—A Study of Socio-cultural Changes in the Detroit Chinese Community from 1872 through 1963 (master's thesis, University of Wisconsin, 1964), 11-12, 15-16.
8. Christian G. Fritz, "Due Process, Treaty Rights, and Chinese Exclusion, 1882-1891," in *Entry Denied: Exclusion and the Chinese Community in America, 1882-1943*, ed. Sucheng Chan (Philadelphia: Temple University Press, 1991), 26-27.
9. Ronald Takaki, *Strangers from a Different Shore: A History of Asian Americans* (New York: Penguin, 1989), 79-131.
10. James Burrill Angell, *The Reminiscences of James Burrill Angell* (Freeport, NY: Books for Libraries, 1911, 1971). For the consequences of the Angell Treaty and how it related to Chinese exclusion, see Fritz, "Due Process," 26-27.
11. Angell, *Reminiscences,* 168.
12. Ohnuki, "The Detroit Chinese," 53.
13. For overviews of the U.S. war in the Philippines and its long-term historical consequences, see Antonio Tiongson, Ricardo Gutierrez, and Edgardo Gutierrez, eds., *Positively No Filipinos Allowed: Building Communities and Discourse* (Philadelphia: Temple University Press, 2006). On the war during its 1899-1903 phase, see Stuart Creighton Miller, *Benevolent Assimilation: The American Conquest of the Philippines, 1899-1903* (New Haven: Yale University Press, 1982). On the U.S. administration of the Philippines, Franklin Ng's PhD dissertation, "Governance of an American Empire: American Colonial Administration and Attitudes, 1898-1917," finished at the University of Chicago in 1971, still rewards consultation.
14. Many of these Michiganders wrote memoirs, diaries, and reminiscences of their experiences in the Philippines. They also preserved records of their activities. Both sets can be

found in the Bentley Historical Library on the campus of the University of Michigan. In 1982, Marjorie Barritt wrote an annotated inventory of these records available as "American-Philippine Relations: A Guide to the Resources in the Michigan Historical Collections," Bentley Historical Library, University of Michigan, Ann Arbor.

15. Takaki, *Strangers from a Different Shore*, 315.

16. Ohnuki, "The Detroit Chinese," 51, 62.

17. Ibid.

18. Ibid., 104 (for the overall sense of burials in Detroit), 105-6 (for information about children's burials).

19. Chelsea Zuzindlak, "Notes on 1922 Chinese Laborers Brought to Detroit by Ford," August 16, 2008. "In 1922, Henry Ford wanted to bring . . . Chinese laborers to Detroit to work for him. . . . Sending out supervisors of his to Hawaii, he instructed them to hand pick the laborers. . . . Postcards exist that document the dialogue between Ford and his supervisors regarding the chosen laborers. The official documents of receipts in Detroit also exist."

20. Arthur Helweg, *Asian Indians in Michigan* (East Lansing: Michigan State University Press, 2002), 15.

21. Ibid., 17.

22. The citations for these two cases are *United States v. Ali*, 7 F.2d 728 (1925) and *Wong Wing v. U.S.*, 163 U.S. 228 (1896).

23. Roger Daniels, *Prisoners without Trial: Japanese Americans in World War II* (New York: Hill and Wang, 1993). Daniels's short history distills the official findings of the report of the Commission on Wartime Relocation and Internment of Civilians. *Personal Justice Denied: Report of the Wartime Relocation and Internment of Civilians* (Seattle: University of Washington Press, 1997).

24. The eventual number of persons who were placed within "WRA custody" was 120,313. This is represented in a chart entitled "The Evacuated People" in U.S. Department of the Interior, *WRA: A Story of Human Conservation* (Washington, DC: U.S. Government Printing Office, 1947), 196.

25. Richard Drinnon, *Keeper of Concentration Camps: Dillon S. Myer and American Racism* (Berkeley: University of California Press, 1987), 50-61. The sentiment can also be found in various speeches that Myer delivered during the war years.

26. U.S. Department of the Interior, War Relocation Authority, *Farming in Michigan*. The copy I studied can be found in its original form in the archives of the Japanese American National Museum in Los Angeles.

27. Ibid., 1.

28. Ibid., 4-5.

29. Ibid., 5-6.

30. U.S. Department of the Interior, *WRA*, 204.

31. Papers of the Japanese American Citizens League Detroit, Bentley Historical Library. Readers wishing to know about the civil rights agenda of the JACL in Detroit during this postwar period should examine the newsletters, bulletins, and board minutes of the JACL Detroit chapter.

32. Thomas Sugrue, *The Origins of the Urban Crisis: Race and Inequality in Postwar Detroit* (Princeton, N.J.: Princeton University Press, 1996), 125-52.

33. Joe Grimm, ed., *Michigan Voices: Our State's History in the Words of the People Who Lived It* (Detroit: Wayne State University Press, 1987), 190-91.

34. Ohnuki, "The Detroit Chinese," 11n1 (for "Chinatown crowd"), 95 (for the razing of Chinatown).

35. A book-length history of the Michigan State University Vietnam Advisory Group is John Ernst, *Forging a Fateful Alliance: Michigan State University and the Vietnam War* (East Lansing: Michigan State University Press, 1998).

36. Ibid., 21-114.

37. Marilyn B. Young, *The Vietnam Wars, 1945-1990* (New York: HarperCollins, 1991), 44, 61. See Sucheng Chan, *The Vietnamese American 1.5. Generation: Stories of War, Revolution, Flight, and New Beginnings* (Philadelphia: Temple University Press, 2006) for a similar assessment.

38. Ernst, *Forging a Fateful Alliance*, 96.

39. *Congressional Record*, 84th Cong., 1st sess., 1955, A2677.

40. Philip A. Hart, "A New Immigration Bill: Its Aim Is to Make Our Laws as Good as Our Practices," *National Council of Jewish Women*, n.d., 5-6. A copy of this essay is in the Michigan State University Vietnam Advisory Group Papers.

41. Japanese American Citizens League Detroit, "Operation 80s," Bentley Historical Library.

42. *Research Survey of the Hmong Health Needs Assessment* can be found in the papers of American Citizens for Justice in the Bentley Historical Library.

43. Sworn statement of Moy Kung Suey, Chinese laborer without Certificate of Residence, case 2242/418, Record Group 85, Great Lakes Region, [United States] National Archives, Washington, DC.

44. Helen Zia, *Asian American Dreams: The Emergence of an American People* (New York: Farrar, Straus and Giroux, 2000), 77.

3

"TELL 'EM YOU'RE FROM DETROIT"

Chinese Americans in the Model City

Chelsea Zuzindlak

It is easy to infer that there was once a Chinatown in Detroit. It is not so easy, however, to flesh out the details and make it real. On the surface, the elements of every American Chinatown are here—fixtures with Chinese lettering, curved roofs, and neon signs for Cantonese cuisine. Yet a glance down Peterboro Street, home to "New Chinatown" in the 1960s and 1970s, shows those days have passed.

Once a metropolis emblematic of the American dream, Detroit is now a paradigmatic case of deindustrialization and urban decay.[1] The effects are apparent on Peterboro. Signs of what, it was once hoped, would become "New Chinatown," an ethnic and commercial district to succeed "Old Chinatown," which was demolished in the 1960s to make way for one of America's first freeways, are invariably scarce.[2]

I first stumbled upon Detroit's Chinatown in 2006 in my second year of university. I was on the way to my first day as an instructor of English as a second language (ESL) at the Association of Chinese Americans' Detroit Drop-in Service Center.[3] Standing at Peterboro and Cass, my curiosity was provoked by an aged pagoda and a sign that read, "Welcome Chinatown." I saw several vacant facades with Chinese characters, a dilapidated neon sign for Chung's Restaurant and, at the far end of the block, another pagoda that appeared to have been firebombed. These sights, coupled with knowledge that a small community of elderly Chinese immigrants still resided here in the Cass Corridor, one of the toughest strips in Detroit, propelled me to ask questions.

I wanted to know who had lived here, what had happened and, most important, why I had never learned about Detroit's former Chinatowns before. Visitors often hear that one of Detroit's distinguishing characteristics is its diverse population—albeit a segregated one. But virtually nothing is known, even by their descendants, of the city's first Chinese settlers, their transformation into American citizens, or "Chinatown." Paradoxically, as Detroit was and continues to be a city arguably defined by race, the stories and experiences of Asian Americans frequently have been omitted from local and regional histories.[4] Thus, a glimpse into the lives of Asian Americans, in this case Chinese Americans, could offer a means of comprehending much more about our shared history.

After my introduction to the "New Chinatown," I rigorously pursued public records and talked with former residents, many of whom had collected and preserved family archives. While I derived a large portion of my research from local newspaper articles, a great deal stems from the memories of people who consented to having their stories and identities publicized.[5] Accordingly, I must thank those who allowed me into their homes and their hearts as they recounted their life histories, filling the gaps left by library research. Without them, this project would have amounted to nothing more than a superficial outline of events.

Yin Ack Yee

[For the] Chinese in [the mid- to late 1800s], like in China in those days, [it was] very difficult to find a job. There was no job. Our agriculture was very bad because it was a hilly country. So what was our biggest industry? Immigration! They must go all over the world, [and do] whatever they can to find jobs, to send money home for support.

My dad [and] my grandfather were here during the railroad days in California. You know, the Union Pacific, the railroad days. And because [my grandfather] was treated so badly, later he brought the family back to China. He said to never go back to the United States again. But after he died, they all came back, you know.

And then my father married. Then he had to come back here to make a living, so it took him ten years before he could go back [to China].

My mother died when I was six. I lived with my aunt for four years, then he [my father] brought me back here to Detroit. He had a business already. He had a laundry on Englewood Avenue . . . corner of Woodward. Woodward and Englewood. I think it was Yee Wah, Yee Wah laundry. . . . I don't know if the building is still there or not. I think maybe [it's] not there anymore.[6]

Hand Laundries and Social Visibility in the Urban North

The first Chinese settler, Ah-chee, arrived in Detroit between 1872 and 1873, soon followed by Lu-how.[7] Though the number of Chinese who migrated to Detroit over the next twenty-five years would be modest compared to other midwestern cities, the newcomers, nearly all of whom opened hand laundries, became the darlings of local journalists.[8] To white Detroiters, Chinese laundrymen were exotic, inviting intellectual curiosity. Fluctuating between inquisitive affirmations and shallow assumptions, *Detroit Free Press* and *Detroit News* reporters frequently probed Detroit's Chinese about their native customs and processes of Americanization.[9] In their columns, reporters' perceptions of their new neighbors surfaced. The religious and cultural traditions of the Chinese laundrymen were often described favorably because the traditions themselves were symbols of the "Great Empire," a dynastic China that retained the splendors of antiquity. In contrast, the "Children of the Sun" received less than positive reviews, especially when they were unwilling to reveal private information about themselves or their lifestyle.[10] What the journalists did not include were the Chinese settlers' firsthand accounts of how they had migrated to Detroit or why they had come. The columns revealed little more than the dates settlers arrived and their initial employment.

Like most cities in the mid- to late 1800s, Detroit attracted both foreign-born immigrants and domestic migrants seeking refuge and jobs. The largest of Detroit's minority populations, black migrants from the South, were symbolic of this movement. The racially discriminatory policies they sought to avoid were in stark juxtaposition with the economic opportunity and perceived freedoms of the urban North.[11] To the Chinese, the image and promise of Detroit also shone as a beacon of hope. Originating mainly from China's Canton region, now Guangzhou city, many Chinese immigrants had initially arrived on America's Pacific Coast to enlist as laborers on sugar plantations, in mines, and on the Transcontinental Railroad.[12]

Their arrival was far from welcomed. Chinese who settled in the West became caricatures for anti-Chinese propaganda that distinguished Asian immigrants from ethnic white immigrants as being inferior and inassimi-lable.[13] This fueled public perceptions of the "Chinese Problem," the threat-ening effect of free nonwhite persons on the developing labor market.[14] In 1882, racial animus toward the Chinese reached the breaking point. The U.S. Congress passed the Chinese Exclusion Act, suspending the entry of both skilled and unskilled Chinese laborers into the United States. Though the ban exempted merchants, scholars, and officials, it still prohibited them from naturalizing or becoming American citizens.[15] During this time when one of the most discriminatory immigration policies in U.S. history was in effect, many Chinese developed a new strategy for survival. They moved east to join the small communities of settlers in Chicago, Detroit, New York, or Boston.[16]

Despite the absence of firsthand accounts from Detroit's earliest Chinese settlers, stories from individuals with comparable experiences can help us to imagine their journey from China to the Midwest. Yin Yee, a World War II veteran and restaurateur, was one such invaluable source.

My meeting with Yee seemed to be fate. My family had long patron-ized his restaurant, which was then managed by his son, and consequently I became well acquainted with the staff. During one of my visits I struck up a conversation with Yee's son about Detroit's Chinatown. It was as if I had struck gold. I quickly arranged a meeting to speak with Yee himself.

Yee welcomed me into a dimly lit room adjacent to the main dining area of the restaurant. The room had once been used for banquets but was now a storage area. We sat at one of the tables that had yet to be deconstructed. On it, Yee had layered black-and-white photos of himself in the service, images of the Chinese American congregation that once met at Central Methodist Church in Detroit, and several certificates of achievement he had earned throughout the years. His face lit up with pride as he fingered through his artifacts, briefly describing each memory.

Yee told of his grandfather and father's initial migration to the United States in what he referred to as the "railroad days." The ill treatment that led his grandfather to leave the United States, he said, compelled his family to remain in China for some time. Although his grandfather insisted that his family "never go back" to America, Yee eventually did, returning with his father to Detroit in the early 1900s.[17]

When I asked Yee, "Why Detroit?" he explained that his father already owned a hand laundry here and that extended family connections existed to provide stability and support. He stressed the importance of hand laundries in an era before the electric washing machine and the opportunity this posed for the Chinese:

> A white shirt was a must. You got to have a white shirt to go to church. You got to have a white shirt to go . . . to work in the office. You got to have a white shirt to enter the court. So people [sent] the shirts to the . . . laundries. And the Chinese open[ed] . . . they call[ed] them hand laundries. They [did] it by hand; [they did] a very nice job. So for most Chinese in those days, as I say, there were not very many jobs open to them. So they had created their own job and supported themselves during that period. We were visible only because of the laundries.

Yee's remark about visibility is striking. With few Chinese living and working in Detroit, those who did migrate were able to network without rousing the anti-Chinese bigotry that had become engrained in the political platforms and social institutions of the West.[18] Moreover, the Chinese were able to exercise entrepreneurship by learning a trade and opening small businesses that served the basic needs of their neighbors.[19] Yee's career did not end in the laundry business. After working and living in his father's laundry as a young child, Yee joined the U.S. Fourteenth Air Service Group at the outbreak of World War II and served in China and India. Later he joined the Chinese American veterans' organization AMVET Post 85.[20] Though he ultimately retired from the business, he still spent most of his days in the restaurant, mingling with patrons.

Dorothy Matsumoto

[In the 1940s,] we all went to elementary school . . . by the famous Holy Trinity Church. That's by, I believe, Sixth and Labrosse, down in Corktown. Chinatown bordered Corktown. It's all gone. Everything is gone. They tore it down when they put in the Lodge [Freeway].

We were very young. I'm talking about ten years old, eleven years old. They had a community center that was run by the city . . . and we called it Neighborhood House. That's where we hung out after school, that's where we played basketball, that's where they sent us to summer camp. For a quarter you could buy a membership for a year. It was at Fourth and Porter, it was a block away [from Old Chinatown].

The Caucasian people came in to eat, you know, at a restaurant or something like that . . . but they didn't hang out there. In Corktown . . . we hung out with the Mexicans, Irish, [and] Maltese. It was a real melting pot down there. And we hung out with them in Neighborhood House . . . it was a meeting place for kids.[21]

Living Together and Apart in Metropolitan Detroit

The dawn of the twentieth century ushered in a new era for Chinese in America. In Detroit, the new century meant the invention of the moveable assembly line and mass production, a tremendous increase in industrial jobs, and a boom in overall population that would lead to a myriad of organizational and housing crises. For the Chinese, the development of Detroit as a modern industrial complex was advantageous because it provided a context in which they could nurture American-born families. Three city blocks conceived of as Chinatown became a locus for change.

In 1922, Faye Elizabeth Smith attempted to detail the dynamics of Detroit's Chinese population in "Bits of the Old World in Detroit." Smith wrote that the "Chinese here are totally Americanized [and] there is no district in which they are grouped." She also noted that "65 percent of the colony own their own homes which are in pretty residential districts."[22] In the early twentieth century, nothing could have been farther from the truth. While migrant families from many backgrounds were seeking to establish residence in Detroit, the Chinese, like blacks, were neither welcomed nor permitted to buy homes in white neighborhoods.[23] Consequently, nonwhite groups settled in ethnic enclaves in the most segregated areas of the inner city.

Between 1940 and 1950, nearly a third of Detroit's blacks lived on the lower east side, an area that extended from the Detroit River to East Grand Boulevard. Called Paradise Valley, the neighborhood was anything but edenic. Though home to a large number of black social institutions, jazz clubs, and clothing stores, the area contained some of the oldest housing in the city and was crowded.[24] Meanwhile, on the lower west side, Chinese immigrants settled along Third Avenue between Michigan and Porter, an area that was quick to be designated Detroit's Chinatown. Most apartments the Chinese rented doubled as their workspace, debunking Smith's claim that the majority owned homes.[25] Bordering two of Detroit's other ethnic neighborhoods, Mexicantown and the once-Irish Corktown, Chinatown exploded with growth. Before World War II, twelve hundred Chinese were reportedly living in Chinatown, a number that more than doubled to thirty-six hundred before the neighborhood was razed in the 1960s.[26] In addition to homes, the Chinese built social organizations, curio shops, and chop suey restaurants, making Detroit's Chinatown a destination for Chinese merchants and community leaders.[27] Of eighty Chinese-owned institutions listed in the state in the *Handbook of Chinese in America* (1946), sixty were in Detroit. Prominent political and welfare groups included chapters of the Chinese Relief Association, On Leong Association, and Kuo Min Tang, three Chinese organizations that maintained posts in every major American city.[28]

Born Dorothy Sue Chee Moy, Dorothy Matsumoto is one of the few living Chinese Americans old enough to remember playing in the streets of her childhood neighborhood, Old Chinatown. Though her immigrant parents were unable to naturalize as American citizens until the Chinese Exclusion Act was repealed in 1943, Matsumoto was born an American as part of a second generation of Chinese in the States.[29] Unlike Chinese immigrants of the first generation, who experienced greater difficulty integrating into American institutions, Chinese American youth had the advantage of attending public schools and community centers, where they learned English and built friendships with children from all over the city. Matsumoto, who played for an all-girl Chinese American basketball team, recalled socializing at Neighborhood House:

> We had dances there. We had a very active social life because we had a basketball team. . . . We had a girls' team and a boys' team. We would play intercity. Our team would go to Toronto and play against the girls from Toronto or Cleveland or Chicago. We would go for the weekends and after the games the whole city would have big dances with us. The same thing when they came here to Detroit to play against us—at Neighborhood House, that's where our home court was—we would have dances after the game. The same thing with the boys' team. We had Caucasian coaches who worked for Settlement House. Dolores Shadd was our coach. She was an African American and she went to Wayne State University. . . . She called us "her girls."

Matsumoto's description suggests that inner-city services, in this case Neighborhood House, may have played a strong role in providing Chinatown's young residents with access and exposure to American popular culture.[30] Having been born and raised in American cities and educated in American schools, second-generation Chinese Americans expected to enjoy the same rights and privileges as white citizens. But the perception that American-born Chinese had surmounted the adversities of their immigrant parents was far from reality.

Matsumoto, who married in 1955, explained the difficulties she and her husband faced as newlyweds trying to find housing outside of Detroit's Chinatown:

> The pressing issue for us at that age was not being able to find a job, not being able to find housing, being discriminated against . . . back in the 1950s, it still existed. We tried to find an apartment that was advertised. We went over there and applied. As soon as we got there they said, "We're sorry, it's been filled." And the next day it was still advertised. I called up and, speaking on the phone, you'd never know that I was Oriental. [They said,] "Oh, yes, we still have an opening." And I told them, "Why didn't you just say you would not rent to Orientals?" The same thing with trying to find a job. Those are the things you hear African Americans say. We put up with it [too].

After several attempts, the couple found a temporary home in a low-income complex on Collingwood just south of Highland Park. After her husband finished his degree from the University of Michigan, they moved to a permanent home in the suburbs of Detroit and started a family.

While the Matsumotos and their peers were shaping what it meant to be American-born Asians outside of Chinatown, Detroit's connection to Pacific Asia was beginning to transform. After the success of the Model T in the early 1900s, the Chinese government solicited Henry Ford's help to build roads and manufacture cars in the Canton region.[31] Ford arranged to hire one hundred Chinese craftsmen and appointed Dr. Joseph Baile from Peking University to screen applicants. Convinced that the American work ideal was superior to any other, Ford insisted that Chinese men hired for the job be American-born and trained in Detroit.[32] Though Ford's initial contracts crumbled due to escalating warfare in China, one hundred Chinese American men stayed in Detroit to work the line in Highland Park's Fordson Tractor Plant.[33]

The fighting in China that had prevented Ford from promoting his enterprise in Canton would eventually hit home for Detroiters. After the attack at Pearl Harbor, Detroit would prove integral to America's success in the Second World War, as the city provided both soldiers and munitions to fight the war to victory. For Detroit's Chinese families, the war already had an impact. More than ten years before the attack of Pearl Harbor, the Japanese Army had already come to occupy much of China's mainland in the Sino-Japanese War, or War of Resistance.[34] Keeping a sharp eye on the international war front, Chinese mothers and wives converted their Chinese Women's Club, a homemaking and social group, into a fund-raising and planning committee. Local Chinese organizations collaborated with the American Red Cross and the United China Relief Fund to raise donations and awareness. Some Chinese Detroiters pooled their money to purchase warplanes built in Detroit for China's National Army.[35]

When President Franklin D. Roosevelt declared war against Japan on December 8, 1941, the news carried both a benefit and a burden for Detroit's Chinese. For Chinatown's men, the war meant they could enlist in the military and achieve "new status in American society."[36] In Detroit, young men joined the Flying Tigers, a special military unit created to help the United States run covert operations in Burma, India, and South China. When they returned to Chinatown at the end of the war, new opportunities awaited. Newly discharged soldiers, among them Yin Yee, applied for U.S. citizenship and took advantage of the GI Bill, which provided college or vocational education to veterans.[37]

For Chinese Americans who did not join the military, there was immense pressure to distinguish themselves from the "other Asian," the Japanese. Wearing large buttons that read, "I am American Chinese," Detroit's Chinese Americans organized anti-Japanese protests emphasizing Japanese wartime atrocities and boycotted products made in Japan.[38] The antagonism this caused between the Chinese and Japanese American communities would not be reconciled until the 1980s.

At the end of World War II, it would seem that the Chinese in Detroit had "become American" in every respect. The most prejudicial immigration policy of the nineteenth and twentieth centuries, the Chinese Exclusion Act, had been repealed in 1943, allowing Chinese immigrants to become naturalized citizens.[39] The facilities and networks of Detroit's Chinatown that enabled first-generation immigrants to nurture families also provided the American-born second generation greater exposure to American values and ideals. In addition, the idea that the Chinese would be strictly confined to restaurants and laundries started to fade, as Chinese Americans were offered modest but notable job opportunities in the factories of Henry Ford and the U.S. military.

However, global economics and racial politics began to breed new ills, and the identity of Chinese Americans in Detroit was to be tested again.

A Home Demolished, Rebuilt, Then Abandoned

Not many of Detroit's Chinese residents were prepared to move when the Detroit Housing Commission condemned Detroit's Chinatown as part of a "slum clearance project" in 1959. The project, which was part of the city's $12.5 million plan to replace aging infrastructure, was tightly linked to the Federal-Aid Highway Act of 1956, the government's commitment to build forty-one thousand miles of interstate highways.[40] In perhaps a convenient marriage of federal and municipal legislation, the city protected middle-class neighborhoods while sacrificing the poorest for highway construction. Thus, in the name of "urban renewal," the city's low-income inner-city housing, primarily the residences of black and ethnic minorities, was razed. Paradise Valley was torn down for the Edsel Ford Freeway on the lower east side and Chinatown for the John C. Lodge Freeway on the lower west side.[41]

Without consultation with Chinatown's residents, the plan to demolish their homes and businesses was set into motion. Leaders of Chinatown quickly organized a task force, developing plans to determine where and when their families and livelihoods could relocate. Henry Yee, owner of Jade Palace restaurant, pushed for the construction of a new Chinatown in International Village, a civic center that would include a multiethnic shopping district with office space and housing.[42] He even considered building a high-rise senior citizen complex to accommodate the elderly first generation of Chinese immigrants. Others opposed being part of International Village, citing funding as an inevitable problem.[43] While some members of the On Leong Merchants Association attempted to pull resources from other ethnic groups, they were ultimately unable to supply the several million dollars needed for the project. In 1962, talks with the developers of International Village failed, forcing the relocation council to consider purchasing private assets. When two buildings were finally acquired in the Cass Corridor, business owners who wished to be a part of it were asked to affirm their commitment.[44] With limited commercial space available and more options in the growing suburbs north of Detroit, only a few of the Chinese-owned businesses chose to move to the New Chinatown.

New Chinatown opened just as long-simmering pressures in Detroit came to a head. Fostered by years of de facto segregation, urban poverty, and a corrupt police force, tumultuous racial tensions between blacks and whites erupted throughout the 1960s.[45] Violent confrontations between radical laborers, both black and white, and conservative white workers became common in the workplace.[46] Similar confrontations occurred on city streets, where black residents were harassed by the city's predominately white police force.[47] On July 23, 1967, when police raided a "blind pig" and arrested more than eighty people, outrage at police brutality reached its breaking point, sparking one of the most destructive urban uprisings in the whole of America. Twenty-four hours later, thirty-three black and ten white Detroiters were dead.[48]

Curtis Chin

We would stay late playing Chinese jump rope and Frisbee and . . . racing. We would also just go walking around the neighborhood a lot. It was a lot safer back then. We'd also play mahjong . . . [and] we collected fish in the fish store.

One thing that really happened . . . at the restaurant across the street from Chung's, which is on the corner where the pet shop eventually took over—I think it was called Bow Wah restaurant—the cook was killed. I think that was probably a turning point, I feel, because up until then, there were still kids playing on the street . . . we would still have a lot of fun. But when that guy was shot, I think after that, everybody was a little more cautious and people started to think about moving out of the neighborhood.[49]

Chinese Americans' bitter inclusion in Detroit's racial politics and security concerns amid rising violence in the Cass Corridor would prove to be the death knell for New Chinatown, hastened by two tragedies.

The first was the killing of Tommie Lee in Detroit's New Chinatown on August 5, 1976. Lee, who had originally settled in Detroit's Old Chinatown, had moved to Cass in 1969 as part of the New Chinatown relocation project. His fatal confrontation with an armed robber was not the first time that he had been threatened with brute force. In 1965, Lee had been shot through the front door of his former restaurant, Lung Fung Chop Suey. The area was undeniably dangerous. Residents who paused on public benches had become targets for hit-and-run robberies, even in broad daylight. Notwithstanding a federal grant that had allotted $300,000 to Chinatown to widen the sidewalks and plant flowerbeds to beautify the neighborhood, the Cass Corridor had fallen victim to all the social ills that ailed the city at large.[50]

Curtis Chin, who spent happy hours of his childhood playing with friends near his family's restaurant at Cass and Peterboro, recalls the ironic effects that community renewal projects had on inner-city crime: "You know those planters? I don't know who decided to put those in, but one thing they did is close down the street. So there was not as much good street parking for our restaurant. But another thing, it also allowed for a sitting area where a lot more drugs could be sold. It was a terrible change." To Curtis, the killing of Lee and the changes that had taken effect in Detroit's Chinatown were enough to break the momentum of the ethnic commercial district. Young children like Curtis were no longer allowed to play outdoors, and visitors from outside the city hesitated to visit the area to savor their favorite Cantonese dish. Detroit's shrinking population created a domino effect of vacant commercial districts, blighted residential zones, and an increase in criminal activity. Those who were able to leave the downtown district did.[51] Those who could not afford to move stayed.[52]

Amid the social and political chaos that surged between blacks and whites in the city, Chinese American Detroiters were in a gray area, pinched between the racialized orthodoxy of the majority and the plight of the minority—a position that would seem to posit a choice: to be part of the "problem" or "nearly preferred."[53]

Grace Lee Boggs, a Chinese American revolutionary who married African American labor activist James Boggs, and who has an essay in this volume (see chapter 6), is a profound example of how some Asian Americans shed the dichotomous racial barriers in Detroit to successfully advocate with blacks during the African American political and social movements of the 1950s and 1960s.[54] Few Chinese Americans could take that course. Their parents having gained the right to American citizenship less than twenty years before, many second- and third-generation Chinese Americans were eager to pursue the educational and career opportunities now open to them. Detroit newspapers seized this opportunity to grossly generalize Chinese cultural behaviors, like humility and discipline, attributing emerging Chinese American success stories to such factors.[55] Identifying Chinese American faces as "model minorities" in this way not only suppressed productive dialogue about the racial tensions in the city but also pitted the Asian American image against that of American blacks.[56]

Almost six years after the killing of Lee, Detroit's Chinese American community was devastated again, this time by the killing of Vincent Chin. Despite the civic mobilization the Chin case brought in its wake, it was too late for the actual Chinese American neighborhood in the city. It had taken too many blows. With only one hundred or so Chinese Americans still living in the Cass Corridor and thousands already settled in Detroit's surrounding suburbs, the cultural traditions, businesses, and sense of community of the Old Chinatown could not be resurrected.[57]

Shenlin Chen

I think overall Detroit is growing and that gives us hope. [That is why we want to] stay in that area. We believe that the presence of a Chinese population is still important. Also, if we already established something, why would we just give up?[58]

Chinese Americans' Role in Transforming Detroit

Today, a smooth and inconspicuous blacktop stretches westward over 2121 Cass Avenue, a plot that formerly housed Chin Tiki, a Polynesian nightclub built by Chinese American architect and engineer Marvin Chin in 1967.[59] The nightclub stood just five short blocks south of New Chinatown and was favored by celebrities such as Barbara Streisand, Muhammad Ali, and Joe DiMaggio. Chin Tiki continued to be lauded for its escapist design and remembered for its authentic Hawaiian floor shows even after it had been vacant for twenty years. The Detroit venue was featured in a widely circulated tribute to tiki culture, Sven Kirsten's *Tiki Modern and the Wild World of Witco*, and was a backdrop for scenes in Eminem's 2002 film *8 Mile*.[60] In 2009, the iconic Tiki palace—and a piece of Detroit Chinatown history—was leveled and the grounds converted into a top-dollar parking lot.

For some Detroiters, the demolition of an iconic but vacant building is viewed as simply the removal of an outdated relic. For others, the razing of landmarks invokes a deep sense of loss, sorrow, and regret, as places associated with the past—childhood, the carefree days of adolescence, or the productivity of working years—are reduced to rubble. In Detroit, where demolition is more common than construction, it is hard to overcome the urge to hearken back to the bygone "golden era" when Detroit's buildings were brimming with workers, wages were good, and the diversity of the city was manifest in ethnic boroughs where the ways of the old country and new country merged. (To be sure, to live in an ethnic enclave was a double-edged sword. On one hand, residents could enjoy cultural and social amenities unavailable elsewhere and profit from the tourist lure of their restaurants, celebrations, and shops. On the other hand, ethnic enclaves perpetuated the "othering" of nonwhites, making it harder for them to integrate into American society at large.) Yet, as the historical record proves, and as the stories and experiences of Chinese Americans illustrate, Detroit has never been and never will be a perfect place.

The mid-1980s in Detroit were marked by soaring unemployment, the callous dislocation of ethnic minorities from the Poletown neighborhood to make way for General Motors' now-derelict Detroit/Hamtramck assembly plant, and the residual effects of "white flight."[61] Against that backdrop, Detroit television station WXYZ-TV adopted a new slogan to uplift the spirit of Detroiters. In an ad featuring snapshots of charismatic citizens enjoying the landmarks and culture of Detroit—including factory workers building cars—the jingle sang, "Stand up and tell 'em you're from Detroit!"[62] The slogan became an instant hit as a motto that "made you proud to be a Detroiter."[63] The motto still holds merit today, even though the cityscape has declined since the 1980s.

Shenlin Chen moved to Metro Detroit with her husband, an engineer, in 1999. At the time, only two Chinese American establishments remained open in the Cass Corridor. One of them, Chung's Chop Suey restaurant, shuttered its doors in 2000 due in part to a steady decline in customers over the course of several decades.[64] Chung's had been a prominent fixture of Detroit's Chinatown, serving up authentic Cantonese fare to local workers and night crawlers for nearly forty years. The other establishment, the Association of Chinese Americans' Detroit Drop-in Service Center, hired Chen as its executive director and continued to operate in the New Chinatown area for twelve more years.

The ACA still operates today at a location on Woodward Avenue in Midtown, near Wayne State University and the Detroit Medical Center. The ACA's core programs have not materially changed since its founding in the early 1970s, but the characteristics of the center's patrons have changed in ways that are overwhelmingly positive for the ACA as well as Detroit. In the 1970s and 1980s, the ACA primarily served Chinese immigrants and their American-born offspring. The center now serves a wider population, including local senior citizens, professional Asian immigrants, temporary visitors from

China, international students, and domestic students studying Chinese language and culture.

The wide spectrum of cultural backgrounds serviced by the ACA is also representative of changes occurring in and around Detroit. Chen has observed that the power of the economy of China has had a considerable impact on southeast Michigan in recent years. She noted that Chinese investors are buying real estate and Chinese-owned companies are opening American branches in downtown Detroit as well as Techtown. High schools and colleges are encouraging their students to learn how to read and write Mandarin so they can seal tomorrow's business deals. Though many of the changes are tied to global phenomena, in Chen's view, the city must reach out to the local Chinese American population if it is serious about its future potential for revitalization and growth.

"Transformation is important," says Chen. "We cannot just stick to what we've been doing over the past ten years or fifteen to twenty years. I see Detroit as a very good [nexus] point or location for people, [specifically] Chinese overseas, who visit [Michigan]. The ACA should be a contact point to connect these two very different populations, local Chinese [Americans] and [Chinese visitors]. I think [the Detroit Drop-in Service Center] is a good [resource] to promote Detroit as well as teach 'outside culture' to Detroiters." Succinctly stated, in its efforts to strengthen its economy, Detroit cannot forget its cultural and social assets—mainly, its population—which undoubtedly factor into a company's or investor's decision to do business with the city. Irrespective of city planning and politics, Detroiters are already tapping into the resources made available to them by Chinese American institutions like the ACA.

It is clear that Chen believes the ACA should never leave Detroit. In fact, she hopes that the organization will expand there and influence positive change. In my view, Chen's vision for the future of the ACA speaks loudly in what it does not say—that Chinese Americans should be proud of their contributions to the city and continue to be stakeholders in the city's progress.

Like Detroit's former Chinatowns, both of which rose and died with the city's circumstances, the history of Chinese Americans in Detroit was at risk of obfuscation. But then eyewitnesses like Yee, Matsumoto, and Chin came forth and willingly shared memories of their past. I have recorded their stories and experiences in an attempt to fill gaps in Detroit's history, to make our shared history whole. In the same vein, Sook Wilkinson and Victor Jew worked tirelessly to compile this book, which has a similar, albeit broader, aim. Presently, Chinese Americans like Chen actively advocate for the inclusion of Chinese American voices in a history that is yet to be written. To those alive and to those not yet born, please consider my humble request: Let us record the voices of *all* Detroiters and share them with the world—to comprehend that which has happened and to anticipate that which will.

Notes

1. In November 1966, Congress passed the Demonstration Cities and Metropolitan Development Act to fund rehabilitation projects in "model" cities. Detroit was chosen, but funding was greatly inadequate to meet the goals of Detroit mayor Jerome Cavanagh to reduce urban poverty and overhaul discriminatory institutions that denied blacks equal opportunity in jobs, housing, and education. Sidney Fine, *Violence in the Model City: The Cavanagh Administration, Race Relations, and the Detroit Riot of 1967* (East Lansing: Michigan State University Press, 2007), 87-88.

2. This essay describes Detroit's two Chinatowns. In discussions of Old Chinatown and New Chinatown, I will refer to each neighborhood as simply "Chinatown" except, for the sake of clarity, when the two are discussed together or compared.

3. In summer 2006, I was hired by the ACA to serve as an ESL instructor for five to ten elderly Chinese immigrants who still lived in the Cass Corridor and regularly attended the Detroit Drop-in Service Center. The center provided health screenings, English classes, computer training, legal aid, and hot meals for senior citizens as well as summer cultural camps for children. In 2011, the Drop-in Service Center moved to a location on Woodward Avenue.

4. To date there are no scholarly publications dedicated solely to the history of Detroit's former Chinatowns or Chinese American residents. My work Detroit's Chinatown: Works in Progress, a Detroit Historical Museum exhibit from April 4 to July 5, 2009, is archived on my website, www.detroitchinatown.org/history. For original research on the sociocultural changes in Detroit's Chinese population before Old Chinatown was demolished, see Emiko Ohnuki, "The Detroit Chinese—A Study of Socio-cultural Changes in the Detroit Chinese Community from 1872 through 1963" (master's thesis, University of Wisconsin, 1964).

5. Because my research has required that I jockey between the communal and the personal, the political and the vernacular, to find balance and wholeness amid potentially conflicting accounts, errors are my own and not the result of my participants' efforts to recount their past.

6. Yin Ack Yee (deceased), interview by the author, Madison Heights, September 19, 2008. In excerpts from this interview and others, original grammatical mistakes have been silently corrected. Words in square brackets have been added for clarity.

7. "John Chinaman," *Detroit Free Press*, January 29, 1873; "Another John," *Detroit Free Press*, February 5, 1873; Victor Lim, *Dining with Chopsticks in Detroit: A Guide to the Chinese Community and Chinese Restaurants* (Detroit: Chinese Publishing House, 1960), 17. In *Dining with Chopsticks*, Lu-how's name is cited as Ku How.

8. In 1880 the Chinese population of Chicago was approximately 567. By 1900, it had nearly doubled to 1,209. In contrast, only 10 Chinese resided in Detroit out of an estimated 120 in the entire state of Michigan in 1880. Though the number of Chinese in Michigan doubled to 240 by 1900, the total Chinese population of Detroit had declined to 3. Susan Moy, "The Chinese in Chicago: The First One Hundred Years," in *Ethnic Chicago: A Multicultural Portrait*, 3rd ed., ed. Melvin G. Holli and Peter d'A. Jones (Grand Rapids: Eerdmans, 1995), 379; U.S. Bureau of the Census, *Report on Population of the United States at the Eleventh Census: 1890* (Washington, DC: U.S. Bureau of the Census, 1895); U.S. Bureau of the Census, *Reports on Population of the United States at the Twelfth Census: 1900* (Washington, DC: U.S. Bureau of the Census, 1901).

9. For columns on the native customs of Detroit's first Chinese settlers, see "The Chinese New Year Day," *Detroit Free Press*, February 5, 1875, 1; "Celestial Celebration: Observance of the New Year by Chinese Laundrymen," *Detroit Free Press*, January 25, 1876, 1; "Servants to the Dead," *Detroit Tribune*, August 12, 1886, 4. For columns on the settler's "Americanization," see "John Chinaman's Christmas," *Detroit Free Press*, December 20, 1874, 1 (Sam Lee celebrates Christmas); "Sayings and Doings," *Detroit Free Press*, April 6, 1875, 1 (one of Detroit's Chinese wears a plug hat); "Sayings and Doings," *Detroit Free Press*, July 25, 1877, 1 (Lung Sing wants to naturalize); "Brevities," *Post & Tribune*, May 19, 1882, 2 (the Chinese attend First Presbyterian Sunday school).

10. The most detailed account of a reporter's interaction with the Chinese can be found in "The Chinese Colony: The Aims, Aspirations and Characters of the Ten Mongolians in Detroit," *Detroit News*, May 18, 1878, 4. Using what I envision as " pit-stop" journalism, a reporter traveled from one Chinese laundry to another to record his conversations with the residents.

11. Thomas J. Sugrue, *The Origins of the Urban Crisis: Race and Inequality in Postwar Detroit* (Princeton: Princeton University Press, 2005), 23.

12. Peter Kwong and Dušanka Miščević, *Chinese America: The Untold Story of America's Oldest New Community* (New York: New Press, 2005), 19-20; Ronald Takaki, *Strangers from a Different Shore: A History of Asian Americans*, 2nd ed. (New York: Little, Brown, 1998), 21-24, 79-87.

13. Kwong and Miščević, *Chinese America*, 95-100.

14. Robert G. Lee, *Orientals: Asian Americans in Popular Culture* (Philadelphia: Temple University Press, 1999), 47-48.

15. Kwong and Miščević, *Chinese America*, 101.

16. Moy, "The Chinese in Chicago"; Ohnuki, "The Detroit Chinese"; Xinyang Wang, *Surviving the City: The Chinese Immigrant Experience in New York City, 1890-1970* (Lanham, MD: Rowman and Littlefield, 2001); Rhoads Murphey, "Boston's Chinatown," *Economic Geography* 28 (1952): 244-55.

17. The fact that Yin Yee's father returned to the United States even in the face of immense political and social opposition is an example of how many early Chinese immigrants were actually "settlers" and not "sojourners." For a discussion of the difference and statistics of migration for Asian and European immigrant communities in the nineteenth and twentieth centuries, see Takaki, *Strangers from a Different Shore*, 10-11.

18. In compliance with the Chinese Exclusion Act, the border along the Detroit River between Detroit and Windsor, Ontario, was tightly monitored. Immigration

inspectors, dubbed "Chinamen chasers," patrolled the border. "Over Bridge of Ice Wily Chinese Seek Forbidden U.S. Land," *Detroit Journal*, January 18, 1910, 1.

19. For a discussion of how Chinese men entered the sphere of domestic labor or "women's work" in an effort to maintain employment in the United States, see Lee, *Orientals*, 104-5.

20. Yee interview. See also K. Scott Wong, *Americans First: Chinese Americans and the Second World War* (Philadelphia: Temple University Press, 2008), 207-8.

21. Dorothy Matsumoto, interview by the author, Royal Oak, August 1, 2008.

22. Faye Elizabeth Smith, "Bits of the Old World in Detroit (No. 5—China)," *Detroit Saturday Night*, March 4, 1922, 4.

23. Yee interview; Matsumoto interview. See also Hayne Leung's account in Sandra Bunnell, "The Dragon Dances: A Century of Chinese in Detroit with a Culture That Will Not Die," *Detroit Free Press Magazine*, January 6, 1974, 12.

24. Sugrue, *Origins of the Urban Crisis*, 36-37.

25. Paul C. P. Siu, *The Chinese Laundryman: A Study of Social Isolation*, ed. John Kuo Wei Tchen (New York: New York University Press, 1988), 58, 207; Takaki, *Strangers from a Different Shore*, 246.

26. Detroit Free Press, *The Detroit Almanac: 300 Years of Life in the Motor City*, ed. Peter Gavrilovich and Bill McGraw (Detroit: Detroit Free Press, 2000), 97.

27. The most prominent individual ever to visit Detroit's Chinatown was Madame Chiang Kai-shek, who had earlier praised the residents of Old Chinatown for their contributions to China during World War II. She came to Detroit in 1958 and then again in 1966. "Accolade from China: Mm. Chiang Kai-shek Praises Colony," *Detroit News*, August 21, 1942; "Madame Chiang Kai-shek Greeted by Miss Lydia Woo at Willow Run Airport," 1958, Virtual Motor City, Walter P. Reuther Library, Detroit; Madame Chiang Kai-shek, "And Now What Image?" an address at the Economic Club of Detroit, April 8, 1966.

28. Ruzhou Chen, *Meiguo hua qiao nian jian* [Handbook of Chinese in America] (New York: People's Foreign Relations Association of China, 1946), 544-47.

29. Many male Chinese immigrants remained bachelors in America until 1930, when the restrictions on Chinese women immigrants were repealed. In Detroit, the ratio of Chinese women to men was 1:100 in 1910 but increased to an estimated 1:10 by 1934 after the repeal. Takaki, *Strangers from a Different Shore*, 101-2; Bunnell, "The Dragon Dances," 6.

30. Neighborhood Houses, also called Settlement Houses or Neighborhood Centers, were a phenomenon of the late nineteenth and early twentieth centuries. Rooted in the foundation of social work, they provided services to immigrant families during their initial settlement in America. Rolland F. Smith, "Settlements and Neighborhood Centers," in *Encyclopedia of Social Work*, 19th ed., ed. Richard L. Edwards, June Gary Hopps, et al. (Washington, DC: NASW, 1995), 3:2129-35.

31. American newspapers portrayed Henry Ford's work in Canton as an attempt to revolutionize China's industry and social conditions. "Ford Can Help Halt Drudgery of Chinese Children, Is Belief," December 13, 1922, and "Ford Help for Chinese Is Sought," December 14, 1922, acc. 7 clipping books, vol. 31, pp. 130 and 141, Benson Ford Research Center, Dearborn, MI.

32. "Ford Plans to Extend Operations to Orient," November 11, 1922, and "Ford Training Chinese for Branch in Far East," December 17, 1922, acc. 7 clipping books, vol. 31, pp. 31 and 140, Benson Ford Research Center.

33. "Ford Trade School Prepares Chinese Students for Career," *Ford News*, June 22, 1923, 3; Mable Lim, interview by the author, Troy, August 26, 2008.

34. Wong, *Americans First*, 33-34.

35. "City's Chinese Hold Meeting: Plan to Buy Planes in Detroit for Use against Japs in Manchuria," *Detroit News*, January 11, 1932; "Local Chinese to Raise Fund," *Detroit News*, February 1, 1932; Philip A. Adler, "Chinese Donate Savings to Help Fight Japanese," *Detroit News*, February 25, 1932; "Chinese of Detroit Aid in Fund Drive," *Detroit Free Press*, June 1, 1938; "Parade to Feature China Relief Drive," *Detroit News*, October 8, 1941; "Chinese Dragon to Dance for City in Cause of Relief," *Detroit News*, October 8, 1941.

36. Wong, *Americans First*, 58-59.

37. Yee interview; Wong, *Americans First*, 61. See also Andy Kozlowski, "Plaque Memorializes Chinese-American Veterans," *Madison Park News*, November 18, 2009, 1A, 15A.

38. "Lucille Lee," December 10, 1941, Virtual Motor City; "Demonstration against Japanese Atrocities," June 13, 1938, Virtual Motor City; "Japanese Boycott by Chinese Pickets," December 18, 1937, Virtual Motor City; "This Life Is in Your Hands!" (anti-Japanese propaganda poster), August 4, 1938, E&M 74D4 325.251, Burton Historical Collection, Detroit Public Library; "Christmas Greetings to American Mothers" (anti-Japanese propaganda poster), c. 1938, E&M 74D4 325.251, Burton Historical Collection.

39. In April 1944, four months after the repeal of the Chinese Exclusion Act, fourteen of Detroit's Chinese residents filed for naturalization. Mr. Henry Tom, Mrs. Fong Shee Lee, Mrs. Fong Lee, and the Soo Hoos, all of whom applied, had sons who were then serving in the U.S. Army and Air Corps. "Detroit Chinese Apply for First Citizenship Papers," *Detroit News*, April 25, 1944.

40. James K. Anderson, "Chinatown in Civic Center Proposed as Tourist Lure," *Detroit News*, November 15, 1959; Carroll Pursell, *The Machine in America: A Social History of Technology* (Baltimore: Johns Hopkins University Press, 1995), 285-86.

41. Sugrue, *Origins of the Urban Crisis*, 47.

42. Robert L. Wells, "Spur International Village Project," *Detroit News*, February 19, 1960; "$3 Million Chinese Village Proposed," *Detroit News*, August 3, 1961; "Unveil Plans for $3-Million Chinatown," *Detroit Free Press*, August 3, 1961.

43. Anderson, "Chinatown in Civic Center Proposed as Tourist Lure"; John Gill, "Chinese Bicker over Plans to Build New Chinatown Here," *Detroit News*, July 13, 1961; John (Jack) Manning, "A New Chinatown Would Vastly Aid Detroit, Jack Manning Says," *Detroit Free Press*, August 25, 1961.

44. John Gill, "Chinese Reject Village Role, Will Rebuild along Cass," *Detroit News*, November 4, 1962; John M. Carlisle, "Chinese Will Hail New Cass," *Detroit News*, May 3, 1963.

45. John (Jack) Manning, "Old Chinatown Born Anew," *Detroit Free Press*, May 13, 1963.

46. Heather Ann Thompson, "Workers, Officials, and the Escalating War for Detroit's Labor Future," in *Whose Detroit? Politics, Labor, and Race in a Modern American City* (New York: Cornell University Press, 2001), 103-127. For a history of the black labor struggle prior to the 1960s, see August Meier and Elliott Rudwick, *Black Detroit and the Rise of the UAW* (Ann Arbor: University of Michigan Press, 2007).

47. On the eve of the 1967 rebellion, 5 percent of the Detroit Police Department was black. Fine, *Violence in the Model City*, 109.

48. Heather Ann Thompson, *Whose Detroit?* 46-47.

49. Curtis Chin, telephone interview by the author, August 19, 2008. Curtis is an Asian American filmmaker based in Los Angeles. He released a documentary with film director Tony Lam on the Vincent Chin murder and the evolution of the Asian American movement. See Tony Lam, dir., *Vincent Who?* (2009).

50. Al Stark, "Will Chinatown Come Back?" *Sunday News Magazine*, November 14, 1976, 14, 15, 45–48.

51. Detroit's population swelled to 1.6 million in 1940 and 1.8 million in 1950. Since then, however, Detroit's population has slowly declined, reaching an estimated 713,777 in 2010. Once America's fourth-largest city, Detroit is now the eighteenth largest. Campbell Gibson, *Population of the 100 Largest Cities and Other Urban Places in the United States: 1790 to 1990* (Washington, DC: Population Division, Bureau of the Census, 1998); *American FactFinder*, s.v. "Detroit, Michigan," http://factfinder.census.gov.

52. Patricia Montemurri, "Chinatown Lost: Forlorn Area Is Buried in the Cass Corridor," *Detroit Free Press*, November 26, 1989, 1J, 6J.

53. Frank H. Wu, *Yellow: Race in America beyond Black and White* (New York: Basic Books, 2003), 292 (positing that Asian Americans are forced to choose between whiteness and blackness as two extremes, with whiteness being the preferred choice).

54. See Grace Lee Boggs, *Living for Change: An Autobiography* (Minneapolis: University of Minnesota Press, 1998). See also Bill V. Mullen, "'Philosophy Must Be Proletarian': The Dialectical Humanism of Grace Lee and James Boggs," in *Afro-Orientalism* (Minneapolis: University of Minnesota Press, 2004), 113-62.

55. John C. Treen, "Juvenile Delinquency Low in Chinese Colony," *Detroit News*, February 26, 1956; Susan Fodor, "'Love and Discipline' Rear Good Children," *Detroit News*, January 20, 1959.

56. For a discussion of Asian Americans and the "model minority" myth, see Wu, "The Model Minority: Asian American 'Success' as a Race Relations Failure," in *Yellow*, 39-78. See also Rosalind S. Chou and Joe R. Feagin, The Myth of the Model Minority: Asian Americans Facing Racism (Boulder: Paradigm, 2008).

57. Montemurri, "Chinatown Lost."

58. Shenlin Chen, telephone interview by author, July 10, 2014.

59. Molly O. Abraham, "Chin Tiki, the South Seas on Cass Ave.," *Detroit News Tempo*, February 2, 1967, 20.

60. John Monaghan, "Cass Avenue's Exotic Chin Tiki Is No More," *Detroit News*, March 11, 2009.

61. See generally Thompson, *Whose Detroit?*; Jeanie Wylie, *Poletown: Community Betrayed* (Chicago: University of Illinois Press, 1990); Susan Welch et al., *Race and Place: Race Relations in an American City* (New York: Cambridge University Press, 2001).

62. Detroit Free Press, *The Detroit Almanac*, 404.

63. Kortney Stringer, "Detroiters Can Sell It: Local Businesses Go All out for TV Commercials," *Detroit Free Press*, April 3, 2006, 1.

64. Jane Rayburn, "Fewer Customers Force Chung's to Close Cass Corridor Location, *Detroit News*, September 5, 2000, 1C.

4

"AMBASSADORS" IN THE HEARTLAND

Asian American Racial and Regional Identity Formations in Michigan

Barbara W. Kim

In "Critical Legal Studies, Asian Americans in U.S. Law and Culture, Neil Gotanda, and Me" (1997), legal scholar and artist Keith Aoki evoked time, demographic concentration, and space to contextualize the relationship between racial/ethnic identities and processes of marginalization and exclusion in his experience as a Japanese American growing up in 1960s Michigan suburbia. What makes his experiences regionally specific ones? How are Asian American experiences constructed historically, socially, and spatially? "My memories of growing up in the midwestern suburban milieu," Aoki writes, "are probably similar to many persons of my generation. However, there are a few discordant shards whose generational universality I doubt. One example is playing war and pretending to kill 'japs' with toy guns, at least until my mother informed me that I was a 'jap' and shouldn't be saying such things. I also recall being excluded from a second-grade Thanksgiving pageant by a teacher who told me that there weren't any Chinese people at Plymouth Rock. She was of Polish ancestry, but my second-grade rhetorical skills weren't up to pointing out that there probably weren't many Polish people eating turkey on that chilly seventeenth century Massachusetts day either."[1]

As late as the 1940s, 90 percent of Asian Americans lived along the West Coast and in Hawaii. This concentration had declined to 46 percent by 2010.[2]

As growing numbers of Asian Americans migrated to and settled in other places, scholars have examined histories and emerging community formations beyond typical Asian American spaces.[3] In particular, the significant number of Asian American studies faculty, programs, and departments established east of California in the 1990s resulted in acknowledgment and criticism of the California-centrism of Asian American studies.[4]

Scattered tales are told of early Asian American settlers in Michigan, Chinese miners in the Upper Peninsula in the late 1800s, or *manongs*, the generation of Filipinos who arrived in the 1920s and 1930s, in Detroit's automobile industry. James Tadae Shimoura, one such pioneer, arrived in Detroit in 1915, completed an apprenticeship at the Ford Experimental Laboratory, and worked at the Ford Chemical Laboratory for the next twenty-one years.[5] Studying the intersections of U.S. regionalism and racial formations reveals the important role the Midwest has played in the construction and destabilization of Asian America in the twentieth century, when the federal government imagined the "heartland of America" as an un–Asian American place devoid of such racial/ethnic identity and community formations and created deliberate policies that reflected this cultural and spatial construction.[6] At two significant moments in Asian American history, the Midwest served as "a good place to disperse two waves of Asian-American population 'unsettlements.'"[7]

Drawing from in-depth interviews with Michigan Asian American residents in the late 1990s, this essay explores regional constructions of Asian American racial and ethnic identities by examining the ways in which respondents located themselves within Asian America and the dominant American society. Against the backdrop of concepts and meanings of U.S. regions, this case study of Asian Americans in Michigan offers the construction of a racialized regional identity that simultaneously transcends and reinforces the color line in the heartland.[8]

The Consideration of Space in Asian American Studies

In *Racial Formation in the United States*, Michael Omi and Howard Winant (1994) criticize the tendencies of scholars to analyze race and racial inequality as manifestations of an underlying (and therefore presumably more important or central) social structure. Rejecting the idea that racial inequality is an epiphenomenal consequence of other social inequalities, they argue that race is an independent fundamental category of social organization, analysis, and contestation in the United States that profoundly and significantly shapes reality, affects policies, and determines material consequences. They theorize racial formation as the "sociohistorical process by which racial categories are created, inhabited, transformed, and destroyed."[9] Sucheng Chan notes that the term *Asian American* is rooted in "political and bureaucratic origins." Student and community activists in the 1960s observed how different groups with Asian ancestry had been subjected to similar racializations and subordination. According to Glenn Omatsu, one of the victories achieved by the 1968 San Francisco State College Third World Liberation Front strike was that it united people of various class and ethnic backgrounds by linking "our experience of racism into a critique of U.S. society."[10]

The Asian American population has been changing in numbers and socioeconomic diversity ever since historian Yuji Ichioka coined the demographic term in the late 1960s to describe a group of diverse ethnic backgrounds within (often defined as those *born* within) the national boundaries of the United States. At the same time, those involved in the Asian American movement linked the idiom to anticolonial and revolutionary movements in the third world.[11] Scholars have called for theoretical paradigms of Asian American studies reflective of the blurring of such rigid geopolitical/ethnonational boundaries as a result of global economic restructuring, continuing developments in communication and transportation technologies, and the transnational movement of people.[12] This attention to the interplay between the local and the global has not only expanded the term *Asian America* beyond the United States but has also questioned the centrality of California and the West Coast in Asian American history and studies.[13]

According to Edward Soja, space—one of "those related concepts that compose and comprise the inherent spatiality of human life: place, location, locality, landscape, environment, home city, region, territory, and geography"—has been marginalized in studying, theorizing, and explaining ideas, categories, structures, meanings, and events. Needed is a reconsideration of spatiality, along with history and sociality, as an equally vital dimension that shapes knowledge and the production of knowledge.[14] Geography encompasses more than the physical terrain of the land; it is intrinsically tied to economic, political, cultural, and social terrains. In the United States, racial and ethnic groups tend to be associated with particular spaces in popular and academic consciousness due to historical settlements, population size, and the relationship with and restructuring of the dominant culture and society. Examples include African Americans in the rural South and the urban North/Midwest, Puerto Ricans in New York, Chicanos in the Southwest, and Asian Americans on the West Coast. Less documented are the experiences and identifications of racialized people outside these well-established maps of settlement, and how they are interpreted through the interplay of local, regional, and national contexts.[15]

The consideration of region in race and ethnic studies raises some general inquiries. What attracted or forced people to migrate and settle in particular areas of the United States? What were the compelling reasons to stay there, and do these reasons result in different types of racial/ethnic identity and community formations? For example, Yen Le Espiritu observes that post-1965 Filipino immigrants were mainly highly skilled professionals who entered the United States as members of preferred occupations subject to employer sponsorship, and this group often settled in the Northeast or the Midwest rather than near the larger, older Filipino American communities in Hawaii, California, and Washington.[16] Similarly, the global context of immigration—the conditions in both the sending and the host country—shaped the flow of Korean American settlement in the United States after the 1965 immigration reforms. In the Metropolitan Detroit area, the Korean community grew from approximately one hundred families prior to 1964 to an estimated thirteen thousand in 1989. Before the early 1970s, an estimated 62 percent of Korean Americans were either students, professors, and members of academic professions or medical doctors, nurses, and other medical professionals. The earliest post-1965 Korean American immigrants to Chicago included a large number of female nurses who entered the United States under the occupational preference of the Immigration Act.[17]

Asian Americans in parts of the Midwest have been excluded from the dominant racial discourse, which critically examines existing racial conditions and stratification. In one study of how postwar politics, economics, and racial inequality led to the contemporary urban crisis in Detroit, the historically limited number of groups such as Asian Americans, Latinos, and Native Americans renders them marginal in the dominant discourse of black-white racial relations.[18] The invisibility of Asian Americans in the traditionally black/white–defined racial discourse warrants a study of how this racialized group, perceived as relative "newcomers" in the racial landscape, is identified, portrayed, and aligned along the color line.

Recent studies in other areas of the country have challenged the West Coast's monopoly in studies of Asian Americans, and the influence of space and region on Asian American racial and ethnic formations continues to be explored in order to understand how these localized Asian American communities see themselves, and how they are seen by those outside their ethnic groups or by Asian Americans elsewhere.[19] Increasing Asian American historical documentation in regions outside the West Coast not only challenges the mainstream perceptions of where Asian Americans live—and what that means to the dominant American cultural ideological and social structures—but expands the study of Asian American history, experiences, and racial formations in the United States.

Respondents and Methodology

The data for this study were gathered through in-depth interviews conducted with forty Asian Americans (twenty women and twenty men) between eighteen and seventy years of age who immigrated to, relocated to, or were born in Michigan.[20] The respondents' ethnic backgrounds were Chinese (9), Filipino (2), Hmong (4), Indian (4), Japanese (3), Korean (14), Taiwanese (3), and Vietnamese (1). First-generation (seventeen) and 1.5 and second-generation (twenty-one) respondents comprised the majority of respondents.[21] Twenty-three of the respondents were born outside the United States and seventeen within the country. Of the native-born group, twelve were born in Michigan.

According to the 2000 U.S. Census, 32.3 percent of Asian Americans in Michigan held a graduate/professional degree or higher, compared to 17.4 percent of Asian Americans in the United States generally, 8.9 percent of the total population in Michigan, and 8.1 percent of the total U.S. population.[22] Eight of these respondents described their family backgrounds as working class, while others described theirs as variations of the middle class. All respondents were either attending college or had some college education; fourteen were working toward or had earned a graduate/professional degree. Current and former occupations included nurses, physicians, teachers, engineers, lawyers, and entrepreneurs.

Defining U.S. Regionalism and the Midwest

In shorthand American popular culture, the Midwest has been described as the heartland of America, alluding to its central location in the North American continental terrain as well as the character of its moral, ideological, political, and cultural terrains. The Midwest has been interpreted historically as the physical and cultural bridge between the overly urbanized and industrialized East and the wild, untamed West—the medium between the overcivilized and undercivilized topographical, ideological, and political spaces. The Midwest is simultaneously genuine and boring, pastoral and provincial, friendly and naïve, solid and square. Although it encompasses states with vastly different topographies, settlements, industries, and economies, the Midwest has become essentialized as a "good," "wholesome," and "moderate" space in popular culture, "the idealized and nostalgically yearned-for self of a nation."[23] The breadbasket image of this region has resulted in a westward migration of the "Midwest" label from states such as Ohio and Michigan, which comprised the original "Middle West," part of the Old Northwest Territory annexed in 1783.[24]

In 2010, 11 percent of all Asian Americans and Native Hawaiians/Pacific Islanders in the United States lived in the Midwest. This is the smallest percentage of Asian Pacific Americans in any region.[25] The U.S. Bureau of the Census defines the Midwest as a combination of two subdivided regions: the East North Central states (Ohio, Indiana, Illinois, Michigan, and Wisconsin) and the West North Central states (Minnesota, Iowa, Missouri, North Dakota, South Dakota, Nebraska, and Kansas). All but one of my respondents said that they considered Michigan a geographical and cultural part of the Midwest.[26] However, they also accentuated this fluidity of region and regionalism in their geographic and cultural definitions of the Midwest. For example, more respondents listed Michigan and nearby states—Illinois, Indiana, Ohio, Wisconsin, and Minnesota—as comprising the Midwest region rather than states such as Iowa, Kansas, and Nebraska further west.[27] Sports fans referred in addition to collegiate and professional athletic conferences and divisions to map the region. For example, many respondents attended college and/or graduate school in Michigan, whose NCAA Division I institutions belong to the Big Ten Conference; the states most frequently cited as midwestern states were homes to other Big Ten institutions.[28]

Some respondents embraced positive stereotypes of the Midwest and Michiganders as ones that accurately described themselves.[29] According to Tank Chun, a second-generation Korean American in his early twenties, Michiganders are "wholesome" and "very laid-back people" who "take things more easy . . . we're good people and we get things done."[30] Allison Oh, another second-generation Korean American, observed, "I've always thought of myself [as] very Midwest. I don't want to be goody-two-shoes-ish, but I think I'm pretty wholesome. . . . I like Michigan, because of [my] family, too, and I like how the kids don't grow up too fast."[31] Luis Delgado, a first-generation Filipino American engineer, agreed that Michigan is a "good place to work and raise a family. I have no complaints. This state has been good to me."[32] Others identified themselves as midwestern on the basis of vernacular (for example, saying *pop* rather than *soda*) and accent.[33] Respondents reported that these

differences became more pronounced when they interacted with nonmid-
westerners or traveled outside the Midwest; second-generation Indian American Vivek Mehta noted, "People say all the time that I have a very Michigan
accent. For example, everyone says that my *a*'s come out very [flat] and I
always get teased about that when I go to see my wife's family."[34] The "great
outdoors" and collegiate and professional sports teams also provided sources
of identification as Michigan residents.

In contrast, others identified themselves as Michiganders and/or midwesterners despite holding some negative stereotypes of the region. They
were therefore torn. While these respondents thought of Michigan as a
racially and religiously homogeneous state, they were simultaneously critical of outsiders—including bicoastal Asian Americans—who held stereotypical views of people in their region.[35] Sarah Chu, a second-generation Chinese
American college student, initially described the Midwest as "not very diverse
. . . the most boring section of the United States," but identified herself as a
midwesterner to counteract the assumption that no one in the Midwest is
"politically aware."[36] Others shared this dualism; they described Michigan as
home and felt proud to be from Michigan and the Midwest, but they also saw
the state or region as "less diverse," "conservative," and "close-minded," qualities they disparaged and from which they often disassociated themselves.
Kim Hoang, a second-generation Vietnamese American, noted, "I was born
and raised in Lansing, which I'm definitely really proud of . . . well, I'm not
proud of Michigan per se. . . . I think of the Midwest as very white and really
religious . . . very conservative Christian."[37] One respondent rejected any state
or regional allegiances due to these perceived characteristics. Phillip Chan, a
second-generation Chinese American college student, recalled his high school
teachers telling him, "'You gotta watch out. [The university] has more of those
Oriental people. And so, when you go there, they're going to come and get
you.' Meaning that they're going to try to recruit me, to become a part of their
clique, or group, or something like that."[38]

In general, respondents identified themselves as Michiganders for technical reasons: they were born and raised in Michigan, had immigrated to Michigan decades ago, and/or paid taxes in Michigan. Maria Cruz, a first-generation
Filipina American who has lived in Michigan since 1955, said, "I don't even think
of midwestern, you know? I'm just from Michigan."[39] Peter Tom, a fourth-generation Chinese American said, "I figure I was born here and I lived here all my
life so [I] classify myself as a Michigander or a midwesterner."[40] However, these
respondents' casual initial answers did not reflect the depth of their familial

roots and involvement in Detroit-area Filipino and Chinese communities. For decades, Cruz served as an officer and member of Filipina/o American and Asian American community organizations while Tom and his relatives have been residents and business owners in Detroit for multiple generations.[41]

Whether they identified themselves with positive cultural images of midwesterners, saw themselves as exceptions to the region's negative cultural images, or described themselves as "just from Michigan," respondents described Michigan as home. Michigan and the Midwest are real places with meanings that shape their lives, and yet their identifications belied the complexity of homemaking for these respondents. Scholars have noted that Asian Americans continue to be racialized as foreigners in the United States, and the data from this study also showed that despite their identification as Michiganders, most respondents had experienced words or actions from non-Asian Americans that questioned their local, regional, and national belonging. In particular, respondents' answers indicated that the small population of Asian Americans in Michigan combined with the state's prevalence of highly educated Asian American professionals regionalized their racial identities. How they make sense of being Asian American in Michigan or the Midwest, and what they reveal about race, class, and U.S. regionalism are analyzed in the next sections.

Demographics and Asian American Identity Formations

Between 1990 and 2000, the Asian Pacific American population grew by 86.5 percent and constituted 2.3 percent of the population in the Midwest and 2.1 percent in Michigan.[42] Respondents welcomed this growth of the Asian American population, as it translated into convenient developments such as Asian markets and restaurants that provided greater choices and access to ethnic goods and products.

First-generation Michigan residents in the study reported that they were satisfied with their careers and family lives. Many, such as Jae Hong Park, who helped establish a church and a school to teach the Korean language, participated in ethnic and panethnic organizations and institutions to serve Michigan's expanding and diversifying Asian American population.[43] Respondents of all ages, ethnic backgrounds, and generations cited growing up with and/or forming associations of coethnic or Asian friends, kin, organizations, and other social networks.

Even so, the small number and low density of Asian Americans in Michigan (a few metropolitan areas with higher percentages exempted) created

78 BARBARA W. KIM

distinctively spatialized experiences. Through stares, racist remarks, and/or physical assaults, whites—and at times blacks—clearly marked the respondents as outsiders and foreigners who were "out of place." For example, May Tsai, who arrived from Taiwan in 1989, remembered dining at a fast-food restaurant with her husband on a trip to Ohio. She noticed—because of the other customers' reactions—that they were the only Asians there. "My husband and I—we were the only people who have different skin. We felt so uncomfortable! Everybody was trying to—they just stared at us, in a subtle way."[44]

Korean American Jin Kyung Park, who immigrated to Michigan in the 1960s, recalled attending a small-town fund-raiser in the late 1970s: "People were just fascinated by us because we are the only Oriental group there. It's all white. So we stopped going there when my younger son asked, 'Why [are] people looking at us like we're animals in a zoo?' . . . And I couldn't tell him about the racial discrimination, because it wasn't actually . . . it was my feeling."[45] Park attributes the white attendees' reaction to racial differences and their "curiosity," stopping short of calling it racial discrimination. Nevertheless, this "curiosity" caused Park and her family to stop going to the Chicken Broil, an annual fire department fund-raiser described as a picturesque example of small-town America. Park's discomfort demonstrates that racialized incidents do not have to be overtly hostile to exclude Asian Americans—even someone like Park, who describes herself as knowing "every corner of my town and every corner of Michigan"—from public spaces and events. In these cases the images of heartland are infused with racial homogeneity and exclusivity.

The basis on which respondents embraced their regional identity resembled that shown in previous studies on symbolic or optional ethnicities. Racialized ethnics such as Asian Americans do not possess the agency to select and exercise their ethnic options without having their claims of home, belonging, and American citizenship constantly questioned or revoked. In contrast, white ethnic Americans are able to choose which particular ethnic traits (or none at all, opting for the "American" identity) and qualities to keep, modify, or discard without their ethnicity jeopardizing their incorporation into mainstream America.[46]

The youngest respondents, those of the second generation born to post-1965 immigrants and refugees, cited the lack of other Asian Americans in their schools and neighborhoods as their most distinctive experience in Michigan. Chi Lee, a Hmong American college student, grew up among working-class blacks, Latinos, whites, and Asians in southeastern Michigan. She had many extended family members and socialized with them on weekends, but growing up, she had few Asian American classmates, a situation she described as "typical." Vivek Mehta, a second-generation Indian American in his late twenties, also grew up as one of the few Asians in his neighborhood and schools. While he experienced some racially derogatory comments, Mehta believed that Asians in his self-described affluent hometown were generally accepted because of their socioeconomic status.

While Lee and Mehta reported little trouble other than occasional slurs, other respondents were physically harassed or beaten by kids in their neighborhoods, whether these were predominantly white, predominantly black, small rural towns, middle-class suburbs, or working-class cities. Korean American Brian Cho, who grew up in small town in northern Michigan, recalled that his older brother, who was more "physically roughed up than I was," spent a summer at their father's friend's house in Chicago to take martial arts lessons. When his brother returned with a bigger physique, "the bullies . . . stopped bothering him," and Cho in his turn was sent to take tae kwon do lessons so he could defend himself.[47] Sarah Chu, a Chinese American who grew up in a small town in mid-Michigan, recalled that she was "picked on a lot; I mean, I didn't get beat up or anything like that, but . . . I was just definitely seen as being different. I didn't feel like I fit in at all in junior high or high school."[48] Lisa Riley, adopted from South Korea when she was six months old, grew up in southeastern Michigan and did not meet other Asian Americans until high school. She related that she was "the only Asian student in my whole school, so I got teased a lot and I was really self-conscious about that."[49]

Allen Chuang, a second-generation Taiwanese American, grew up in a predominantly white suburb in mid-Michigan. He joined Taiwanese and Asian American student organizations in college and after graduation worked with similar groups at another university. For Chuang, one consequence of growing up as "one of the few" Asian Americans or "the only" one was that he did not have "a racial identity"—which he defined as being "comfortable and confident in being Asian American"—until his junior year of college. He hypothesized that "geography might have something, something to do with stuff. Like California, West Coast being close to Taiwan, whether it's relatives or influences . . . having an Asian American newscaster, those kinds of things—Asian American newscasters and Asian American TV shows, or Asian American channels—because I had none of that."[50]

Vietnamese American Kim Hoang had only one Asian classmate until a small wave of Vietnamese, Laotian, and Hmong refugee families moved into her hometown in the late 1980s. Despite the cultural and linguistic gaps she saw between herself and her newly arrived peers, Hoang started an Asian American club at her high school because "I felt like it was really important that we had some kind of forum to be proud of who we were." In college, she worked with other student activists as an officer in Vietnamese American, pan-Asian, and feminist organizations. Hoang pointed out that growing up, she had a group of friends from various racial and class backgrounds, but Asian Americans remained invisible in the black/white racial context. Unlike Chuang, Hoang articulated and developed an "Asian American racial identity" prior to college; but like Chuang, she defined racial identity as an option that is more accessible in places with larger and concentrated Asian American populations.

> Because it's so dichotomized—black and white. Asian Americans, for the most part, can't be Asian American. Really, the only option is to be white, I feel. Had I grown up, or had other Asian Americans grown up, in California, I think there would have been more niches to fall into: whether you wanted to be like—and I'm stereotyping—the Asian American artsy, really into poetry and performing arts, or the activist, . . . the Asian American professional, the Asian American science nerd. You know, you had all those niches. In Michigan, because there weren't that many Asian Americans around, the expectation is that you would hang out [with whites] . . . you're going to be lonely if you only hang out with the only other Asian person—if there was that.[51]

From the perspective of these second-generation Michiganders, demographics in Michigan and the Midwest created a distinctively regional experience for Asian Americans. Although some studies on second-generation identities try to quantify the degree of ethnic and racial identification through language usage and racial/ethnic backgrounds of their friends and other social networks, the discussions indicated that for many, such ethnic and racial options did not exist in their childhoods.[52] However, pointing out this lack of options did not mean that the respondents wished they lived elsewhere. Chi Lee, who attended a Hmong New Year celebration in California in the late 1990s, suggested that Michigan demographics offered an alternative, more "realistic" perspective of Asian American experiences than that available in areas such as the West Coast with its higher concentration of Asian Americans because nationally, Asian Americans comprised just more than 4 percent of the total population in 2000 and might not live in or near ethnic enclaves in which they could choose to interact only with coethnics.

For [Californian Asians], it seems like they have a sense of the world being Asian. . . . In Michigan . . . you can stick with your clan, but you know that there is this outside world too. I think it matters more so for my parents and the old generation to see others like them around all the time, because that's what they were used to. I don't think that they deny the fact that they're living here, in a different world, because at work or at school, they have to deal with it, and at home, they come back to their communities the same again.[53]

Sandy Yu, an active member of Chinese and Asian American civil rights organizations in the Metropolitan Detroit area, observed how living in Michigan gave her a perspective of California as a unique Asian American place. Other Michiganders echoed what Yu voiced: when there is a critical mass of Asian Americans to participate in political and community activism, other Asian Americans may not feel the need to do so because that mass creates a sense that Asian Americans are no longer numerically, culturally, and politically marginalized:

You can take California in two ways from our perspective in the Midwest. They've got the numbers; they should be able to get things done. But secondly, when you live in California . . . you see a lot of [Asian Americans] so you don't feel like you need too much [to organize] . . . there's enough of you around. So how can anyone discriminate against you, because when you're walking in the shopping mall, there is three or four walking there with you . . . ? I think you can see California in many different ways. The numbers are a blessing and the numbers are not a blessing.[54]

Previous scholarship documents how immigrant and multigenerational Asian Americans have been racialized as foreigners across the United States, even as Asian Americans uncover historical roots and grow in numbers and socioeconomic diversity.[55] In fact, many of my respondents had lived in different cities and towns across Michigan and other states. They preferred to reside within the boundaries of urban metropolitan areas whose non-Asian residents were perceived as more educated and exposed to racial and cultural diversity, like Pawan Dhingra's second-generation Asian Americans living in Dallas, Texas.[56] While some respondents expressed that they would have been more "comfortable and confident" about their racial/ethnic identities earlier in their lives had they lived in places with a large concentrated Asian American population, others said that their experiences in Michigan offered a more realistic perspective of a racial group that was growing fast but still comprised less than 5 percent of the total U.S. population in 2000. The responses suggested that in general, Michiganders and midwesterners' perceived lack of awareness about Asian Americans and the recollections of racial marginalization in childhood, the workplace, or in public spaces intensified the respondents' sense of racialization. The interviews also indicated that most respondents viewed Michigan and the Midwest as home, describing theirs as a *spatialized* racial experience, and not a lesser or less authentic version of a West Coast–centric narrative.

The Persistence of the Model Minority Image

According to the 2000 census, Michigan Asian Americans were more likely than other Asians or the total population in the Midwest and the United States to have higher incomes and hold a bachelor's degree.[57] In recent decades, Asian Americans who have settled in Michigan have done so primarily because of educational and occupational factors. For example, Ann Arbor, home to the University of Michigan's largest campus, had the highest percentage of the Asian American population in the state. In 1990, Asian Americans and Pacific Islanders made up 7.7 percent of the city's population; by 2000, this had grown to 13.1 percent.[58] Many respondents were aware of this socioeconomic profile of Asian American Michigan residents and believed that in general, non-Asians view Asians as smart, hardworking, and successful—the model minority, a minority group whose members achieve upward mobility and success through cultural values that stress strong work ethics and education. That Asian Americans are seen in this way is neither new nor limited to the Midwest or Michigan.[59] Respondents equally embraced and criticized this image. However, even those who identified positively with the perception recognized it as a stereotype. Not all Asian Americans are wealthy, professional, and highly educated. Furthermore, many professional respondents told anecdotes of racial, cultural, or gender discrimination and marginalization in the workplace or in public spaces, indicating that upward mobility and socioeconomic achievement do not erase differences and discrimination based on other social identities. Simultaneously, discussions about who fits or does not fit the model minority stereotype revealed fissures within Asian American communities along the lines of class, ethnicity, and (Asian) regional origins.[60]

Kim Hoang, who came from a working-class family, noted that "the perception of Asian American is that if you're Asian American, your father probably [is] a doctor or engineer or something like that, and you're well to do, upwardly mobile. . . . I think that there's the assumption that I'm upwardly mobile because I'm Asian American."[61] Joe Miyamoto, a second-generation Japanese American retiree, noted that Asian Americans are not "monolithic" and that the model minority image is "false." But he found it flattering that "Caucasians . . . have a positive prejudice against Orientals. I think it's kind of ego-boosting here, as opposed to the West Coast." [62] Myung Woo Lim, a Korean American engineer who works for a major automobile corporation, speculated that "positive prejudice" resulted from the efforts of first-generation Asian immigrants like himself who had to prove themselves as harder working than (native-born white) Americans to enjoy a similar level of job security.[63]

But working harder does not always translate into upward mobility and socioeconomic success, according to Peter Tom, a business owner who grew up in Detroit's Chinatown. Tom noted how the model minority stereotype overlooks merchants and laborers in the Asian American population. "I think [Asians] are perceived as hard workers. I think the majority of Asians don't mix that well, except maybe the professionals. And [non-Asians] think that most Asians are wealthy, too. It's pretty false. . . . Why do I think that their thinking is false? Because I see it."[64] A fourth-generation Chinese American, he noted that the model minority stereotype may be applicable to Asian professionals—such as those who came as students and skilled workers from northern China and Taiwan—but less to the (Cantonese) merchants and laborers from southern parts of China who comprised the majority of the pre-1965 Detroit Chinese population as well as more recently arrived labor immigrants. Second-generation college student Amit Jain, whose father came to Michigan in the late 1960s as a graduate student, faulted wealthier Indian Americans for ignoring the concerns of newer and less established Indian immigrants. "That's sort of an issue that needs to be addressed more in the Midwest, and I think we're not thinking about that more now," he said. "I think in the New York/New Jersey area, people have realized that a little bit, because [the socioeconomic diversity] is so much more predominant."[65]

Class divisions also challenged the Asian American stereotype that college students had growing up in different sections of urban and suburban Michigan. Serena Choi, a second-generation Korean American from an upper-middle-class southeastern Michigan suburb, pointed out that Asian American students are seen as "curve-busters" who all attend elite colleges or universities, which could create a backlash from the dominant society. But Chi Lee, the Hmong American woman from a working-class city near Detroit who attended the same university as Choi, said that she did not know Asian American students were stereotyped as smart or rich until she came to college. She attributed the difference to class, distinguishing between "suburban" and "city" Asian Americans. Lee observed, "I think [Asian students on her campus] have a stereotype of them being the smart people. And back at home, it's totally different. Back at home, they are more of the quiet people, the ones that are—the ones who don't do very well in school, but they always do the work."[66]

Tae Young Han, a 1.5-generation Korean American who grew up in southeastern Michigan, criticized professional Asian Americans who claim their American identity through class and not through race. One cost is the deterioration of relations among Asian Americans and other minority groups in Michigan.

> I think if you're willing to play by the rules . . . go to a professional school, be quiet, don't talk about race at all, you can get along fairly well here. But that causes problems with other minority groups, especially blacks, who see Asians as sellouts. People who think they are white and better than black people, um, of course, many of them do think that. And that has caused a lot of problems that way.[67]

The respondents' concerns about backlash or race/ethnic glass ceilings also indicated the precarious positioning of model minorities who are accepted as long as they do not threaten the dominant group members. Even as first- and second-generation professionals attributed their reputations as hard workers to the fear of linguistic and racial/ethnic discrimination from their mainstream coworkers, adhering to the model minority stereotype is a way to gain social and economic acceptance from middle- and upper-middle-class whites, who are seen as "true" Americans.[68] In the wake of the civil rights movement and deracialized immigration laws, Michigan attracted students and highly trained engineers, scientists, physicians, and other professionals to its urban industries. "Old-timers," those who had arrived prior to 1965, also benefited from the lifting of institutionalized discriminatory policies. (Many respondents recalled times into the 1960s when they or their parents could not buy homes in particular sections of Detroit or the surrounding suburbs because of discrimination.)

The model minority image revealed intraracial divisions and tensions marked by national, political, linguistic, social, and economic differences, such as the invisibility of working-class Asian Americans. Yet, in numbers and in political clout, Asian Americans as a group were invisible in the historically black/white racial discourse. Historically, Asian Americans of various ethnic backgrounds have been defined as members of every racial classification under the legal lens but, like Latinos and Native Americans, their experiences have been for the most part peripheral in the American racial discourse formed "largely through inequities and conflicts between blacks and whites."[69] The status of Asian Americans shifted between black and white in the racial spectrum depending on history, place, and context. In Michigan, they are, in respondent Luis Delgado's words, "the minority minority." The suburban, well-educated, and professional respondents may be integrated socially and economically into neighborhoods and workplaces, but they are invisible as "almost whites" and visible as "foreigners." Meanwhile, urban poor and working-class Asian Americans remain invisible as Asian Americans due to the model minority stereotype. Michael Shin, a second-generation Korean American, shared that blacks and whites he encounters on the streets assume he is a foreigner or call him "Bruce Lee"—the enduring male Asian American stereotype as the martial arts expert. But in the workplace, he encounters a different set of assumptions: white colleagues treat him as nonwhite, while black colleagues think that he is almost white.

A lot of African Americans think that even though you're Asian, you're not considered a minority—that white people treat you better than the African Americans, that you're promotable far more than, say, your African American colleague. But that's not true. In fact, when you talk to a Caucasian, a Caucasian perceives you as a minority. . . . Case in point, in a particular workplace . . . a lot of the jokes in the work environment was that the Caucasians were getting brand-new furniture and the African Americans were not. And I remember several times, a couple of people came into my office and looked around, and they said, "Where's your new furniture?" And I said, "What new furniture?" and they said, "Wow, you're not one of them?" That just kills me![70]

As the "Rust Belt" has lost thousands of jobs due to declining manufacturing and industrial relocation since World War II, Detroit has attracted fewer immigrants than other places in the United States such as Los Angeles, Chicago, Miami, and New York.[71] So despite the presence of other racial/ethnic groups such as Arab and Latino Americans, the racial discourse in Michigan in the latter twentieth century has been a story of native-born black/white relations.[72] According to researchers, pervasive patterns of residential segregation are interpreted as indications of racial/ethnic competition and tensions, whereas low patterns are interpreted as racial/ethnic assimilation. While scholars have argued that the de facto residential segregation of whites and blacks in American cities has contributed to growing racial inequalities, Asian Americans in Michigan (who arrived as a diverse group of students, skilled workers, resettled refugees, and sponsored family members) exhibit a combination of high socioeconomic status and high levels of suburbanization, two conditions that lower residential segregation.[73] However, such lower residential segregation does not address the stereotypical portrayals of Asian Americans as foreigners and the model minority. How do the participants, then, actively respond to these intertwined themes of small population size and foreigner/model minority image? Their sense of precarious acceptance leads to the next theme: the image of Asian Americans as "ambassadors" in Michigan and the Midwest.

Negotiating Race, Class, and Gender Identities and Representations

Respondents often encountered people in Michigan who had little or no previous interaction with Asian Americans. That made them more self-reflective, aware that their words and actions could have an effect on how these Michiganders perceived all Asian Americans. As a result, willingly or unwillingly, they became "ambassadors" for Asian America as a whole. Some, like second-generation Choi, resented this ascribed duty to be a representative.

> A lot of people in Michigan have so few Asians in general to interact with, so they never get to know them as a person, and when they do meet one as a person, like me, any bad experiences we have together, they'll generalize it to all Asians, and not see it as a personality flaw on my part. It's almost like I'm an ambassador to all white persons.[74]

Yumi Shin, a 1.5-generation Korean American, was also conscious that her behavior and actions in the workplace—where she is one of the few Asian American women in her profession—would be used to generalize behaviors and actions of all Asian Americans. However, she considered this unavoidable ambassadorship a necessary duty so that other Asian Americans would be treated with respect and fairness. Particularly concerned about the intersections of racial and gendered stereotypes, she consciously tried to challenge two stereotypes—the perpetual foreigner and the submissive Asian woman—because "I think a lot of people automatically assume an Asian American female not to be assertive. . . . The last thing I want to do is portray this submissive Asian female person."[75]

Janice Okada, a third-generation Japanese American and a Michigan native, described her efforts to teach awareness about the heterogeneity of Asian America not only in the public school curriculum she helped develop but also in everyday encounters with non-Asian teachers and students in a region of the state with a growing Southeast Asian population.

> Your typical educator in the classroom . . . , unless they had some experience, they don't really know the difference between Asians and Asian Americans]. Like kids might say to me, "Well, in your country, do you eat sushi?" or they might say to me, "In your country, do you wear Western clothes?" And I say, "Well, in my country—*this* is my country." They don't know.[76]

Other respondents said that Asian Americans should interact with non-Asians with the particular goal of breaking down racial and ethnic barriers. Second-generation respondents who had friendships with people from different racial/ethnic groups while maintaining their own ethnic, cultural, and religious ties tended to support this type of ambassadorship. Mehta said, "I think it will be up to strong individuals in different communities to try to dispel the fear. I guess another thing is, people in minority ethnic groups need to focus on inviting outsiders to their group as opposed to excluding them."[77] Another self-described ambassador acutely aware of the invisibility and lack of representation of Asian Americans is Tom Martinez, who is of Latino and Taiwanese descent. Most respondents talked about interactions between Asian Americans and non-Asian Americans in the suburbs and small towns across the state, but Martinez, who grew up in predominantly black or racially mixed neighborhoods, addressed Asian, Latino, and black interactions in Detroit. A teacher at a predominantly black high school in Detroit, Martinez recalled how his students believed that he must be black because he lived in the city:

> They're like, "If you're Chinese, then why are you in Detroit?" Well, because I want to be. "But you're not black."

So already it's ingrained in them, these divisions. . . . So actually, I brought my kids up to a [Chinese culture show] because I wanted to show them, like—you're not going to like all of us. . . . But there's something different outside of food and nails. And it was funny because by the end of the second day, it was like, "Mr. M., the Chinese are just like black people." I didn't quite see that. I said, "Black people may be like Chinese people." . . . That's what I love doing, doing out there. Being that middle person, I can do it. I can go on and take both worlds.[78]

The "food and nail" reference stemmed from Martinez's perception that like other Detroiters, his students' interactions with Asians in the neighborhoods are with immigrant entrepreneurs who operate small businesses such as takeout restaurants and nail salons. But while he tried to challenge his students' one-dimensional images of Asian Americans, Martinez also confronted middle-class peers he met through Asian American student organizations in college who construed the world as a binary of Asian and white. Martinez noted that other Asian Americans wanted to join white fraternities while he wanted to join a black one. "And then, the interracial dating thing, you know—they're always talking about in terms of white, and I'd be talking about, well, what if someone is Dominican?" Other respondents discussed ambassadorship chiefly in terms of Asians and the dominant white society. Martinez saw his role as challenging stereotypical encounters between predominantly suburban, middle-class Asian Americans (or immigrant Asian American merchants) and other people of color, often from working-class backgrounds, in Detroit.

Respondents cited the absence of a large Asian American population as a distinctive feature of the midwestern or Michigan experience. That, in turn, created ambassadors, either reluctant or willing, who became representatives of their racial or ethnic group whose actions and behaviors could potentially affect how non-Asians perceived and treated Asians in the future. Invisible in the black/white discourse but nonetheless visible as racial others, respondents learned to "walk circumspectly" around racial and economic fault lines and strategize ways to challenge racial, class, and gendered stereotypes in everyday encounters with non-Asians.[79]

But respondents did not merely walk circumspectly. They were actively involved in social networks, campus organizations, ethnic associations, and American Citizens for Justice, formed in the wake of the 1982 murder of

Vincent Chin.[80] Examples of their social and political activism committed to helping fellow Michigan Asian Americans included providing social services for Chinese senior citizens, mobilizing student activists on their university campuses, hosting fund-raising events for Asian American political candidates (including those from outside Michigan), providing immigrant business owners with language assistance to resolve legal or bureaucratic issues, forming and teaching heritage language schools for the second generation, fundraising for ethnic community centers, and mobilizing around local, national, and international events. Drawn by the history of Asian American activism and attracted to the larger, demographically concentrated Asian American populations, organizations, and resources on the coasts, Chu and Hoang said they wanted to move to such "Asian American communities" but eventually return to Michigan to work for social change in the state and region. These ambassadors not only negotiated racial, ethnic, gender, and class identities and representations, they also committed themselves to shape and sustain their regional communities in Michigan and the Midwest.[81]

Racialized Ethnics and Regional Identities

As Michiganders and as midwesterners, the respondents confronted many of the same issues that Asian Americans experience elsewhere in the nation, such as the prevalent images of the model minority and the forever foreigner. But many contrasted themselves in particular with their West Coast and East Coast counterparts, perceived as living in areas with large Asian American populations. Kathleen Wong (Lau), writing about Asian American community in the Southwest, claims that West Coast frameworks have dominated mainland Asian American literature and politics; physical ethnic enclaves and institutions (such as Chinatowns, Manilatowns, Japantowns, and Koreatowns) are used to gauge the authenticity and maturity of racial/ethnic communities and identities when in fact these are "localized" and regionalized formations.[82]

Taking this dominating West Coast framework into account, the respondents dialectically negotiated their regionalized racial/ethnic identities as they interacted with non-Michigan/midwestern Asian Americans and non-Asians in Michigan/the Midwest. Such intersections of race, geography, and identity take into consideration negotiations of immigration histories, class, gender, ethnicity, and representation of place and people.[83] For example, citing a regional Michigan/midwestern cultural identity and echoing regional studies literature about the Midwest, many respondents said that they saw themselves as more "wholesome," "down-to-earth," and "laid-back" than their coastal counterparts, and first-generation residents were generally satisfied with their careers and the quality of life of themselves and their children in Michigan.

However, the interviews revealed that for many second-generation respondents, growing up as one of the few or only Asian Americans meant that they had to choose between a black or white identity rather than an Asian American one. This created a sense that their experience—in contrast to the West Coast/East Coast models—was a spatially distinctive one. Yet the ratio of Asian Americans to the general population in Michigan is closer to that in the United States as a whole than that in bicoastal metropolitan areas. In another finding, the high representation of Asian Americans in professional, managerial, and technical fields as a result of post-1965 immigration reforms and policies has resulted in a sharper sense of being the "model minority."[84] In fact, the concentration of Asian Americans with high socioeconomic status and education levels suggested to some respondents that Asian Americans in Michigan are even *outmodeling* their counterparts elsewhere in the nation. Yet this sense of achievement denies the existence of socioeconomic diversity and splits along class, ethnic, and national lines within Michigan Asian America, demonstrating the precariousness of belonging in the heartland through socioeconomic means.

The intensity of the simultaneous visibility and invisibility of Asian Americans in Michigan, despite the apparent economic, occupational, and residential integration, indicates the enduring power of cultural meanings in American regions and the interplay of race and class in determining who is included or excluded in the heartland. For the respondents, regional identity was contextualized by race. Michigan is their home by birth or by migration. Although some were critical of their home state, most expressed love and pride. Respondents held allegiances to local sports teams, appreciated the beauty of Michigan's great outdoors, had traveled extensively throughout the state, and spoke with a regional accent, but they still found their regional and national identities questioned by non-Asians. The lack of a "critical mass" and the tendency to be rendered invisible in some contexts and to "stick out like a sore thumb" in others resulted in two contradictory experiences. Asian Americans were accepted because of their small numbers, especially against the backdrop of black/white relations, *and* Asian Americans faced more blatant discrimination because their small numbers made their physical and cultural differences more visible against racially homogeneous neighborhoods, workplaces, and other public spaces. But the respondents, as individuals and as participants in networks and organizations, actively negotiated representations of racial, ethnic, gender, and class identities as they acted as ambassadors and as Michigan residents committed to fostering and fighting for the cultural, social, and political concerns of Asian American communities locally and regionally.

Victor Jew argues that the characterization of midwestern values as "central, standard American values" did not come about accidentally; it was a nativist promotion of the territory, which was described in 1912 by University of Wisconsin sociologist Edward Alsworth Ross as lying "beyond the ken of the insweeping tides from southern Europe and the Orient." This xenophobia translated into the endorsement of whiteness as central and standard America.[85] This study of Asian Americans in Michigan and the Midwest—the nation's heartland—documents how space and region, with other multiple social identities, intersect to construct and maintain the continued significance of race in contemporary American society. It links locations, meanings, and the presence/absence of "critical masses" to processes of racialization. In this manner, Keith Aoki's "midwestern shards of memory" are not aberrations outside "authentic" Asian American communities but experiences that need to be examined in their historical, social, and spatial contexts within the ongoing political project of defining race, citizenship, and belonging in the United States. This essay and this volume as a whole serve as documentation and analysis of Asian American experiences in Michigan and the Midwest as sites of such contestation.

Notes

1. Keith Aoki, "Critical Legal Studies, Asian Americans in U.S. Law and Culture, Neil Gotanda, and Me," *Asian Law Journal* 4 (May 1997): 19.
2. Elizabeth M. Hoeffel, Sonya Rastogi, Myoung Ouk Kim, and Hasan Shahid, *The Asian Population: 2010,* U.S. Census Bureau, 2010 Census Briefs, C2010BR-11, www.census. gov/prod/cen2010/briefs/c2010br-11.pdf.
3. Gary Y. Okihiro, *The Columbia Guide to Asian American History* (New York: Columbia University Press, 2001); Eric Lai and Dennis Arguelles, *The New Face of Asian Pacific America: Numbers, Diversity, and Change in the 21st Century* (San Francisco: *AsianWeek* and the UCLA Asian American Studies Center, 2003). Both census data and the respondents' discussions indicate the historical and contemporary importance of the greater metropolitan area of Chicago in Asian America. Respondents gave Chicago as an example of ethnic enclave, community, and a place to go for various ethnic goods, services, and resources unreplicated elsewhere in the region.

4. Victor Jew, "Making Homes in the Heartland," in Lai and Arguelles, *The New Face of Asian Pacific America*; Stephen Sumida, "East of California: Points of Origin in Asian American Studies," *Journal of Asian American Studies* 1, no. 1 (1998): 83-100.

5. Detroit JACL newsletter, September 1962, pp. 3, 7, Detroit Japanese American Citizens League Collection, Michigan Historical Collections, Bentley Library, University of Michigan, Ann Arbor. See also Easurk Emsen Charr, *The Golden Mountain: The Autobiography of a Korean Immigrant, 1895-1960*, 2nd ed. (Urbana: University of Illinois Press, 1996); Huping Ling, *Chinese St. Louis: From Enclave to Cultural Community* (Philadelphia: Temple University Press, 2004).

6. Victor Jew, "Attempts at Mapping Changing Landscapes and Shifting Borders: The 'Midwest' and Asian American History," in *Asian Pacific Americans and the U.S. Southwest*, ed. Thomas Nakayama and Carlton E. Yoshioka (Tempe: Arizona State University, 1997); Sumida, "East of California." In the 1940s, the War Relocation Authority resettled incarcerated Japanese Americans throughout the Midwest in hopes that they would assimilate more quickly into the dominant American society away from prewar community social ties and institutions. After 1975, federal departments and agencies created a Southeast Asian diaspora throughout the Midwest and the nation in order to avoid the depletion of economic and social support services in one area of the United States.

7. Jew, "Making Homes in the Heartland."

8. Also see Barbara W. Kim, "Race, Space, and Identity: Examining Asian American Racial and Ethnic Formations in the Midwest" (PhD diss., University of Michigan, 2001).

9. Michael Omi and Howard Winant, *Racial Formation in the United States: From the 1960s to the 1990s* (New York: Routledge, 1994), 55.

10. Sucheng Chan, *Asian Americans: An Interpretive History* (New York: Twayne, 1991); Glenn Omatsu, "The 'Four Prisons' and the Movements of Liberation: Asian American Activism from the 1960s to the 1990s," in *The State of Asian America: Activism and Resistance in the 1990s*, ed. Karen Aguilar-San Juan (Boston: South End, 1994). In 1968, African American, Latino, American Indian, and Asian American members of the Third World Liberation Front staged a five-month strike against San Francisco State College to establish the first School of Ethnic Studies in the nation. The student and community activists sought to change how people of color had been marginalized and silenced within canons of American history, scholarship, and contemporary society. According to Omatsu, the Asian American movement and "consciousness" arose from the recognition that Asian Americans, like other people of color, had been racially set apart and marginalized or excluded from full participation in the dominant society. See also Karen Umemoto, "'On Strike!' San Francisco State College Strike, 1968–1969: The Role of Asian American Students," *Amerasia Journal* 15 (1989): 3–41.

11. Okihiro, *The Columbia Guide*, 133.

12. Arif Dirlik, "Asians on the Rim: Transnational Capital and Local Community in the Making of Contemporary Asian America," *Amerasia Journal* 22 (1996): 1-24; Sau-ling C. Wong, "Denationalization Reconsidered: Asian American Cultural Criticism at a Theoretical Crossroad," *Amerasia Journal* 21 (1995): 1-27.

13. Okihiro, *The Columbia Guide*, 133; Sumida, "East of California," 85-86.

14. Edward W. Soja, *Thirdspace: Journeys to Los Angeles and Other Real-and-Imagined Places* (Cambridge, MA: Blackwell, 1996), 1. See also Thomas F. Gieryn, "A Space for Place in Sociology," *Annual Review of Sociology* 26 (2000): 463-96. Gieryn argues that place, distinguishable from space, matters in the study of social processes and phenomena because it has (1) a unique and recognizable geographical location; (2) a compilation of things or objects that exist in material form; and (3) associated meaning and value.

15. For example, see James DeVries, *Race and Kinship in a Midwestern Town: The Black Experience in Monroe, Michigan, 1900-1915* (Chicago: University of Illinois Press, 1984). DeVries studied the lives of a few blacks who at the turn of the century populated Monroe, a small, rural town in southeastern Michigan near the Ohio border. Although the trend in the Northeast and the Midwest was to follow the Jim Crow segregation system developed in the South, Monroe did not adhere to strict segregationist policies because the town simply did not have enough black citizens to pose a serious threat to the predominantly white community, unlike in Chicago or Detroit. But DeVries notes that the lack of segregation did not translate to equality. The descriptions of the blacks in the town, preserved in newspapers, resonate with national perceptions of blacks as the "child-negro and the beast."

16. Yen Le Espiritu, *Filipino American Lives* (Philadelphia: Temple University Press, 1995).

17. Byung Ha Song, "The Immigrants' Residential Settlement Process: The Case of Koreans in the Detroit Region" (ArchD diss., University of Michigan–Ann Arbor, 1990); Jung-Sun Park, "Identity and Politics in a Transnational Community: A Case of Chicago Korean Americans" (PhD diss., Northwestern University, 1997). But since the late 1970s, more Korean and other Asians who are either small-business owners or blue-collar workers have settled in the Midwest and other regions of the United States due to changes in U.S. immigration law that restricted occupational immigration and increased family reunification slots (although occupational immigrants also have entered through family reunification sponsorship). This has resulted in a greater and normalized socioeconomic diversity among Asian Americans.

18. Thomas J. Sugrue, *The Origins of the Urban Crisis: Race and Inequality in Postwar Detroit* (Princeton: Princeton University Press, 1996).

19. Okihiro, *The Columbia Guide*. Surveying the literature, Okihiro observes that studies of Asian American histories in other regions have not challenged the dominant California narrative. Referring to contemporary "centers" of Asian American population numbers and percentages, sizeable populations of Asian Americans exist outside Hawaii and the West Coast, including in the Midwest; examples include New York, Chicago, and the Washington, DC area. However, six out of ten areas with the highest Asian American populations were in California and Hawaii in 2000. For an example of a study that explores the intersections of race, space, and class, see Pawan Dhingra, *Managing Multicultural Lives: Asian American Professionals and the Challenge of Multiple Identities* (Stanford: Stanford University Press, 2007).

20. Interviews were conducted in July 1998 and April—August 1999. The names of potential respondents were initially gathered from various agencies, community and university organizations, and personal recommendations to access different social networks. Then snowball sampling was used: each respondent was asked to refer two persons to be contacted for the study. Interviews lasted from forty-five minutes to three and a half hours, and respondents were asked numerous questions about

immigration and settlement histories in Michigan, social networks, impressions of neighborhoods in which they lived, "ethnic/cultural" markers and practices that were stressed in their lives and, if applicable, in their children's lives, and impressions of race relations in different spatial contexts as defined by the respondent (neighborhoods, schools, cities, regions, and so on). Interviews were conducted at locations convenient to the respondent, such as cafés, restaurants, shopping malls, homes, and workplaces. All respondent names in this study are pseudonyms.

21. Seventeen are first-generation Asian Americans; seventeen are the "new" 1.5 generation (defined as born outside the United States and immigrating between the ages of six and twelve) or second generation (children of post-1965 immigrant parents in their twenties and early thirties); four are older second generation, in their forties, fifties, or seventies; one is third generation; and one is fourth generation. In this study, discussions of self-identified 1.5-generation respondents were similar to second-generation respondents in their age cohort.

22. Eric Lai, "Socioeconomic Trends in the Midwest," in Lai and Arguelles, *The New Face of Asian Pacific America*.

23. Jew, "Making Homes in the Heartland," 47.

24. See James R. Shortridge, *The Middle West: Its Meaning in American Culture* (Lawrence: University Press of Kansas, 1989).

25. Hoeffel et al., *The Asian Population: 2010*. At different points in the chapter, 2000 census figures will be referenced in order to contextualize the demographic numbers and percentages current at the time of the interviews.

26. One respondent said that he did not think Michigan was a part of the Midwest because it was a part of the Eastern Standard Time zone.

27. Shortridge, *The Middle West*. In a survey of one thousand college students locating the Midwest region on a U.S. map, Shortridge found that students from the Midwest were most likely to conceptualize the region around their home state. For example, Iowa natives were likely to designate that state as the center of the Midwest and less likely to include Ohio—the easternmost state included in the region—as a part of the Midwest.

28. However, only one respondent speculated that Pennsylvania (Pennsylvania State University joined the Big Ten Conference in 1990) is in the Midwest, based on this argument.

29. The author used "Michigander" (noun) to refer to the people of Michigan in forms and interviews but "Michiganian" (adjective) to refer to Michigan residents, as some respondents preferred the latter term.

30. Tank Chun, interview by the author, Ann Arbor, May 18, 1999.

31. Allison Oh, interview by the author, Ann Arbor, August 19, 1999.

32. Luis Delgado, interview by the author, Dearborn, August 10, 1999.

33. Respondents who gave examples of regional vernacular and accent as markers of their spatialized identities used "midwestern" and "Michigan" interchangeably. Kathy Kim, interview by the author, Ann Arbor, July 12, 1999; and John Lee, interview by the author, Ann Arbor, August 24, 1999.

34. Vivek Mehta, telephone interview by the author, August 14, 1999.

35. Respondents in their twenties with non-Protestant or no religious affiliations tended to stress the religious homogeneity of Michiganders/Midwesterners.

36. Sarah Chu, interview by the author, Ann Arbor, June 25, 1999.

37. Kim Hoang, interview by the author, Ann Arbor, June 5, 1999.

38. Phillip Chan, interview by the author, Ann Arbor, July 29, 1998.

39. Maria Cruz, interview by the author, Dearborn, August 11, 1999.

40. Peter Tom, interview by the author, Detroit, July 21, 1999.

41. James M. Anderson and Iva A. Smith, *Ethnic Groups in Michigan,* Peoples of Michigan (Detroit: Ethnos, 1983), Michigan Historical Collections, Bentley Library; Sandra Bunnell, "The Dragon Dances: A Century of Chinese in Detroit with a Culture That Will Not Die," *Detroit Free Press Magazine,* January 6, 1974. By 1876, Detroit had fourteen Chinese laundries, collectively referred to as the "Mongolian colony" by the local newspapers. Stores providing Chinese goods and services were in business as early as 1918 catering to the early Chinese settlers, who worked as houseboys, servants, and cooks or operated laundries and restaurants in the area. This Chinatown, located in Detroit on Third Avenue between Michigan and Howard (where Peter Tom grew up), thrived from the 1940s until 1961, when the Detroit Housing Commission decided to raze the existing Chinatown and rebuild Chinatown as a part of International Village. The plans for International Village fell through, and the remaining few businesses and organizational buildings of Detroit's Chinatown were moved to the corner of Cass and Peterboro in 1962, the current home of the Association of Chinese Americans Drop-in/Outreach Center and Chung's, Michigan's oldest Chinese restaurant. The Detroit Chinatown is a symbolic reminder of the ethnic enclave that once was located in the city but now has scattered throughout the suburbs surrounding Detroit as well as across the national border to Windsor, Ontario.

42. Jew, "Making Home in the Heartland."

43. Jae Hong Park, interview by the author, Ann Arbor, June 29, 1999.

44. May Tsai, interview by the author, Detroit, August 9, 1999.

45. Jin Kyung Park, interview by the author, Ann Arbor, July 7, 1999.

46. For a discussion of white Americans and optional ethnic identities, see Mary Waters, *Ethnic Options: Choosing Identities in America* (Berkeley: University of California Press, 1990). For discussions of racialized ethnics and ethnic identities, see Pawan Dhingra, "Being American between Black and White: Second-Generation Asian American Professionals' Racial Identities," *Journal of Asian American Studies* 6, no. 2 (2003): 117–247; Nazli Kibria, *Becoming Asian American: Second Generation Chinese and Korean American Identities* (Baltimore: Johns Hopkins University Press, 2002); Mia Tuan, *Forever Foreigners or Honorary Whites? The Asian Ethnic Experience Today* (New Brunswick, NJ: Rutgers University Press, 1998).

47. Brian Cho, interview by the author, Ann Arbor, June 6, 1999.

48. Sarah Chu, interview by the author, Ann Arbor, June 25, 1999.

49. Lisa Riley, interview by the author, Ann Arbor, July 15, 1999.

50. Allen Chuang, telephone interview by the author, July 2, 1999.

51. Kim Hoang, interview by the author, Ann Arbor, June 5, 1999.

52. See Jennifer Lee and Min Zhou, *Asian American Youth: Culture, Identity, and Ethnicity* (New York: Routledge, 2004) for discussions of determinants of identity choices among Asian American youth.

53. Chi Lee, interview by the author, Ann Arbor, June 7, 1999.

54. Sandy Yu, interview by the author, Livonia, July 31, 1999.

55. See Dhingra, "Being American between Black and White"; Marina Espina, *Filipinos in Louisiana* (New Orleans: A. F. Laborde, 1998); Tuan, *Forever Foreigners*.

56. Dhingra, "Being American between Black and White," 126.

57. Eric Lai, "Socioeconomic Trends in the Midwest," in Lai and Arguelles, *The New Face of Asian Pacific America*. Asian Americans in Michigan had the highest percentage of income greater than $100,000 (29.7 percent), compared to Asians in the Midwest as a whole (23.3 percent), the general midwestern population (14.1 percent), and the national Asian population (23.1 percent). The overall poverty rate for Asians in the Midwest is 13 percent, compared to the general midwestern rate of 10.2 percent. Asian poverty rates are the highest in Wisconsin and Minnesota, especially among the Southeast Asian population. Of persons twenty-five years and over in 1999, 85.6 percent of Michigan Asian residents were high school graduates, 61 percent were college graduates, and 32.3 percent had obtained a graduate/professional school degree.

58. Jew, "Making Homes in the Heartland." Throughout the interviews, many respondents favorably compared Ann Arbor to other cities or towns they had lived in in Michigan, if not the whole region. Asian American Ann Arborites commented on the greater presence of other Asians/Asian Americans within the city limits even in comparison to immediately neighboring towns, and if they experienced acts of prejudice or discrimination, they attributed these to "out-of-towners." In September 2005, officials at the University of Michigan investigated a racially motivated incident in which two white male students allegedly assaulted two Asian American students walking near campus. One of the white students allegedly urinated on the Asian students from his balcony and then used racial slurs. A coalition of students, faculty, and staff demanded, among other things, that university administrators increase dialogue about hate crimes and assess the status of Asian American students, faculty, and staff on campus. Karl Stampfl, "Coleman Condemns Urinating Incident," *Michigan Daily*, September 23, 2005.

59. The model minority concept is controversial; its supporters view it as a positive recognition of Asian American achievement from the dominant society, while its critics argue that statistics, especially those on education levels, occupation categories, and household income levels, inaccurately paint a rosy picture that obfuscates the disproportionate percentages of Asian Americans who have little formal education, are in poverty, and hold low-wage occupations. Critics also argue that by emphasizing individual success and a group's "innate" cultural values, the model minority stereotype obscures the persistent prejudice and institutional racism that disenfranchise Asian Americans regardless of socioeconomic background. Other critical analyses contend that the popularity of the model minority concept (with its implication that racial minorities can overcome institutional discrimination through individual effort) coincided with the civil rights and the Black Power movements that sought to change institutions that systemically and structurally oppressed racial minorities. As a result, the portrayal of Asian Americans as the "good" minority—in contrast to bad or "undeserving" minorities—fuels competition among people of color and resentment toward Asian Americans. See Chan, *Asian Americans*; Kibria, *Becoming Asian American*.

60. For examples in the Chinese American community, see Ling, *Chinese St. Louis*; and Chuen-rong Yeh, "A Chinese American Community: The Politicization of Social Organization" (PhD diss., Michigan State University, 1989).

61. Hoang interview.
62. Joe Miyamoto, interview by the author, Ann Arbor, August 4, 1999.
63. Myung Woo Lim, interview by the author, Ann Arbor, July 6, 1999.
64. Tom interview.
65. Amit Jain, interview by the author, Ann Arbor, July 28, 1998.
66. Lee interview.
67. "Tae Young Han," interview by the author, Ann Arbor, July 27, 1998.
68. Pensri Ho, "Performing the 'Oriental': Professionals and the Asian Model Minority Myth," *Journal of Asian American Studies* 6, no. 2 (2003): 149-75.
69. Angelo Ancheta, *Race, Rights, and the Asian American Experience* (New Brunswick, NJ: Rutgers University Press, 1998). In the nineteenth century, Californians tried to assign Mexicans and Chinese to the three existing racial categories (white, Negro, and Indian). In *People v. Hall* (1854), the California Supreme Court ruled that Chinese were Indians and therefore barred from testifying against whites in court, in the same way "no black or mulatto person, or Indian, shall be permitted." *People v. Hall*, like most significant court rulings involving Asian Americans, clearly delineated between white and nonwhite persons and allocated political rights accordingly.
70. Michael Shin, interview by the author, Detroit, July 8, 1999.
71. Alejandro Portes and Ruben Rumbaut, *Immigrant America: A Portrait* (Berkeley: University of California Press, 1990). In 1987, Chicago was the only midwestern metropolitan statistical area (MSA) to appear on the list of the three principal destinations of the eight largest immigrant groups; it was the third most popular city for Koreans (38). In 1990, Michigan was home to the tenth-largest Filipino population (1.8 percent), tenth-largest Japanese population (1.3 percent), and ninth-largest Asian Indian population (2.9 percent) in the nation. See also Herbert Barringer, Robert Gardner, and Michael Levin, *Asians and Pacific Islanders in the United States* (New York: Russell Sage Foundation, 1993).
72. Sugrue, *The Origins of the Urban Crisis*, 13.
73. Joe T. Darden, "Asians in Metropolitan Areas of Michigan: A Retest of the Social and Spatial Distance Hypothesis," *Amerasia Journal* 12, no. 2 (1985): 67-77; Douglas Massey and Nancy Denton, *American Apartheid: Segregation and the Making of the Underclass* (Cambridge, MA: Harvard University Press, 1993); Mark Langberg and Reynolds Farley, "Residential Segregation of Asian Americans in 1980," *Sociology and Social Research* 70, no. 1 (1985): 71-75. Langberg and Farley found that Asian-white segregation scores were lower than Asian-black segregation scores in all thirty-eight MSAs in 1980, and Asian-white segregation scores were lower than Asian-Latino segregation scores in twenty-three of the thirty-eight.
74. Serena Choi, interview by the author, Ann Arbor, April 24, 1999.
75. Yumi Shin, interview by the author, Farmington Hills, August 13, 1999.
76. Janice Okada, interview by the author, Ann Arbor, August 17, 1999.
77. Mehta interview.
78. Tom Martinez, interview by the author, Ann Arbor, June 5, 1999.
79. Sonya Rose, *Which People's War? National Identity and Citizenship in Britain, 1939-1945* (New York: Oxford University Press, 2003). Rose discusses the dilemma of Jews who faced anti-Semitism during World War II in Britain. Although aware that Nazi Germany was exterminating Jews, British citizens opposed extending refuge and

citizenship to people whom they saw as inherently and forever alien and "un-British." In letters written to national newspapers, they also accused Jews of instigating anti-Semitism themselves with their actions and behaviors. As racial others, Jews in Britain had to "walk circumspectly" so as not to call attention to themselves, and yet this careful attempt to be inconspicuous signified the inability to become British.

80. Out of the forty respondents, twenty-seven cited the Chin murder as one of the most significant events involving Asian Americans. See Helen Zia, *Asian American Dreams: The Emergence of an American People* (New York: Farrar, Straus and Giroux, 2000).

81. Barbara W. Kim, "The Ties That Bind: Asian American Communities without 'Ethnic Places,'" *Ethnic Studies Review* 30 (2008): 75-92.

82. Kathleen Wong (Lau), "The Asian American Community in the Southwest: Creating 'Place' in the Absence of Ethnic 'Space,'" in Nakayama and Yoshioka, *Asian Pacific Americans and the U.S. Southwest*, 83.

83. See Rick Bonus, *Locating Filipino Americans: Ethnicity and the Cultural Politics of Space* (Philadelphia: Temple University Press, 2000); and Brian Graham, *In Search of Ireland: A Cultural Geography* (New York: Routledge, 1997).

84. Vijay Prashad, *The Karma of Brown Folk* (Minneapolis: University of Minnesota Press, 2001).

85. Jew, "Attempts at Mapping Changing Landscapes and Shifting Borders," 52.

5

GENEALOGY OF A DETROIT CHILDHOOD

Min Hyoung Song

In 1975 my family immigrated to Detroit from Seoul. I was five years old. After a period of struggle, as my parents sought shelter and took on a variety of working-class jobs, my father landed a slot as an assembly line worker at a General Motors plant. It was difficult, tedious work that could often be hazardous, especially if the equipment was not safely maintained or if the company pushed employees to work too fast and too long. It was also an amazing position, with a good hourly wage, dental and health insurance, and retirement benefits. It was the very kind of job that enabled numerous working families to propel themselves into the ranks of a generously defined middle class and to contribute to an all-too-brief moment in American history, now suffused with nostalgia, when the curve of economic well-being bulged into a conspicuous bell shape rather than the miserly, asymmetrical hourglass figure of today's income and wealth statistics. By the time my father was hired, this kind of industrial labor had already grown scarce as production turned toward automation, subcontractors, and sites in the Sunbelt and beyond the nation's borders. In the wake of severe job losses, the dark side of industrial capitalism—never invisible—became glaring, as evidenced by continued segregation, crumbling urban infrastructures, ghostly vacant buildings, burned-out lots, and polluted rivers. Worst of all were the eerie silences created by the missing people.

I can't do justice to what it felt like to grow up in the long shadow of one of the nation's worst urban crises. An absence is always hard to put into words. And certainly it's hard for some of us, accustomed as we are to tales of success and upward mobility and inevitable progress toward brighter futures, to pay proper heed to a narrative that has a different kind of trajectory. Something is missing and what is missing doesn't fit into the stories we like to tell ourselves. Jerry Herron explains, "Detroit used to stand for success, and now it stands for failure. . . . This is the place where bad times get sent to make them belong to someone else. . . . But the same things that make Detroit immediately, if disagreeably, representative also make it very hard to know because the 'truth' about the place comes in prearranged forms, often with little relevance to actual fact or feeling."[1] These words speak eloquently to the problem of writing about a place that so many have agreed to overlook, an unpleasant part of the scenery best turned away from as one whizzes by on the expressway. The concrete embankments and dividers help keep the view from us. The high speeds the expressway enables and the roar of the engine cocoon us in manufactured dreams of progress, technological prowess, and security, which the sight of what lies beyond the road would only spoil. Also, I want to be certain not to claim more knowledge than I have. If anything, researching this topic has been an exercise in humility, as the fact of my having grown up in Greater Detroit has turned out not to be a privileged vantage point from which I can speak about its recent past.

In this essay, then, I seek to contribute to the ongoing conversations that linger over what others have understandably wanted to pass over swiftly. I do so by drawing on my personal history because this enables me to cover a lot of ground very quickly, and to do so from a perspective produced by, and caught in, the global flows of surplus labor let loose at the same time the city of Detroit was plunging into economic crisis. This essay is not, however, about me. I do not dwell on the details of my life, nor do I provide a thick autoethnographic account of Asians in the Midwest. I am more interested in what lies beyond my self's limits to gaze at what shapes such limits. In short, my personal history is a starting place for a working outward, so as to place at the center of attention my personal history's conditions of possibility.

Perhaps this is only a typical immigrant habit that I've picked up and haven't learned to let go: to deflect attention away from myself because too much attention can be a dangerous thing. Or it might simply be a matter of personal taste, as I dislike the voyeurism that might motivate readers of a memoir. In either case, my reticence to make my life the main focus of this essay is also, and just as importantly, motivated by my wish to avoid what Rey Chow has called our contemporary tendency to "interiorize." By this she means a self-referential spiraling inward into our subjectivities or, conversely (and perhaps even a bit counterintuitively), the denial of ourselves as selves completely.[2] Against either total self-absorption or self-abnegation, I would like to keep at the forefront the traces of the self that mobilize my interest in Detroit while not allowing those traces to become the central focus.

Toward the goal of realizing such a balance, this essay examines how my family participated in the late twentieth-century flows of surplus labor that contributed to the racial and ethnic diversity of Detroit. These flows made the region a kind of underappreciated contact zone between different peoples. Then I consider how Detroit's urban crisis intersects the national transformation of urban to suburban dominance. By stressing my family's move to the suburbs during my midchildhood, I seek to provide a nuanced understanding of how such a transformation was, ironically, made possible by the system of industrial output, infrastructure, use, maintenance, and cultural significa-tion with which the city's name has become synonymous. Next, I consider how the specificity of the city's urban crisis and the growth of its suburbs connect Greater Detroit to other parts of the world. Together, these aspects of the discussion help me to clear space in the critical literature—which I find at once heroically focused on a history that few seem to want to think about and limited by a fixation on black-and-white racial confrontations and suburban-urban spatial divides—to explore how my own personal his-tory has been made possible by phenomena that seem so completely about something, and someone, else. I clear space not to make myself more visible but to understand better the density and dynamism of these phenomena of race, economic restructuring, and geographical transformations. This essay's contributions to an understanding of these phenomena is (I hope) twofold: on the one hand, to disrupt what is ready-made or, as Herron puts it, "pre-formed" and, on the other hand, to make connections between topics that ordinarily occupy separate domains of knowledge.

The story of how Detroit "used to stand for success and now . . . stands for failure" is well rehearsed. In the 1920s, Detroit was the fourth-largest city in the United States, after New York, Chicago, and Philadelphia. From the American South and from all over Europe, black and ethnic white workers arrived in large numbers, formed new social and cultural blocs, and fought over the $5-a-day jobs Henry Ford famously promised.[3] By 1943, Detroit boasted nearly 2 million residents and remained solidly in fourth place among American cities. The Second World War provided an unprecedented opportu-nity for the city to push its industrial capacities to new heights, as factories whose output had been slowed by the Depression began to turn out "military hardware, airplanes, tanks, and other vehicles, making Metropolitan Detroit one of the birthplaces of the military-industrial complex."[4] Work was plentiful, and workers became more diverse as migrants from abroad and from other regions of the country, such as Appalachia and the Deep South, continued to move into the city, hardened into complex and layered blocs, and struggled with increasingly inadequate housing.[5] Simultaneously, those who could afford to and who were of the right race and ethnicity followed a familiar pattern, established as early as the 1920s, of movement out of the city into already established suburbs or into new developments rapidly created by the fast-expanding demand. Employers also began to set up shop elsewhere, locating workplaces closer to where workers were living. This out-migration of residents *and* workplaces was the most visible indicator that by the 1950s the city of Detroit, like many industrial places, was headed for trouble. By the time Christine Choy and Renee Tajima began filming their 1988 Oscar-nominated documentary *Who Killed Vincent Chin?* which powerfully captures the climate of racial and economic claustrophobia gripping southeastern Michigan during the years in which I was a teenager there, the city was well on its way to seventh place among U.S. cities, with barely a million people within its municipal limits.[6] In 2010, the city of Detroit had dropped to eighteenth place, with around seven hundred thousand people.

Beyond the story of racial violence, activism, and judicial wrangling the film wishes to tell, however, what makes *Who Killed Vincent Chin?* memorable is the urban crisis it graphically evokes and the way this crisis ties the region of Greater Detroit to the Pacific.[7] As the work of scholars such as Laura Pulido, Cynthia Young, Bill Mullins, and many others has sought to recover, an interracial and international perspective was an essential part of the U.S. Third World Left that blossomed during the late 1960s and early 1970s in places like Los Angeles, New York, and Detroit.[8] Such a perspective is clearly expressed in the groundbreaking film *Finally Got the News*, produced in 1970 as a collaboration between New York Newsreel and members of the League of Revolutionary Black Workers to highlight efforts to organize black workers in Detroit into an independent union.[9] Near the beginning, a narrator appears in a living room decorated with posters of Malcolm X, Che Guevara, Angola, and Mao. The deliberate inclusion of these posters in the frame asks viewers to consider how the local conflicts addressed in the film are part of struggles signified by these readily accessible icons. The international theme is picked up again at the end, when a narrator states that black revolutionaries must seek to organize black workers wherever they might be found, from Detroit to Bolivia, South Africa, and beyond. The makers of the film obviously have a capacious definition of what it means to be "black."

In Dan Georgakas and Marvin Surkin's *Detroit: I Do Mind Dying*, the classic work about Detroit's postwar political radicalism (published the same year my family arrived in Detroit), the focus on black autoworkers is explicitly linked to the influx of nonwhite immigrants as cheap labor. Their analysis needs to be quoted at length to capture the breadth of their perspective:

> The new Arab immigrant workers of the late 1960s felt that the UAW [the union the United Automobile Workers], like most American institutions, was hostile to them. . . . They were like the Puerto Ricans, Chicanos, Filipinos, and West Indians employed in other American industries and localities. They were also a part of a larger world pattern. Beginning in the 1950s, European capital had made massive use of cheap immigrant labor. Black Africans, Turks, Greeks, Arabs, Yugoslavs, Italians, and Spaniards had found work in northern Europe, France, Switzerland, and northern Italy. They frequently were forced to live in separate compounds and were paid wages inferior to those of domestic labor. . . . Similarly, in the early 1970s, American capital began to import cheap labor for specific industries. In the East, along with Puerto Ricans, who had been immigrating for years, there were large influxes of South Americans and various Caribbean peoples, particularly Haitians, Jamaicans, and Dominicans, each with their own culture and language. On the West Coast, the cheap labor was primarily of Mexican and Asian ancestry.[10]

These two examples suggest that contemporary critical discussions centered on the migration of peoples and capital pick up the threads of a conversation that was already long established in places like Detroit, as assembly line workers, union organizers, and intellectuals with deep roots in the labor community sought to understand how their struggles could be local and global at the same time. It is instructive to place the international outlook found in an especially striking segment of *Who Killed Vincent Chin?* within this tradition of thought. Interrupting a television news clip of local residents lining up at a suburban dealership to take turns bashing a Japanese import with a sledgehammer, a drawing reminiscent of Second World War propaganda appears on the screen. It depicts a flying car with slant eyes, buckteeth, flat nose, and oversized ears that double as wings. In the background, there is the symbol of the Rising Sun. The car is dropping a bomb on a city labeled "Detroit."

By suggesting that this segment's critique of race thinking fits neatly alongside an intellectual tradition firmly rooted in earlier social struggles, I hope to highlight what a racially and ethnically complex place Detroit was during the period of these earlier conflicts and how these continue to haunt our understanding of the city. For African Americans and their many nonblack allies, the 1960s and early 1970s were both a time of tense conflict, to which events like the Twelfth Street riot and the Algiers Motel incident readily attest,[11] and a time of hope that change was finally coming to their city: that police violence could be curtailed, that informal housing segregation would come to an end, that jobs would be shared more equally, that their kids could go to school without running a gamut of hate, and that they would with the election of the city's first black mayor finally have a fair say about how things were run.

Grace Lee Boggs's powerful memoir *Living for Change* recalls the Chinese American author's intellectual introduction to radical politics through American philosophical pragmatism. Holder of a doctorate in philosophy from Bryn Mawr, Boggs became involved with ever-splintering Marxist groups, worked with C. L. R. James, Raya Dunayevskaya, and Kwame Nkrumah, and participated in grassroots organizations like the Freedom Now Party. She had a lifelong partnership with respected African American activist and author James Boggs. Her experiences embodied complex heterogeneities irreducible to a simple black-and-white perspective and captured some of the fever of this era, when Detroit beckoned with industrial activity, bustling crowds, and radical labor activity threatening the bloated UAW from the Far Left.[12]

By the end of her book, however, the hopefulness of the author feels more depressing than either the defensiveness of Mayor Coleman Young's autobiography *Hard Stuff*, or the bleakness of Ze'ev Chafets's *Devil's Night*, a hard-boiled account of Detroit in the 1980s.[13] The optimism that suffuses Boggs's *Living for Change* seems out of sync with the crisis of depopulation and job loss that gripped the city as the 1970s gave way to the Reagan years. In 1980, unemployment hovered at around 15 percent, with about a quarter of all minorities and well over half of all black teenagers out of work. When a local cable company announced six job openings, a thousand applicants lined up outside its door.[14]

Shortly after my father landed his slot at GM against such odds, my family moved out of Detroit to the enclave of Hamtramck, which is surrounded by Detroit but independent from it. This meant that my vantage point as a child was not the best, obscuring my ability to bear direct witness to the changes Detroit proper underwent during the late 1970s and 1980s. I wasn't personally there, for instance, to see firsthand the ways in which the city resisted and failed to resist the numerous Halloween eves when arsonists, whether hired by building owners or caught up in a moment of carnival, burned down many of its buildings. I was in Hamtramck, however, when a building erupted into flames near our two-family house. A crowd formed on the street, circling around the firefighters as they worked. It was broad daylight, sunny and warm, nowhere near Devil's Night. My father was home on a rare day off. We stood together, his presence reassuring and large. I was very young. I never learned what caused the fire. But I did learn that fires are eerily fascinating and will draw people of various backgrounds together, often with a solemn yet friendly mood, an inexplicable sublimity that only destruction and catastrophe can enable. I also noted the air of normality that pervaded the crowd. We looked not with awe or fear but resignation.

Hamtramck also suffered during the years of economic restructuring and population loss, but it suffered less than its neighbor, and for this reason my family must count itself lucky to have moved there. Even as its traditional Polish base of citizens began to leave in greater numbers and jobs became scarcer, Hamtramck was fortunate because it somehow kept a greater percentage of its former residents than the surrounding city and also because it succeeded in drawing new immigrants. Not only Poles but Yugoslavians, Czechs, Albanians, Jews, Koreans, Chinese, Thai, Arabs, Ukrainians, Bangladeshis, and so forth kept moving into its neighborhoods, running its shops, and maintaining the semblance of a pedestrian-friendly downtown. Of course, there were also many African Americans who wanted to stay close to Detroit living there and many new immigrants who eventually moved, even as they continued to work in Hamtramck, as my family did. According to the 2010 U.S. Census, Hamtramck, with a median household income well below the national average, remained a strikingly diverse place: 53.6 percent white, 19.3 percent African American, and 21.5 percent Asian. In addition, 43.1 percent of its population was foreign born in 2010.[15]

It's not yet clear to me how, if at all, this dynamic mix of peoples affected the formation of the Dodge Revolutionary Union Movement, the first and most active of its kind, which organized a Chrysler plant within Hamtramck and led to the eventual formation of the League of Revolutionary Black Workers. Nor is it clear how much the influx of immigrant labor or the movement of factory work elsewhere might have contributed to the movement's dissipation by the mid-1970s. Did new arrivals contribute to the powerful mass democratic movements sweeping through Detroit in the 1960s and early 1970s, or were we a kind of advance reactionary guard robbing it of its momentum?

Shortly before my father was laid off, my parents opened the first of what would turn out to be a series of small businesses, each more or less a step up the hierarchy of establishments that reigned on Hamtramck's Jos. Campau Street: a wig shop, a women's clothing store, a dime store (perhaps more of a lateral move), and finally a men's clothing store. Even though Hamtramck is as close to a hometown as I have, it's important for me to resist any urge to romanticize the life of an ethnic entrepreneur, which was, and remains, hard. There was constant friction and fighting, and I still resent all the many dull hours I spent helping out. I vividly recall how rude and distrustful my parents were as storekeepers. I recall how the worst racist comments I have ever heard came from African American customers, although whites were hardly models of rhetorical circumspection. And how relationships among blacks, Asians, Arabs, and whites, while not as bad as it might seem from afar, could never be characterized as a colorful mosaic anyone would want to celebrate. More than literature, as I had expected when I began writing this essay (biased as I am by my training as a literary critic), it is sociology that has done the most to capture the dynamics of such social interactions.[16]

Nonetheless, sociology has not been fully up to the task. The worst memory I have of my childhood took place in Hamtramck, the intensity of which no work of sociology, much less fiction or memoir, has ever been able to approach. One cold Saturday morning, my parents, my sister, and I arrived at the store my family had just opened. My mother worked at the store on weekday mornings until my father finished his early-morning shift and joined her in the midafternoon. We all worked together on Saturdays unless I could come up with some credible excuse for avoiding it. We arrived that morning to find that someone had punched a hole through the window to steal some cheap costume jewelry. The thief must have cut his or her arm on the jagged glass, for there was a thick, wide trail of blood leading from the window all the way down the sidewalk. I have never seen so much blood before or since. After that morning, my parents always made sure to remove anything expensive from the display and to cover up the rest with cardboard so passersby wouldn't be tempted. Soon thereafter, we moved to the suburbs.

Go in any direction away from Hamtramck's tiny business district and the landscape gives way to roaring highways, dilapidated houses, and empty lots that attract garbage, weeds, and much, much worse. Urban renewal, fire, city demolition to prevent vacant houses from being used for illegal purposes— all have left their mark on Detroit. They have destroyed the irreplaceable,

removing infrastructure that might have drawn the adventurous and nostal-
gic who have gentrified so many other U.S. cities and, saddest of all, they
have paved over historic regions of the city where so much of its fate had
been fought over and determined. I'm thinking most explicitly of places like
Paradise Valley and Black Bottom. Hastings Street, the most famous late-
night gathering place for African Americans in the city, is now under the I-75
Expressway that connects downtown to the northern suburbs. These are the
places where many African Americans were restricted to reside alongside
immigrants of numerous nationalities, where Motown Records originated,
where the Nation of Islam got its start, and where Malcolm X was nicknamed
"Detroit Red."[17] I'm also thinking about the Chinatown that was razed to build
the Lodge Freeway, which connects traffic between downtown and the northwest suburbs.[18] It is true that much of what was destroyed was poorly built,
dangerous to inhabit, and would have been demolished even without urban
renewal. But there's a difference between destroying individual buildings,
working within the fabric of a city block, and razing whole neighborhoods for
highways, phantom high-rises, and industrial parks.[19]

The most grievous case of lost infrastructure occurred near Hamtramck.
The victim was a traditionally Polish neighborhood of two-story frame
houses, shops, civic centers, and a beautiful Catholic church. It was also one
of the most integrated areas in the city. Although known as Poletown, half
its population was black and many others were of Slavic and Arab descent.
Over the years, urban renewal slashed through its fabric. The I-94 freeway cut
out one swath and I-75 another, but still the area had hopes of knitting itself
back into something more coherent and vibrant, with many actively seeking to rehabilitate rundown-looking streets. Unfortunately, just as such plans
were being formed, Chrysler announced it was closing Dodge Main, where
the Dodge Revolutionary Union Movement originated. At the same time,
General Motors announced plans to close two other plants in the city and to
replace them with a new plant on the old Dodge Main site. To do so, however,
GM insisted that Hamtramck and Detroit had to level 465 acres and displace
about sixteen hundred residents so that it could build a much larger, more
modern factory based on designs for one built in the much less populated
plains of Oklahoma.

Detroit mayor Coleman Young's administration closed ranks with state and
federal authorities, the local news media, the courts, and the Catholic hierarchy
to take advantage of new legislation to speed up the workings of the state's
eminent domain law. Within eight months, they planned to relocate residents,

bulldoze buildings, fill holes, and prepare the site for GM to build a new Cadillac plant, all to preserve thirty-five hundred jobs against the net loss of thousands more when GM's two other facilities closed. By moving quickly, project proponents hoped to establish a sense of inevitability, thereby making the vigorous local campaign against the seizures and demolitions appear quixotic. This campaign, eventually aided by a team of lawyers affiliated with Ralph Nader, fought a hard and public battle against the city and GM, culminating in the occupation of the Immaculate Conception Church. Resistors, largely elderly Polish residents and young activists as well as Nanu Ashar and his family, Indian immigrants from the suburb of Troy, held their ground for several days. On July 14, 1981, police, including a SWAT team, swooped into the church in the middle of the night to arrest them. Ashar and his family, including two young children, were treated worst. "Ashar's wife's sari was torn and her glasses trampled. Police handcuffed her abruptly, shouting, 'Goddamned woman' and threatening that her children would be taken away from her."[20] *Detroit Free Press* staff photographers David C. Turnley and Taro Yamasaki captured much of what happened that night in their vivid, almost eerily beautiful photographs.

Amazingly, in addition to the millions the city would eventually have to pay through a combination of federal block grants and loans to undertake this project, one that cost far more than it would have to rehabilitate the neighborhood, Young and the Detroit City Council approved $200 million in tax abatements after GM threatened to build the plant elsewhere. In exchange for this generosity, GM delayed construction for more than a year before finally building the most modern factory it could. Suggestions by local activists and homeowners that the plant could coexist with the neighborhood had been brushed aside as impractical. After its construction, the plant proved unnecessarily large, the automation largely inefficient, and much of the land where people had once lived went underutilized as a parking lot.[21] Predictably, the plant contributed to a glut in automobile production capacity and did very little to stem a tide of economic hardship, even as GM topped the Fortune 500 list for the second year in a row in 1987. It did so by closing more plants, laying off workers, forcing concessions, moving work to Mexico, and pursuing joint ventures in places like Korea.[22]

I was too young to understand fully what my parents and our customers were talking about while all of this was going on. Only later, as I began doing research for this essay, did it dawn on me that they were talking about the survival of a city that others had already declared dead. Such a declaration is, of course, largely hyperbole. Not only does such a pronouncement consign hundreds of thousands of residents to social death, what James Kyung-Jin Lee defines as "the metaphorical placeholder for a terrain of political absence,"[23] it also obscures the ways in which Detroit is the heart of the four-county Metropolitan Detroit. The city itself is sprawling, occupying 143 square miles. Roads radiate out of downtown from the banks of the river from which the city gets its name, puncturing remnants of a street plan borrowed heavily from Charles L'Enfant's design of the U.S. capital.[24] In his Pulitzer Prize–winning novel *Middlesex,* Jeffrey Eugenides observes the traces of this design, a vision of what the city might have become if it hadn't been "dedicated to money":

> And there it is: half a hubcap of city plaza, with the spokes of Bagley, Washington, Woodward, Broadway, and Madison radiating from it. That's all that remains of the famous Woodward plan. . . . Judge Woodward envisioned the new Detroit as an urban Arcadia of interlocking hexagons. Each wheel was to be separated yet united, in accordance with the young nation's federalism, as well as classically symmetrical, in accordance with Jeffersonian aesthetics. This dream never quite came to be.[25]

Beyond the city limits, the grid becomes more pronounced. Land is demarcated into square miles, and major roads to the north are labeled by the number of miles they are located away from the original city center. Eight Mile Road, the dividing line between city and suburbs, is the most famous. The title of the film *8 Mile,* loosely modeled after rapper Eminem's life, draws upon its local cultural significance, as did Coleman Young during his 1974 mayoral inauguration when he famously declared, "I issue a warning to all those pushers, to all rip-off artists, to all muggers: It's time to leave Detroit; hit Eight Mile Road!"[26]

The development where my parents resided before their retirement, their last house in Michigan before they moved south, is a typical—if grander— example of all the places we lived in the suburbs. Large houses stand alone in the middle of a plot of land, surrounded by grass that requires constant watering, mowing, and spraying against weeds. Because no one wants other commuters cutting through his or her street, entry is restricted to two points. My parents thus had to drive along numerous curvilinear streets, each almost as wide as a four-lane highway, before they reached the collector road. Once there, they had to fight heavy traffic, often backed up for miles during the busiest times of the day and all through the weekends.

All this meant that no matter what my parents were doing or wanted to do, it required a car. Indeed, since the mailboxes in my parents' subdivision were all clustered together in one place, mail service itself became almost exclusively drive-through. It is easy to imagine how the open spaces, modern conveniences, and new construction offered by the suburbs must have felt like a welcome change.[27] Certainly for my parents, who were children during the Korean War, who were teenagers during the worst years of poverty that afflicted the newly divided peninsula, who lived as young adults under the forced austerity of Park Chung Hee's autocratic drive toward export-oriented modernization, and who endured one small apartment after another upon arriving in the United States, the manicured lawns of the ready-made suburbs brimmed with promise.

On the other hand, during long periods of the day, especially in the winter when the grass is hidden under many inches of snow, the silence in the suburbs is absolute, uncannily similar to the silence of the streets in Detroit. Paul Clemens, in his memoir about growing up white in a city that had become majority black, observes, "White Detroiters of a generation or two before mine acted as if the city from which they came had become, against their will, a universe lost, and thus the yardstick against which everything else—sterile suburbs, slum cities—would forever be slightingly judged."[28] Such nostalgia for an unremarkable white supremacy helps to explain a lot of the angry affect shaping political debate in this part of the country. Especially among those who live in the more working-class suburbs near the city limits, which also happen to be the most predominantly white, there is a pervasive sense of dispossession, of loss-of a present that never lives up to memories of the past, undoubtedly sugarcoated by time. For many of a certain generation and their children, suburbia is a place they felt forced to endure, refugees squatting in temporary quarters hastily put up on the outskirts of a hometown they have helped feed, whether inadvertently or not, to the fire.

What are the costs of this diaspora? The city of Detroit became more dangerous after half its population left and its tax base collapsed. The problems the city suffered were easy for those who left to ignore because they could always blame those problems on black mismanagement and crime.[29] The suburbs grew, but in a frenzied pattern, so that these developments seemed to age quickly— although many have also aged nicely. Historic districts and cityscapes were leveled to make way for the roads people used for their exit, and now roads and houses are being built over delicate wetlands and farmland. Good jobs continue to vanish as economic restructuring moves production overseas in search of ever-cheaper labor and further automates what's left, and it seems it won't be long now before even the white-collar jobs follow the factory jobs. Indeed, the whole region of southeastern Michigan is losing population, as unemployment soars and economic opportunities in the Sunbelt and further west promise a new beginning. Old Michigan friends visiting my parents in suburban Atlanta, with its rapidly expanding enclave of ethnic Koreans, were enchanted by what they found and dreamed of moving there—if only the real estate market hadn't grown flat and made it nearly impossible to sell their houses (this is before Greater Atlanta experienced its own real estate hardships).

Another severe cost of this diaspora may be the ways in which life in both the suburbs and the city, which long ago had to give up its trolley system (the last rails were ripped up in 1956), depends so much on cars for transportation. Yes, those who made their way back into the city may find that their homes are bigger than the ones their parents or grandparents left, but they still must drive to go to work, to shop, to reach entertainment. As any stranded child or chauffeur-parent can explain, being without a car means that one can't go anywhere or do anything—one can't even attain the basic necessities.

A final, and still untotaled, cost of suburbanization may thus be the ways in which this pervasive phenomenon contributes to environmental problems that are now reaching global proportions. No matter how clean our cars get or how efficiently they sip gasoline (and cars are not nearly as clean or efficient as they could easily be), the damage to our environment caused by our dependency on them, among a host of other ingrained habits of behavior enabled by automobile travel, has already been done as all that burned hydrocarbon cooks our atmosphere. And we keep adding more.

All of these costs revolve around what sociologist John Urry calls *automobility*, a term that evokes both "the humanist self as in the notion of autobiography" and "objects and machines that possess a capacity for movement, as in automatic and automation." Building on this double meaning, the term "demonstrates how the 'car-driver' is a hybrid assemblage of specific human activities, machines, roads, buildings, signs and cultures of mobility. . . . What is key is not the 'car' as such but the system of these fluid interconnections."[30] In short, an individual car lacks meaning or function without its being embedded in a complex network of production, maintenance, support, perception, and so forth, all of which make owning and operating a car possible, desirable, and even essential for survival. Obviously, Greater Detroit, because of its dominance by the U.S. automobile industry, continues to play a significant role in shaping and sustaining such a system of automobility.

John Dingell, my congressman when I was an undergraduate at the University of Michigan, is a good example of how the region contributes to this

system. He served Michigan's Fifteenth U.S. District for sixty years, making him the longest-serving congressman in U.S. history—an even more
extraordinary circumstance considering that his father had served as a representative for the same district from 1933 until his death in 1955.[31] Over the
years, Dingell has been a powerful, consistent voice in favor of policies that
benefit U.S. automakers. He led calls for reform of the Chinese yuan and the
Japanese yen as a way to curb automobile-import competition, once asking
President George W. Bush to file a complaint with the World Trade Organization over the way China's monetary policy pegs the yuan to the dollar.[32]
Reacting to the news that Toyota was poised to succeed GM as the world's
largest automobile manufacturer, Dingell insisted this was caused by U.S.
automakers having to pay the full cost of employee health care and by the
strength of the yen. When pressed further, he said, "If Toyota's worldwide
production surpasses General Motors, it will simply provide further evidence of the need for the U.S. government to pursue policies that maintain
and strengthen the U.S. industrial base."[33] Although Dingell is notable for
his many other accomplishments in Congress over a long career, it is hard
to imagine that he would have been able to hold onto his seat if he were less
supportive of the U.S. automobile industry. This unwavering support has
underwritten Dingell's involvement in shaping national energy policy. It
has also made him a staunch apologist for the automobile industry, a fierce
critic of its many rivals in Japan and the rest of the Pacific, and selective
about the kinds of environmental legislation he will support.[34]

In many ways, however, despite Dingell's apparent power, his strenuous
efforts on behalf of the U.S. automobile industry suggest how weak Greater
Detroit's hold on the very system of automobility it made possible has
become. By the late 1970s, the industry already found itself flagging in competition with rivals in the Pacific. This led to a terrible climate of racial anxiety, which in turn fostered the infamous 1982 beating death of Vincent Chin.
Ronald Ebens, a foreman at a Chrysler plant, was overheard saying to Chin
at a local strip club, "It's because of you little motherfuckers that we're out of
work." Later, Ebens and his stepson, who was laid off at the time, caught up
with Chin in a McDonald's parking lot. The son-in-law held Chin from behind
while swung at his head with a Louisville Slugger, a Jackie Robinson special,
no less. Chin later died from his injuries. For this murder, Ebens and his stepson both received three years' probation.[35]

I vividly recall from my childhood the controversy surrounding Chin's
murder, as the local news focused on it for a long time and my parents often

engaged in heated discussion about what it meant for them. My uncle, who would eventually become president of the Korea Society of Greater Detroit, convinced many (but not my parents) to engage in public protest against the verdict. To my knowledge, my uncle's role in the protest was as overtly political as anyone in my extended family ever became. This lack of public political assertion was not a matter of indifference or passivity as much as it was a barometer of how disenfranchised we felt. It was simply safer to keep our mouths shut and our thoughts to ourselves, especially since no one cared what we had to say and we didn't know what craziness we might encounter if we started to say what was on our minds.

This didn't mean, of course, that we had no thoughts. My parents talked a lot about politics on the other side of the Pacific and on occasion even wondered how these might be linked to the many tumultuous changes happening around us. It was hard not to speculate about the connections. One memory stands out in particular among the many occasions when my parents said something, or made a telling motion, indicating how keenly observant they were. In 1992, we bought a Honda Accord. It was our first Japanese car, something my father purchased reluctantly because he had grown up worshipping big American-made cars. Shortly after we brought the car home, my father and I stood over its open hood to inspect its immaculate new engine. He pointed out how much more sophisticated engines had become since he'd built them in a factory in Detroit, so much so that he couldn't tell anymore what function each part was meant to perform. He also called attention to how the different parts were clearly labeled as having been manufactured all over the world: Germany, Canada, Mexico, Japan (and maybe even Korea; I don't recall which specific countries were represented), only to be shipped to a factory in Tennessee where the parts were put together. What was it exactly, he asked, that made this car Japanese? He shook his head in wonder, words eluding him.

Notes

1. Jerry Herron, *Afterculture: Detroit and the Humiliation of History* (Detroit: Wayne State University Press, 1993), 9.
2. Rey Chow, *The Age of the World Target: Self-Referentiality in War, Theory, and Comparative Work* (Durham: Duke University Press, 2006), 22.
3. Kevin Boyle, *Arc of Justice: A Saga of Race, Civil Rights, and Murder in the Jazz Age* (New York: Henry Holt, 2004), 156-58. Figures regarding population and city ranking from the U.S. census.
4. Thomas J. Sugrue, *The Origins of the Urban Crisis: Race and Inequality in Postwar Detroit* (Princeton: Princeton University Press, 1996), 19.

5. Heather Ann Thompson, *Whose Detroit? Politics, Labor, and Race in a Modern American City* (Ithaca: Cornell University Press, 2001), 9-27.
6. Christine Choy and Renee Tajima, *Who Killed Vincent Chin?* (New York: Filmakers Library, 1988).
7. It's also worth noting how far back the ties between Detroit and the Pacific go. For instance, see Thomas Campanella, "The Civilizing Road: American Influence on the Development of Highways and Motoring in China, 1900-1949," *Journal of Transport History* 26, no. 1 (2005).
8. Many radical political activists in the United States during the late 1960s and 1970s were influenced by the rise of the Third World Movement, which made decolonization a central goal of political organizing in countries that aligned neither with the West nor the Soviets during the cold war. These activists saw in this movement a model for political organizing in the United States that took the struggles of racial minorities seriously, saw their experiences as structurally interconnected, and encouraged an international perspective. See Bill Mullen, *Afro-Orientalism* (Minneapolis: University of Minnesota Press, 2004); Laura Pulido, *Black, Brown, Yellow and Left: Radical Activism in Los Angeles* (Berkeley: University of California Press, 2006); Cynthia Young, *Soul Power: Culture, Radicalism, and the Making of a U.S. Third World Left* (Durham: Duke University Press, 2006).
9. Stewart Bird, Rene Lichtman, and Peter Gessner, *Finally Got the News* (Brooklyn: First Run/Icarus Films, 1970).
10. Dan Georgakas and Marvin Surkin, *Detroit: I Do Mind Dying; A Study in Urban Revolution* (New York: St. Martin's, 1975), 80. In this context, it is important to note that Greater Detroit contains "the largest, most highly concentrated population of Arabs in North America," and perhaps even, as I have heard friends and neighbors say, in the world outside the Middle East. Andrew Shryock and Nabeel Abraham, "On Margins and Mainstreams," in *Arab Detroit: From Margin to Mainstream*, ed. Nabeel Abraham and Andrew Shryock (Detroit: Wayne State University Press, 2000), 18.
11. On July 23, 1967, the Detroit police tried to shut down an illegal after-hour bar (known locally as a "blind pig") located on Twelfth Street, where much of the city's African American nightlife migrated after the destruction of Hastings Street. In the melee that followed, hundreds gathered on the street and violence soon erupted across the city. Similar in character to the 1965 riot that swept through Los Angeles, the "Great Rebellion," as it became widely known, resulted in thousands of arrests, hundreds of deaths, and millions of dollars in property damage. Federal troops were eventually brought in to stop the violence. Three days after the police action that initiated the riot, the Detroit police entered the Algiers Motel, which had a reputation for criminality but was also a convenient place for those who worked in the nearby Twelfth Street neighborhood, and killed three black men, also abusing other guests. Although the officers involved in the shooting were eventually acquitted, a separate "people's tribunal" was set up in one of Detroit's most prominent black churches and the officers involved were symbolically found guilty of murder. Suzanne Smith, *Dancing in the Streets: Motown and the Cultural Politics of Detroit* (Cambridge, MA: Harvard University Press, 1999) 181-208.
12. Grace Lee Boggs, *Living for Change: An Autobiography* (Minneapolis: University of Minnesota Press, 1998); James Boggs, "Black Power—A Scientific Concept Whose

Time Has Come," in *Black Fire: An Anthology of Afro-American Writing*, ed. LeRoi Jones and Larry Neal (New York: William Morrow, 1968); James Boggs, *The American Revolution: Pages from a Negro Worker's Notebook* (New York: Monthly Review, 1963).

13. Ze'ev Chafets, *Devil's Night and Other True Tales of Detroit* (New York: Random House, 1990); Coleman Young and Lonnie Wheeler, *Hard Stuff: The Autobiography of Coleman Young* (New York: Viking, 1994).

14. Jeanie Wylie, *Poletown: Community Betrayed* (Urbana: University of Illinois Press, 1989), 29, 30.

15. www.factfinder.census.gov.

16. See in particular Edward Chang and Jeannette Diaz-Veizades, *Ethnic Peace in the American City: Building Community in Los Angeles and Beyond* (New York: New York University Press, 1999); Won Moo Hurh, *The Korean Americans* (Westport, CT: Greenwood, 1998); Claire Jean Kim, *Bitter Fruit: The Politics of Black-Korean Conflict in New York City* (New Haven: Yale University Press, 2000); Kwang Chung Kim, ed., *Koreans in the Hood: Conflict with African Americans* (Baltimore: Johns Hopkins University Press, 1999); Jennifer Lee, *Civility in the City: Blacks, Jews, and Koreans in Urban America* (Cambridge, MA: Harvard University Press, 2002); Pyong Gap Min, *Caught in the Middle: Korean Merchants in America's Multi-ethnic Cities* (Berkeley: University of California Press, 1996).

17. For an in-depth discussion about cultural life in black Detroit after the Second World War, see Smith, *Dancing in the Streets*. Also, for an informative historiographical essay on the same topic, see Suzanne Smith, "'Boogie Chillen': Uncovering Detroit's African-American Cultural History," *Michigan Historical Review* 27, no. 1 (2001), 93–107.

18. Sugrue, *The Origins of the Urban Crisis,* 168-74; Arthur Woodford, *This Is Detroit, 1701-2001* (Detroit: Wayne State University Press, 2001) 168-74.

19. One of the most well-known discussions about the destructiveness of urban renewal that favors automobile travel over neighborhoods is Marshall Berman, *All That Is Solid Melts into Air: The Experience of Modernity* (New York: Simon and Schuster, 1982). For a more recent discussion about the South Bronx, see Jeff Chang, *Can't Stop, Won't Stop: A History of the Hip-Hop Generation* (New York: St. Martin's, 2005), 41-65.

20. Wylie, *Poletown,* 189.

21. Ibid., 213. In addition to Wylie's book, see the documentary George Corsetti and Jeanie Wylie, *Poletown Lives!* (Detroit: Information Factory, 1982). Also see David Fasenfest, "Community Politics and Urban Redevelopment: Poletown, Detroit, and General Motors," *Urban Affairs Quarterly* 22, no. 1 (1986): 101–23.

22. Wylie, *Poletown,* 214-15.

23. James Kyung-Jin Lee, *Urban Triage: Race and the Fictions of Multiculturalism* (Minneapolis: University of Minnesota Press, 2004) 2.

24. Woodford, *This Is Detroit,* 39.

25. Jeffrey Eugenides, *Middlesex* (New York: Picador-Farrar, Straus, and Giroux, 2002), 80.

26. Quoted in Bill McGraw, *The Quotations of Mayor Coleman A. Young* (Detroit: Wayne State University Press, 2005.

27. Sugrue, *The Origins of the Urban Crisis.* Also see Jane Jacobs, *Dark Age Ahead* (New York: Vintage-Random House, 2004), 139.

28. Paul Clemens, *Made in Detroit: A South of 8-Mile Memoir* (New York: Doubleday, 2005), 78.

29. Such problems also help to obscure the difficult times rural small towns have been enduring. For discussion of the connected plight of inner cities and rural small towns, see Ruth Wilson Gilmore, *Golden Gulag: Prisons, Surplus, Crisis, and Opposition in Globalizing California* (Berkeley: University of California Press, 2007).

30. John Urry, "The 'System' of Automobility," *Theory, Culture and Society* 21, nos. 4–5 (2004): 26.

31. Dingell Sr. is remembered most by historians for a letter he wrote to President Roosevelt in the days before Pearl Harbor, in which he suggested that "if it is the intention of Japan to enter into a reprisal contest . . . [then] we remind Nippon that unless assurances are received that Japan will facilitate and permit the voluntary departure of this group . . . the Government of the United States will cause the forceful detention or imprisonment in a concentration camp of ten thousand alien Japanese in Hawaii; the ratio of Japanese hostages held by America being one hundred for every American detained by the Mikado's Government." George McJimsey, ed., *Documentary History of the Franklin D. Roosevelt Presidency,* vol. 9, *US-Japan Relations, January–December 1941* (Bethesda, MD: University Publications of America, 2000), 350. The letter goes on to note that there are another 150,000 Japanese in the United States who can be held in "reprisal reserve" should Japan up the ante once again. What's shocking, of course, is the ease with which the Michigan congressman is willing to barter Japanese Hawaiian lives as if they are expendable and cheap, a hundred of them equal to "every American."

32. Mark Drajem, "U.S. Seeks Growth in China," *New Zealand Herald,* 2005, www.nzherald.co.nz/business/news/article.cfm?c_id=3&objectid=10335331.

33. Micheline Maynard and Martin Fackler, "Toyota Is Poised to Supplant G.M. as World's Largest Carmaker," *New York Times*, December 23, 2006.

34. Most recently, when newly elected Speaker of the House Nancy Pelosi announced the formation of a committee to study and bring to public attention the threats of global warming, Dingell was reported to have been furious to have his power encroached upon in this way. He said, "We're just empowering a bunch of enthusiastic amateurs to go around and make speeches and make commitments that will be very difficult to honor." "Pelosi Seeks New Panel on Global Warming," *Houston Chronicle*, January 21, 2007, www.chron.com/default/article/Pelosi-seeks-new-panel-on-global-warming-1556240.php. He later announced that his own committee would discuss the issue. He was also the congressman who introduced legislation into the House that became the 1990 Clean Air Act Amendment. Its environmental impact is mixed, helping to prop up the enthusiasm for ethanol as an alternative fuel. See Jonathon Adler, "Clean Fuels, Dirt Air: How a (Bad) Bill Became Law," *Public Interest* 108 (1992), 116–31.

35. For more about the Chin case, see Helen Zia, *Asian American Dreams: The Emergence of an American People* (New York: Farrar, Straus, and Giroux, 2000). Zia, a reporter in Detroit when this incident occurred, went on to become an important figure in the political debates that followed. Incidentally, the bat Ebens used to kill Chin was a Jackie Robinson special. This is a small irony in that Robinson, who grew up in Pasadena, was close friends with a multiracial group of "other blacks, Japanese, and Mexican members of the Pepper Street gang." Daniel Widener, "'Perhaps the Japanese Are to Be Thanked?' Asia, Asian America, and the Construction of Black California," *positions: east asia cultures critique* 11, no. 1 (2003): 150.

PART II

Legacy Keeping and Memory Keepers

Victor Jew

A resident of Michigan since the 1940s, Toshiko Shimoura has a lot to remember. The story of her life is a transcript of how large-scale events shaped lives, both her own and those of many Asian Americans during the Second World War and after. Shimoura was not born in Michigan. She grew up near the San Francisco Bay area of northern California and, had events transpired differently in the winter of 1942, she may have stayed there for the rest of her life. Before February 1942, she had never thought of moving to the Midwest or spending the rest of her life in Detroit. But in the wake of the U.S. entry into the Second World War after the Imperial Japanese Navy attacked Pearl Harbor on December 7, 1941, she and more than one hundred thousand other Americans of Japanese descent found themselves forcibly moved from their homes on the West Coast. Starting in February 1942 and continuing through the spring and summer of that year, those one hundred thousand West Coast Japanese Americans moved and moved again as decisions mandating their removal were made through executive orders from the White House enabling legislation by Congress and military decisions from the U.S. Army's Western Defense Command.

Shimoura did not move directly to Michigan from her home in Fremont, California. First she was moved to the Army's Assembly Center, then she was transferred to the War Relocation Authority's Central Utah Project, known otherwise as Topaz, "the jewel of the desert." At the Central Utah Project she heard about the War Relocation Authority's program to permit incarcerated college students to finish their educations at schools in the Midwest, the East Coast, and the South. Taking advantage of that student leave program, she went to Michigan State College, thus starting her path to becoming a public health microbiologist.

History changed Shimoura's life dramatically, but the written and published history of Asian America in Michigan (and the Midwest) has always been lacking. For people like Shimoura, it was important to preserve history through memories, stories, and passed-on knowledge. That is why part 2 groups Shimoura's contribution and seven others under the rubric of memory keepers and legacy keeping. The eight contributions in part 2 tell various kinds of history, but they do so primarily in the form of memories passed on as local knowledge. These legacies had to be preserved because no one else in Detroit (or Lansing or Ann Arbor) was going to keep them alive.

At the time these legacies were written and submitted, Michigan had not created a public place for marking the Asian American presence in the state. With no permanent Asian American museum in Michigan as in other locales (Chicago has a Chinese American Museum in its Chinatown, Los Angeles is home to the Japanese American National Museum, and Seattle and New York have Asian American museums), the legacy keepers in part 2 *are* Michigan's cultural resources for remembering its Asian Americans. There is no doubt that the memories in part 2 need to be studied by historians to contextualize them and to compare them with other sources, but that conversation begins here, with the publication of these essays. These memories—of pioneer Japanese midwesterners, of the first Korean Detroiter, who was superintendent of physical education at Condon Junior High School from 1918 to 1923, of the diversity of Asian Indians in Michigan—constitute a cultural lifeblood whose preservation is remarkable. In retrospect, it would have been as easy to obliterate these as it was to bulldoze Detroit's old Chinatown in the early 1960s. The legacy keeping preserved and now shared here is a testament to the importance of keeping such remembrances "on the ground" as local knowledge.

I return to Toshiko Shimoura. Starting and ending this introductory essay with her life helps us see the power of making the kinds of connections that keep memories alive. In 1991, Toshiko Shimoura had a chance to complete that circuit of memory and history when the *Los Angeles Times* sent a reporter to Detroit to write about the city's continuing struggle to adjust to Japanese automobile imports—and, by implication, its Japanese American residents. During Shimoura's interview with the journalist, the two of them gazed at one of Detroit's cultural treasures, *Detroit Industry,* the fresco mural painted by Diego Rivera in 1932 that adorns all four walls of a court in the Detroit Institute of Arts. Pointing to a figure on one of the murals, Shimoura remarked, "That's Mr. Hirata. James Hirata. . . . He was a tool-and-die man." Identifying the Asian face in *Detroit Industry,* she recalled what local Japanese American memory had long known, that Mr. James Hirata, the "tool-and-die" man, brought key hands-on engineering knowledge to the making of the B-29 bomber at the Willow Run Plant during the Second World War.

Such an act of keeping memory becomes richer yet when its implications are explored. Diego Rivera painted Mr. Hirata in 1932, meaning that "tool-and-die man" was a member of the pioneer generation of Japanese Americans who ventured to the Midwest prior to the larger midwestern resettlements of Japanese Americans during the war years of 1942-46. That historical point makes James Hirata more than just the sole Asian face in *Detroit Industry.* And more connections are found when we consider details of Shimoura's life. After she resettled in the Midwest, she married a Michigan man, James Shimoura. James Shimoura was a native Detroiter; his father, a "true automotive pioneer," had traveled from Tokyo to Dearborn in 1911 to work for the Ford Motor Company. It would be that pioneer's daughter-in-law, a native Californian, who would connect the two strands of Japanese American history in Michigan: the pioneers, as represented by the elder Shimoura, his son James, and James Hirata, and the resettlers who came to Detroit as a result of the war. Toshiko Shimoura's life experience connected both strands, and when she recounted the local knowledge (treasured by Detroit's Asian Americans) that the bespectacled figure in *Detroit Industry* had a name and a history, she bore that past forward. Toshiko Shimoura became the transmitter of that local memory—all she had to do was point and remember.

History and memory. Inextricably entwined, they operate in indispensable ways to keep cultural persistence and witness alive for individuals and communities. Here are eight such efforts.

6

THE MAKING OF
AN ASIAN AMERICAN DETROITER

Grace Lee Boggs

When I came to Detroit from New York in 1953, I had no idea that I would still be here more than fifty years later, still working at the age of ninety plus to transform Detroit into a twenty-first-century city with a thriving local economy and diverse and lively communities.

The main reason I'm still here and active is that shortly after I arrived, I married Jimmy Boggs, an African American Chrysler worker, activist, and writer. We were partners in struggle for forty years until his death in 1993.

On my own, a Chinese American female born above my father's restaurant, I would never have perceived myself as someone who could make a difference in Detroit or any American city. When I was growing up, first in Providence, Rhode Island, and then in New York City, Chinese Americans were a tiny, almost invisible minority. And the best a woman could aim for was to become a teacher or a nurse.

By contrast, Jimmy, who was coming of age in the "movement" climate of the mid-twentieth century, was very conscious that the blood and sweat of his ancestors had made possible the rapid economic development of this country. By the time we met, he had already embarked on the fight to ensure that his people would be among those deciding the political and economic future of the United States.

Boggs, who wrote this essay in 2009, is grateful for and encouraged by the number of Asian Americans she has seen stepping into leadership roles in more recent years.

We couldn't have been more different. I was not only Chinese American but from the Big Apple. My ideas had come mostly from books, and I spoke with a New England accent. Jimmy had grown up in the Deep South, in the little agricultural town of Marion Junction, Alabama. The saying "You can take a person out of the country, but you can't take the country out of a person" might have been coined for him. He spoke "Alabamese," telling audiences that they had better succeed in their struggle to understand him because one day they would have to understand a billion Chinese. As a child, he had been the scribe for his mostly illiterate community, and he never lost his connection with the people of his past. We spoke, wrote, and engaged with the same issues, but his style and ideas came mostly out of his life experiences and those of his people.

After graduating from high school in the middle 1930s, Jimmy moved to Detroit and was hired at the Chrysler-Jefferson plant at the beginning of World War II. An assembly line worker for twenty-eight years, he was very conscious of himself as someone who had lived through two distinct epochs: first the agricultural, and now the newer one featuring industry and automation. When we met, he was profoundly troubled by the speed with which technology was eliminating factory jobs, especially for young people. But he was also beginning to envision the new, more livable cities that could be created by working people if they spent less time making a living and instead focused on taking responsibility for one another, for their communities, and for the planet.

I found Jimmy's combination of concern and vision irresistible.

A United Nations Family

As an Asian American married to an African American for so many years, I am often asked, "How did Jimmy's family and community and your own respond to the marriage?"

Jimmy's mother, brothers, nephews, and nieces not only accepted me, they warmly welcomed me into the family. Overnight, in line with old southern custom, I became Daughter Grace, Sister Grace, and Auntie Grace. They all lived in Chicago and we visited back and forth.

I also felt very comfortable with Jimmy's friends and coworkers in Detroit, many of whom were from the South, including some with whom he had grown up in Marion Junction. In those days, there were few signs in the African American community of the black nationalism that would later make relationships with blacks so potentially sensitive. I may have been more acceptable as a person of color myself, although I was always careful to keep clear the distinction between the discrimination experienced by Chinese Americans and the hell African Americans had endured.

I didn't feel I was seen as "exotic," possibly because during World War II Americans had gotten used to working alongside "Orientals," as they were still called. Many blacks had also served in Korea during that war, which had recently ended without a victory for the United States. Some had returned with Korean wives. To children, however, I was a novelty. They wanted to play with my hair because it was so straight. Recently, a woman in her late forties came up to me at a meeting and said that she still remembers when she first met me in the 1950s. "You were the prettiest thing I had ever seen."

My oldest friend in Detroit is Ellen Richardson, a black woman from Mississippi who, back in 1953, had recently married a Detroiter. Jimmy and I were the godparents of their daughter, Stephanie, born in 1954. I have never over the years felt the tension in my relationships with black women that is often present in bonds between white and black women. That tension is rooted in long years of black women serving as mammies and domestic workers: nurturing Miss Ann's children, doing her laundry, mopping her floors. My black friends and I could come to our relationships fresh because Asian American and African American women have little or no history to overcome.

When people discover that my husband was African American, they almost always ask whether we had children. We had no children of our own, but Jimmy had plenty of children from his first marriage so I have a lot of grandchildren and great-grandchildren. I sense that my questioners are disappointed, partly because of natural curiosity about how our offspring would look. Personally, I never wanted to have children because raising children is a full-time job and I always saw my role as being out in the world rather than in the home. It has even occurred to me that one of the reasons I married Jimmy was that he wasn't likely to want more children; it was tough enough to support those he already had. For years after we were married, he used to get up at 3:00 a.m. to walk to one job cleaning a bar, then take the streetcar at 6:00 to work on the line at Chrysler. The first thing he did every payday was send a money order to the Friend of the Court for child support.

Reactions to our marriage in my own family varied. My brothers Harry and Eddie lived in Detroit and had been friends with Jimmy before I met him. Harry was married to Julie, a Japanese American. Around the same time that Jimmy and I got together, Eddie married Averis, a fellow worker from a small town in Georgia. He was welcomed into her close-knit poor white family the same way I was welcomed into Jimmy's. Averis and Jimmy got along famously, talking and laughing about the experiences they had in common growing up in the South. We all took pride in our United Nations family. Eddie especially respected Jimmy because he was "the kind of leader who didn't overwhelm you, who let you think for yourself, and who did not expect others to minister to his needs." My sister Kay, who lived in New York, and my brother Bob, who eventually settled in Hawaii, met Jimmy only a few times, but they always sent best wishes to him in their letters.

On my few visits to New York, I never discussed my marriage with my father, who also avoided the issue, having learned through long experience not to intervene in matters he was powerless to influence. I don't think he ever anticipated that his children would marry anyone who was not Chinese. Yet almost all of us did just that. When we were young, he used to warn us that the only whites who would have anything to do with Chinese were "lowlifes" or "riffraff." When my brother Harry first began to date Julie, we considered telling my father that she was really Chinese but didn't look it because she had been raised in Hawaii. Later, when he came to live with us in Detroit, I marveled at the way my father related to Julie, Averis, and Jimmy. It seemed to me that he trusted them as much or even more than he trusted us, his own children.

Asian Americans who have come of age in the last thirty years find it hard to imagine that there ever was such a gulf between Chinese Americans and Japanese Americans that Harry and Julie's marriage could be an issue. I have to remind them that the term *Asian American* didn't even exist prior to 1969. People who looked like us referred to ourselves and were referred to by others according to the national backgrounds of our parents: Chinese Americans, Japanese Americans, or Filipino Americans, the main population groups in those years. The idea of intermarriage between individuals from these groups, and especially between Chinese and Japanese Americans (in the Pacific, the Chinese and Japanese had been at war since the invasion of Manchuria in 1931), was as remote as that of intermarriage with Caucasians.

Becoming Asian American

It was only after the Black Power movement and the black rebellions inspired a new pride in all people of color that we repudiated the stereotype of ourselves as the "model minority." We created our new identity as Asian Americans to announce our resentment of racial discrimination and our refusal to accept the "divide and rule" policies of the power structure. The term *Asian American* bristled with the defiance inherent in rebellion: the rebellion of Asian women against our portrayal as "exotic," of Asian men against the efforts of white society to desexualize them, and of Asian artists against the deadening of their creativity by the suppression of their ethnic identity.

Out of this new radical spirit came an explosion of creativity in community and campus organizing, in literature and the arts, especially on the East and West coasts. Poets, writers, and artists became cultural workers, helping to raise and shape community consciousness. Students wrote papers and scholars wrote books on the exploitation, oppression, and marginalization of our forebears. Our ancestors were forced to work as labor on railroads, mines, and farms. They were cheated, by racist legislation, of the right to naturalization and citizenship, to own land, to marry Caucasians. And then they were herded into internment camps during World War II. As our consciousness was raised, new publications poured off the presses. Asians from different national backgrounds began dating and marrying.

However, by the time the Asian American movement burst onto the scene, I had become so active in struggles inside the African American community that some FBI records speculated that I was Afro-Chinese!

Up South

When I arrived in Detroit in the 1950s, the city was still considered "Up South." After the passage in 1949 of the Public Accommodations Act by the Michigan legislature, it was illegal for restaurants and coffee shops to refuse to serve blacks. But housing was still blatantly racist. For example, in the west-side neighborhood at Blaine and Fourteenth Street where I sublet an apartment from a friend, blacks could buy houses (usually on land contract) but were not allowed to live in the apartment houses right next door. I was actually evicted after Jimmy started visiting me. It was only after thousands of apartments had been vacated by whites fleeing to the suburbs by way of the newly built Lodge and Chrysler freeways that blacks were allowed to rent these apartments—at twice what whites had been paying, naturally.

In the 1950s, Detroit's population was about 2 million. Today it is about seven hundred thousand. In the 1950s, the ratio of whites to blacks in Detroit was 80 percent to 20 percent. Today it is exactly the opposite. By the 1960s, in the wake of white flight to the suburbs, the racial split was about 50-50. Yet despite their shrinking numbers, whites still ran everything: city hall, the schools, the fire department, and the police force, which last acted like an occupation army, humiliating and brutalizing blacks at will. It was to correct this blatantly undemocratic situation that blacks began organizing the Black Power movement in the early 1960s.

I was very much involved in the movement in Detroit. I was one of the main organizers of the 1963 Grassroots Leadership Conference at which Malcolm X made his famous speech. I was also the coordinator of the all-black Michigan Freedom Now Party, which ran a full slate in the 1964 election but got only a few thousand votes because in those days if you called someone black, you had to be ready for a fight.

In the 1960s, Jimmy was putting in a full day's work at Chrysler-Jefferson, so he was less involved in day-to-day organizing. But he did a lot of thinking, speaking, and writing about the new challenges that were being created by the struggles against racism and the radical changes in the economy. In his first book, *The American Revolution: Pages from a Negro Worker's Notebook*, he warned that the high-tech elimination of so many jobs was creating a lot of "outsiders" who could not be expected to accept their expendability peacefully.

In July 1967, thousands of these "outsiders," outraged by a police raid on an after-hours drinking club on Twelfth Street, now Rosa Parks Boulevard, erupted in widespread burning and looting that could only be subdued by calling in federal troops and the Forty-second Airborne. During the five days of violence, 42 people were killed, 1,189 were injured, and more than 7,000 were arrested.

The media and the power structure called the 1967 explosion a "riot," but most black Detroiters called it a "rebellion" because it was such a righteous response to the abuses of white power. Moreover, it achieved what all our Black Power agitation and propaganda had failed to do: it fostered a tremendous pride in blackness and eventually led to the election of a black mayor, because even the existing power structure recognized that a white administration could no longer maintain law and order in the city.

When the nation's rebellions erupted in 1967 and 1968, Jimmy and I had been in the radical movement for a combined total of nearly sixty years but had never found it necessary to distinguish between a rebellion and a revolution. Now, with the "civil disorders" exploding all over the United States being described as the "black revolution," we coauthored our first book, *Revolution and Evolution in the 20th Century*. We made it clear that while rebellions break the chains that have been holding the corrupt system together, they do not provide the leap forward in the evolution of social responsibility and creativity that is essential to a revolution.

Transforming the City

In 1973, Coleman A. Young was elected Detroit's first black mayor. A former autoworker and Tuskegee airman, Young was a charismatic and forceful militant who had been closely associated with the left wing of the labor movement. As the new mayor, he acted decisively to reverse the racism embedded in the fire and police departments and in city administration. But he had no idea what to do about the growing numbers of young people without adequate employment: one could no longer drop out of school in the ninth grade and get a job in the plant making enough money to raise a family.

Thus, in 1981, with the support of the United Auto Workers unions but overriding community opposition, Young demolished a whole community in Detroit (Poletown, with 1,500 houses, 144 businesses, 16 schools, and a hospital) to provide General Motors with the space to build a plant, which the company promised would provide 6,000 jobs. The Poletown plant never delivered more than 3,500 jobs and GM cut workers at its other plants.

A few years later, the city experienced the next casualty of declining jobs. Because the invention of crack had created a "drug economy" in the inner city, kids started saying, "Why stay in school with the idea that one day you'll get a job making a lot of money when you can make a lot of money now rollin'?" The result was a huge spurt in school dropouts, street violence, and homicides. In 1986, 43 kids were killed and 365 wounded. This led to the founding of Save Our Sons and Daughters (SOSAD) by Clementine Barfield, whose sixteen-year-old son, Derrick, had been killed and her fourteen-year-old son, Roger, wounded in street violence. For nearly ten years, I edited the monthly SOSAD newsletter and Jimmy contributed a regular column.

To meet this crisis Young, still hoping to reindustrialize Detroit and still viewing the crisis mainly in terms of jobs, proposed a casino industry, which he said would provide fifty thousand jobs. We managed to defeat his proposal by forming Detroiters Uniting, a broad antigambling coalition of community groups, blue-collar, white-collar, and cultural workers, clergy, political leaders, and professionals who together embodied the rich ethnic and social diversity of Detroit. In the course of the casino struggle, Young called us "naysayers" and demanded, "What is your alternative?"

Recognizing the legitimacy of Young's challenge, Jimmy made a speech titled "Rebuilding Detroit: An Alternative to Casino Gambling" (see boggscenter.org) in which he projected a vision of a new kind of city, one where Detroiters would take responsibility for creating the local enterprises that would ensure our livelihoods instead of continuing to depend on the promises of corporations, which had no loyalty to the city, to provide us with jobs.

To give a sense of how that new kind of city could be created, in 1992 we founded Detroit Summer, a multicultural, intergenerational youth program to rebuild, redefine, and respirit Detroit from the ground up. Since 1992, Detroit Summer has been involving young people in planting community gardens (side by side with a loose network of elders, many of them born and raised in the South, who call themselves the Gardening Angels), rehabbing houses, and painting public murals. The initiative also offers opportunities for youth to expand their minds and imagination through workshops and intergenerational dialogue.

We were delighted to discover that Dr. Martin Luther King Jr., in response to the urban rebellions and after extended conversations with young people in the Chicago ghetto, had earlier projected "direct action Self-Transforming and Structure-Transforming Programs" for young people "in our dying cities" along the same lines as Detroit Summer.

Over the years, because of the pioneering activities of Detroit Summer and of local residents who have transformed the increasing number of vacant lots into spaces to grow their own food, there is a growing acceptance in Detroit of the idea that instead of buying everything from the grocery store, we can begin to build a healthier, more self-sustaining city by planting community gardens.

Thus, now a collaborative exists, consisting of the Detroit Agricultural Network, the Greening of Detroit, Michigan State University-Extension, and Wayne County. These groups work with individuals and organizations to coordinate and support hundreds of community gardeners, agricultural training programs, and garden cluster groups in many neighborhoods. The Catherine Ferguson Academy, a public high school for teenage mothers on the near southwest side, the 4H Community Center on the east side, and the Foundation for Agricultural Resources in Michigan (FARM) in the north end all serve as neighborhood resource centers. Students in the architectural department at the University of Detroit Mercy have created a twenty-minute video envisioning how two and a half square miles of land on the east side of Detroit, from I-94 to the river and between East Grand Boulevard and I-75, could be rebuilt as a community based on urban agriculture.

One of the most important contributions of Detroit Summer is that it provides the new model of education that is urgently needed to give our young people a sense of continuing participation in creating change. To stem the catastrophic 50 percent dropout rate in our inner cities, we must go beyond the top-down factory model of education created at the beginning of the twentieth century to supply industry with a disciplined workforce. We must replace it with a concept of education as an ongoing process that enlists the tremendous energies and creativity of schoolchildren in rebuilding and respiriting our communities and our cities.

Just imagine how safe and lively our streets would be if, as a natural and normal part of the K-12 curriculum, schoolchildren were taking responsibility for maintaining neighborhood streets, planting community gardens, recycling waste, rehabbing houses, creating healthier school lunches, visiting and doing errands for the elderly, organizing neighborhood festivals, painting public murals. The possibilities are endless.

This is the fastest way to motivate all our children to learn and at the same time turn our communities, almost overnight, into lively neighborhoods where crime is going down because hope is going up. By giving children a better reason to study than just to get a job or to advance their individual fortunes, by showing them how to become useful citizens, we will also get their cognitive juices flowing. Learning will come from practice, which has always been the best way to learn.

Asian American Detroiters in the Making

When I arrived in Detroit in 1953, the only visible Chinese community was the downtown Chinatown near Howard and Abbott. It was bulldozed to make room for the John C. Lodge Freeway, just as the downtown black community on the east side, known as Black Bottom or Paradise Valley, was being demolished to build the Chrysler Freeway. At the same time, a new Chinatown was emerging near Wayne State University at Cass and Peterboro. That is where for many years Detroiters like myself used to go to buy Chinese groceries or to eat at Chung's or the Golden Dragon. In the past twenty years, however, this new midtown Chinatown has almost disappeared as Chinese Americans joined the white exodus to the suburbs.

In l969-70, when Asian Americans were inspired by the black movement and the anti–Vietnam War movement to organize themselves, I was one of the founders of the Asian Political Alliance (APA) in Detroit. There were only six of us, three Japanese and three Chinese, including my brother Harry. To the average Caucasian, we may all have looked alike, but we were very aware of the differences in our backgrounds, both of ethnicity and whether we were American born or Asian born. We stayed together for less than two years, but it was one of the most enjoyable periods of my political life. Our program was very modest. We discovered things about each other and about ourselves by studying Chinese history and Japanese history. Each month we showed films like *The East Is Red* that attracted a varied group of Asians, especially Chinese from China who had been fearful of showing too much interest in the Chinese revolution. But in the darkness of a movie hall, they would break into smiles as they witnessed the tremendous changes taking place in their homeland.

We held workshops to help young American-born Asians both discover and create their identity. We also participated in anti–Vietnam War demonstrations locally and nationally, shouting "Yellow is mellow!" and blasting the racism and imperialism of U.S. aggression in Asia.

Working with Asians was unlike anything that I had known in the white or black community. For the first time in my life, I was meeting regularly with political people who shared my background as an Asian American. The experience made me much more aware of how Asians have been marginalized, not only in American society in general but also in movement circles because, until very recently, we have been so few and far between.

The most striking difference was the respect that young people showed for me as an elder. Thus, when I attended the Asian American Reality Conference at Pace College in New York in 1970 as a representative of APA, I was asked to make the closing speech, something that had never happened to me in all the years that I was involved in the black movement. In my speech, which was off the cuff, I found myself speaking like an elder to the mostly college-age audience, drawing lessons from my experience in the movement. The speech has been printed in a pamphlet titled *Asian Americans and the U.S. Movement*. Reading it today, I am amazed at how didactic I was.

The Asian American movement that had begun on college campuses in the late 1960s took on new life in reaction to the murder of Vincent Chin in 1982. Chin, a twenty-seven-year-old Chinese American Detroiter, was killed on the eve of his wedding by two unemployed autoworkers, Ron Ebens and Michael Nitz. This was at a time when the U.S. auto industry was in a recession because both in this country and abroad, Japanese-made cars were increasingly preferred to those made in the United States. Anyone who looked Japanese was personally blamed and held accountable for the predicament of GM, Ford, and Chrysler—and their workers.

Ebens and Nitz did not serve one full day in jail and paid only a $3,780 fine for the murder. This blatantly racist verdict sparked the creation of American Citizens for Justice, a broad coalition joining Asian American suburbanites, Chinatown residents, and university students and professors and supported by other groups like the Urban League and the Anti-Defamation League.

I was not active in American Citizens for Justice, but when my autobiography, *Living for Change*, was published in 1998, Asian American campus activists became interested in my life as a veteran Asian American campaigner who had been deeply involved in the African American struggle and was currently engaged in Detroit Summer.

Among these activists were Californians Scott Kurashige and Emily Lawsin, who now teach at the University of Michigan but live in Detroit. They have worked with members of the Metro Detroit Asian American community and with Asian American students at neighboring universities to create an Asian American presence in the city. The efforts of all these Asian Americans attracted more than two hundred participants to a historic three-day Vincent Chin Twentieth Year Remembrance and Rededication to Justice event in June 2002. Out of this event came the Detroit Chinatown Revitalization Workgroup which, in the summer of 2003, collaborated with Detroit Summer and the local On Leong Chinese Welfare Association to create a mural memorializing the movement for justice for Vincent Chin and depicting the history of social movements and political struggle in the community,

A group of community members gathered in Detroit Chinatown on July 24 to celebrate the conclusion of a summer initiative. The Detroit Asian Youth Project, an unprecedented summer youth program, brought together eight Asian American youth from Detroit to engage in community-based projects and explore issues of history, politics and identity over a six-week period.

In 2004 the work group convened a forum called Bridges to the Future: Asian Americans and Community Organizing in Detroit, bringing more than fifty community organizers together to discuss community building and Asian American history in Detroit. Ellen Somekawa and Debbie Wei of the Philadelphia-based Asian Americans United shared lessons learned from their own urban youth program, which works primarily with the Asian American community.

Out of this forum came the idea of a youth initiative, the Detroit Asian Youth Project, that would provide a space for young Asian Americans to engage in community-based projects and develop political awareness. In the summer of 2005, Asian American youth, primarily from the Southern Asian American community on the northeast side of the city, again worked alongside Detroit Summer youth, tending organic urban gardens. They made their own T-shirts and developed a sense of the city's diversity by visiting Mexican Town, Indian Village, the Heidelberg Project, and Chinatown with its Vincent Chin Mural.

The closing ceremony, which the young people planned themselves, was very moving. It included a Hmong dance in traditional dress followed by a dance to pop music. Participants described how much the project had meant to them. "It changed me. I now know what I want to do," one young man said. Participants articulated the lessons learned: "A community is where everyone comes together to make it safer and a better place for everyone." "It is a place where you can express your thoughts and feelings."

7

THREE LEGACY KEEPERS

The Voices of Chinese, Korean, and Indo-American Michiganders

Tai Chan, Tukyul Andrew Kim, and Kul B. Gauri

Tai Chan: Detroit's Chinatown and the Current Chinese Community

The first Chinese lived in Michigan in the mid-1800s. Early immigrants were not organized for the most part, tending to focus on their own family businesses or their employers. Nonetheless, George Lim Poy, president of the Four Seas Club in Detroit, recalled a fund-raiser at a Chinese restaurant in 1928 when more than $20,000 was raised in support of the new Chinese government. That was a very impressive sum back then, since there were only a few hundred Chinese in Michigan and their earning power was limited. It was later learned that similar fund-raisers by Chinese Americans in Hawaii and California fueled the victorious revolution over the Qing Dynasty in 1911. Madame Chiang Kai-shek came to Detroit in 1935 to thank the Chinese Americans personally and to report that democracy was alive and well in the new Republic of China.

It was not until the 1930s that the location on Michigan Avenue and Third Street evolved as Detroit's Chinatown. It was during the 1920s that the Four Seas Club was formed. It was more or less a social club where the Chinese would get together for dinner and to play mahjong. However, the Chinese community in the Detroit area remained small.

As the economy recovered after World War II, Detroit was a pleasant city in which to live. On weekends, Chinese Americans would go to Belle Isle with their families and enjoy the outdoors. To some, Detroit's Belle Isle was even better than New York's Central Park because it had more water and green space as well as picnic areas, a greenhouse, a zoo, and an aquarium. It was a model for the Michigan state parks in the counties north of Detroit.

In 1961, as part of an urban renewal plan, the City of Detroit razed the original Chinatown to make way for the John C. Lodge Freeway. Chinatown was moved to the current location at Cass Avenue and Peterboro Street, west of Woodward Avenue. Jin Chin was a visionary businessman who owned both Chung's restaurant and the Wah Lee grocery store at Cass and Peterboro. Through hard work, he made enough money to support his family and sustain his businesses in Detroit's Chinatown for almost forty years. Unlike other Chinese communities in larger U.S. cities, however, Detroit's Chinatown never reached the critical mass required to launch a vibrant ethnic community. There were never more than a dozen families living there, and they gradually moved to the suburbs. The Chung restaurant closed in the late 1990s, leaving only the sign. Sadly, even long after the riots in 1968, some of the buildings on Peterboro Street remain empty.

Discouraged by the decline of the city after 1968, Jin Chin took a risk the next year and built a new restaurant in Troy, a northern suburb. The City of Troy had incorporated only thirteen years earlier as a bedroom community when developers were converting farmlands to subdivisions to meet the growth of professionals working for the automotive industries.

It was not always a simple matter for Chinese Americans to move to the suburbs, however. Ray Lim, a resident of Detroit since the 1930s, recalled looking for a home to buy in the Detroit suburbs. More than once, Lim would walk up to a house with a "For Sale" sign and knock on the front door, only to be greeted by a firm voice announcing, "This house has been sold." The house would stay on the market for months, and eventually a white family would move in.

The Chinese started moving out of Detroit after World War II, and only a few hundred elderly Chinese lived in Chinatown in the 1980s. They frequented the On Leung Club on Peterboro Street, essentially a community center for retirees to drink tea, reminisce, and play mahjong. As time passed and these seniors had fewer friends and family members still living in the city, they grew depressed and their quality of life suffered. Two physicians, Silas Cheuk and Pang Man, responded by launching the Chinatown Drop-in Center. They provided free medical help and, because they spoke Chinese, they were able to cheer the seniors while meeting their physical and psychological needs. The center was a historic project of the Association of Chinese

Americans (ACA), with funding provided by the State of Michigan Mental Health Department.

The ACA was formed in 1974, a year before what became its parent group, the Organization of Chinese Americans (OCA), was formed in Washington, DC. Doctors Alex Mark and K. L. Wong were the founders of both. Over the years, the ACA and OCA have worked well together on many initiatives. The OCA has more than thirty chapters in the United States and one in Hong Kong. Its responses to social issues such as the murder of Vincent Chin and the unjust accusation of Dr. Wen Ho Lee for leaking government secrets were immediate and significant.

In 1990 the national convention of the OCA, with the theme of Emphasizing Diversity in the 1990s, was held at the Hilton in Novi, Michigan. The convention was unconventional, going beyond the traditional scope of providing services to Asian communities. Many speakers insisted that it was time for the Asian community to become more assertive within the surrounding society. The message was that America could be transformed—and for the better—by integrating Asian culture and heritage in the new century. The Chinese community was inspired to stand up and be counted.

Besides the ACA, there are more than thirty nonprofit Asian Pacific American organizations in the greater Detroit area. There are seven Chinese schools in the area offering Chinese language, arts, and culture classes to both children and adults. Some organizations, such as the Chinese Senior Citizens Group, are essentially social clubs with a single agenda: to meet regularly for lunch. Others are professional societies with a focus on networking and career development. These include the Detroit Chinese Engineers Association (DCEA), the Detroit Chinese Business Association (DCBA), the Asian Pacific American Chamber of Commerce (APACC), and the Chinese Association of Greater Detroit (CAGD). These organizations are key bridges between the APA community and China. The groups host governmental and business delegations to keep each other current on business developments and political reforms. In addition, several alumni associations of key universities in China, such as Tsinghua, Shanghai Jiaotong, and Jilin universities, have active alumni chapters in Michigan. These cultural and professional organizations play important roles in the networking and assimilation of Asian/Pacific American immigrants in Michigan, assisting the business development of Chinese companies and facilitating professional exchanges that are mutually beneficial to China and the United States.

Tukyul Andrew Kim: Korean Americans in Michigan

The first Korean resident in Michigan was Huh Sung. He was a member of the Young Men's Christian Association in Seoul. He attended the YMCA College in Springfield, Massachusetts. He graduated with a degree in physical education and served as the superintendent of physical education at Condon Junior High School, Detroit, from 1918 to 1923.

Another early settler was Joseph K. Deyo. He worked in the schools as a violinist and music teacher.

Jhung Yang Pil and his wife, Lee Hwa Sook, founded Jhung-Ahn & Co. in Detroit, starting a limited partnership with Ahn Jae Hong, Joh Dae Heung, Joh Oh Heung, Choe Eung Ho, Lee Won Shik, Jeon Deuk Ki, and Yoo Jin Ik in March 1925, with a capital investment of $30,000. The company produced Oriental foods until 1953. Jhung and Lee also served on the financial committee of the provisional government of the Republic of Korea in Shanghai, China, during the Japanese occupation of Korea. The Republic of Korea granted them the posthumous honor of the Order of National Independence in 1995. They were buried at the national cemetery in Dae-jon, Korea. Their daughter Mary is a pediatrician in Ann Arbor, Michigan.

In early 1920s, Lim Byung Chik (Colonel Ben C. Lim) worked at the Ford Motor Company in Highland Park, Michigan. Lim actively participated in the Korean independence movement. Upon the liberation of Korea in 1945, Lim returned to his homeland and became minister of foreign affairs for the Republic of Korea. Later, he served as the Republic of Korea's ambassador to the United Nations.

Considerable numbers of Korean scholars have studied at the University of Michigan, Ann Arbor, and then returned to Korea and served with academic distinction. Dr. Choi Kyu Nam became president of Seoul National University, Dr. Koh Whang Kyung became president of Seoul Women's University, and Dr. Lee Won Cheul became director of the National Weather Observatory.

Whang Chang Ha (Harry Whang) stands out as a patriot and one who helped organize the Korean community in Detroit. In 1919 Whang participated in the March 1 independence movement demonstration in Pyong-yang. Exiled to Shanghai, he came to the United States to study at the University of Chicago. He then moved to New York City, working on his master's degree in philosophy at Columbia University while serving as the secretary of the Korean Students Division of the New York YMCA. In 1928, the Student Volunteer Mission held its national conference at the Masonic Temple in Detroit.

Whang attended the conference with ten Korean student delegations and met some twenty Korean residents of Detroit.

In 1933, Whang and his wife, Helen, moved with their three children from New York to Detroit, where they started an indoor garden department at the J. L. Hudson department store. Their successful enterprise blended the artistic touch of Korean culture with the beauty of nature. Whang oversaw the department until his retirement in 1966, all the while steadfastly pursuing another dream: independence for Korea. He worked selflessly to build a Korean community in Detroit with a strong Korean national identity. He organized the Detroit chapter of the Korean National Association (Dae-Han-Keuk-Min-Hoe), a substructure of the provisional government of the Republic of Korea.

After the Japanese attack on Pearl Harbor on December 7, 1941, and the U.S. entry into World War II, the provisional government of the Republic of Korea declared war against Japan. Whang Chang Ha organized Korean Detroiters to march under the banner Patriotic Koreans in Detroit. Forty-three Korean immigrants marched down Woodward Avenue in downtown Detroit, hoisting both the Korean and American flags. The demonstrators denounced the Japanese attacks and demanded victory over Japan and the liberation of Korea. With this bold parade, the Koreans in Detroit raised $1,250 to buy a military ambulance for use in the war against Japan. The *Detroit Free Press* praised the march in an editorial, stating that the Koreans in Detroit, although small in number, participated in the war against the Japanese Empire with a great impact.

At last, the Japanese Empire surrendered unconditionally to the Allies. The Japanese were forced to retreat from the territories they occupied to their four main islands. Thus Korea became liberated. The United States and the USSR created the 38th parallel on the waist of the Korean peninsula as a demarcation line of where each country stationed its army in Korea: the USSR in the north, and the United States in the south.

Who could have imagined that the 38th parallel would divide the nation and its people into North Korea and South Korea, causing the separation of families, the tragic Korean War (June 25, 1950–July 27, 1953), and horrible destruction, including over 4 million people killed. A brutal Communist dictatorship rules in the north even today.

In Detroit, Whang Chang Ha, with the support of Detroit mayor Albert Cobo, organized the Korea Relief Committee of Michigan in 1950. The committee mobilized to bring aid to refugees and help with reconstruction of the war-torn country. In cooperation with Kiwanis International, Whang also organized a project to send five hundred cows to Kang Won Do Province in South Korea.

As a new relationship between Korea and the United States developed, waves of Korean students began to arrive to study in U.S. universities and colleges. The University of Michigan, Michigan State University, Wayne State University, and the University of Detroit Mercy have drawn many students from Korea. In addition, Detroit-area hospitals, such as Henry Ford, William Beaumont, Harper Grace, St. John, St. Joseph, St. Mary, and Providence, have opened internship and residency training programs for Korean medical students. As students from Korea arrived, first-generation Korean Detroiters welcomed them with warm hospitality. Especially notable is Mary Kim Joh, a former professor at Ewha Women's University in Seoul, who served as an affectionate bridge between the old-timers and the newcomers.

Opportunities for Koreans to immigrate to the United States have multiplied. The revised U.S. Immigration Act of 1965, activated in 1967, expanded the annual Korean immigration quotas from two hundred to twenty thousand. There were only about six hundred Koreans in Michigan in 1970; in 2014, the estimated numbers are about thirty thousand residents in addition to thousands of Korean students. As the Korean American community expanded, the Korean American Cultural Community Center of Michigan was established in 2003 at 24666 Northwestern Highway, Southfield, by the grassroots campaigns of Korean Americans. It serves as the center of community life, housing the Korean-American Association of Metro Detroit, the Honorary Consulate of the Republic of Korea, and the Korean Library. It provides cultural and educational programs, fellowship activities, translation and counseling services, and various information sharing. It is a unique characteristic of Korean immigrant life in America that the church has always been at its center. As the spiritual foundation of the United States was laid by the solid faith of the Puritan Pilgrim fathers, so the Korean churches' ministry is enhanced as their members lay their spiritual foundation of immigrant life in solid Christian faith. The first Korean Christian church in Michigan was launched at a prayer meeting in the basement of the Woodward Avenue Presbyterian Church in Detroit by the Reverend Whang Kwan Il, Professor Rhee Choon Jai, Kim Kee Taik, and Kim Choon Kyu, on May 28,1967. This congregation became the Korean Presbyterian Church of Metro Detroit, 27075 West Nine Mile Road, Southfield.

In 2014 there are forty Korean Protestant congregations in the tri-county Metro Detroit area as well as in Ann Arbor, Battle Creek, Kalamazoo, Lansing, Grand Rapids, Flint, and Saginaw, all under the umbrella of the Michigan Council of Korean Churches, which was formed in 1976. There is also a Korean Roman Catholic Church.

Historically, Korean Americans have been only a small percentage of Michigan's population, but their limited number includes heroes who have supported both the Republic of Korea and the local community. As the community has grown, we have remembered our roots. Just as Korean Michiganders of the past struggled for Korea's freedom from Imperial Japan, today we continue to work, hope, and pray for the reunification of North and South Korea. Yet in creating local Korean cultural organizations and vibrant church communities, we have also laid down new roots here in Michigan, our adopted home.

Among such Korean American heroes, Nam Sang Yong of Ann Arbor ought to be cited. When he was a high school junior in Korea, the tragic Korean War broke out. The North Korean army invaded his hometown, Dae-Jon, which is located in the middle of Korean peninsula. When the Communist army retreated, it kidnapped his father, taking him to North Korea. As the second son of eight children in the family, he supported his mother to keep the household going. Upon high school graduation, with a desire to help rebuild the war-torn country, he entered the College of Engineering, Department of Architecture at Seoul National University.

After his college graduation, he was admitted as a graduate student to the Department of Architectural Engineering and City Planning at the University of Michigan in 1964. When he arrived in Ann Arbor, he had $4 in his pocket. Upon receiving a master's degree in architecture and city planning from the University of Michigan, he found a job in the city of Ann Arbor.

He married Hong Moon Sook, who had graduated from the College of Nursing, Seoul National University. They are members of the Korean Church of Ann Arbor. Nam Sang Yong served the congregation as an ordained elder. He and his wife, devoted to their work and treasuring their frugal lifestyle, started purchasing apartment buildings one after another, eventually establishing the Nam's Building Management Company. By the grace of God, they achieved their American dream! Nam Sang Yong, however, was also pursuing another dream—to establish the Center for Korean Studies at the University of Michigan, similar to the university's famed Center for Chinese Studies and Center for Japanese Studies. Prayerfully, he accumulated $20,000 for the endowment fund. When he proposed the establishment of the center, the university, touched by his affection for his alma mater as well as his devotion to his homeland, graciously accepted his historic proposal. On August 31, 2010, the historic inaugural service of the Nam Center for Korean Studies of the University of Michigan was held at the heart of the main campus.

Nam Sang Yong and his family loved their adopted hometown Ann Arbor. Thus, he gave all his children names beginning with the letter A. His two sons, Andrew and Anthony, carry on their father's dreams.

Kul B. Gauri: Indian American Michigan

The first Indian influence in the United States came in the form of ideas. Translations of the Indian scriptures and stories about India arrived on America's shores before any contact was made between the people of the two countries. Interest in India increased after the visit of Swami Vivekananda, the "Cyclonic Monk," in 1893, when he attended the Parliament of Religions in Chicago. He journeyed extensively in the United States, traveling to the East and West coasts. In 1894, he visited Detroit as the guest of Frances Bagley, the wife of former Michigan governor John J. Bagley.

Although there is some reference made to an Indian who came to the United States as a maritime worker in 1790, little more is known of him. The first group of Indian immigrants to the United States came from British Columbia (then part of the British Empire) to Washington state and then to California in the early part of the twentieth century. These were mostly middle-class Sikhs, originally from the Indian state of Punjab. In British Columbia they had worked in the lumber industry, but they moved south to escape hostility and violence.

Following riots, a small group of Indians from Bellingham, Washington, was evicted from the state in 1907. They were called "unassimilable, really foreign, exotic people." This sparked further riots all along the Pacific Coast, often attributed to job competition with the local population.

Migrating to California, they took up farming, but they continued to face anti-Asian sentiments. The expansion of the auto industry in Detroit, including the tempting wage offer of $5 a day made by Henry Ford in 1914, attracted some Asian Indians, mostly Sikhs, to Michigan from California. There were also some studying at the University of Michigan at that time.

The history of civil rights struggles among Asian Indians in the first half of the twentieth century parallels that of other minorities. Discriminatory laws in force through 1946 worked against Asian Indians, barring them from the right to become U.S. citizens. When legal restrictions were relaxed in that year, it is estimated, about fifteen hundred Asian Indians remained in the United States—a greater number had left the country because of discriminatory laws and open hostility.

The second wave of Asian Indian immigration came after the passing of the Immigration Act of 1965. The act relaxed earlier racist and discriminatory practices. Because the new law was based upon applicants' qualifications, students and highly educated professionals took advantage of it. By 1970, universities, professional institutions, and manufacturing industries eagerly sought skilled workers. Michigan, with its well-established educational institutions, auto industry, and hospitals, became a magnet for scientists, engineers, and doctors.

These new immigrants, with highly professional backgrounds and a command of the English language, tended to be very mobile in their jobs and thus free in their choice of residence and settlement. The earlier model of immigrants settling in "ethnic enclaves" did not appeal to them. As Arthur Helweg wrote, "They were independent of the cultural borders, because they were fluent in the English language and skilled in dealing with bureaucracies and corporate structures."[1]

Asian Indians in Michigan come from different regions of India and have varied backgrounds. They represent different religions, classes, and castes, and speak sixteen different languages. What many have in common, however, is that they make uniquely self-confident immigrants, armed as they are with mastery of the English language and desired technical skills.

The growth of the Asian Indian population in Michigan from 1970 to 2000 was astounding. In 1974, there were 3,561 Asian Indians in Michigan. By 1980, the number of people who claimed to have been born in India grew to 8,879. By 1990, the number was 13,286. In that year, the number of people claiming Asian Indian ancestry was 23,485. The census of 2010 showed 77,132 Indian Asians living in Michigan, more than triple the number from 1990, making them the largest Asian American group in Michigan, with 0.8 percent of the state's population. Most chose to live where the jobs were, in the southern part of the state along the I-94 and I-96 corridors.

While the economic benefits enjoyed by these skilled workers are immense, they in their turn contribute to the Michigan economy. Helweg estimated that each foreign-trained doctor saves the state of Michigan at least $6 million in educational costs, and each engineer saves $2 million.[2] There is also a contribution in dollars and research from graduate students in major universities.

The community as a whole shows little proclivity or interest in engaging in business. But there are some instances of successful ventures. Singh Brothers, a residential building company, has been around for some time and is quite reputable in southeast Michigan. Syntel, a computer technology company specializing in business and management applications since 1972, is another major venture in the area. Another notable business is Lotus Bank Corporation, established in 2007.

Vattikuti Technology provides computer technology solutions in health care and other industries and has some affiliates in India. Its sister organization, Vattikuti Foundation, is a philanthropic body that helped establish Vattikuti Urology Institute, which provides robotic surgery at Henry Ford Hospital.

The Indus Center for Academic Excellence in Southfield has provided tutoring and academic support to high school students since 1995. Its students have frequently won awards at the national level, including the Michigan Math Prize. On an individual level in academia, the elevation of Dr. M. K. Moudgil as president and CEO at Lawrence Technological University is notable.

In the political domain, only a few efforts to date have been made to participate in the local and national arenas, but the case of Samir (Sam) Singh, mayor of East Lansing (2005–7) and a state legislator since 2012, is probably a precursor of a future trend.

To maintain the sights and sounds of the old country, many Asian Indians participate in ethnic *melas,* or gatherings, to celebrate a variety of events. These activities, rooted in regional and linguistic affinities, offer emotional support as well as social pleasure. At one time there were twenty-five organizations meeting in regular melas in the Metro Detroit area and more than one thousand nationwide. Paradoxical as this may sound, these local gatherings result in a lack of civic and political unity at state and national levels.

In the Metro Detroit area, a linear progression is evident—from a social group with symbolic ethnic identity to the establishment of mature institutional structures like temples, gurdwaras, and mosques. This process has been relatively free of the conflicts, discrimination, and intolerance so often encountered by populations immigrating into a new locale. It is probable that, along with the prized employment skills Asian Indians possess, the Western fascination with Eastern religions, particularly prevalent during the latter part of the twentieth century, may have contributed to a benign acceptance of Asian Indians relative to other immigrant groups.

To date, the skills and values of these immigrants have served them well in their new home. But there will probably be new concerns and dilemmas for the next generations to face. These will likely involve an erosion of traditional values, a growing trend toward individualism in the younger populations, and the strains of coping with old age in a manner not experienced or seen by the present generation. Time will tell when these issues will emerge and how Asian Indians will surmount them.

Notes

1. Arthur Helweg, *Asian Indians in Michigan* (East Lansing: Michigan State University Press, 2002), 24-25.
2. Ibid., 26.

8

THE HISTORY OF NIKKEI (JAPANESE) IN DETROIT

Toshiko Shimoura

At a time when most Japanese were seeking their American dream on the West Coast and in Hawaii, there was a small influx of Japanese into the Detroit area. The turn of the twentieth century witnessed the first arrival of youthful, entrepreneurial Japanese to the state of Michigan, particularly Detroit. Two further waves of Japanese immigration followed. In each period, the new population had a unique reason for coming.

Years of arrival	Population	Cultural background
1900 to 1924	Early pioneers	Immigrants from Japan—issei
1944 to 1950	Internees just released from U.S. government relocation centers	Issei (first generation), nisei (second generation), and sansei (third generation)
1970 to present	Japanese nationals with business interests, especially in the automotive field	Educated Japanese expatriates intending to live in Detroit area for a limited time and then return to Japan

1900 to 1924

Immigrants from Japan in the early 1900s were mostly single young men, ready to start new lives in the land of opportunity. Some who were eager to plant their roots in America married white American women, and a few returned to Japan and brought back Japanese wives. Many, however, remained lifelong bachelors.

The pioneers worked at various occupations. James Sasakura, who worked for Ex-Cell-O Corporation, invented the waxed milk container. He was an accomplished tool-and-die maker who later joined Tucker Motors to help develop the Tucker automobile. James Hirata, a tool-and-die engineer, was an expert with Johansson gauges whose expertise was important during World War II in building B-29 bombers at Ford's Willow Run plant. He appears as an engineer in Diego Rivera's industrial mural at the Detroit Institute of Arts. James Tadae Shimoura worked as a chemist in rubber research at Ford Motor Company. Taizo Kokubo was an optometrist and gift shop owner who imported many gift items from Japan. He became a generous donor to the Japanese community.

Some Japanese chose to return to Japan, as was the case of Tokumatsu Tamura, who worked for Dodge Motor Company. An introspective man, Tamura enjoyed the freedom of living and working in Detroit, but his thoughts often wandered back to the country of his birth. After much contemplation, he returned to Japan, where he put his knowledge of modern technology learned in Detroit's automobile industry to use, founding Tamura Seisakusho in Tokyo. At first the company specialized in radio, but Tamura later became an expert in transmission. Today, Tamura Corporation still operates in Tokyo.

Early immigrant Japanese spread out across the Detroit metropolitan area so that no Japantown ever formed. Occasional social gatherings included summer picnics where Japanese American children enjoyed meeting each other. There were no ethnic churches to offer weekly meeting places. Some joined local Christian churches, but most laboring people chose no church at all. There were no organized Buddhist churches, and at any rate the concept of weekly worship was not a priority.

For the most part early Japanese families, in spite of ethnic intimidation and racial discrimination, gradually learned the American way of life. They studied English at night school and became productive members of their communities.

Education was very important to first-generation Japanese immigrants, or issei. Their nisei children were strongly encouraged to attend college but were influenced by their American peers, and many took on the lifestyles of their Caucasian friends.

Holidays were a joyous time for all. Most American holidays and religious holidays were celebrated with American friends. Within their homes, major Japanese holidays were observed such as New Year's, Girl's Day and Boy's Day. The most eagerly awaited holiday was New Year's, when traditional Japanese foods were prepared and parents enjoyed the day with their children. Other Japanese holidays were talked about among issei parents, but they rarely became a part of the family tradition. In many ways, Michigan nisei children were deprived of the richness of the Japanese culture enjoyed by their West Coast and Hawaiian cousins. As they grew older, many became interested in learning more about their history and took pride in their Japanese heritage.

The U.S. Asian Exclusion Act of 1924, or, as it is usually named in history textbooks, the Immigration Act of 1924, effectively terminated further immigration of Japanese to the United States.

1944 to 1950

The bombing of Pearl Harbor in 1941 and the beginning of World War II with Japan had a profound effect on the demographics of Japanese Americans living in California, Oregon, and Washington. With the forced evacuation of all 120,000 persons of Japanese descent from their homes and placement in ten relocation centers, the dynamics of this whole group was changed. The incarceration made no distinction between Japanese American citizens, who were born here, and noncitizens of the older generations. West Coast Japanese and Japanese Americans spent most of the war in these camps.

Toward the end of the war, when the internees were being released, the big problem was that they had nowhere to go. Most had lost their homes in the government-forced "resettlement." Some families chose to return to their former hometowns, in spite of the hostile atmosphere. Others opted to venture east. Employment opportunity was an important factor, and Detroit was an industrial city with jobs to offer.

In 1944, families began to trickle into the Detroit area. In some instances, one family member would come in advance to scout out if the area was hospitable. The Central Methodist Church in Detroit, the Highland Park Baptist Church, the YMCA and YWCA, the Quakers, and the International Institute of Metropolitan Detroit stand out as institutions that generously helped newly arrived, displaced families and allayed their apprehensions. Prewar resident James T. Shimoura opened his home, offered advice, and helped new residents find homes.

At that time, Detroit's Cass and Canfield area was the central gathering place where Japanese American families could find temporary living quarters. As time passed and they became more self-reliant, families scattered throughout the Detroit area. A Japantown never materialized, in part because the horrific experience on the West Coast made new Japanese Detroiters reluctant to gather in groups that might attract attention.

Family and friends kept in touch in their new community, but many had virtually no larger social network. It became apparent that an organization to serve their needs was necessary. The Detroit chapter of the Japanese American Citizens League was formed in 1946. The league, which had started in 1929 in San Francisco, focused on the welfare and civil and human rights of Japanese and Japanese Americans. Nationally, it served to connect all disenfranchised people and meet their needs.

Associations such as the Motor City Golf Club, a bowling league, men's and women's investment clubs, a blood bank, the Japanese American Youths (JAYS), dinner groups, and craft groups were organized. All have gone by the wayside except for the Japanese American Citizens League, which continues to serve as a conduit between local Japanese Americans and the national organization, keeping people apprised of national happenings and issues. The league's ideal of creating "Better Americans in a Greater America" continues to serve as a guide.

A lesser-known group of Japanese who came to Detroit were war brides, the wives of American soldiers during the U.S. occupation of Japan and during and after the Korean War. Their cultural adjustment to Detroit was very difficult. The International Institute helped guide them. The Cherry Blossom Club was formed so the wives could socialize, share experiences, and feel the kinship of others like themselves. War brides did not often mingle with the rest of the Japanese American community.

Unquestionably, the evacuation of the Japanese from their homes during the war had lasting effects. Some lived with the psychological scars for years. Some found their financial standing irrevocably damaged. Others experienced their relocation as an opportunity to expand in new directions. Many Japanese Americans found jobs in Michigan that had not been available to them in the West, in spite of their education and qualifications. Some nisei left the camps to attend colleges in the Midwest or the East, while others sacrificed their education to help their families get back on their feet financially. Many Japanese had been farmers on the West Coast before being uprooted, and a few resumed that occupation. Several families settled in the Capac and Washington, Michigan, area, where they grew vegetables for Detroit markets.

The second wave of Japanese Americans did not organize a church as other Asian groups had. For a time, a small congregation met with a Japanese minister at Highland Park Baptist Church, but when the minister was called away the group ended. Churchgoing nisei joined local church communities.

When the Detroit Buddhist Church lost its minister, church leaders brought in a reverend from Cleveland once a month. These gatherings served both religious and social purposes. The potluck meal after the service was an important part of the fellowship. In recent years, membership has dwindled to a few families, and young people are not filling the void. The congregation's needs are met today by a minister from Chicago, who visits to conduct special services.

Christian issei who spoke only Japanese gathered at a private home once a month for a meeting of the Detroit Kyo-Yu-Kai, a Christian fellowship group. Here again, food played an important role after the service.

As first the issei and in their turn the nisei aged, their families took responsibility. The aged and infirm required no help from social agencies because either their needs were met at home or they were placed in retirement facilities under the supervision of their sansei children.

1970 to the Present

Japanese immigration to Michigan slowed to a trickle after the immediate postwar period. The next wave of Japanese came not to live but to work for a time and then return home to Japan. With the arrival of many Japanese nationals with business interests in the region came a bonus for resident Japanese Americans—a proliferation of Japanese restaurants and grocery stores. From the original Kado's and Kuwahara's grocery stores, the number has grown to a half a dozen or so stores, giving the community a wider and fresher choice of Japanese cuisine. Japanese food is no longer a rarity, reserved for special gatherings and holidays; it can be enjoyed any day. Food is an important and gratifying part of culture, not only for itself but for the childhood memories of family special occasions it triggers. And on a practical note: no longer is it necessary to drive to Chicago for supplies!

There is no denying, though, that the second and third generations of Japanese Americans have drifted from tradition and cultural practices. Theirs has been a typical American upbringing of Boy Scouts, Girl Scouts, Little League, and school activities. However, because of their outward appearance,

Japanese Americans still feel reluctance and lack of total acceptance in some situations. This situation points to the value of identity securely based on the knowledge of who one really is.

The sansei and yonsei (fourth generation) usually adhere to typical American rituals for important life events. In weddings, for example, the usual customs are followed, whether the couple chooses the blessing of the church or a civil ceremony. The formality of a traditional Japanese wedding is unheard of in the United States. Even in a Buddhist ceremony in America, a wedding is very similar to the customary American observance, save perhaps for the ritual of exchanging the sake cup and partaking of the *san-san-kudo*.

Today it is a rare Japanese American who marries within his or her ethnic group. Out-marriages are the norm. Not only has this changed the structures of individual families, it is altering the landscape of the Japanese American community as a whole as members of this once close-knit population now share in the associations and interests of their Caucasian relatives. The change has come about in just one generation. One wonders what the ramifications will be in succeeding generations, and whether Japanese Americans will disappear as a distinct demographic group.

Nonetheless, the Japanese maxims of duty, obligation, honor, courtesy, and filial piety have not totally faded increasing Americanization. These principles were so strongly stressed by the issei they still find a place in the hearts of succeeding generations of Japanese Americans. They seem to be qualities deeply embedded in the Japanese psyche.

In the decades after World War II, it became apparent to the Japanese American Citizens League that U.S. history books carried little information regarding the wartime evacuation and incarceration of West Coast Japanese and Japanese Americans. To help educators understand and teach this history, a curriculum guide was prepared by the league's education committee and made available to educators everywhere. Curriculum workshops have been held in several cities, including Detroit. Invitations were sent to secondary social studies teachers in southeastern Michigan. This successful workshop was held at the University of Michigan's Dearborn campus. As a result, a number of high school teachers have requested speakers from the league's Detroit chapter to personally speak of their experiences.

In 1980, Wayne State University's Ethnic Heritage Project invited the league to participate in the Manoogian Hall Project to reflect the ethnic diversity of the university. The league enlisted architect Hideo H. Fujii, who generously contributed his design and time, to construct the Japanese Center

Room at Wayne State. The room remains a symbol of goodwill from the Japanese people of Detroit.

Two vastly different events brought Japanese Americans in close association with the Chinese community and other Asian groups—the Far Eastern Festivals and the Vincent Chin case.

The Far Eastern Festivals brought together Chinese, Korean, Filipino, South Asian, Japanese, and other Asian groups for the first time. These groups created summer events in the 1970s and 1980s at Detroit's riverfront Hart Plaza. The food, dances, cultural exhibits, and martial arts were a great attraction and provided goodwill and good times for the greater community.

The tragic Vincent Chin murder case was the most significant event in the history of Michigan's Asian community. The broader racial implications of the Chinese American's murder and the lenient sentences given to his killers united all the subgroups of Asians, although they had often been at odds with one another in the past. The miscarriage of justice generated a fiery national and international response. American Citizens for Justice was formed, becoming a nationally recognized force in fighting injustice and bigotry.

The history of the Japanese in Detroit spans over a century. From the early arrival of pioneer immigrants to the coming of evacuees from the relocation camps in the western deserts to the recent appearance of Japanese businesspeople, the Japanese American presence is a proud legacy that will remain an important part of Detroit.

9

FROM HAMMERED-DOWN NAIL TO SQUEAKY COG

The Modern Japanese American Experience in Detroit

Asae Shichi

Japan-Bashing: The Reality Show

Thirty years ago, cross-cultural differences were not well understood by the general American population. In the economic slump of the early 1980s, especially in Michigan's regional economy, where the American automotive industry was losing its competitive edge to Japanese automakers, it did not take much to ignite the fire of Japan-bashing into a raging fury. In 1982 there was the murder of Vincent Chin, a Chinese American who was killed by two Americans who believed he was Japanese. TV screens conveyed the faces of angry American autoworkers as they pounded on Japanese cars with sledgehammers. "We beat them in the war! We'll beat them again!" we heard them shout. It was reported that some people driving Japanese cars became the targets of highway shootings. A student told me that his father would "kill" him if he found out that his son was studying Japanese. He said that when he visited his father, parking his yellow Toyota in the driveway, his dad would cover the car with a big sheet: "Don't let the neighbors see this!" he would exclaim.

Media reporters were eager to interview Japanese businesspeople and their families, but they couldn't find anyone who was willing to talk. Where was the Japanese community in Detroit? Unlike in San Francisco or Los Angeles, there was no big ethnic shopping center, Japantown, or Buddhist temple in the Detroit area. Other than Novi, Japanese people didn't live in one specific area.

The "community," if it could be called that, remained quite elusive. Japanese companies in Michigan told their Japanese employees not to speak out or grant interviews because they didn't want to become visible targets for bashing. "Let's all be quiet and wait for the storm to pass," they said.

As the old Japanese proverb goes, "The nail that sticks out will be hammered down." But the American saying goes, "The squeaky cog gets the oil." Some of us who were not connected directly with the business community, and who were therefore free from this gag order, decided to be the squeaky cog. Some of us felt that such bashing stemmed from lack of real knowledge about Asian culture, especially Japanese culture. Economic issues, in this case the so-called unfair trade practices of Japanese car manufacturers, were the underlying cause, but the matter was likely exacerbated by the lack of thorough explanations about these issues from the Japanese side. Some of us felt the need for more effective face-to-face communication with the American public. To be elusive, to hide and be quiet could only make the situation worse, we believed. And the scenario everyone dreaded was a repeat of the 1982 Vincent Chin case, which had taken place here in Detroit.

At the height of Japan-bashing, the program *Kelly & Company* on Channel 7, WXYZ-TV, came up with the idea to air a live discussion among several guests, followed by audience participation. I was invited to participate as a guest representing the Japanese community. I had been interviewed by the media before, and they knew that I was not affiliated with any automotive companies and therefore would speak up freely. As I entered the building, I passed a big group of UAW workers from the Willow Run plant, which had recently closed. I could feel the emotion of these angry, agitated men, so intense that it almost seemed a physical emanation. Whether they meant to threaten me or not, I felt very intimidated.

During the show, Dr. George Friedman, who had just published a book titled *The Coming War with Japan* (1991), gave his prediction that Japan was preparing for a full-scale war with the United States within ten years. Several local automotive executives offered their views on the unfair trade practices of Japanese car companies. A young Korean student told the audience she was continually harassed because of being mistaken for a Japanese person. At a shopping mall someone had yelled at her, "Because of you, my family member lost a job!" "What could I say," she told the audience, "Other than 'I'm Korean, and I drive an American car?'"

Dr. Kaz Mayeda, a prominent second-generation Japanese American researcher at Wayne State University, got tough, reminding the audience that it was the tenth anniversary of Vincent Chin's murder. "If we have to, we'll take up arms to prevent this sort of thing from happening again."

The laid-off UAW workers I'd passed were seated in a group not very close to the podium, and they raised their hands and took turns speaking during the show: "We need our jobs! The Japanese auto manufacturing companies are moving into the Midwest with hundreds of parts makers trailing behind them, and we *are* losing our jobs!"

The air was tense with anger and frustration—precisely the atmosphere the producer must have wanted. The more confrontation, the better! The studio was not the Roman Colosseum, but I imagined the directors of the show whispering among themselves: "Let's see how the gladiators fight!" "I thought I might not come out alive at one point," I later confessed, only half joking, to a friend. When it was my turn to speak, I was very much aware that I was the "face" of Japan for the audience. Dr. Mayeda had already talked about getting his gun to defend his community. I wanted to appeal to the reason and conscience of our audience. I was reminded of my first impression of America while I was in graduate school in New York, full of hope and joy, getting to know this country. Where was that America that I knew? I explained to the audience that I had always viewed America as strong and Americans as proud, creative, and generous of spirit. "I still trust the Americans to get back that pride and strength again."

Several people in the audience voiced anger against their own government and their bosses, who were interested only in short-term profits. "We are putting Japanese parts in the cars we are making and calling them American cars! That's what we are doing!" As this middle-aged worker expressed his bewilderment, he got much support from the audience.

Then another middle-aged man, who introduced himself as an automotive engineer, stood up and quietly stated: "We brought this on ourselves. We've been a bit lazy. We didn't work as hard as we should have. We are the ones who have to share the blame." Whether the TV station deliberately invited this man, knowing he would be a catalyst, I never knew. But his speech became the turning point. More people joined him and supported his view, and one could feel a sudden change inside the heated studio: one moment intense hatred, the next a great calm.

It was a TV show. But what took place in the show was real: real people, real feelings, a real exchange of thoughts and emotions. People are biased. We all are. But there should be opportunities to get these feelings out in the open and talk about them. Information is important. But engaging in conversation, hearing all sides, and meeting as human beings is the first step toward understanding and, hopefully, reconciliation.

The Sushi Eaters of Clawson

Today there's a little Japanese grocery store that may be the symbol of how Japanese Americans in Detroit have become part of the mainstream. It's in a small town named Clawson, nestled between the bustling corporate city of Troy and trendy Royal Oak. It's a quiet town, even on the busier weekdays. Driving along Fourteen Mile Road, you might not note the names of the establishments you're passing: a few pizza shops, car maintenance places, small eateries, and the like. What makes this street attractive to certain drivers is a nondescript store called Noble Fish, a Japanese grocery store where people can eat authentic sushi at a reasonable price or pick up the takeout sushi of their choice.

At Noble Fish, they sell Japanese-style tofu, rice, green tea, locally grown and imported Japanese vegetables, packs of instant seasoning for sushi, frozen slices of sukiyaki meat, and a fine assortment of rice crackers and sweets. Near the register, a chilled display case is packed with rolled sushi to go. Sushi is the store's main draw for local shoppers who are not Japanese. Unlike the sushi packs displayed in ordinary American grocery stores these days, this sushi is prepared onsite by Japanese sushi chefs. And best of all, it's cheaper.

Noble Fish is unlike other grocery stores in that customers can sit down, order their sushi combinations, and eat them right there. The place is always crowded with local people—high school students seeking a bite of exotic food during lunch breaks, businesspeople treating their coworkers, neighborhood men who look like factory workers. They form a long line for this treat, filling up the narrow aisles of the tiny store. Occasionally, one sees Japanese people eating here, but usually most of the sushi-eating customers are non-Japanese. The store has gotten so popular that neighboring stores have taken to rather aggressively protecting their parking spaces from Noble Fish customers: the next-door hardware store hired a security guard to threaten sushi eaters trying to park in hardware spaces.

The store acts as a gossip corridor for the regular Japanese customers who shop here. One is bound to run into someone one knows, since this is the only Japanese grocery store in the vicinity. There are a few similar stores in Novi and Livonia, but there are not many others that can provide the needed fresh produce and frozen food items.

Non-Japanese Asians shop here as well when they are looking for specific ingredients. Normally, they prefer Chinese or Korean grocery stores if they are looking for ordinary soy sauce, tofu, dried shrimp, and so on, as they are much cheaper elsewhere. For most people, seaweed is just seaweed—any black sheet of seaweed will do for their sushi. Not so, however, with the purists, who seek seaweed "harvested and processed in Japan" because they believe there is a significant difference in taste. This holds true with rice, tofu, soy sauce, vinegar, salad dressing, sake wine, and other items. Japanese brands tend to be two to three times more expensive than non-Japanese brands. These are not, of course, the most expensive gourmet brands like the ones chosen by the iron chefs of TV fame. The shoppers learn to compromise, though, knowing that there is a limit to what is available when living abroad, and one learns to be grateful to obtain fresh tofu, ready-to-slice fresh tuna filets shipped weekly from the East Coast, or Japanese cucumbers and eggplants harvested fresh at Kuramoto's, a Japanese farm near Windsor, Ontario, just across the Detroit River.

Of the many Asian faces you'll see here, some shoppers are Korean, some Chinese, some Japanese. How does one tell the difference between the three ethnic groups? If you are Asian, just stand there and watch. A Chinese person will ask if you are Chinese. A Korean person may look at you but won't say anything. A Japanese, typically, glances at you then simply looks away, for this is the age-old Japanese way to deal with someone you don't know.

But there is more than just one kind of Japanese person living in Metro Detroit today. Drop into Noble Fish and you will meet the three different kinds of Japanese populations who live in this area: the Japanese Japanese, the Japanese American, and the shin-issei.

The Japanese Japanese
The first and by far the largest number of people belong to the Japanese Japanese group. They are Japanese from Japan, temporarily residing here for two to five years but planning to eventually return to Japan. Some from this Japanese Japanese group hold permanent visas, but their number is not very large. Most work for Japanese companies and bring their families, including school-age children. They send their children to local English-speaking schools during the week but keep them studying in their native language at all-day Japanese School on Saturdays or enroll them in one of the private Japanese prep schools. I call this group Japanese Japanese in contrast to the Japanese American population.

Generally, the Japanese Japanese live as close to the way they live in Japan as possible. Most watch Japanese TV news programs via satellite every day. They like popular Japanese sitcoms, read Japanese newspapers, and eat Japanese food every day. I was once surprised to learn a young Japanese mother I was talking to didn't know about an impending snowstorm. She said she was not aware of such weather changes because she never watched local weather reports on American television.

The Japanese Americans

The next-largest population is the Japanese American group. Of Japanese ancestry, they may be the second-, third-, fourth- or even fifth-generation descendants of immigrants who came to the States before World War II. Because the largest number of prewar immigrants settled on the West Coast, the number of Japanese Americans who came to live in Michigan is small. Most came when the Japanese American concentration camps closed at the end of World War II. In a paper, "Japanese," written for presentation, Prout and Shimoura described the situation: "Following the end of World War II, many Japanese-Americans and their families found their way to the Detroit area, away from the anti-Japanese sentiments in their former homes on the West Coast. Many found opportunities to continue their college educations in friendly Michigan colleges, while others found employment with sympathetic businesses."[1]

Some Japanese Americans married non-Japanese, and this trend continues to rise, as noted by demographers Larry Shinagawa and Gin Yong Pang. "In the early post war period, interracial marriages were predominantly between Japanese immigrant women and white men. In the 1960s and 1970s, marriages between American-born Japanese Americans and white Americans became the dominant intermarriage pattern. In the 1980s, there was a shift towards marriages to other Asian Americans. In 1990, marriages with other Asians rose to become the majority of Japanese American intermarriages."[2]

I am not going to discuss here the significance of this particular trend of intermarriages, although it is fascinating. I am interested in whether the language (or languages) of such couples is handed down to their children. Just from my own association with various intermarriage couples, I can say that the children of such couples are distinctly American in language and mannerisms, and often in appearance as well. Unlike the Chinese and Korean communities, which are dedicated to maintaining their own languages in foreign countries, Japanese American communities have not been so keen about requiring their young to study the Japanese language. In "Japanese," Toshiko Shimoura notes, "Language has not been a common thread because most Japanese-Americans are second-, third- and fourth-generation. Very few speak or understand the language."³

The most obvious explanation for this is the deep wound inflicted by internment during the war. Japanese Americans had a far stronger motivation to blend in with the larger American community than other ethnic groups. They did not wish to stand out as Japanese. In such a situation, naturally, the language was the first to go.

The question of identity has been a difficult issue for many second-generation Japanese Americans. I heard a second-generation man say, "I am not a *Japanese* American. I am a Japanese *American*." This probably sums up the view of many members of the second generation, who may look Japanese on the outside but who are American on the inside.

Third- and fourth-generation Japanese Americans, however, are more open and curious about their Japaneseness. Many would like to find out what real Japanese values are, and some want to become fluent in the language that their grandparents spoke. Self-identity is a personal issue, but it is also a social issue. At a Youth Conference in Salt Lake City in the summer of 2005, identity was at the heart of the discussion among young third- and fourth-generation Japanese Americans. They learned that they could talk openly about their concerns and that they are not alone in their quest. Although they are inheritors of a history of injustice, they learned that "they can go beyond the past and become leaders to create a more acceptable society."⁴

The central active organization for Japanese Americans in the Detroit area is the city's chapter of the Japanese American Citizens League. The organization's more than two hundred members gather for activities and enjoy friendships. Although the median age of those in the local group, as in other chapters, has been going up, it is much hoped that the younger generation will participate and keep the organization moving forward.

The Shin-issei

There is another group of Japanese Americans: the wave of immigrants who came after World War II. They were born in Japan and moved to the United States for business or as doctors and researchers in hospitals and universities. When they obtained citizenship and became Japanese Americans, they began to use the term *shin-issei*, "the new first generation," to distinguish themselves from prewar immigrants.

The number of people in this group is quite small in Michigan. On the West Coast, there are enough of them to form their own chapter within the Japanese

American Citizens League. Their children are known as *shin-nisei*, "the new second generation" and *shin-sansei*, "the new third generation." Members of the new wave have less complex identity issues. They know they are totally Japanese inside and out. Although they are legally American and have adopted the lifestyle of the community they live in, they feel more at home speaking and reading Japanese. Their children tend to be bilingual, although English is considered their primary language. Usually, mothers communicate with children in Japanese at home while the siblings use English among themselves. Their number is estimated to be quite small, although it is gradually increasing.

How Many Japanese?

In the metropolitan area of Detroit, the 1990 U.S. Census cites 10,680 Japanese and Japanese Americans, including 4,000 temporary residents. In the 2000 census, under the category of Japanese, there were 11,288, although it is hard to know exactly who was included in this number. According to Lai and Arguelles, "[A]ll individuals who are here on temporary visas such as college students and business people and their families are included in the Census as the 'foreign-born' Japanese-American population," whether they intend to stay on to become Japanese Americans or not.[5] The 2000 census also identified people born of one Japanese parent and one of another ethnic group. Their number is listed as 15,745.

Since the opening of the office of the Consulate General of Japan in Detroit in 1993, we have a more accurate count of the Japanese population. Table 1 compares the number of temporary residents and permanent residents in Michigan in 1995.

The number of temporary residents reflects the trends of Japanese automotive businesses. In large cities such as New York and Chicago, Japanese business offices have been declining in number for the past several years. This decline reflects basic changes in business practices on the Japanese side over

Table 1

1995	Total number	Male	Female
Temporary residents	5,791	2,953	2,838
Permanent residents	798	265	533
Total	6,589	3,218	3,371

Source: Consulate General of Japan, Detroit.

Table 2

Year	Number of Japanese companies
1999	375
2002	352
2003	343
4-year gain/loss	-32 or -8.5%

Table 3

2003	Total number	Male	Female
Temporary residents	7,653	3,999	3,654
Permanent residents	1,389	477	912
Total	9,042	4,476	4,566

the previous twenty years. It used to be quite rare for manufacturing sectors to do business directly with overseas customers. The trading companies, so-called *sogo shosha*, handled negotiations and selling, while the manufacturers simply relied on the service of this go-between.

When the trend shifted and manufacturers started to relocate overseas, they began dealing with clients directly without relying on the shosha. In Michigan, likewise, certain sectors reduced their workforce, but the manufacturing sector has expanded both facilities and workforce because most of the working population is tied to automotive and related businesses.

In tables 1 and 3 above, the male-female ratio of temporary residents does not show a significant difference, but there is a considerable difference among permanent residents. Females outnumber males almost two to one. The trend continues and, in 2003, the total number of permanent residents increased to 477 men and 912 women.

What does this mean? Apparently, there are many single Japanese women who have obtained permanent residency to pursue their careers in Michigan. Additionally, the number of Japanese women married to non-Japanese has increased.

Now, the most recent data show the total count of the Japanese population as 12,027 as of January 2014. A similar breakdown of the Japanese population to show the male/female ratio of the permanent residents or the ratio of permanent visa holders versus nonholders is not yet available for 2014. We can only predict similar trends will continue since one does not see notable changes in the work environment back in Japan for women.

Education of Children in the Michigan School System

About 80 percent of Michigan's Japanese population resides in the Detroit/Ann Arbor–area counties of Oakland, Wayne, Macomb, and Washtenaw. During the period when the Japanese population rapidly increased, around 1990, there was a high concentration of Japanese schoolchildren compared to other ethnic groups in certain areas where the Japanese chose to live, mainly because of proximity to good schools and Japanese grocery stores.

These children did not advance in English proficiency as rapidly as other Asian children. Knowing they would return home to Japan soon, their parents put a higher priority on their children maintaining their Japanese-language and study skills. Although many of the children excelled in mathematics, this did not compensate for the lack of language skills. Not only did problems persist in everyday communication in the classroom, some of the children exhibited serious behavior problems: because they were not able to express themselves verbally, they sometimes acted out physically (especially when they were teased or picked on). Teachers and administrators were exasperated and pleaded for help.

When it became clear that many area schools were having similar problems with the Japanese children, Michigan's Department of Education started to get involved in finding solutions. Dr. Chapman, director of the department, asked me to join in the effort to help teachers. I proposed to run workshops for school administrators and teachers to explain some basic differences between Japanese and American ways of doing things, such as communication patterns within the classroom, approach to education, and many related issues.

For instance, in Japan children are taught not to look directly into the eyes of a speaker. This is an age-old custom of showing respect in many Asian countries, but it can be misunderstood by American teachers, who think that Japanese students are not taking them seriously. Another example is that Japanese children don't ask questions when they do not understand, a concept often not understood by Americans. This custom is based on a deep-rooted feeling of shame for showing one's ignorance, also common in Asian countries.

For teachers, gaining awareness of different customs and learning that their Japanese students should not be judged by American standards of behavior alone are big challenges—but ultimately big steps forward in communication. Getting release time for teachers and administrators to attend such seminars and workshops was arranged through the Department of Education, and I enjoyed working with these educators, who were so eager to learn. I also had to make sure that Japanese mothers are well informed about the customs and norms of school life here, and emphasize the importance of teaching their children basic communication skills in English.

Today, orientation sessions are held for Japanese parents before the beginning of school year to introduce them to the way things are done in American schools. Cultural adjustment remains a concern for teachers, children, and parents, but at least today we know about the issue. More Japanese mothers are participating in school communities and becoming aware of the cultural difficulties their children face. Awareness has also grown among the teachers and administrators of local schools.

Birth of the Women's Club

Experiences such as these were behind the formation of an organization that would reach out to the American community to explain Japan and its culture. There was the Japan Society of Detroit, which had been formed in 1972 with the primary aim of creating a Saturday school where Japanese children could study in Japanese. Now, some of us women wanted to create our own group to enable better communication with the community and to help newcomers from Japan get settled more comfortably. In 1991, the Women's Club was created under the umbrella of the Japan Society of Detroit as an independent organization, open to any woman who wanted to promote these causes and who could speak Japanese. Some 130 women joined at its inception: permanent residents, temporary residents, Japanese Americans, and some Americans. Later the club became a nonprofit organization and was called JSD Women's Club.

From its beginning, the club has showcased Japanese culture to area communities. Its most active component, a choral group, has presented numerous concerts. Tea ceremony experts performed at Cobo Hall in Detroit and at the state capitol in Lansing. Dancers, calligraphers, and *koto*, Japanese lute players, went to schools, retirement homes, and businesses to share their skills.

The club became the "nail that sticks out." With its help we've learned a good deal about our own culture and community while educating and learning from the American people in the community. Many Japanese women who had never dreamed they would talk about their culture in English or demonstrate folding paper cranes to American schoolchildren learned the joy of sharing through such exchanges. Until recently, wives of temporary residents were not allowed to work, so they were happy to participate in activities that gave them opportunities to get to know American people firsthand.

One of the most important accomplishments of the Women's Club was the publication of *Info Michigan,* a guidebook of some 140 pages in Japanese to help newcomers get settled here without too much stress. We started gathering pertinent information as soon as the club got started, and with the help of a word processor and Kinko printer published our first edition. It covered essential information on legal, medical, and educational matters that a newcomer should know and provided a shopping guide to area markets and maps of recreational facilities, including public golf courses. How to drive in Michigan in the wintertime, what to expect when one has a car accident, how to tell your child's school when your child is sick, how to make medical appointments . . . all these helpful tips were given so that newcomers would be able to cope with these new situations with some confidence. We kept updating information, and in 2014 published the work's sixth edition in response to popular demand. Apparently ours is the most comprehensive guidebook published in Japanese. We receive requests from other states as well. We are pleased that our organization has been able to make a difference, helping people who need such assistance.

Japan Business Society of Detroit

The 1993 establishment of the Consulate General of Japan's office in Detroit was a major event for the Japanese community in Michigan, creating an official representative of Japan to reach out to the community as well as protect its people. The Japan Society of Detroit became the Japan Business Society of Detroit in 1997, expanding its corporate membership. In 2014, 253 companies were corporate members along with 1,600 employees of those companies and about 40 individual members. A fund-raising and fund-distributing organization called the JBSD Foundation has contributed money to various cultural, educational, artistic, scientific, and charity organizations in the Metropolitan Detroit area. By the end of year 2013, it had contributed over $1 million to such organizations since 1991. The foundation also awards $30,000 each year in scholarships for qualified schoolteachers and students for firsthand living experiences in Japan. JBSD cosponsors the Japan Festival every year with the Women's Club, a huge event in the fall presenting a cultural show and workshops in Novi.

Contribution of Japanese Companies to Michigan's Economy

A 2003 survey undertaken by the Consular General's Office showed that over two-thirds of Japanese companies in Michigan are in manufacturing, with 60 percent in automotive and automotive parts manufacturing. A considerable number of their employees, 30,065, or 94 percent of the total workforce, were American in 2003. In 2013, a little over half (55 percent) of the Japanese companies were in manufacturing, 64 percent of them in automotive and automotive-related manufacturing. The employee breakdown of 37,020 workers shows the same trend, with 95 percent of workers, or 35,197, local and 1,823 Japanese. The manufacturing plants steadily contribute to Michigan's economy.

Table 4

Year	Total employees	U.S. employees	Japanese employees
1990	25,500	23,950	1,550
1995	36,330	34,730	1,600
1999	35,234	33,476	1,758
2002	34,823	32,955	1,868
2003	31,970	30,065	1,905

Sources: Compiled from the 1997 and 2001 *Michigan Economic Guide,* published by the Japan Business

Although the majority of these Japanese employees return to Japan, some stay and become part of the Michigan community. Their number is increasing gradually, although not dramatically, compared to other ethnic groups. In due time, it is hoped, there will be a sizable group of Japanese Americans participating in community affairs as U.S. citizens and as members of the Asian community in Michigan.

Conclusion

All three groups of Japanese in Michigan—the Japanese Japanese, the Japanese American, and the shin-issei—have come a long way since the Japan-bashing days of the late 1980s and early 1990s. Together, we've proven that the Japanese adage "The nail that sticks out will be hammered down" just doesn't apply when it comes to defending our culture and our people in America. By standing up for ourselves, we have become a vibrant and relevant part of Metro Detroit's vast, diverse community.

Notes

1. Elaine Prout and Toshiko Shimoura, "Japanese," September 6, 1998, 1.
2. Dean S. Toji, "The Rise of a Nikkei Generation," in *The New Face of Asian Pacific America: Numbers, Diversity and Change in the 21st Century,* ed. Eric Lai and Dennis Arguelles (San Francisco: *AsianWeek* and the UCLA Asian American Studies Center, 2003), 77.
3. Prout and Shimoura, "Japanese," 2.
4. *Pacific Citizen,* July 1-14, 2005, 2.
5. Lai and Arguelles, *The New Face of Asian Pacific America,* 76.

10

BANGLADESHIS IN HAMTRAMCK

Durriya Meer

In order to understand the Bengalis of Bangladesh, it is necessary to give a brief sociopolitical and geopolitical history. Bangladesh, literally the land of Bengal, is in its most basic form the product of the British colonizers of the Indian subcontinent and their motto: Divide and rule.

In 1905, under the British Raj, the viceroy of India, Lord Curzon, divided India's western state of Bengal solely on the basis of religion: West Bengal was Hindu; East Bengal, today's Bangladesh, was Muslim. In 1947, India was partitioned into Pakistan and India. East Bengal, renamed East Pakistan, became the eastern wing of Pakistan—again, only because West and East Pakistan had majority Muslim populations. Other than religion, though, East Pakistan had little in common with West Pakistan. In fact, East Pakistan shared linguistic, social, and cultural practices with neighboring West Bengal. Natives of both West Bengal and Bangladesh call themselves Bangali, or the anglicized Bengali. They speak Bangla, or Bengali, although the dialects are different. Even today, it is not uncommon to meet someone in West Bengal who speaks fondly of a childhood in some village that is now part of Bangladesh or vice versa, recalling the pain of having to choose between religion and culture.

Bangladesh is born of blood. Under West Pakistan rule, Bangladeshis[1] had little or no freedom to speak their native language, to travel, or to exercise many other civil liberties. The people of present-day Bangladesh are the only ones in history who fought a civil war to preserve their language. On February 21, 1952, there was a violent uprising because West Pakistan wanted to make Urdu the official language of Bangladesh. To this day, February 21 is commemorated by Bangladeshis all over the world as Language Movement Day with the song "Amar bhaiyer rokte rangano ekushe February" ("February 21 Is Colored with My Brother's Blood").

In 1971 the country fought a violent war to finally gain complete independence. It is estimated that the Pakistani army killed about 3 million Bangladeshis during the war. In many ways, East Pakistan was as much a colony under West Pakistan as the Indian subcontinent had been under the British Raj. When Bangladesh won independence, it had to rise from under the yoke of being colonized twice: first by the British Raj and then by West Pakistan.

Bangladesh is a small country, about the size of Wisconsin, with a population estimated at 166,280,712 in 2014.[2] In its relatively short history of independence, Bangladesh has seen considerable turmoil in the form of both natural disasters and continual political unrest. After the war of independence, Bangladesh had to reestablish its identity. The land of Bengal had always prided itself on its cultural and intellectual heritage, but the country had suffered severe losses. Bangladeshis with the means to do so had immigrated to the United Kingdom in the 1960s as war became imminent. Most of Bangladesh's intellectuals had been killed during the war. Thus, at independence, Bangladesh had been deprived of both its intellectual and social elite; most who were left were of the lowest economic strata.

I first learned of Hamtramck, Michigan, when I was an intern at Michigan State University in 2001. Feeling isolated in this country, I was desperately looking for people (and food!) from my native country. Some Bangladeshi students I met in East Lansing told me about Hamtramck. I assumed that, as in many other towns, there would be one little Bangladeshi grocery store huddled among a vast array of Indian stores—a small establishment that sold halal meat and Indian spices and called itself Indo-Pak-Bangladeshi to attract a larger array of South Asian clients. I certainly did not expect Little Bengal, as Hamtramck has been nicknamed.

As I drove down Conant Avenue, it was hard to contain my excitement: I saw store after store with neon and hand-painted signs written in Bangla! Hamtramck was comparable to what I had seen only in New York City, a true Bangladeshi Bangali neighborhood! Perhaps even more striking was how the flavor of the neighborhood changed every few yards: from eastern European to Arab to Bangladeshi. In a segregated city like Detroit, it amazed me to find such an integrated enclave.

Among Asians, even South Asians, Bangladeshis were late immigrants to the United States. Bangladeshis did not start coming until the late 1980s, with the vast majority arriving from the 1990s on. There were several reasons for this influx in the 1990s. First, political unrest was worsening. Second, a growing socioeconomic elite, the nouveau riche, had come to money suddenly and now had the means to send their children to a better education and life. Third, the United States had started the Diversity Visa lotteries in which people from certain countries, including Bangladesh, could try their luck at getting an immigrant visa.

Earlier Bangladeshi immigrants came at a time when Indians made up the largest number of immigrants from South Asia. This earlier generation of Bangladeshi Americans, because their numbers were so few, had to become completely "Indianized." These are Bangladeshis quite familiar with popular Indian culture such as Hindi movies, styles, and fads from Mumbai or Delhi, who use the generic term *Indian* to refer to everything South Asian. It is disturbing that yet today, on a highly diverse and aware campus such as the University of Michigan, *South Asian* equates to *Indian* and *Indian* equates to South *Asian.* Little or no attention is paid to the other countries that make up South Asia, and their unique social and cultural contributions.

Indianized Bangladeshis thrived among the South Asian community as well as in the larger Michigan social structure. But I think they lost a sense of brotherhood and sisterhood with the Bangladeshis who came in the 1980s and 1990s, especially those who were less privileged. Talk to almost anyone in Hamtramck and they will tell you that those who did well in their new home care little about the plight of those who came later. Later immigrants were seen as FOBs—people "fresh off the boat")—less polished, less cultured, and less sophisticated. It didn't matter how educated they were, what class they belonged to, or how long they had been in this country. More recent immigrants describe Indianized Bangalis with the phrase "Nijederke khoob bhalo mone kore," which means "They think they are better than us." A manifestation of internal oppression? Perhaps. It seems as though Indianized Bangalis guard their American identity by dissociating themselves from newcomers.

Among later immigrants, many of whom came illegally, the first stop was New York City, where they found a community built by the few who had come before. Internalized oppression existed in New York, but there were enough people arriving at the same time that a sense of community was not hard to find. The Big Apple offered myriad employment opportunities, most popular among them driving a taxicab or restaurant work. As individuals settled in the United States, they arranged to bring their families over and created their own version of Bangladesh in New York.

This changed. Bangladeshis found they were unable to prosper in New York, especially driving cabs in the wake of 9/11, and thus Hamtramck experienced a Bangladeshi influx—an exodus from the New York perspective.

According to the U.S. Census Bureau, the 2.1-square-mile City of Hamtramck had an estimated population of 22,100, a slight decrease from 2000. About 7,000 to 10,000 are from Bangladesh and Pakistan. About 900 students registered in the Hamtramck school system speak Bangla or Urdu (the national language of Pakistan is still spoken in some areas of Bangladesh) as their native language.

A walk down the streets of Hamtramck is a treat; the city showcases cultural and ethnic diversity and integration. In the course of a few blocks one encounters women in flowing saris, dark-eyed children, groups of young men playing soccer, mosques, a Bangladeshi cultural center, restaurants catering to east European, Arab (especially Yemeni), and Bangladeshi and Pakistani palates. The mosques and the new flavors and sounds symbolize Hamtramck's transformation.

Hamtramck seems to have emerged as a destination favored over New York. If you ask "Hamtrackers" how this happened, they don't know. It is puzzling that a small, rundown town virtually surrounded by a gritty and segregated city has become home to groups of people claiming different racial, ethnic, and religious backgrounds. But the city does have advantages over New York. Southeast Michigan, specifically Detroit and its surrounding areas, offers job opportunities in small auto parts and electronics factories. Housing is relatively inexpensive. Hamtramck is close to good universities and community colleges, so second-generation Bangladeshi Americans can get a good education without leaving home. The city is small, so it lacks the impersonality of New York. The key element, however, is the enclave itself. Most Bangladeshis in Hamtramck are from Sylhet in northeastern Bangladesh, and those who take the route to Hamtramck via New York are from that region. This testifies to the strong ethnic, sometimes ethnocentric, bond that characterizes Bangladeshis.

However, the fear of being targeted because of race and religion—or of being deported because of illegal status—remains high among the Bangladeshi Muslim community in Hamtramck. Even for those who have the right to be in the United States, settlement and integration into Hamtramck has challenges. For years, ethnic minorities were unwelcome in this historically heavily Polish American enclave. In 2002, a Bangladeshi American became the first Asian American elected to the Hamtramck City Council. Shahab Ahmed had first run in 1999 but lost amid allegations of discrimination in the elections. The U.S. Department of Justice sent monitors for the city elections in 2001. In the aftermath of 9/11, however, Ahmed lost again. Justice officials said they "had not seen such blatant violations of Voting Rights Act since the 1960s." In 2002, Ahmed's optimism and persistence paid off when he was finally elected to the city council. Ahmed's victory was not his alone; it was a triumph for the entire Bangladeshi community.

Bangladeshi Muslims in Hamtramck created an uproar in this historically Catholic city in 2004, when elders of one Bangladeshi mosque asked the city council for permission to broadcast the *adhan,* or Muslim call to prayers. Opponents of the proposal, some of whom came in on buses from out of state to protest, said the two-minute recordings, which would be broadcast from loudspeakers five times a day, would constitute a public nuisance. Muslims countered that the adhan serves the same purpose church bells do for Christians, and the broadcasts merely represented the right to practice their religion. Permission was granted, although detractors argued that such concessions allow ethnic minority immigrants to retain their own culture rather than assimilate into the majority culture. For the Bangladeshi population in Hamtramck, this was a huge symbol of acceptance and integration into Hamtramck and their new homeland.

That the newcomers have caused ripples in the traditionally white, Catholic city is obvious. Some ripples have added to the colors of a city that has welcomed and become home to immigrants from across the globe—Bosnians, Yemenis, and other Arabs, and now the Bangladeshis. But the repercussions have been serious. As the numbers of Bangladeshis increased, they became targets of hate crimes. In February 2006, a group of teenagers attacked the Bangaldeshi mosque and Islamic Center Al-Islah. The attack heightened fear and deepened schisms among the racial and ethnic groups in Hamtramck.

Bangladeshis have always had a very strong sense of ethnic identity. Newcomers in Hamtramck are embraced by old-timers in the area as *amar doorer shomporko* ("my distant relative"). Given that most are from the same part of Bangladesh, Sylhet, people feel connected, whether they are related, acquaintances, or strangers. One has only to walk into a Bangladeshi store on Conant Avenue in Hamtramck to feel a sense of homecoming.

On the other hand, the tight-knit community that makes it comfortable for Bangladeshis to navigate the demands of everyday life has prevented them from adapting to the larger culture. As an ethnic Indian who grew up in Bangladesh, I move fluidly between these two communities. But those who identify as ethnic Bengali from Bangladesh stick with their own people. There are reasons for this. Many don't speak any language other than Bangla. For many, this is their first time in a foreign land and culture. Those who came on the Diversity Visa, who sold everything they had to make a new life here, look to other Bangladeshis for acceptance and comfort. I find this phenomenon truer for ethnic Bangalis from Bangladesh than for many other South Asian communities. I lived in Windsor, Ontario, for a few years, and experienced the same phenomenon there.

This strong ethnic bonding and the resulting lack of fluidity between the Bangladeshi and outside communities have left some people vulnerable. In 2005, the employee assistance program of a large company contacted me to help a Bangladeshi woman whose husband, an employee of the company, had passed away suddenly. This woman spoke no English, had no clue how to manage finances, and could not drive. This situation is not unusual, especially for women.

This ongoing codependence among Bangladeshis has created a comfort zone that very few want to leave, even after they gain legal status. The years it took to become permanent legal residents while living in virtual hiding meant that in some cases people believed it was too late to learn English or adapt to the ways of their new homeland. By this time, many had become dependent on their children, American by birth, to negotiate the competing demands of the Bangladeshi and majority American cultures.

As a psychologist at the University of Michigan, I see many second-generation Bangladeshi American students. As is true in other immigrant groups, this generation is caught between cultures. Second-generation Bangladeshi Americans have their feet on two boats, one flowing with the current, the other against. One boat represents the freedom of attending a prestigious university, looking forward to accomplishments and dreams. The other is the burden of family responsibility.

These students' most common concerns are depression and anxiety at being unable to manage the competing demands of family and academics. Although they are now at school, familial demands are often so strong that it is as though they have never left home. Their weekends are generally devoted to fulfilling family responsibilities such as grocery shopping, attending family or social functions, and attending to younger siblings or elderly relatives. For the family, their child's life at the university is a foreign, inexplicable world. When the parents lack legal status, the situation is even more complicated. For the students, there is no good solution. They do not have the choice of not taking care of the family that depends on them. Nor do they have the option of not doing well in school, because a good degree is their path to a better life.

Just as their parents feel lost in American society, Bangladeshi American students get lost in the vastness of the university. Their numbers are few and therefore their voices are silent or unheard. Some find acceptance through religious identity, in groups such as Muslim student associations. Others, notably the more Indianized ones, disappear into the folds of South Asian student organizations largely dominated by Indians. History seems to be repeating itself with this generation.

One thing that can be said for Bangladeshis is that they are resilient. For many, the fear of being caught or deported is constant. For others, the competing demands of school and family pull them in different directions. But these are a people who have survived one natural disaster after another, one unstable government after another in Bangladesh. According to a recent British Broadcasting Corporation survey, Bangladeshis are among the happiest people in the world, more so than Westerners, with all their material comforts. And to me, there is no doubt that they bring this resilience and cheerfulness with them when they come to the United States. If they did not, there would not be a Little Bengal or a Shahab Ahmed in Hamtramck, Michigan.

Notes

1. For ease of reading, in this chapter the terms *Bangladeshi* and *Bangali* (or *Bengali*) are used interchangeably. Strictly speaking, Bangali refers to an ethnic group while Bangladeshi refers to national origin. So there are Bangladeshis who are not Bangali (such as ethnic Indians who stayed in Bangladesh after 1947) and Bangalis who are not Bangladeshi (such as the Bangalis of West Bengal).
2. www.cia.gov/library/publications/the-world-factbook/geos/bg.html.

11

A BRIEF HISTORY OF FILIPINO AMERICANS IN MICHIGAN

Emily P. Lawsin and Joseph A. Galura

Despite a history of more than one hundred years in Michigan and over four hundred years on the U.S. continent, very few people know about the Filipino American experience. This chapter aims to offer a brief introductory overview of the history of Filipinos in Michigan.

The earliest documented record of Filipinos in the continental United States dates back to the year 1587 and is related to the Spanish galleon trade between Mexico and the Philippines. In the Spanish records, Filipinos were referred to as "Luzon Indians" and were sent ashore to scout out the area of what is now Morro Bay, California.[1] The first Filipino American communities were found in the bayous of Louisiana, where "Manilamen" jumped ship from the galleons and formed eight settlements as early as 1765.[2] As a result of the Spanish-American War of 1898, Spain ceded the Philippines, Guam, Cuba, and Puerto Rico to the United States. However, the Philippines' struggle for independence, first from Spain, began with the 1896 Philippine Revolution. It extended to the Philippine-American War, which began in 1899, on the eve of the U.S. Congress's vote to ratify annexation of the Philippine islands. After Filipinos became U.S. nationals, a wave of immigrants came to the United States, including what was then the Territory of Hawaii. These early *Pinoy*— Filipino American male—and *Pinay*—Filipina American female—immigrants

Parts of this article originally appeared in Lawsin and Galura, *Filipino Women in Detroit: 1945–1955, Oral Histories from the Filipino American Oral History Project of Michigan* (Ann Arbor, MI: OCSL Press, 2002).

included thousands of migrant and plantation laborers, students, military personnel, civil servants, and some families.

As early as 1876, naturalists and botany professors at the University of Michigan began traveling to the Philippines to collect plants and fauna from the islands. Years later, University of Michigan professor Dean C. Worcester began anthropological studies of the Philippines. After the Spanish-American War, Worcester served as secretary of the interior from 1901 to 1913 on the Philippine Commission, a body appointed by the president of the United States to exercise legislative and executive powers in the Philippines. Worcester suggested a competitive exam be instituted to choose elite students from the Philippines to study in the United States. The first three Filipino students arrived in Ann Arbor, Michigan, in 1900. In 1903, the *pensionado* program for government-sponsored students began sending more Filipinos to American universities and colleges. They were followed by hundreds of self-supporting students, many of whom remained in the United States. The University of Michigan also accepted some of the first Filipina students, including Barbour Scholars. Because University of Michigan scholars were directly involved in the colonization of the Philippines, to this day the university holds an immense collection of Filipino artifacts and archives.

Moreover, Frank Murphy, mayor of Detroit, became the last governor-general of the Philippines during the colonial period, governing from 1933 to 1936, the last year as high commissioner. He later became governor of Michigan, U.S. attorney general, and U.S. Supreme Court justice. When he returned to Michigan from the Philippines, he brought many artifacts and participated in many Filipino American community functions. These artifacts are housed in the Frank Murphy Museum in Harbor Beach, Michigan. In the early 2000s, Annalissa Herbert and Adelwisa Agas Weller began cataloguing the museum's Filipiniana collection, with the help of Filipino American residents of Harbor Beach and University of Michigan students, as part of a community service-learning project.

During the 1920s and 1930s, many of the earliest Filipino laborers in Michigan immigrated first to Hawaii, San Francisco, Seattle, or Los Angeles, the major ports of entry for Filipinos at that time. Met with racism, discrimination, the Great Depression, and poor working conditions on the plantations of Hawaii, the fields of the West Coast, and the canneries of Alaska, these Filipinos sought employment or education elsewhere. Many had heard about the booming auto industry in Detroit and traveled there by train.[3]

In Detroit, many worked at the car factories of Hudson, Ford, Chrysler, and Chevrolet. Some worked at the post office, department stores, hotels, fraternity houses on college campuses, or the Detroit Boat Club. Like Filipinos on the West Coast, Filipinos in Detroit were underpaid, so they shared rooms at boardinghouses or rented one-bedroom apartments in which as many as seven people lived. As had the pensionado students before them, many of the Filipinos enrolled in technical schools and colleges such as the University of Michigan, University of Detroit, and what is now Wayne State University. They formed regional, religious, and mutual-aid associations, organized social activities, and published newsletters and newspapers.

After lengthy congressional debates, the Tydings-McDuffie Act of 1934 promised the Philippines independence in ten years and limited the number of Filipino immigrants to fifty per year. World War II actually delayed Philippine independence until 1946.

When the war broke out, many Filipinos in Detroit joined the U.S. Army or Navy. Like their counterparts on the West Coast and Hawaii, most army recruits served in the First and Second Filipino Infantry Regiments, stationed in the Philippines. A select few, such as Atilano Galura, remained in Michigan to work for government defense contractors, engineering firms, or rubber and steel plants.

By war's end, the image of Filipinos in American popular culture had moved from that of savages or "Little Brown Monkeys" who needed to be colonized to "Little Brown Brothers" who had fought for U.S. and Philippine freedom. Many servicemen stationed in the Philippines brought their wives to the United States, taking advantage of the War Brides Act of 1945, which temporarily waived quota restrictions for alien spouses and dependents of U.S. service personnel.[4] Between 1945 and 1952, over 117,000 persons entered the country under the War Brides Act, among them several thousand Asians.[5] Subsequent waves of Filipina/os settled after World War II, and even more after the passage of the Immigration and Nationality Act of 1965, which lifted race-based exclusionary laws.

In our first book, *Filipino Women in Detroit: 1945-1955*, we profile the life histories of three Filipino American women who settled in Detroit immediately after World War II: Tomasa Parinasan Balberona, Rosalina Castillo Regala, and Isabel Aguilar Galura.[6] In the introduction, we discuss how there were other Filipino women in Detroit, most notably Presentacion Ygay (1910-2004), who immigrated in 1938, and Evangeline "Nena" Lopez (1915-2007), who also immigrated in the 1930s. Ygay was a former schoolteacher on the island of Cebu, Philippines, who married Melquiedes Ygay, a U.S. civil servant. As well as raising children, she worked for Detroit's post office and later in a doctor's office. With five other Filipinas, including Tomasa Balberona (née Sheppard) and Nena Lopez, she became one of the founders of the Filipino Women's Club of Detroit in 1952. Similarly, Nena Lopez and her husband, Joaquin, and Rosalina Regala and her husband, Richard, became host families to many Filipinos—men and women—who migrated to Detroit from the Philippines and other parts of the United States. The Lopez family often housed Filipino American families from Chicago, such as the Alayus, who visited Michigan during the summers for Filipino American softball games.[7]

During their history in Michigan, Filipino Americans were forced to find ways to survive the pervasive climate of racism. As in other major cities, they formed many organizations to help them. One of the earliest, the Philippine Michigan Club, was founded by University of Michigan students in the 1920s. Later, in the 1970s, after the declaration of martial law in the Philippines, students and community members in Ann Arbor formed the Philippine Study Group (PSG) to discuss and understand the political situation of the Philippines. Since then, the group has evolved to become the PSG Student Association (PSGSA), which organizes campus events on Philippine and Filipino American issues, while the active undergraduate group on campus is the Filipino American Students Association (FASA).

Off campus, organizations like the Pangasinan Club, the Filipino Women's Club of Detroit, and the Federation of Filipino Americans established roots in the community as far back as the 1930s, 1950s, and 1960s, respectively. Working with other groups, they helped organize the annual Far Eastern Festival in downtown Detroit's Hart Plaza and the Rizal Day Banquet and Balls. The federation even had a clubhouse in Detroit until the 1980s. During the Philippine martial law era of the 1970s-80s, activists with ties to the Katipunan ng Demokratikong Pilipino (KDP), Friends of the Filipino People (FFP), and Movement for a Free Philippines (MFP) organized rallies and forums in Ann Arbor and Detroit. In 1974, the Philippine Cultural Center Organization, followed by the Filipino American Community Council (now known as FILAMCCO) began a fund-raising drive lasting over twenty-five years to establish a Filipino community center. In 1984, FILAMCCO, in cooperation with the University of the Philippines Alumni Association of Michigan, established the Paaralang Pilipino Language and Cultural School. After decades of meeting in homes, churches, and recreational centers, Paaralang Pilipino is now housed in Southfield at the Philippine American Community Center of Michigan (PACCM), which opened its doors in 2001.[8] The FILAMCCO organization continues to sponsor the Rizal Day Banquets and serves as an umbrella association of over fifty Filipino organizations in the Metropolitan Detroit area alone.

Although there are thus so many ties between the Philippines and Michigan, very little has been published about the history of Filipino Americans in the state.[9] Fred Cordova's *Filipinos: Forgotten Asian Americans* includes excerpts of oral histories that Nancy Ordoña Koslosky conducted in 1981 with pioneers Rufino Dumo, Balbino "Bill" Bibat, Jose Mallare, and Victorio Mallare, all of whom immigrated to Detroit between 1924 and 1926.[10] In 2000, the Philippine Nurses Association of Michigan published *The Filipino Nurse: The Dream and the Promise*, a book with interesting poems, stories, and brief glimpses into the lives of twenty Filipino nurses. In 2007, the association published a sequel titled *Living the Promise*.[11] In 2003, Duke University Press published historian Catherine Ceniza Choy's *Empire of Care: Nursing and Migration in Filipino American History*, which includes a chapter analyzing how Filipina American nurses were falsely accused of poisoning patients at the Veterans Administration Hospital in Ann Arbor during the 1970s.

We are thankful to Cordova, the Philippine Nurses Association of Michigan, Choy, and other researchers, such as Eva Fizette and Marita Ectubañez, who wrote her senior thesis on the early Filipino American community of Detroit.[12] According to Ectubañez, the Philippine Historical Society of Michigan, led by Fizette, began an oral history project titled Living Treasures to document the experiences of Michigan's earliest Filipino immigrants. In 1996, Fizette interviewed old-timers such as Vicente Rivera, Presentacion Ygay, Letty Manzano, Feliciano Lictawa, Dionisio Casing, and Fred Gorospe. The Philippine Historical Society of Michigan has since disbanded but in 2004, some of its former members helped charter the Michigan chapter of the Filipino American National Historical Society, hoping to revitalize, continue, and archive the historical society's projects.

Today, Filipinos make up the second-largest Asian American population in the United States. In 2010 the U.S. Census counted 22,500 Filipinos in the state of Michigan. But as time passes, the generations of the old-timers and their children are lost to us—and with them, their stories of the early days. This is why we feel an urgency to uncover more local history before it is too late.

Notes

1. Lorraine Jacobs Crouchett, *Filipinos in California: From the Days of the Galleons to the Present* (El Cerrito, CA: Downey Place, 1982), 9-11.

2. Marina E. Espina, *Filipinos in Louisiana* (New Orleans: A. F. Laborde, 1988). Espina notes that Lacfadio Hearn and J. O. Davidson wrote about a Filipino settlement in "St. Malo: A Lacustrine Village in Louisiana," *Harper's Weekly,* March 31, 1883, 198. See also Marina E. Espina, "Seven Generations of a New Orleans Filipino Family," in *Perspectives on Ethnicity in New Orleans,* ed. John Cooke (New Orleans: Committee on Ethnicity, 1979), 33-36.

3. Letter from Larry Navarro Lomibao and Anita Braganza Lomibao to Melissa Lomibao, November 6, 2000. Larry Lomibao immigrated to Seattle in 1927, resettled in Detroit in 1935, and lives in retirement in the Philippines. *Mabuhay* to our student Melissa, a third-generation Pinay, for her inspiring research.

4. Public Law 271, Ch. 591, 59 Stat. 659 (December 28, 1945). In her oral history interview, Tomasa Balbarona refers to this act. The Fiancées Act, Public Law 471, also temporarily admitted alien fiancées or fiancés of members of the armed forces of the United States in 1946 (Ch. 520 [June 29, 1946]). For more on Filipino American war brides, see Emily Porcincula Lawsin, "Beyond 'Hanggang Pier Only': Filipino American War Brides of Seattle, 1945-1965," *Filipino American National Historical Society Journal* 4 (1996): 50-50G.

5. David M. Reimers, *Still the Golden Door: The Third World Comes to America* (New York: Columbia University Press, 1985), 22.

6. Joseph A. Galura and Emily P. Lawsin, *Filipino Women in Detroit: 1945-1955; Oral Histories from the Filipino American Oral History Project of Michigan* (Ann Arbor, MI: OSCL), 2002, www.umich.edu/~mjcsl/volumes/filipinos.html.

7. Terry Alayu, telephone interview by Emily Lawsin, April 9, 2001.

8. For more on Paaralang Pilipino and the Philippine American Community Center of Michigan, see www.paccm.org.

9. In his classic short story "Scent of Apples," Ben Santos writes about a lonely Filipino farmer who travels thirty miles west to Kalamazoo, Michigan, just to see another Filipino during World War II; see Bienvenido N. Santos, *Scent of Apples: A Collection of Stories* (1955; repr., Seattle: University of Washington Press, 1979), 21-29. Antonio J. A. Pido includes some references to Michigan Filipinos in his book *The Pilipinos in America; Macro/Micro Dimensions of Immigration and Integration* (New York: Center for Migration Studies, 1986). Additionally, newspapers, letters, and the personal papers of early Filipino Americans in Michigan can be found in the University of Michigan's Bentley Historical Library.

10. Fred Cordova, *Filipinos: Forgotten Asian Americans* (Dubuque, IA: Kendall-Hunt, 1983). *Maraming Salamat* to Dorothy Laigo Cordova, the founder/executive director of the Filipino American National Historical Society and the former director of the Demonstration Project for Asian Americans' oral history project in Seattle, for sharing the full transcripts of the Dumo, Bibat, and Mallare interviews.

11. Virginia Skurski, ed., *The Filipino Nurse: The Dream and the Promise* (Detroit: Philippine Nurses Association of Michigan, 2000), and *Living the Promise* (Detroit: Philippine Nurses Association of Michigan, 2007).

12. Marita Ectubañez, "The Filipino American Community in Detroit: Expressions of Identity" (senior honors thesis, University of Michigan, 1997). *Maraming Salamat* to Adelwisa Agas Weller for sharing this source.

.

PART III

Culture and Heritage

Sachi Koto

As a third-generation Japanese American, I find a deep sense of commonality with the writers of these chapters in part 3 pertaining to culture and heritage. They remain closely connected to their Asian roots, though removed by thousands of miles and perhaps generations from where their lineage began, some having never even laid eyes on the lands of their ancestors. The closeness grows deeper as each writer is reminded of ties to his or her heritage through such everyday matters as the preparation, presentation, and consumption of food.

After living in Tokyo away from my Atlanta home for ten years, I was often homesick for real "American food." To make matters worse, authentic American ingredients and kitchen equipment were not readily available in Japan. In this section, Kook-Wha Koh expresses these very sentiments as she writes about her mother's insistence on preserving her Korean customs and culture through cooking in Michigan, despite the obstacles presented by lack of authentic spices and cooking utensils. As an immigrant's daughter, Kook-Wha continues this tradition as she strives to carry on her mother's cooking techniques and customs in preparing meals for her own children—the next generation in Michigan.

Anna M. Shih takes a different approach to traditional cooking techniques and tastes, bringing a more eclectic quality to Asian cuisine. Her creative preparations have just the right amount of Eastern and Western flavors
and spices—blended with culinary and cultural know-how. With her chapter
title "How to Cook Like a Banana," don't expect Anna to follow the traditional
methods of preparing dishes and recipes.

I grew up in the Deep South in the aftermath of World War II. It was not
the most conducive place or time to learn the Japanese language or culture,
and to be honest it was not a real interest of mine until I matured and came
to appreciate my ancestral roots. Frances Kai-Hwa Wang felt much the same,
as early on she was not overly enthusiastic to learn her parents' language.
However, Frances's mother knew it was absolutely essential that she learn
Chinese to fulfill her life as a Chinese American. She gave her daughter an
incredibly lasting gift of culture and pride that is now being passed on to her
grandchildren in Michigan.

Michigan has the same diversity of Asian American populations as
other states. In addition to Chinese Americans and Japanese Americans,
Koreans and Korean Americans have a presence in Michigan, as do the latest refugee resettlement groups who have arrived since 1975. Hmong Michiganders have built their presence in Detroit as well as on the western side
of the state in Holland.

Jeffrey Vang's essay, a combination of personal reminiscence and larger
context, illustrates how Hmong Michiganders take up the public challenge
to represent their community, both to themselves and to their non-Hmong
neighbors. As a key public figure in Michigan's Hmong American community, Jeffrey Vang brings hard-earned experience and achievement to his role
as cultural mediator. He was the first Hmong to join the U.S. Public Health
Service as a commissioned officer and the first Hmong appointee to the Governor's Advisory Council on Asian Pacific American Affairs. In his essay, as
in his life's work, Vang communicates his sense of the Hmong past to others
in the state, beginning his account with questions many fellow Hmong raise
at the outset of their life stories: "Who are the Hmong?" and "What are their
origins?" He also interlaces his account with personal interjections of "According to my grandfather" and "I remember."

Due to their tenacity and unwillingness to leave ancestral cultures
behind, these writers represent the keepers of Asian culture and perpetu-
ators of our heritage. I salute those who have persevered, even through
the lack of essential culinary items and ingredients, and used creativity

and resourcefulness to continue cooking traditionally for the next generation. Hooray for Frances and other students who did their Chinese-language homework on Friday nights while others were out partying. As we third-, fourth-, and future-generation Asians nurture and develop our children, I can only hope that we look back and admire those who have pioneered the way for us and that we appreciate their struggles to keep our cultures and heritage alive.

12

HOW TO COOK LIKE A BANANA

Anna M. Shih

I'm making something different for dinner tonight: Chinese food. Chicken and broccoli stir-fry with garlic sauce sounds like a good, healthy meal after a weekend of errand running.

When people learn I enjoy cooking, they invariably glance at my slanted eyes and ask, "Oh, what kind of food do you cook? Chinese?" While I understand that this is a fine question for sustaining small talk, I want to inform them that being Chinese does not genetically incline me to make stewed chicken feet. I don't even own a wok. The few times a year I do make Chinese food, I make it the same way my mom does—in a sauté pan.

Making tonight's dinner, I follow a recipe for "Chinese-Style Garlic Sauce" from a cookbook called *Get Saucy* by Grace Parisi (clearly not a Chinese person). Parisi describes the sauce as being "a standard in Szechuan cuisine." That's a new tidbit of information for me because I normally think hot and spicy when I think of Szechuan food. While the majority of books and articles about Chinese food are still written by Chinese authors, there are also many non-Chinese Chinese food experts, such as Nina Simonds and Barbara Tropp, who teach me plenty of things about my own ancestral cuisine. While I'm thankful that Chinese food is interesting enough for Westerners to study it, it's hard to shake off the twinge of guilt I feel knowing that they care more about my own culinary cultural background than I do.

In my lifetime, I've owned only four Chinese cookbooks, compared to over two hundred dealing with other types of cooking. One of my Chinese cookbooks came with my mom's old West Bend electric wok (a sacrilegious tool for anyone who takes Chinese cooking seriously).

Like any person who cooks Chinese food only occasionally, I need a crutch as I venture into foreign cooking territory. My everyday dinners are simple: a protein, pan sauce, and a vegetable, or maybe soup and salad. I can make both of these staple meals without a recipe. Stir-fries are just as simple conceptually, but I still need outside help when it comes to the cornstarch-thickened sauce. I double-check the recipe and measure my sauce ingredients carefully because I have no idea what the proper ratio of liquid to cornstarch should be. Too little cornstarch, and the sauce will be too runny to coat the food. Too much, and the sauce will turn thick and pasty. Of course, my mom can hit this ratio every time using her eyeballs as the only measuring tool.

Despite my clumsiness at making Chinese food, I'm no stranger to the kitchen. Earlier in the day, I made apple crisp (from local apples) and a pan of kale crunch, which involves baking kale leaves with Parmesan cheese and salt until they're as crispy as potato chips.

Growing up in southeastern Michigan meant I had no experience of a large, distinct Chinese community beyond my parents' social circle. Mom and Dad emigrated from Taiwan to the United States in the 1960s and started their lives together in Detroit along with a few other Chinese families. At the time, Detroit did not have an established Chinese immigrant infrastructure, which might have shielded us from interacting with non-Chinese people day to day. That, and my parents' zest for discovering things in their new country, made it easy to embrace the culinary knowledge of other cultures. Stereotypical American food, like the potato chips I used to feed to the neighbor's dog, was viewed and tasted with a sense of curiosity rather than prejudice, making Chinese food only one of many options offered to me as my own tastes developed.

Chinese food writing in magazines involves misty-eyed retellings of childhood memories laden with old-world foods—probably to fuel the romantic fantasies of readers dreaming of culinary cultures more fascinating than their own. My own real-world experience, though, is more eclectic than exotic. I do have a few magazine-ready memories, like when Mom and I would make dozens of pot stickers for dinner. I kneaded flour and water together until it was smooth and supple, and Mom rolled pieces of the dough into neat little circles that were slightly thicker in the middle. She pleated the wrappers around a seasoned mixture of pork and napa cabbage spiked with sherry, then fried half the dumplings and boiled the other half. At the table, I asked for *jiang-yuo/ma-yuo/tsu* (soy sauce, sesame oil, vinegar) dipping sauce as if were all one word. We also had plenty of breakfasts that consisted of rice porridge, *xi-fan* in Mandarin, enriched with dried fish or pork, peanuts, and pickled radish.

But I find that other memories stemming from living in the Midwest are as influential as my Chinese heritage in my current attitudes toward food and cooking. Oatmeal-raisin cookies made from the recipe on the Quaker Oats box were just as much a part of Mom's culinary repertoire as her Chinese dishes. Lunchtime in our Detroit home could mean Campbell's tomato soup with saltines and Little Debbie Banana Twins as easily as anise-scented "looed" eggs and stir-fried vegetables with dried shrimp. There was no sign that said, "This is Chinese food" versus "This is American food." It was all "Mom's cooking."

Like many other Chinese families at the time, we went to Asia Merchandise in Warren to buy most of our food, but our food outings didn't stop there. My parents used to take me to the Little Caesars Pizza Treat on Livernois near McNichols to watch the cooks hand-toss pizza dough to order. MCL Cafeteria at Tel-Twelve Mall in Southfield, which existed before food courts invaded malls everywhere, was also a treat for us, offering quintessential midwestern food choices like roast beef, baked cod, fried chicken, green beans, broccoli and cheese, and fabulous bread pudding with raisins. Mom would usually order the "Jack Benny plate," which had half-sized portions at half price, to accommodate her smaller appetite. Shish kebab at the now-defunct Syrian Palace near the GM Tech Center was my favorite meal whenever Dad brought me along to visit his friends in the area.

This culinary open-mindedness probably grew out of necessity as my immigrant parents tried to assimilate in a region with a sparse Chinese community and a reputation for insularity. They encouraged me to be "American" and speak perfect English because I was in America, not in China or Taiwan. This American focus spilled over into my reading habits as I became interested in food that was more comforting than exotic. I devoured the descriptions of cooking in late-1800s America in the Little House on the Prairie book series; I even tried to make some of the foods described in the stories. I also made cheese balls from a recipe in the *Charlie Brown Cookbook*. As a result, I learned how to make so-called American food before I learned how to make Chinese food. Among the first dishes I made completely on my own were creamed chipped beef and chicken à la king, both from Robin Mather's columns in the *Detroit News* in the 1980s.

Desserts were an obsession of mine during college, despite being practically nonexistent in Chinese cooking. Chinese meals end with fruit, like oranges or melon chunks, yet I learned how to bake enough cookies and other sweets for a fifty-guest dessert party at my sorority house. Mom and I also had a years-long tradition of making trays of baklava at Christmastime using a recipe given to us by our pastor's Lebanese wife. Tasters raved about our baklava, proving that it wasn't any less delicious or less Middle Eastern from being assembled by Chinese hands. The baklava recipe is one of my most cherished, and to this day I find it easier to make baklava than pot stickers.

Some of my relatives would probably disagree with me on whether an inclusive approach to the foods of other cultures is a positive character trait. Although my parents unabashedly enjoy non-Chinese food—Dad has a weird penchant for Big Boy, and Mom says that the United States has the best ice cream and orange juice she's ever tasted—their attitudes are different than those of many of our West Coast relatives. To them, and many other Chinese people, any food that is not Chinese within a narrow definition is "American" and viewed with a disdainful sniff, as if inferior. I'm sure there are food snobs who agree with them, but I believe that a big misconception about ethnic cooking is that authentic food is somehow necessarily better food. Many cooks go to great lengths to stay true to a rendition of a dish that some food authority deems "real" without thinking about what surely should be the most important consideration of food: whether it tastes good. Having been exposed to many different cuisines means that I can incorporate the best aspects of all of them in my own cooking and eating habits.

For example, the chicken soup of my childhood is not something I ever want to eat again. Sure, it was quick to make because it involved simply dropping chicken pieces into water and bringing the water to a hard boil. No matter who made it, though, it was always a thin, greenish-gray broth with dots of oil floating on top and usually accompanied by kelp and bone-in chicken pieces still clad in their pale, slimy skins. Compare that to "American" chicken soup: the golden, greaseless cold remedy with broth made from roasted chicken and filled with vegetables and boneless chicken chunks. I find the American version much easier to love, even if it is more complicated to make.

I suspect that in areas where there is a large Chinese population, it is easy to isolate yourself and avoid tasting anything beyond the Chinese food you already know. But in Metropolitan Detroit, the smaller and more fragmented Chinese community makes it nearly impossible to avoid encountering the many other foods that are available. Mom, Dad, and I go to La Shish far more often than to all the area's Chinese restaurants put together (in fact, I can't remember the last time we ate Chinese food at a restaurant together), and my Hungarian boyfriend introduced me to the joys of veal paprikash and kolbasz. Polish food, Greek food, Indian food, and other cuisines are inescapable in Metropolitan Detroit, and my taste experiences are richer because of it. Hungarian paprika, Indian black mustard seeds, chipotle powder, Japanese *furikake* and Chinese five-spice powder all share space in my spice cupboard, ready to accommodate any cooking whims I have.

As I cut the broccoli for my stir-fry dinner, I'm aware that Chinese cooking purists would sneer at the knife I'm using. It's a *santoku* knife, made popular by Rachael Ray on Food Network, and it's a far cry from the Chinese cleavers that "real" Chinese cooks use. I suppose I could blame my mom for that one too, although she prefers to use a large chef's knife to chop the ginger, garlic, and scallions that go into nearly every dish she makes. Neither of us will employ a traditional Chinese cleaver because we both feel the bulky rectangular shape makes it too difficult to control. We've watched with amazement as Martin Yan wields his cleaver like a magic wand on TV, mincing and chopping with ease, but even that shining example isn't enough to convince Mom or me to pick one up.

Traditional Chinese cooks would probably accuse me of cooking like a "banana": yellow on the outside but white on the inside. I don't start each cooking session with the Chinese essentials of ginger/garlic/scallion and peanut oil, nor do I need to have a twenty-five-pound bag of rice to get me through the month. Most of the food I make can be classified as "upscale home cooking": simple, flavorful dishes with no identifiable ethnic allegiance. I was in college before I made dinners that had any resemblance to my mom's, and even then the stir-fries I cooked in my West Bend wok included bottled sauce made by House of Tsang. When I look at recipes to try, I don't even think about where they might be from, at least not at first. Good food is good food, and no single culture or country has a monopoly on that.

Putting together my stir-fry for dinner is an easy affair, especially with a large, very hot sauté pan and a big spatula standing in for the traditional wok shovel. I'm proud of the final result: the vegetables are seared and tender crisp and the sauce glossy but not gloppy like so many Chinese takeout sauces. It doesn't matter that the recipe came from a book that also has recipes for barbecue sauce and béchamel. When I sit down for dinner with my stir-fry, rice, and chopsticks, I feel a little more Chinese at that moment.

But that doesn't stop me from having Michigan apple crisp instead of an orange for dessert.

13

MY MOTHER AND THE KIMCHEE JAR

Kook-Wha Koh

From 1973 to 1996, my mother stayed with us in America. She helped take care of her four grandchildren and prepared authentic Korean food for us. In making our meals, she strictly followed the traditional ways she had been taught by her mother and her grandmother. She did not want to adjust her recipes to the different circumstances of a U.S. kitchen. She didn't always have the right ingredients, tools, and conditions here in Michigan, but she did her best.

One of the most labor-intensive foods my mother prepared was *kimchee,* a variety of red, spicy pickled vegetables. It's a distinctively Korean dish and a national symbol, just as sushi belongs to Japan and hot dogs to America.

Traditionally, we make different kinds of kimchee for different seasons. In the summer we make *nabaak* kimchee with thinly sliced turnips and lots of juice. Nabaak kimchee is usually a clear, watery kimchee garnished simply with salt, garlic, ginger, green onion, and red pepper powder or chopped red pepper. Served cold, nabaak kimchee is refreshingly cool in the steamy, humid weather. The other popular kimchee in summer is *oyee* (cucumber) kimchee because cucumbers are in season and we can get small, fresh pickle cucumbers easily and at a reasonable price.

The autumn and winter are time for *baechoo* (pickled cabbage) kimchee and *kakdoogi* (pickled turnips). The seasonings are almost always the same— salt, ginger, green onions, garlic, small marinated shrimp or anchovies, fruits (usually pears), nuts (walnuts and chestnuts), red pepper powder, and fresh chopped red peppers.

The recipe for kimchee also depends on what province one is from and one's family traditions. In the southern part of Korea, the kimchee is spicier and saltier than in North Korea. The winter in North Korea is bitterly cold; if you put the same amount of salt in your kimchee there as in South Korea, it would take much longer to marinate to the right taste. Kimchee in the south is saltier to preserve it in the warmer weather. There is no written recipe for preparing kimchee. Each family has its own unique preparation methods handed down through the years from mothers, grandmothers, and great-grandmothers.

My mother, trying to prepare winter kimchee in Michigan just the way her mother had taught her, ran into her first obstacle in the matter of peppers. A spicy red pepper powder is an essential ingredient of kimchee. One can use red pepper powder and fresh chopped red peppers together. In Michigan, we found that for red pepper powder we could use chili powder from local grocery stores—Farmer Jack, Kroger, or Meijer's. But my mother believed that the chili peppers available at the stores might be two or three years old and thus they lacked the hot spicy flavor vital for kimchee. With no truly fresh chili peppers at hand, my mother had to improvise. Bell peppers do not yield the requisite spicy taste, and red pena peppers are *too* hot and spicy—they will burn your mouth—so she had to mix several varieties together to get exactly the right taste. Every autumn I would go to the Eastern Market in Detroit and buy four bushels of red peppers—one of bell peppers, one of banana peppers, and two of pena peppers for the preparation of winter kimchee.

In late October, my mother spread out three to four blankets in the backyard on which to dry these four bushels of peppers. The strong spicy smell kept the rabbits, squirrels, and even the neighborhood dogs away. Our neighbors, curious, asked us many questions. I tried to explain but I don't think they understood. They wondered how people could eat so many red peppers without making holes in their stomachs.

For a couple years we were lucky. The weather cooperated and my mother successfully dried the red peppers under the sun. Then she cut them, took out the seeds, and put the dried skins into a blender to make the powder. Unfortunately, one year in October we had so much rain that she couldn't dry the peppers outside, so she put them in the living room to dry near the heating vent. Although she did this in the daytime when everyone was out at work or school, the smell of peppers nevertheless pervaded the house. That autumn everyone in the family had a difficult time breathing.

When we cut the peppers and took out their seeds, it was difficult to pierce the skin without wearing a face mask and Playtex gloves. Our hands burned as if we had plunged them in steaming hot water. And of course our noses were burning, too. My mother ground the dried skin in a blender while nobody was home but come evening, even if we opened every window, the pepper smell would not dissipate. For weeks my youngest daughter especially complained about the "yucky" smell. My mother, however, was happy even through this difficult process. Her hands were rough with many wrinkles and brown spots, but she was preparing the fresh red pepper powder to make winter kimchee for her family.

It was an annual event in our family to prepare winter kimchee over the Thanksgiving holiday—enough to yield a four-month supply for the winter. Merely assembling the ingredients takes two to three days. Required are two or three boxes (about forty heads each) of Chinese cabbage, one box of turnips (about fifty), bundles of green onions, extremely small marinated shrimp, garlic cloves, ginger roots, and—of course—homemade red pepper powder.

On the first day of preparation, we left the cabbage soaking in salt water overnight. Meanwhile, we shredded turnips into the thickness of knitting yarn or angel hair pasta. Then we put all the other ingredients, a mixture called *yangneum*, on the shredded turnips. Cleaning the cabbage and draining the water, we placed the yangneum between the layers of cabbage leaves and deposited the whole into containers to marinate.

We used five-gallon plastic buckets to contain twenty-five to thirty gallons of kimchee. Where to keep the buckets while the kimchee marinated was a problem. My mother thought the temperature in the garage fluctuated too much in the Michigan winter: either the kimchee was becoming sour before the winter was over or it was freezing. But in the refrigerator the temperature was too cold for proper marination. Her idea was to bury the kimchee buckets in the backyard: this was the way they stored kimchee in Korea, especially in North Korea, in her time. My husband and I were not wild about this idea, but my sons dug up the ground and buried the pails of kimchee as soon as we made it. And it worked. After a couple months under the ground at a constant temperature of around 40° F, the kimchee was marinated just right. We started eating from the end of January and continued until the end of March. The taste was unbelievably fresh. Kimchee is eaten with meals, like relish or pickles, mostly with a bowl of rice. When we eat it, we cut it to bite size.

So my mother found a way to stick to two out of her three kimchee traditions. She made fresh red pepper powder and marinated the kimchee under the ground during the cold winter months. The last frustration was the container. She did not like keeping the kimchee in white plastic pails, which she considered suitable only for chemicals or oils, not food. In Korea she had put marinated kimchee in dark brown ceramic jars that have a very shiny outside surface. Usually these ceramic jars are between five and seventy gallons in size. They have heavy ceramic lids so it is safe to put them outside—no dogs or other animals can lift the lids, nor can the wind blow them off. The contents are secure.

My mother decided she wanted a ceramic porcelain kimchee jar. She thought this would make the taste of the kimchee even better. Again, she wanted to follow her traditions. We could not find the type of kimchee jars she wanted anywhere in Detroit, but my husband and I did not consider this a serious issue; we believed my mother was fairly happy with what she had.

One summer she had a chance to go back to Korea to visit her adopted son and her younger brother. When we picked her up at Detroit Metropolitan Airport she was carrying a heavy round item. "Mom, what is it?" I asked. "Kimchee jar," she answered. I couldn't believe it; I was completely speechless. She had carried this bulky ceramic porcelain kimchee jar, weighing about twenty pounds, from Korea to Detroit.

With the arrival of this kimchee jar, our kimchee was the best in the Korean community in Detroit. At least we thought so. More important, my mother could now faithfully keep three traditions for making winter kimchee: fresh red pepper powder, underground marination, and storage in a ceramic porcelain jar.

In the summer of 2001, we moved from West Bloomfield to Northville and many household items were thrown away or donated to the Salvation Army, including my mother's tofu frame and her pounding jar for making powder. But I could not part with this special kimchee jar. I brought it to our new home and currently I'm using it as a flowerpot. But someday when my workload is lighter, I will make kimchee for my family in this kimchee jar, remembering our family tradition.

14

GOING BACK TO CHINESE SCHOOL

Frances Kai-Hwa Wang

It All Started . . .

I cannot believe that I am going to Chinese school again. It's been fifteen years since I finally graduated from San Jose Chinese Language School. Now I find myself sitting at the back of my four-year-old's preschool class at the Ann Arbor Chinese Center of Michigan. I'm furiously scribbling down the words to the songs and rhymes the children are learning, using my own mad mix of Chinese characters, *pinyin* (the mainland China romanization system I learned in college), *zhu ying* (the Taiwan phonetics system I learned in Chinese school), and English, so that I can help my daughter practice at home during the week. The fact that I'm writing with a blue crayon isn't making this any easier.

After class, I fax the homework and the weekly note from the teacher to my mom in California so she can tell me what it says. Then we completely forget about Chinese school until Friday afternoon, when we rush to finish the seven pages of homework before class starts. My daughter whines, "Chinese homework is too hard." I agree. It is hard for me, too, but with a dictionary and a page of translations e-mailed from my mom, I force her to go on, hoping she does not become permanently put off by the experience.

This feels strangely familiar.

I hated Chinese school. Everyone did. Every Saturday morning from 10:00 a.m. to noon we had to be at Branham Junior High School in San Jose, California, composing sentences and learning phrases. No sleeping in, no cartoons, no

Parts of this essay appeared in earlier versions at imdiversity.com/asian-american-village.

going out with friends, no special school events, no sports. Saturday morning was reserved for Chinese school. Of course, that also pretty much ruined Friday nights, too, committed to a mad dash to finish this week's Chinese school homework, sitting at the kitchen table with a dictionary on one side and my mother on the other. "How do you write this word? What is that word? How do you use this phrase in a sentence? What does that mean?" It was excruciating.

American friends did not understand and always felt sorry for those of us forced to attend Chinese school. I remember one blond girl in high school insisting that the principle of Saturdays off from school was "a constitutional right." Jewish friends understood as they had to go to Hebrew school on Wednesday afternoons to prepare for their bar and bat mitzvahs. We never discussed what we actually learned, just that we had to go. It was a rite of passage, a dreaded yet bonding experience all the Chinese and Jewish kids had to endure. We knew even then that it was something we would probably force on our own kids when the time came.

I could not wait to graduate from high school so that I would not have to attend Chinese school anymore—and then, as soon as I started college, I took Chinese classes again—second- and third-year Chinese at UC Berkeley. In my junior year, I went to Beijing to study at the School for Overseas Chinese. In graduate school, I petitioned to fulfill my language requirement with Chinese classes instead of German or French, which in retrospect would have been so much easier, and spent another summer taking intensive Chinese. My teachers always chastised me for having the best spoken Chinese but the worst written Chinese. I could participate in class and orally state all the right answers, but I barely passed the written exams. I just could not keep the characters in my head.

Even after so many years of study, I still cannot really read and write Chinese. My spoken vocabulary does not easily extend past topics of family and home. I forget new words and idioms as soon as I learn them. When writing thank-you letters, I have to look up almost every word in the dictionary. I am very good at guessing meaning and context from the few words and particles I can read, though, and I can bluff my way through signs and menus and letters from grandparents.

But I can speak the language, for which my mother gets all the credit. I am so proud when Chinese people ask if I am from Taiwan or the mainland, and how many years it has been since I immigrated. They are amazed that an ABC, an American-born Chinese, can speak Chinese without an accent. My Chinese friends love to introduce me to other Chinese people: "Can you believe she is an ABC?" The other people gasp, "You speak so well! You do not have that 'ABC accent.' What is your secret?" After a lifetime of not being a good enough Chinese girl (too outspoken to interest any Nice Chinese Boy or his parents), I am suddenly a model for what they want their children to become. It is very unsettling.

Nevertheless, I am still too embarrassed to let on that I cannot read and write Chinese very well, so whenever my daughter's Chinese school passes out a notice or wants a form filled out, I hold the page in front of me and look at it thoughtfully, pretending I can read it, before tucking the sheet away in my bag for faxing later to Mom. Sometimes, if I need to know right away (like the time we had to vote and I could not figure out which box meant yes and which no), I sneak over to a trusted friend and quietly ask her what it says. Other times, I pretend the words are too small or too poorly photocopied for me to see. Chinese school officials ask me, "Didn't you see the giant sign in the front lobby?" "Oh, right, of course, I remember now," I lie.

On the one hand, I view this experience as a second chance for me. If I sit in the back of the room and pay attention for the next fifteen years, maybe I can learn it right this time, from the very, very beginning. But at the same time, if, after so many years of studying Chinese, I am struggling to keep up with the preschool class (these three- and four-year-olds in the class know so many words that I do not—like *ostrich* and *rhinoceros*), what chance is there for my third-generation multiracial girls to be able to learn it at all? Or does that really matter?

When my children were born, I thought the best I would be able to do is to build a solid enough base to hardwire the language into their brains' neural networks so that after they forget it, they will be able to learn it again in college and possibly avoid having an accent. But now, they can communicate with their great-grandparents who do not speak English, they are unembarrassed and unafraid to teach their "American" (they call them "English") friends how to say different things in Chinese, and they see the world as a multilingual place. I am reluctant to let them lose that.

My mom tells me not to be so frantic, reassuring me that if I create the interest, my daughters will want to learn the language in college. She also reminds me that a big part of Chinese school is simply to be with other Chinese children, to see three hundred people with black hair and to not feel like a minority. "And when they become young adults, they can make friends." As I begin to chuckle at the relentless matchmaking of Chinese parents, she protests, "Not just to marry, but good friends—close like cousins."

Does Chinese school really make its students family? Certainly I took many different kinds of lessons that did not affect me as deeply as Chinese school. Regardless of whether we retain what we learn, enduring the school together helps us create the bonds with other Chinese Americans that come so naturally for our immigrant parents. Being surrounded by people who share the same cultural norms as our parents makes those norms seem a little less eccentric. It gives us a safe community in which to be Chinese American children. Going through Chinese school is an important part of being an American-born Chinese, if only because we all have to do it. It has become a part of our Asian American culture.

So far, my girls actually like Chinese school (except for the homework, of course). However, I am the only American-born Chinese parent in the school. It will be interesting to see if other ABCs, the oldest of whom are now coming of age and having children themselves, will continue to send their children to Chinese school. I hope so.

Becoming a Part of Chinese School

It has been five and a half years since I first started going back to Chinese school with my children. My oldest daughter, now eight years old, is in the second-grade class, my second daughter is six and in the first grade, and my youngest, three, started preschool this year. Chinese school has now become the most important thing we do. All our other lessons, activities, plans, and social events come after Chinese school homework and classes on Friday nights. On Saturdays, a Chinese tutor comes to our home to give additional lessons in reading, speaking, and listening comprehension. Our summers are structured around Chinese summer camp and Chinese art camp in San Jose, California, near my mom's house.

My oldest daughter now reads and writes Chinese better than I do. When I show her how to write a word, she always asks, "Are you sure? I better look it up in the dictionary to be safe." When my second daughter needs help with her homework, she asks her older sister, not me. My three-year-old is so excited to finally be able to attend her own class at Chinese school (after going every week with her sisters since she was two weeks old) that she asks me every morning when she wakes up, "Today we go to Chinese school? Why not?"

Even my own Chinese has improved dramatically. When I was asked to read "The Lord is my Shepherd" in Chinese at my grandmother's funeral, my father asked me if I understood a word, hsing, which means "to walk." I answered that of course I did, and I began to recite a children's rhyme (all the while marching in place and swinging my arms at my sides as I learned at my kids' Chinese school): "Hong deng ting, lu deng hsing" (Red light stop, green light walk). I can read Chinese a lot better now, too, but when I do not recognize the words, I pretend to quiz my daughters: "Can you read this for me? What is this word?" My oldest daughter is starting to figure out my tricks, though.

My children's closest friends at public school (we call it English school or *ying wen hsue Hsiao*) also attend Chinese school, so they ask each other every day, "Did you finish your homework yet? Are you ready for the test this week?" Sometimes they help translate for new Chinese students who do not speak English. Sometimes they even speak Chinese together at school just because they think it is fun. Or they "trade words" with their friends who go to Korean school. They compare lunches and envy the girl who has dumplings (*jiao zi*) or wheat glutens (*mian jing*) or rice balls (*fan tuan*). They are especially proud at Lunar New Year's when they can dress up and perform the dance and songs they learned at Chinese school for their "English" schoolmates. If the Chinese school dance troupe has scheduled a performance on the same day as a soccer game, a quarter of the second-grade girls' soccer team is missing.

Once when I gave a presentation about Chinese culture at my daughter's school, the teacher asked me to teach the class to count in Chinese. Afterward my daughter and two of her Chinese school buddies were giggling in the corner because I wrote the number 3 on the blackboard wrong—the middle line was too long. I told them that I was so pitiable because I had never had a chance to go to Chinese school until I was twelve years old, and by then it was too late. They listened very seriously, and my daughter's friends went home and told their mommies how terrible it was that I was not able to go to Chinese school and did not even know how to write "3" properly.

As my children do, I now collect all of my friends from Chinese school, too. Many are officers, board members, and parent representatives, and almost everybody now knows my embarrassing secret—that I cannot read and write Chinese very well (although many still do not believe it; they think I am just being modest). Although I keep declining official roles because I do not feel that my Chinese is good enough, the school has finally found a special role for me: I now write all the official English correspondence. I cannot really translate because I cannot read Chinese well, but if they tell me what a letter needs to say and in what kind of tone, I can do it, and much more quickly and cleanly than anyone else. Instead of feeling like an imposter and hanger-on, now I'm proud I can make my own contribution to Chinese school.

My oldest daughter recently had a homework assignment to write some sentences: "I like Chinese school because . . ." or "I do not like Chinese school because . . ." I was a little worried about what she might write, but I was very pleased to discover that the things she liked about Chinese school outnumbered the things she did not by five to one. The only thing she disapproved of was, pre- dictably, "too much homework." Nonetheless, she now does a page of Chinese homework every day without being nagged and without any help.

I have always worried about raising my children in Michigan because there are not a lot of Asian Americans here and Vincent Chin was killed less than an hour from where we live. I did not want my children to struggle with being "different" or have to deal with racism at a young age. However, thanks to Chi- nese school and the friendships we have developed there, we have found a safe and nurturing community for all of us. The Chinese community in Ann Arbor may be smaller than that in San Jose, but everybody knows us and everybody watches out for us. My children are proud of their Chinese heritage and culture and secure in their sense of identity. Although they are multiracial, there can be no doubt about their Chineseness. That they can also speak, read, write, and understand Chinese is an added bonus—an incredible bonus—that would not have been possible without the security and strength that comes out of our Chinese school relationships. Chinese school has become our anchor.

Our Chinese school recently held a storytelling contest in which the chil- dren were given a set of pictures and thirty minutes to prepare a story—with no adult help and only dictionaries for reference. It was a real test of their Chinese skills. My children (in only the first and second grade at the time), although they were so much younger than everyone else, placed fourth out of twenty-eight teams whose members were third through eighth graders. We were even prouder when we learned how excited everyone was for them, and how many people were cheering for them behind the scenes.

Beyond Chinese School, beyond Translations

The high-pitched, little-girl giggles sail up to me from downstairs, where the kids have all congregated with my dad for the afternoon. Snippets of conver- sation fly up to me—a joke here, an explanation there, a few random phrases that make me worry about what they are doing down there, and a few rough pauses while my youngest daughter tries to get her mouth around the Chi- nese vocabulary she needs. My dad tells a joke that you have to understand Chinese to get, and the kids all get it and laugh uproariously.

I am delighted to notice that, left to their own devices, the kids are choos- ing to speak Chinese (Mandarin) with my dad. It is not easy for them. Their English is much quicker and, like all kids, they find it tempting to lapse into it. Unlike some families in which the grandparents do not know any English, my parents understand and speak English perfectly well. Still, their Chinese is stronger. Therefore, my parents come across differently in English, and the kids would miss the nuances of their personalities and the full flavor of their stories if they communicated only in English.

Even Little Brother, just eighteen months old, is entertaining the troops as he begins to learn to speak Chinese: *chou chou* (stinky), *bi zi* (nose), *hsiang jiao* (banana), *hsieh hsieh* (thank you . . . which he says whenever he gives *you* something), *nah sheh me* (What dat?), and the one that thrills most of all, *Gong Gong! Gong Gong! Gong Gong!* (Grandpa! Grandpa! Grandpa!).

I am often both criticized and praised by my family and friends for putting too much pressure on the kids to learn Chinese. They go to Chinese school, they have a Chinese tutor, they go to Chinese summer school and Chinese summer camp, they take Chinese dance lessons, Chinese art lessons, Chinese kung fu lessons, and more. They always have lots and lots of Chinese homework. They even have a Chinese piano teacher and Chinese babysitters. I am constantly explaining to my kids that although it takes a lot of effort now, in the end, being fully bilingual in Chinese and English will open all sorts of doors for them—twice as many people they can meet, twice as many books they can read, twice as many jobs they can have. However, it is difficult to explain facts of the world economy and job security to a five-year-old. All they know is there's a thick booklet of Chinese school homework they have to work on every day this summer before they can go on to fifth, fourth, and first grades in the fall.

But these sweet and tender moments my children are sharing with Gong Gong are so moving, so precious, that I'm convinced I am indeed on the right track. So today I point out to the kids an argument they can appreciate better: that with both Chinese and English, they can tell twice as many jokes.

When my oldest daughter, now ten, went to France and Italy with my mom last summer, she discovered firsthand how useful her Chinese was. Her three years of after-school French classes were no help whatsoever. However, even when the two were down to their last few euros, they could always be sure of a hot bowl of noodle soup, a plate of dumplings, and friendly assistance in the many Chinatowns and Chinese restaurants they found. Sure, a lot of people in Europe know English, but with Chinese, there is no translation involved (plus the food is better).

Our friend James, an American-born Chinese who does not speak Chinese, was thrilled when we introduced him to the one good Chinese restaurant in town. He had a fabulous meal there when his mom came to visit from New York—and he ordered in Chinese. However, when he later went by himself and ordered in English, the quality of the food mysteriously declined.

James believes that because he cannot speak Chinese, he is served the same indifferent food as white diners. He is dejected because he knows how good the food could be—he can even see it on other tables—but it is just out of his reach. We tease him endlessly about this.

My earliest memory is of my mother calling me in Chinese. I cannot see her face, but her voice comes clearly out of a dense fog: quiet, with a hint of longing. She calls out to me by my Chinese name, Kai-Hwa. Her voice is young and gentle, and I picture her as she was in her twenties—long black hair, horn-rimmed glasses, vintage 1960s Jackie O–style fashions. That is the memory I call up whenever I need to feel her close, wrapped all around me like protective fog. Although I use both my English and Chinese names, my Chinese name feels more like family and home.

Last week at the Puna Fresh Foods grocery store in Kea'au, Hawaii, the kids blurted out something before running off to investigate the gumball machines at the front of the store.

The mostly Hawaiian-looking lady at the checkout smiled wistfully as she scanned our groceries and said, "That's sweet; it's been a long time since I heard that."

My dad and I looked at each other and then back at her, completely blank. We had no idea what she was talking about. None.

She explained, "I used to have a Gong Gong and Po Po. I haven't heard anyone use those words in a long time."

My dad and I had not even registered that the kids had just called him "Gong Gong" because it came out so naturally. Yet the look on the lady's face clearly showed that "Grandpa" just is not the same as "Gong Gong," nor "Grandma" the same as "Po Po." Translations only go so far.

My mom has recently started trying to get the kids to call her "Lao Lao" instead of "Po Po" because our family is northern Chinese, and that's the term northerners use for their maternal grandmothers. However, Lao Lao just does not sound right to me because my own maternal grandmother was southern Chinese—even if my grandfather was northern—and hence we all called her Po Po. My mom also called her own grandmother Po Po. It is really tough for me to get my head around such a dramatic change, so I drag my feet and refuse to discuss the issue.

It is the feel of a word in the heart that gives it its real meaning, beyond dictionary definitions and regional differences. This is the gift I really want to give my children: enough proficiency to be able to feel the words . . . as well as to get the jokes.

15

MEDIATING THROUGH MEMORY

The Hmong in Michigan

Jeffrey Vang

Where do the Hmong come from? It is believed that the Hmong, known as Miao to the Chinese, lived prosperously in southwestern China for several thousand years.[1] They had their own kingdom, rules, and written language. They fought off the Chinese for many centuries, but eventually the Chinese prevailed and destroyed the Hmong civilization. Even in defeat, however, the Hmong were resourceful. By migrating from the plains to rugged mountain areas and living in virtual isolation from the Chinese government, they preserved their identity and culture for the next several thousand years.[2]

Then the Manchu Dynasty came to power during the mid-1800s, and it began an oppressive campaign against the Hmong. According to my grandfather FaiDang Vang, oral history passed down through the generations indicates that thousands were killed and families were separated. Those Hmong who surrendered remain in China today, many living in the rural areas of the southwest. Current population estimates range from 2.8 to 5 million.[3] The older generation still speaks the Hmong language, but the younger generation has lost culture and language through assimilation.[4]

Not all Hmong surrendered during the Manchu Dynasty's campaign of terror. Those who resisted emigrated south into French Indochina, Vietnam, Laos, Burma, and Thailand.

The Persecution of Hmong in Laos

The journeys of the Hmong expatriates were filled with painful tears, according to my grandfather, a former Hmong *tasseng* (canton administrator) in the city of Muong Ngat, Province Xieng Khouang, Laos. Many Hmong families lost loved ones to starvation and illness on their way south out of China. My great-great grandmother, Nyia Xiong Vang, survived the journey to Laos with her two sons, Tong Khue Vang and Chia Long Vang. Her husband and other family members were massacred as they migrated south. The survivors arrived at a village called Phue Xa, Province Xieng Khouang, before they moved to Nong Het, a city in north-central Laos, east of the Plain of Jars. Most of the Hmong refugees arrived and settled in this region from the mid-1800s to the early 1900s.[5]

Around 1893 (no one knows for sure), the French imposed a heavy tax and other duties on the Hmong.[6] (The French colonized Laos, Vietnam, and Cambodia from the mid-1800s until they became independent in 1954.)[7] In protest Chao Pa Chay led a revolt in 1919 called Rog PimPab (Mad War) against the French. The rebellion ended in 1921 after Chao Pa Chay was killed.[8] After the rebellion, the French allowed the Hmong to govern themselves through the system of tasseng in Nong Het.[9]

During this time, there were three Hmong clans: the Ly, Lo, and Moua. The Lo Clan was granted the Hmong tasseng (leadership authority) first; later it was given to the Ly. Each clan wanted authority, and an ongoing power struggle erupted between the Lo and Ly.[10] During World War II, the Ly Clan and Moua Clan remained loyal to the French while the Lo Clan sided with the Japanese, who took over the country.[11]

At the end of World War II, the French reoccupied Laos. The country fell into civil war, with the government-backed Royal Lao Government (RGL) party fighting the Communist-supported Lao People's Democratic Republic (Lao PDR).[12] The North Vietnamese, occupied in an ongoing battle against French "imperialism," sent forces to assist the Lao PDR in their struggle against the Royal Lao Government.[13] The Ly and Lo clans took opposite sides in the struggle: the Lo Clan joined the Lao PDR and the Ly Clan supported the Royal Lao Government and the French to resist the spread of Communism. The fighting between the French and North Vietnamese ended in 1954.[14] As a result, Vietnam, Laos, and Cambodia gained independence from French colonization. As the French pulled out from these southeast Asian countries, the Americans tried to take over what they had left behind, leading to the Vietnam War in the 1960s.[15]

The Hmong were drawn into the Vietnam War through the activities of the American CIA. "A CIA agent, identified only as 'Colonel Billy,' went to the jungles to look for Vang Pao, the Hmong military leader, who had been a soldier since his early teens. . . . When Colonel Billy found Vang Pao in 1960, he asked if the Hmong would be willing to help stop the Communist advance into Laos."[16] The Hmong troops' missions were threefold: (1) to fight against North Vietnamese forces in Laos; (2) to interdict movement of the enemy and supplies on the Ho Chi Minh Trail; and (3) to rescue U.S. flyers shot down over Laos.[17]

The Hmong, under the leadership of General Vang Pao, became involved with the CIA's secret war in Laos from the 1960s until 1975. Many Hmong men served as soldiers, including my father and his brothers, uncles, and grandfathers. Some were trained in Laos while others were sent to Uldon, Thailand, the American headquarters. The Hmong "fought on as best they could, with child soldiers, confident that the United States would not forsake them and would finally prevail. . . . Thirty percent were fourteen years old or less, and ten of them were only ten years old . . . another thirty percent were fifteen or sixteen. . . . The remaining forty percent were forty-five or over. . . . Where are the ones in between? . . . They're all dead."[18]

In 1972, approximately 70 percent of all American air strikes took place in Laos and the Ho Chi Minh Trail. Many Hmong troops and civilians, including women and children, were killed during combat. "Americans did not try to force more Laotians to fight because American military advisors in Laos were now fully aware that the RLA (Royal Lao Army) could not fight well. The Hmong were the only effective indigenous fighting force in Laos—one estimate had it that 20 percent of the Hmong who enlisted were killed, another estimate, seventeen thousand Hmong troops and fifty thousand Hmong civilians perished during the war."[19]

I was two in 1975, and I can remember hearing the bombing and my sister taking me from our hut to an underground bunker. My parents and other family members suffered greatly during the war. Many relatives were killed by the bombing, starvation, or illness brought on by constantly moving from place to place. When members of my extended family returned to our village after the war, many were without parents, children, wives, and husbands. My family's experience mirrored that of thousands of Hmong families torn apart by the war.

At war's end in May 1975, more than ten thousand Hmong waited to be evacuated from Long Cheng, the CIA's secret base in Laos. Tragically, "only one plane load of people was taken out by the C-130, which did not return to pick up any more passengers."[20] As a result, thousands of Hmong were rounded up by the Lao Communist government and sent to "seminars." According to the propaganda, these seminars were to teach people job skills, but in actuality, as witnessed by my father, NengKai Vang, a former soldier trained in Uldon, Thailand, as a forward air guide (FAG), they were concentration camps. There were several located around the country, such as in the provinces of Sam Neua, Attapeu, and Vang Vieng. There are no reliable estimates, but many Hmong in the concentration camps died from torture, lack of medical care, or starvation.[21]

Approximately forty thousand Hmong from across the country managed to escape to Thailand.[22] Many more escaped to Thailand until the refugee camps were finally closed in 1992.[23] They traveled by foot through the jungle—a journey of several grueling weeks. My family fled to Thailand in 1984, when I was eleven. I remember it took us about two weeks to reach the Mekong River and safety. We trekked through the rugged jungle, eating whatever my parents found along the jungle floor. It rained day and night and we were constantly soaked. At night when we stopped to rest, my mother and grandmother built a campfire, and we would all sit around it to dry. I, a young child, usually fell asleep by the fire. In the morning, we went on again in the rain. We encountered the nastiest rain forest crawlers and creepers: termites, ants, bees, jungle-floor leeches, snakes, and mosquitoes. The worst were the mosquitoes, ants, and leeches. The only way to remove the jungle-floor leeches was to sprinkle salt and hot pepper on them. Often we simply let them feed on us—when they got full, they dropped off.

Not everyone who tried to escape made it. Many were hunted down and killed by the Lao Communist government soldiers. Others died from starvation or drowned trying to cross the mile-wide Mekong River.[24] The Hmong who did not surrender to the Lao Communist government or escape to Thailand fled to the country's most rugged mountainous areas such as Phou Bia massif, the highest mountain range in Laos.[25] Many of them, including children and women, died from starvation or lack of medical care or were killed by government soldiers.[26]

The documentary film *Hunted Like Animals* by filmmaker Rebecca Sommer depicts the ongoing genocide perpetrated by the Lao Communist government. This documentary was to be shown before the United Nations in May 2007, but the screening was blocked by Vietnam. Supporters of the filmmaker were successful in having it shown in Manhattan that month and again at the

University of Wisconsin in Madison and at the Hmong Community Center in Sacramento, California.[27]

Hmong in Laos—Our Culture

According to Laos Census 2005, there were approximately 450,000 Hmong in Laos, representing 8 percent of the population of the country.[28] When the Hmong arrived from China, they settled in isolated areas away from the Laotians. They usually lived up in the mountains or highlands of Laos, Vietnam, Thailand, and Burma.[29] From my own recollection, the Hmong chose to live in the mountains or other isolated areas for two reasons: such locations are peaceful and provide a refuge from ethnic persecution, and they offer land to grow crops. Most Hmong are farmers and traditionally education is not a high priority—only a few of those who came to Laos were educated. Children are expected to help on the farm and do not go to school. Some children were educated during the reign of the French colonial government in Laos, but they were from wealthy families. Only rich families could afford to send their children to schools in the cities and not many primary schools existed. According to my father, education for Hmong children did not become widespread until during the Vietnam War, when many primary schools were built with the support of the CIA. The number of Hmong students enrolled in schools "rose from 1,500 students in 20 schools in 1960, to 10,000 students by 1969."[30] For instance, my aunts and uncles were sent from the family village of Ban Nam Song, Province Xieng Khouang, to Vientiane, the capital of Laos, for schooling during the 1960s and early 1970s.

Hmong farming in Laos follows "slash-and-burn" practices. I remember that my parents chopped down and burned giant trees, bamboos, and banana plants before planting corn, other vegetables, rice, and opium. My parents grew the corn to feed the pigs and chickens, the rice and vegetables to feed the family, and the opium as a cash crop enabling them to buy clothes and other essential items.

Although many Hmong people grew poppy as a main crop, only a few became addicted. My grandfather FaiDang Vang and his brothers did, not by choice but as a consequence of social customs. My great-grandfather, Tong Khue Vang, was the first Hmong tasseng in the district of Muong Ngat, Province Xieng Khouang, Laos, during the French colonial government in the late 1930s to early 1940s. He entertained many visitors, and it was the convention to offer guests opium as a sign of welcome. My grandfather and his brothers prepared the ritual smoking and were expected to smoke with the guests.

I know from personal experience that poppy was a very difficult crop to grow. I remember how hard my parents used to work for months on the farm. It rained a lot and they had no shoes, so their feet were always infected with fungus and covered in insect bites during the fall farming season each year. In bad years, it rained so hard that their crops were entirely washed away down the hillside. During a good year, I remember, we had purplish and white flower poppies that stood taller than I. Poppy flowers are one of the most beautiful flowers I have seen in my life, and their fragrance is lovely. I would help my parents collect the opium from the poppy fruits in the cold morning before sunrise. My grandfather and I hunted squirrels that tried to eat the poppy fruits.

Once my parents had collected the opium, my father and uncles would travel to Vietnam to trade it for silver bars, coins, and fabrics. Merchants came to our village, selling clothes that my parents could buy for the family for the New Year Celebration.

Most Hmong families, including mine, really had no idea about the primary use of opium. We were not aware of its dangerous potential until we came to America. All we knew was that it was a good source of income for families to buy commodities and that it sometimes caused addiction in the elders who smoked it. Smoking among women and young people (both of opium and cigarettes), however, was as a general rule discouraged.

My parents, like other Hmong, worked very hard—usually from dawn until dusk, seven days a week. There were no such things as weekends or holidays, except the Hmong New Year in December. Older children were expected to take care of their younger brothers and sisters. Grandparents were expected to help look after the children as well as the livestock at home while the parents were out working at the farms, sometimes for several weeks or months at a time. To this day, many Hmong families in Laos still live in isolated areas. Their children have never seen a car, a bike, or an airplane. So it was with me when I was little; I did not see these things until my family fled to Thailand in May 1984. Today some Hmong families in Laos have moved to the cities, where they are business owners or government workers. Their children are receiving an education.[31]

In 1952 something extraordinary happened in Laos: the creation of a written Hmong language. The writing system, now known as the Romanized Popular Alphabet and used throughout the world today, was the work of Dr. William Smalley, Dr. Linwood Barney, and Father Yves Bertrais, Christian missionaries who wanted the Hmong people to be able to read the Bible. The three mastered Hmong phonics, leading to the written language and the conversion of many Hmong families to Christianity.[32]

The mainstream Hmong religion is ancestral worship.[33] Illness is believed to be caused by the person's spirit being out of the body, a bad spirit occupying the body, or deceased ancestors attempting to attract the attention of the person or family members. The afflicted individual usually seeks help from a shaman, who travels into the spiritual world to bring the spirit back to the body, appease the bad spirit, or pacify the deceased ancestors, whatever is needed. The shaman usually requires the sacrifice of an animal (usually a pig or a chicken). The Hmong also believe in reincarnation. They have practiced their beliefs for thousands of years, from their time in China to Laos, the refugee camps in Thailand, and now in the United States.

In Hmong culture, four special events are celebrated during a person's lifetime.[34] When a child is born, the family has a naming ceremony and soul calling to welcome the newborn. When a couple marries, the wedding ceremony unites their families. After the couple has its first child, a ceremony gives the father an honorific name to welcome him into full familial responsibility. His parents-in-law are invited to provide the name. For example, my birth name is Lee Vang. After my wife and I had our first child, my name changed to Yong Lee Vang. This naming ceremony is similar to adding "Sir" to a person's name. The fourth special event is the funeral ritual, when many animals are sacrificed for the dead and a reed pipe is played to guide the departed soul back to deceased ancestors. The Hmong believe that sacrificed animals are given to the dead to take to the next life. The funeral ceremony lasts three days.

Hmong in Thai Refugee Camps

After the Vietnam War ended in May 1975, thousands of Hmong fled Laos, escaping by foot to Thailand. The exodus took place in three waves.[35] In the first, 1975-77, most refugees were former soldiers of the secret army and their families. They arrived at the refugee camps Ban Nam Yao and Nong Khai. According to Sheng Thao, my aunt, life in the camps was terrible. They had barely any food or shelter. Sanitation was poor. Many people lived in tiny huts. Fortunately, my aunt's family immigrated to Philadelphia in 1976 through the sponsorship of a Lutheran church.

The second wave was 1978-82, "a period when both lowland and highland Laotians fled drought and crop failure, compulsory farm collectivization enforced by the Lao Communist Government, and attacks on the resistance movement."[36] These refugees were sheltered in the Ban Vinai camp. According to relatives, conditions there were much better than in Ban Nam Yao. People were allowed to leave the camp to find food for their families. They were able to set up their own shops. Furthermore, family members who had settled in America earlier were able to send money to help them buy necessities. Although many families lived in poverty, their children had the opportunity to learn how to read and write Hmong, Laotian, and English from former soldiers and educators who had fled Laos after the war. The United Nations High Commission for Refugees supported this educational program.[37]

The third wave of Hmong refugees was 1983-86, when more former soldiers and their families sought asylum from the brutalities of the Lao Communist government. These refugees were placed at Chiang Kham camp. My family was part of this wave. When we arrived in Thailand in 1984, a Thai official working for the United Nations High Commission told us that we would be the last refugees legally allowed to enter the camp. Many families came after us, but they did not have the legal documents required to enter the refugee camp. "By 1987, about 75,000 Laotian refugees were known to be in Thailand. Of these, the majority—about 54,000—were hill tribe people, mostly Hmong in Ban Vinai and Chiang Kham camps."[38]

I recall that life in the refugee camp at Chiang Kham was difficult, very difficult for the Hmong. People were kept in the camp by a barbed-wire fence guarded by Thai police. Anyone who attempted to climb the fence was put in jail or beaten. My brother was jailed for a week for buying an ice cream from a vendor on the outside of the fence, and my uncle was locked up for buying firewood to keep his wife and newborn child warm in December. He was finally released the day his family left for America.

The Thai officers of the camp considered Hmong refugees animals and treated us horribly.[39] Most people wouldn't have survived without help from the UN commission and their families already in America. Fortunately, most refugees spent only a short period of time at the camp before coming to America. Many families were sponsored by Lutheran or Catholic churches in the United States, others by their families who had immigrated in the late 1970s and early 1980s. A Lutheran church sponsored my family, bringing us to Minneapolis in 1986.

However, there were refugees who did not want to come to America. They had heard many stories about the issues that families abroad faced, such as isolation, family problems, the high cost of living—even cannibalism. I remember hearing such stories when I was in the camp as well. Those refugees who did not want to come America, especially those at Ban Vinai, fled to the northern part of Thailand when the camps were closed in 1992. Others went to a Buddhist temple in Thailand called Wat Tham Krabok. They felt the temple would provide them with a safe "sanctuary" to start a new life outside the camps. They also believed that their leader during the Vietnam War, General Vang Pao, would someday return and lead them back to their homeland. Such a dream was shattered when General Vang Pao passed away in January 2011. Since then, some of these families have decided to come to America after spending many years in Thailand.[40]

Hmong in Michigan—The Challenges

Most Hmong immigrants arrived in America in early 1976. American churches, Lutheran, Catholic, and others, sponsored most families. The 2010 U.S. Census estimated that 260,076 Hmong people live in the United States. The vast majority live in California, Minnesota, Wisconsin, Michigan, and North Carolina. There were 91,224 Hmong in California and 66,181 in Minnesota, while Michigan has about 5,924, a decline of almost 2,000 from 2005 estimates.[41]

According to ZongDoua Xiong, an active member of the Hmong community in Michigan, five families arrived in mid-Michigan in April 1976, settling in Frankenmuth, Midland, Bridgeport, Pigeon, and Pontiac. Around that time, several Hmong families came to the Detroit metropolitan area as well.

Life in America began a new chapter for the Hmong people. The Hmong, used to living in the nineteenth century in Laos and Thailand, were brought into the twentieth in America. Changes in their environment, culture, technology, and daily life activities created many issues and problems.

One early problem was literacy, especially among adults. Back in Laos and in the camps, they did not have the opportunity to attend school. They could never have guessed they would end up in a new land where literacy is essential for survival, so they were illiterate when they arrived in Michigan. Since the Hmong written language had been created so recently, this generation learned everything orally. Some former soldiers were able to read and write in Lao and Hmong and understand a little English, but the typical Hmong family could barely communicate with U.S. sponsors, doctors, schoolteachers, and social workers. There were no established Hmong families nearby to help the newcomers adjust. They did not know how to use the phone to call for help; the very utilities in the house were foreign to them.[42] Their lives had been turned upside down.

For the most part, sponsors communicated through action, modeling to the families how to grocery shop, visit medical offices, or register their children in school. Furthermore, illiteracy prevented the immigrants from driving or making use of public transportation. Sponsors had to help Hmong families for several years before they could take care of themselves.

Isolation created more problems for the earliest Hmong families in Michigan. Back in Laos, the Hmong community was usually led by a clan leader who made major decisions for the community. The Hmong had a saying: "In a big forest, there must be a big tree; in a clan, there must be a leader." There are eighteen clans within the U.S. Hmong community—Chang or Cha, Cheng or Chue, Fang, Hang, Her or Heu, Khang, Kong, Kue, Lo or Lor, Ly or Lee, Moua, Pha or Phang, Tang, Thor or Thao, Vang, Vue, Xiong, and Yang—but when Hmong families arrived in Michigan, they were by themselves. In Thailand and Laos, families of the same clan had lived near each other; now these new arrivals in Michigan did not have any idea where the other families had gone. They had no way of communicating with or helping one another. They did not have a clan leader. Who would help them if there was a problem within the family or a big decision to make? They did not have a shaman or herbalist to help them when they were sick.

Moreover, the Hmong encountered severe culture shock in their new land. They found that even traditional family roles and rules were now subject to different interpretation. For example, the patriarchal family structure no longer existed; women were now expected to share important roles in the family and society. Parents who disciplined their children by their traditional methods, such as spanking for misbehavior or disrespect, felt hopeless, unable to understand why they could face trouble for such an action.

As more and more Hmong families arrived in Michigan and across the country, other problems emerged, foremost among them health issues. "Western diseases" such as heart disease, diabetes, cancer, stroke, and high blood pressure struck many Hmong families. From my observations over the last twenty years in Michigan, I believe the rise of these diseases is directly related to changes in diet and physical activities. Food intake has changed from vegetables and fruits to meat and fatty food. Back in Laos, I remember, my family rarely ate meat except during the New Year Ceremony, following a death in the family, or after the sacrifice of an animal for the shaman to bring the spirit of an ill person back to his or her body. Here in the States, Hmong families adhere to the typical American diet, with its emphasis on meat, fatty food, soft drinks, sweets, and alcohol. Such items were not available in Laos.

Patterns of physical activity have changed dramatically as well. In the homeland, the Hmong worked very hard every day of the year—and their work was of a physical nature. Whatever they ate they used as a source of energy for their daily activities. Now, Hmong people in Michigan still work very hard to feed their families, but their work has changed from the strenuous backbreaking kind to office and light manufacturing work. They no longer have to chop and clear giant trees for farming or carry home fifty to one hundred pounds of food harvested from the fields. The walking the Hmong used to do has been replaced by driving. Like members of the larger American society, they simply do not get the exercise they should for optimum health. The results of these changed dietary and exercise habits are clear in the higher incidence of diseases previously rare among the Hmongs.

Additional reasons for declining health may be different beliefs about the causes of illness, lack of insurance, and language barriers.[43] Many Hmong families, especially those of the first generation, still seek help from a shaman rather than a Western doctor when sickness strikes. Western medicines are often misunderstood and mistrusted. Some Hmong believe hospitals and physicians are only interested in taking their money. When first-generation Hmong do go to a doctor for help, they often must rely heavily on family members, usually their children, to interpret. Confusion and lack of trust often result because so many current health problems are unfamiliar to them since they were not common in their homeland. Or the patients' interpretation of what the doctor is trying to communicate may be faulty because of limited English proficiency. Compounding the problem is that this same limited proficiency keeps most first-generation Hmong in low-paying jobs where there is no medical insurance. Others have their own businesses, but it costs too much to buy insurance for the family.

Youth gang violence is another serious problem within the community. According to Richard Straka, a writer for the FBI's *Law Enforcement Bulletin*, "the Hmong gangs started forming in St. Paul and Ramsey County, Minnesota, in the mid-1980s . . . by a group of teenage friends who played on a soccer team . . . to protect themselves and other Hmong youth from the racism occurring in their schools and neighborhoods."[44] The Hmong gangs spread from Minnesota to other states, including Michigan. I remember in the late 1980s and early 1990s, we had the Bloods and the Crips here in Michigan.

The Bloods' gang color was red while the Crips' was blue. These two groups fought not only one another but other ethnic groups, such as African American or Laotian gangs. They stole money, cars, and televisions, sometimes from their own families. During community events, such as a New Year's celebration or a soccer tournament, they would start shooting or fighting. I remember a five-year-old girl was struck in the head with a bullet once; fortunately, she survived. The parents of these gang members were afraid of their own children and did not know what to do. Such problems would have been unthinkable in Laos. Those who committed serious crimes were sent to prison. As time went on, many teenage troublemakers grew to adulthood and disassociated themselves from the gangs. Also, there are more positive role models within the Hmong. As a result, Hmong gangs are not as prevalent as before.

Another obstacle for the Hmong people in Michigan and other states is the conflict between generations. Many first-generation Hmong fear their children are out of control. They blame the American system for the children's misbehavior because they believe if they were allowed to discipline their children as they see fit, problems like gangs, smoking, and talking back would not exist. Most second- or third-generation Hmong call their parents "oldies" who do not know anything.[45] In Wisconsin and California, some conflicts between parents and children have been so severe that the parents committed suicide. The roots of the conflicts are divergent desires between the generations. Many in the second and third generations want to live the American dream; influenced daily at school and work and by the media, they want to assimilate into the dominant society.[46] Conversely, their parents are trying to preserve their culture.

Many Hmong families came to Michigan to work in the auto industry. Unfortunately, as factories moved out of the state, many families have moved as well, especially to states like Oklahoma, Arkansas, and Missouri. Today, Michigan cities with the largest Hmong populations are Warren and Detroit, which have the most, Lansing in second place, and Pontiac with the third-largest community.

Hmong in Michigan—The Successes

The Hmong community has experienced its share of problems in Michigan and across the United States. However, the community has also accomplished much. The Hmong in Michigan are known for their thriving businesses. The first Hmong restaurant, CheePeng, opened in July 1981. Located in Petoskey, it is operated by six partners (Nou Ying Kue, YouaGe Hang, WangTru Hang, ZongDoua Xiong, Chue Lee Hang, and Wang Chao Kue). Since then, Hmong families in Michigan have opened more than a hundred restaurants around the state, serving mostly Thai and Chinese cuisine, although there are also several sushi bars. Other businesses owned by Hmong include dry cleaning, office cleaning, Oriental grocery stores, realty, plumbing, a medical clinic, and auto repair shops. Hmong outside of Michigan, especially in Minnesota and California, own other types of businesses, including funeral homes, nursing homes, law firms, newspapers, flower shops, chiropractic clinics, dental clinics, jewelry shops, clothing stores, grocery stores, Hmong museums, and social service organizations. The Hmong in the Southwest and South own fish, poultry, cattle, pig, and flower farms.

Hmong children in Michigan have performed exceptionally well educationally, considering that their parents are not well educated. For example, WaChong Kue was the first Hmong student to attend the University of Michigan in 1981, and Kao Thao was the first at Michigan State in 1982. Several other leaders are worth noting:

- Dr. Ia Yang Kue received her degree from the Michigan State University College of Osteopathic Medicine and owns the first Hmong medical clinic in Fraser, Michigan.
- WaNeng Kue graduated from Michigan State University in 1987. He was the first Hmong to receive an engineering degree in Michigan.
- Bobby Yang received a medical degree from outside the state and his brother, Paul Yang, was the first Hmong to earn a law degree in Michigan.
- Yee Chang Hang was the first Hmong to graduate from West Point, in 1991.
- Nao Toua Chang, Michigan's first bilingual Hmong teacher, taught at William Robinson Elementary in Detroit in the 1980s.

I myself graduated from Wayne State University's College of Pharmacy and Allied Health and earned a doctorate of pharmacy from Shenandoah University, Winchester, Virginia. In September 2005, I was the only Hmong officer deployed to Gulfport, Mississippi, to support in the aftermath of Hurricanes Katrina and Irene.

Hmong outside of Michigan have received a variety of degrees, and many work in the medical, dental, and law fields. Some have gone into politics, such as Minnesota state senator Mee Moua, the first Hmong woman to hold such a position, Cy Thao, the first Hmong male state representative in the country, and Paul Lo, the first Hmong superior judge. Hmong people live all over the world: in Africa, Asia, Australia, Europe, North American, and South America. Dr. Yang Dao is the first Hmong person from Laos to receive a PhD from France, and Dr. PaoZeb Vang succeeded in having the ethnic Hmong registered at the United Nations in 1996.

The Hmong in Michigan established a community center in 1982 on Detroit's east side. Nou Soua Kue was its first president, from 1982 to 1985. The center's purpose at that time was to help new refugees negotiate interactions with immigration services, social services, health care, and housing. When my family arrived in Michigan in 1988, the organization took my mother to see social services and requested assistance from churches to help my family procure beds, sofas, and a television.

The center also helped find a place for Hmong families to celebrate their New Year. The Hmong New Year is the year's main celebration for Hmong families. Back in Laos, families have huge feasts. Traditionally, this is the only opportunity for young men and women to meet each other with an eye to marriage. It is also the only time when Hmong families rest. The families, believing that each individual has a soul, have a soul calling for everyone. During the New Year's celebration, it is customary to bring all the souls of the family together to the home through the use of two pairs of chickens (male and female), a dozen eggs, and a burning stick. The Hmong also decorate their altars with new rooster feathers. This altar, usually located on the north side of the house, ensures protection and good fortune for the home. Family members are careful not to spend money for three days after New Year's Eve; spending money during this time will result in spending lots of money through the entire year instead of saving. In Michigan, most New Year's celebrations in the 1980s and 1990s took place at Mount Zion Church, Detroit high schools such as Osborn and Denby, and the Michigan State Fair Ground on 8 Mile Rd in Detroit. Lately, the celebration has been held at the Bishop Gallagher Athletic Complex in Fraser, Michigan.

In recent history, the Hmong people had no land or language of their own. What they had in the distant past was taken from them by more powerful people. The Hmong struggled for freedom from China, which took them to Laos. Then they escaped from Laos to Thailand and from there, to America and beyond. In each country, they incorporated some of the new culture to become a part of the Hmong culture. Although there are inevitable conflicts and problems within the Hmong American community, in time, the Hmong people will prevail. I truly believe that the Hmong people have assimilated into the American culture well and they, like many other Asian ethnic groups, will continue to be educated and to prosper.

Notes

1. Paoze Thao, *Mong Education at the Crossroads* (New York: University Press of America, 1999), 29–34.
2. John Duffy et al., *The Hmong: An Introduction to Their History and Culture*, Culture Profile no. 18, June 2004, 4, www.culturalorientation.net/library/publications/the-hmong-culture-profile.
3. Sucheng Chan, ed., *Hmong Means Free: Life in Laos and America* (Philadelphia: Temple University Press, 1994), 1.
4. Thomas S. Vang, *A History of the Hmong: From Ancient Times to the Modern World Diaspora* (Morrisville, NC: Lulu, 2010), 118.
5. Ibid., 136.
6. Ibid., 138.
7. *French Indochina History*, http://en.wikipedia.org/wiki/French_Indochina.
8. Vang, *A History of the Hmong*, 151.
9. Chan, *Hmong Means Free*, 8.
10. Ibid., 9.
11. Duffy et al., *The Hmong*, 5.
12. Chan, *Hmong Means Free*, 10.
13. Ibid., 21.
14. Vang, *A History of the Hmong*, 168, 211.
15. William M. Leary, *CIA Air Operations in Laos: 1955–1974*, www.cia.gov/library/center-for-the-study-of-intelligence/kent-csi/vol43no3/pdf/v43i3a07p.pdf.
16. Chan, *Hmong Means Free*, 30.
17. J. G. Learned, *The Hmong*, part 2, *Hmong in Laos—Bloody Trails to Uncertain Freedom*, www.north-by-north-east.com/05_04_2.asp.htm.
18. Ibid.
19. Chan, *Hmong Means Free*, 38–40.
20. Ibid., 45.
21. Ibid.
22. Ibid.
23. Vang, *A History of the Hmong*, 408.
24. Duffy et al., *The Hmong*, 7.
25. Chan, *Hmong Means Free*, 45.
26. Vang, *A History of the Hmong*, 352–53.
27. Rebecca Sommer, *Hunted Like Animals*, 2007, www.rebeccasommer.org/.
28. Lao PDR, 2005 Census, www.sunlabob.com/data/documents/energy_issues/LG-10-07-Population_census-2005.pdf.
29. Chan, *Hmong Means Free*, 1.

30. Duffy et al., *The Hmong*, 26.
31. Gary Y. Lee, *The Hmong of Laos: Overview of Their Transnational Adaption*, http://members.ozemail.com.au/~yeulee/Topical/hmong%20of%20laos.html.
32. Vang, *A History of the Hmong*, 189.
33. Duffy et al., *The Hmong*, 14.
34. Ibid., 15.
35. Ibid., 19.
36. Ibid.
37. Ibid., 28.
38. Ibid., 19.
39. Vang, *A History of the Hmong*, 308.
40. Ibid., 408.
41. www.hmong.org/page33422626.aspx.
42. Margaret P. Allen et al., "Working with Immigrants and Refugee Populations: Issues and Hmong Case Study," *Library Trends* 53, no. 2 (2004): 301–28.
43. Helda Pinzon-Perez, "Health Issues for the Hmong Population in the U.S.: Implications for Health Educators," *International Electronic Journal of Health Education* 9 (2006): 122–33; Stanford School of Medicine, *Patterns of Health Risk: Hmong*, http://geriatrics.stanford.edu/ethnomed/hmong/health_risk_patterns/index.html.
44. Richard Straka, "The Violence of Hmong Gangs and the Crime of Rape," *Law Enforcement Bulletin*, February 2003.
45. Tamara L. Kaiser, "Caught between cultures: Hmong Parents in America's Sibling Society," *Hmong Studies Journal* 5 (2004–5).
46. Straka, "The Violence of Hmong Gangs."

PART IV

Life Journeys

Pratyusha Tummala-Narra

The life experiences of Asian Americans have remained largely invisible to non-Asians living in the United States and elsewhere. The myth of the "model minority" that has been routinely applied to various Asian groups in the United States has contributed to a silencing of the complexity characterizing Asian American identity. This section, "Life Journeys," offers powerful glimpses into the lives of Asian Americans and serves to transform any singular lens of the Asian American experience. While devoted to the specific experiences of Asian Americans in Michigan, the essays in part 4 share the common task of breaking the silence that keeps the humanity of all Asian Americans from being heard. In this part we hear the details of trauma, loss, change, and joy that fill the inner lives of Asian Americans, both of these contributors and of Asian Americans in general.

Several themes emerge from the writings and artistic works in this section, including the traumas of generational migration across history, the invisibility of internal struggles, the changing nature of identity, and the resilience of Asian Americans.

The authors in this section highlight the ways in which many Asian Americans are raised to keep a low profile, work hard, and keep silent about injustice and racial discrimination. The authors discuss how silence can contribute to invisibility, and how invisibility can become a liability to the physical and psychological safety of Asian Americans. Being invisible can be a double-edged sword: invisibility can lead to an illusory sense of harmony within mainstream society where no immediate threat is posed to one's sense of safety. In this sense, invisibility offers protection against negative attention that can lead to violence and humiliation, such as in the cases of Vincent Chin's murder and the backlash against South Asians after the terrorist attacks of September 11, 2001. The result is fluctuating feelings of belonging and alienation. Catherine Chung speaks to these issues as she recounts a harrowing incident of hostility near East Lansing in which an act of schoolyard aggression left more than physical scars.

The essays in "Life Journeys" explore the challenges of multiple kinds of Asian American experiences. Jen Hilzinger, a Caucasian American, writes about her experience of adopting and raising her children, who are of Chinese and Korean origin. Lynet Uttal remembers what it was like to grow up *hapa*, or "mixed," in Ann Arbor and how being the daughter of a Jewish American professor and a Japanese mother shaped her. Katherine M. Lee describes her fifteen-year separation from her father, who lived in Detroit while she and the rest of her family remained in Hong Kong. Her family's predicament stemmed from the stringent gatekeeping that characterized U.S. immigration policy toward Asians after World War II, a peculiar situation that will surprise readers today because it occurred *after* the congressional repeal of the Chinese exclusion laws.

Dylan Sugiyama explores the ironies of history's persistence when he discusses the legacy of the Japanese American internment and how it haunted his family's life journeys. Likewise, Kyo Takahashi of Detroit reflects on how those ironies shaped his life as he followed a culturally stressed life journey. Born in Japan, he came to the United States and worked as an art director for advertising firms whose clients were American automobile manufacturers, a professional situation that allowed him to see firsthand the growing hostility to competitive imports in the 1970s. That decade saw history affecting other Asian-derived communities, and Mimi Doan-Trang Nguyen shares how her life journey as an American began on April 30, 1975, when the larger historical moments of the U.S. departure from Southeast Asia and Southeast Asian refugee resettlement combined to influence new life journeys for those from Vietnam, Laos, and Cambodia.

The idea that Asian American identity involves a dynamic process of change across one's lifespan is revealed in Elaine Lok's photos and writing, as she shares her vision of connecting with her family and her Asian identity. Lok's work reflects the need that we all share as human beings to discover the unknown aspects of our unique identities by reconnecting with previous generations. In a similar vein, Emily P. Lawsin's poetry reveals the critical importance of knowing one's past, which includes familiar people, places, objects, and sounds from one's country of origin. Her poem complements Lawrence G. Almeda's prose as he remembers what it was like to be marked as "different" and Filipino in Rochester, a suburb of Detroit.

Finally, a life journey that proved to be a twenty-year public ordeal is encapsulated in the remembrance of a single day by Ti-Hua Chang. He remembers the day Lily Chen, the mother of Vincent Chin, left the United States and its "Gold Mountain" promise to live out her last days in her homeland of China. She would never see her son's killers brought to justice because all attempts to call out the racial hate that had animated his killing were defeated. Her life journey would end where it began, and Gold Mountain would prove to be a place of bitter disappointment.

The authors in this section celebrate their connection with past generations and immediate family even as they welcome the opportunity to create new communities. They remind us that the past is a way to understand the present, and they look toward a promising future for Asian Americans, not only with respect to their material well-being but also to the endurance of their voices. "Life Journeys" speaks to the resilience of Asian American communities, families, and individuals. In the past, this resilience has been misinterpreted as the alleged passivity and unidimensionality of the "model minority." These authors challenge us to consider that resilience involves reconnection to the past, recognition of the sacrifice of previous generations, the negotiation of shifting cultural identities, the raising of children who must survive in two or more cultural environments, and the building of new communities.

16

GROWING UP IN MICHIGAN

Lawrence G. Almeda

My palms began to sweat as I realized the magnitude of the embarrassment about to befall me. Mrs. Saucer, my first-grade teacher, had decided to try a lousy gimmick to get us lined up single file for gym class. As she tried to guess what the kids had had for breakfast, I felt strangely alone.

You see, I grew up in the 1970s and 1980s in the suburbs of Detroit. I attended an elementary school in what was then Rochester, now Rochester Hills. My friend of Korean descent, Youngjean, and I were the only Asians— the only minorities, for that matter—in our entire class of about thirty-five. At that time, Rochester was a midsized community with small businesses, woods, and fields. The town was middle class, mainly blue-collar.

That afternoon, Mrs. Saucer decided to line us up in order of what we'd eaten for breakfast. She would name a breakfast food and those who had consumed it were granted permission to stand and fall in line. The honor system was assumed. She probably innocently thought the exercise would be a fun and interesting way of getting the class's attention and encouraging participation from each child. However, she forgot two points: (1) Like most citizens in my community, she didn't know anything about any Asian cultures; and (2) I'm Asian.

Cereal. Eggs. Toast. Inexorably, my classmates left their seats and joined the gym line. Mrs. Saucer's "pancakes or waffles" rounded up four more, leaving me and Youngjean the only students still seated. As those four shuffled toward the end of the line, I looked around in horror, knowing that practically all eyes were on me.

As Mrs. Saucer's guesses became increasingly esoteric, it was clear to me that she would never, ever guess my breakfast dish. However, I could see that my distress and her inevitable failure were not yet clear to her; from the look of determination on her face, it was apparent that Mrs. Saucer believed she had invented a great game of challenge and deduction. It took several more dreadful guesses, including classic American dishes such as eggs Benedict, French toast, and Cream of Wheat, before she finally started to understand the game was lost. I remember my feeling of isolation.

I'd known from the start of this disaster that admitting what I'd had for breakfast—fried rice, which was by far my favorite dish—would be very embarrassing, but until that moment I hadn't realized just how public a mortification this was going to be. Finally, Mrs. Saucer walked over to me and quietly asked what I'd had for breakfast. I answered softly, for her ears alone, "Fried rice." Innocently, she then announced, "Okay, those of you who had *fried rice* for breakfast, please fall in line." A painful silence filled the room as I stood up, looking determinedly at the floor, and joined the line, knowing that all eyes were on me—or possibly on Youngjean, because I then heard Mrs. Saucer's confident voice: "And those who had *fried rice with shrimp,* please fall in line."

I was born in Staten Island. My parents emigrated from Manila, Philippines, to the Big Apple. It was the 1960s, and in the States the demand for doctors was high, so high that positions were being filled by physicians with degrees from foreign medical schools. My father was one such physician. Thus, with English as their second language, my parents-to-be journeyed halfway around the world to America to make a new life—a better life, as they saw it—for themselves and their future family. It has taken me literally decades to fully appreciate the courage and determination such an endeavor required. I now understand. I now understand, mostly, why a lot of things happened the way they did.

In 1968, when I was a year old and my sister three, my parents, still very young, moved the family to Michigan. Apparently, my father had some vision of living in a rural, wooded area. I later wondered why he was attracted to Rochester, since rural, wooded areas do not seem to draw too many Asians today. Nevertheless, Rochester was his choice, a convenient driving distance from his office and the hospital at which he practiced.

As a toddler and small child, I was oblivious to the distinguishing features of the Filipino and other Asian cultures. Of course, I had no substantial experience with any other culture, so there was no reason for me to even have noticed. However, it took only a few days in the first grade to recognize the obvious as Youngjean and I stared at each other, realizing that no one else ate fried rice for breakfast. My parents never really prepared me for this. I guess they did not know how to broach the topic or did not feel it was necessary to discuss the situation—the situation that I was brown and everyone around me, more or less, was white.

In my household, my parents spoke Tagalog, the main language in the Philippines, to each other but were a little reluctant to speak their language or teach their culture (excluding food) to my sister and me. They generally spoke English to us. Years later, they told us they regretted not teaching us the language or culture. But they admitted they were concerned that if we grew up bilingual like them, we would develop Filipino accents. This concept was apparently extremely common among many Filipino immigrants. They believed that a foreign accent would result in discrimination similar to what they had experienced. In hindsight, a number of outcomes occurred in my life at least partially because of my lack of exposure to Tagalog or the Filipino culture. Had I been familiar with my cultural heritage, I would have from the beginning independently distinguished myself from the rest of my first-grade classmates as a Filipino American. Instead I had to discover it through Mrs. Saucer's game, an experience I can only describe as traumatic. It was the moment when I finally realized that I did not look like most of my classmates. I subsequently concluded they must have recognized our differences instantaneously.

Today, I have three sons, aged four, two, and eight months. My wife (also of Filipino descent) and I have learned that communicating to each of them what to expect in a situation prepares them, calms them, and minimizes the unexpected. I believe that this practice would have helped me enormously growing up in Michigan.

Although I may seem to place responsibility on immigrant parents to prepare their second-generation children for the environment in which they will live, I believe community, government, and business leaders also have a role to play in educating the Asian American population at large. My parents could have done only so much to prepare me for my environment. Many immigrants are like my parents were, new to the country and are not familiar with U.S. systems and procedures. Additionally, the governments and environments from which Asian and non-Asian immigrants left or escaped might make them unfamiliar with the rights that this country provides.

Community, government, and business leaders have the resources and knowledge required to educate the whole community. Through education I believe we could avoid, or at least minimize, ignorance like that of my first-grade teacher, no matter how innocent. The way I see it, as citizens of this country we want the United States to continue to be the leader of the free world, and diversity is one of our unique strengths. We need to continue fostering human rights here at home. The passing of civil rights laws in 1964 did not cure the ills of racism. At the very least, basic awareness and understanding of existing ethnicities and cultures across the country are imperative.

When Vincent Chin was killed in 1982 I was fifteen. His killing shook the Asian American community, including my family. Although my parents never really sat me down to discuss this matter, I could tell that they were deeply troubled by news of the murder. So was I. Other than the clear fact that the beating was related to race, I initially could not put a finger on exactly what disturbed me about it, nor could I put my anger into words. Sometime later, in college, I finally realized that the scope of my anger was twofold. First and obviously, an Asian American was killed for purely racial reasons. The Japanese were producing products that were in direct competition with Americans, many of whom responded by bashing the Japanese, including Japanese Americans whose families had been for several generations loyal and patriotic citizens of the United States. That part was easy to figure out.

Second and less obviously, the two perpetrators had mistakenly targeted Vincent Chin as a Japanese American. In addition to their failure to understand the dynamics of an ever-changing business market, the two were ignorant and grossly mistaken in classifying people of Asian descent as a whole—as if Asia was only one country. If (for example) the French had been the ones producing automobiles that fiercely competed against American automakers, I highly doubt that these men would have simply assumed any Caucasian person was a Frenchman. The killing of Vincent Chin was a massive political and racial issue for Asian Americans, especially those in the automotive area, but to me the issue went much deeper.

The murder of Vincent Chin, along with the country's generally mild reaction, opened my eyes to how non-Asian Americans in Michigan possibly had perceived me—not as an individual but lumped together with all other Asians. As an Asian American of Filipino descent, I know that Chinese, Japanese, and Filipino people and cultures are overwhelmingly different in ways analogous to the differences among English, Spanish, and French cultures. I cannot tell you the number of times growing up in Michigan, especially in the 1970s and 1980s, I was mistaken for Chinese or Japanese. I was never mistaken for Hmong, Malaysian, or Thai (to me, that would indicate some knowledge of Asian cultures), only Chinese or Japanese. In fact, some people would ask me, "So are you Chinese or Japanese?" I would occasionally be identified by racist youths with racial terms identifying an individual of Chinese or Japanese descent.

In hindsight, knowing the issues America faced back then, such racist comments do not bother me much, since the kind of people who made them are so easy to spot. More than likely they had racist fathers who blamed "foreigners" for "stealing" their jobs. On the other hand, I was bothered that non-Asian Americans mistakenly identified me as Japanese or Chinese. In high school, my buddy was planning to introduce me to a girl he knew. When he mentioned that he had told her things about me, I was curious and asked him to elaborate. "I said that you are captain of the varsity wrestling squad, from Rochester, a good guy . . . and that you are Chinese." I remarked, "That first part is right, but I'm not Chinese—I'm Filipino." He answered, "Oh, you're all the same to me." I was floored. Even my own friend was not aware that there are substantial differences between Asian countries and had merely associated me together with all other Asians. If my friend felt that way about me, what could I expect from the general public? But in fairness, what was my friend able to learn about Asian cultures in school? Close to nothing.

The responsibility of educating the community at large falls on the shoulders of our community, business, and government leaders; they must implement such awareness training in schools, businesses, and public settings—beginning in primary school classrooms. From the third grade on, my classmates and I were taught the histories of various European countries, including England, France, and Spain. The histories of Asian countries were left a complete mystery. I remember asking Mrs. Schwartz, my fourth-grade social studies teacher, why we did not study the Philippines or other countries in the Orient. Her response was essentially that the histories of "Oriental" countries were not taught because our Founding Fathers had not come from there. Although I did not speak up and disagree with her, her answer was not acceptable to me for reasons too complex for me to put into words at the time.

However, I do remember the Philippines being mentioned at least once a year from about the third grade through the sixth. In social studies, we learned and were reminded each year about the magnificent Ferdinand Magellan, who journeyed to countries around the world until he was killed by Philippine natives, ending his final voyage. Every year I had to brace myself for minor beatings or harassment during recess. Nothing I could say would ever convince these grade-schoolers that I was not related to Lapu Lapu "the Magellan killer" nor did my family help organize the ambush of his shipmates. I just absorbed the typical "Why'd ja do it?!?" questions and the shoves and light hits that followed.

Each country in Asia is rich with historical events, leaders, and legends still to be learned by Americans. There are volumes of data on the science, industry, food, language, government, military, and more in each of these countries. Today, there are strong incentives to learn more about Asian countries and cultures. For example, as the automotive industry changes with an Asian-influenced global economy, it is important to understand the various Asian cultures that are practiced by Asian Americans today. As Asian companies continue to grow and maintain businesses in Michigan, we should more actively embrace educating our people. It will help grow our community and economy and, best of all, improve the majority's understanding of people of Asian descent.

17

SHOVELING AND HEAVING

Michigan's Manangs and Manongs

Emily P. Lawsin

For the pioneer Pinays and Pinoys

When I moved here [Detroit] from the West Coast, I felt like the cousin from
the Philippines who has never seen snow.

Their hands, like my nanay's: the color of worn sandpaper.
Their eyes, gray from perpetual overcast clouds.
Their hair and hearts, singed from Detroit's incinerator fires.
Five or more decades of Michigan winters take their toll
on their bent backs and brown arms,
shoveling and heaving
shoveling and heaving
the white snow until their children come home.

Their dreams, like my tatay's: to fish for a better life, postwar;
or like my nanay's: for an education, suspended by evacuation.
Their jobs, like my lolo's: post office guards.
Or pounding steel for a factory's cars.

Pumping gas while changing diapers.
Changing hospital bedpans on shifts no other nurse dares want.
Designing bombers, engines, and fighter jets for a country
whose neighborhood militias often chased them out,
whispering, "No Filipinos Allowed,"
shoveling and heaving
shoveling and heaving
until they could pay cash to own their own home:
many forced in subdivisions or the far east side.

They teach me to grow umpalaya / bittermelon and kabocha / squash:
"Protect them from frost. Pray and swallow," they say.
Like planting rice: sifting our harvest,
sifting our pride,
we shovel and heave
we shovel and heave
the biting cold snow.

"Anak, you eat now," they say, even to us adults.
Their Ilocano, Kampampangan, or Tagalog accents
all buried under a hint of Midwest twang.
Their children, our kababayans, grew up
playing quiet violin and baseball,
compared to our kulintang and West Coast basketball leagues.
All of us American-born learning only cuss words and names of food.
Sweat tears on my cheek as I realize how
we picked berries and apples, while they
shoveled and heaved,
shoveled and heaved
mounds of iced snow off their backs and their homes.

Now a new generation sails into this harbor
The Great Lakes draining the Pacific of their brains;
washing dishes or flipping burgers,
pending visas and board exams,
they learn to study and leave,
they learn to shovel and heave
the hard snow, much better than me.

So we plant rice together,
teaching this history, these her-stories,
shoveling and heaving
shoveling and heaving,
melting pounds of white snow from our backs and our homes.

18

ADOPTION AS CRUCIBLE

Jen Hilzinger

My husband and I adopted two children, one from China and one from Korea. We are Caucasian. We're often approached by strangers with questions, usually Caucasians but sometimes folks of other ethnicities. "Is her father Chinese?" "Yes," I respond and quickly walk away, lost in a reverie imagining the Asian husband I don't have and what he might look like, how he spends his leisure time, and also what he might want for dinner tonight. Children are not the only ones who fantasize.

But I know full well that my flip response hasn't really answered the question; what the questioner really wanted to know was "What exactly is your relationship to this Asian child and how did you come together as a family?" But I do not feel that any stranger has a right to our family's information simply because we are conspicuously unrelated biologically. "Was your child delivered via C-section or vaginally?" might be a similarly inappropriate and jarring question to a parent.

Adoption is often portrayed in the media as risky or sensational. Either birth parents suddenly decide not to relinquish their rights and want their baby back after months or sometimes years (a statistically rare occurrence, although the media would have you believe otherwise), or some actress is playing Mother Theresa rescuing the orphans of the world. I can assure you, while our story of coming together as a family is absolutely riveting to myself and my husband and on a good day even our children, others might find it a little short on drama. We just wanted to be parents. Unlike some other families, we had not exhausted all fertility routes before choosing adoption. It just seemed right. I have learned that this information belongs to our family how-ever, and I share it only when I am comfortable.

I am not alone in my experience of really way out, intrusive questions. Most transracial adoptive parents and adoptees themselves have heard things they'll never forget, even though the questioner most likely forgot on the way out of the grocery store or movie theater. Many questioners demonstrate shocking ignorance and racism. And these comments don't come only from the general public, either—horrifically, and sometimes most painfully, they can come from within our family as well. "Will she speak in 'baby Chinese'"? a distant relative asked me of my ten-month-old daughter. Some questions you do not even answer. There is simply way too much education needed here. I was not up for the task at a holiday party. Avoiding this relative before she mercifully left was the best option. Again and again we are reminded by the world that we don't fit. Our simple presence allows people to feel as if we are fair game for these intrusions.

I was not attuned to racist overtones in conversations through personal experience or even through secondhand knowledge. As Caucasians, we very often don't even recognize racism when we see it. Perhaps we're hoping that if it is not in our homes or our hearts, it will not exist in society either. Thus I lacked real skills to tease apart the complexities of these encounters. I knew that through adoption, my husband and I were forever altering the trajectory of our new child's life. We did not do this lightly or without a thought to our obligations in the adoption. But as in many things that are important in one's life, I quickly found that adoption was changing the trajectory of *my* life.

Adoption issues have been well researched. I am aware that to develop healthy self-esteem my children need to know their identity and how to rec-ognize and cope with the issues of loss that surround their adoptions into our family. For them to come to us, there had to be an initial loss of their birth family, and in the case of international adoption, that loss is compounded: birth language, country, and culture are forfeited as well. As a transracial adoptive parent, I simply cannot ignore the tools my children need to be brave enough to face these harsh realities of loss; they must have a strong idea about what being Asian in America entails and how that relates to them. The history, present, and future of Asian America are relevant concerns in which our adoptive families must be involved and educated. This, too, is information our children need.

Along with education, our children need many strong role models to be able to visualize their own success. Without these, they may believe that being Asian means being adopted. Or that being Asian means just being one kind of Asian—which, they might conclude, is not the kind they are.

Inside the four walls of our home, we are not different at all. We are all just Hilzingers—a regular family. But in the grocery store, or anywhere out in public, we are Caucasian and Asian. A mixed family. Different. Interesting. And the level of ignorance that greets us can be devastating. If you are Asian American, chances are you also have stories of the tremendous ignorance and possibly hatred that faces you almost daily. If you are a transracial adoptive parent, chances are that you have been surprised by the reactions you get in public. Even seemingly innocuous reactions or comments can leave you feeling like you need a shower—and quite possibly new friends and a new community.

There Are My Experiences and Then There Are My Kids'

Both my children's adoptions were amazing and miraculous events in my life. I became a mom, a dream I'd had since childhood. The reality for our infant children, most likely, is that those days were among the scariest of their lives—new parents, new smells, new noises, new everything. Probably they came to us with serious abandonment fears and anxieties, the perfect beginnings for attachment issues. All good parents whose children have experienced a loss have to learn specific skills in reaching out to their kids so they can gradually learn to love and trust. Adoptive parents are no different.

I have grown in my role as a mom, incorporating my children's needs into my own, as it should be. I have had to develop a more hardened response to intrusive questions. I am particularly proud of my lovely blank stare. I must now protect my children from unwanted encounters that may lead to negative feelings in my kids. And I must be their stalwart advocate in the event they are attacked, either physically or with words of hate. Ignoring racism is not an option anymore. And allowing racist jokes and comments to go unacknowledged in my presence is also not an option. These were always uncomfortable experiences for me, but now it has become my duty to challenge them. Being a mom empowered me to make changes in my behavior.

Racism and Adoptism—Minority within a Minority

Adoption doesn't end when all the paperwork is signed; it continues to play a large part in our lives and always will. Adoption issues have sculpted my children and my family and are just one of the aspects of parenting in which we've educated ourselves. I've had wonderful mentors over the years, although often I still have had to learn the hard way. Shame-filled rages are *not* an efficient way of getting your child to eat her peas. On the other end of the parenting spectrum, "stepping on eggshells" around a child who is dealing with the unfairness of being adopted is another horrible way to be a family and often creates children who feel super powerful over adults. I know both of these scenarios intimately. We've made all of the mistakes.

I have also learned the hard way when it comes to choosing adoptive parenting mentors. Having the open mind required to look for solutions as an adoptive parent sometimes can set us up to be misled by those who claim expert status. Some had strong opinions and weak experience; the "expertise" of some was entirely self-proclaimed. Checklists and step-by-step instruction manuals do not apply to parenting. If you want to find out how to raise healthy adopted children into adulthood, find someone who has done it. If you want to learn how to teach your kids about racism and aid them in creating healthy identities, which include their race, find someone who has experienced it and is teaching these valuable lessons to their own children.

Another Layer—Racial Identity

The fact is that we as parents are missing certain key pieces of information that our kids need to learn. We have to go to the real experts sometimes. But we cannot send our children alone. Nor can we wait for them to grow up and figure it out on their own.

We are their parents. Even though we don't have the information that only experience teaches, we can find those who do and reach out to them. We have to become connected to our children's ethnic community and learn the ways that these groups have handled issues like dual identity and racism. We have to admit that our society is racist. We have to dig up the racist views that we still hang on to ourselves and look them square in the eye, and then set them aside to become comfortable with everyone of color. It was only after I did this—and dedicated myself to continually renewing my efforts that I was able to really see people as people. Dividing lines have disappeared and my life, friends, and community have changed.

I used to believe that any type of talk about race was racist, and conversations on the subject made me uncomfortable. I considered myself "race neutral," totally color-blind, and thought this was the way to raise my family. I am ashamed to admit that before I became the mom in an Asian American family, I thought that maybe there was still racism against African Americans, but certainly not against Asians. I had definitely subscribed to the "model minority myth," and it was undoubtedly going to drive an enormous wedge in my family if I didn't unpack my racist ideas and confront them. I had to just plain grow up and drop my idealism: all that was going to do was teach my kids how to ignore problems.

With the patient help of wonderful friends and mentors, I began to see the world through the experience of a minority in our society. What I saw made me guilty, mad, and incredibly sad for my children. I mean, my kids are absolutely perfect: how could it be that someone might not see that because of the way they look? How were they going to even attempt to maneuver through racism without feeling Asian? Were they really going to think of themselves as Caucasian? Could they ignore their race?

Could I?

In a moment of pure openness and slight desperation, I called the local Chinese Missionary Alliance Church in my area. My daughter was nine months old, and already I had received enough strange looks and awkward smiles from strangers to know that I needed some Asian American allies. I was beginning to understand that I had to reach beyond our four walls to teach my beautiful daughter everything she was going to need to know. So I called. The answering machine kicked on and what was said was all in Chinese. I assumed that at some point the voice on the machine said, "Leave a message after the beep," so I left my name, number, and a lighthearted inquiry if someone might like to come and talk to a small group of parents with babies adopted from China. I tried not to let on the real fear motivating my call: that adopting this precious bundle was perhaps more than I could handle. I received a call about two hours later from the pastor of the church, speaking English, who gave me the name and number of a young woman recently arrived from China, a former teacher (like me!) who he thought would love to come and talk. Little did I know that this woman and I would become best friends after a few years of top-down conversations in which I was her student and she my teacher.

We were so different in many ways. She and her family had lived through the Cultural Revolution. Her father, considered a "rightist" by the Chinese government in the 1960s and 1970s, was sent to the countryside for reeducation like so many of his counterparts. I had only read about such things. Although she and I were roughly the same age, I couldn't believe how different our upbringings had been. And yet how similar our outlooks on life are today. I grew to know and love her and her family through her tales of life in China and what it is like to be Chinese in the United States. One day she said, "I would like to be Emily's A-yi." "Okay," I said cheerfully. My Chinese had grown and I knew she was offering to be my daughter's "auntie." No child can have too many loving aunts.

Over the past ten years, I've grown to understand the real meaning of A-yi. My friend has proven a stalwart protector of my daughter—ever vigilant of her education, improving her understanding of China and being Chinese in America, and letting her in on tricks and secrets about mathematics and logic—passions they share. I trust her implicitly and when, five years ago, her own beautiful daughter was born, I finally had the chance to repay some of what she has given me and my children. Feeling the burden of responsibility that only mothers can feel, she said, "I've helped you figure out how to raise your Chinese American daughter, now you need to help me raise my Chinese American daughter." I still get chills when I think about it. Today we continue to create a new and unique friendship, a bond based on our tremendous love for our children. It is staggering how much we share as we both try to negotiate two cultures, two countries.

A-yi has experienced the rough edges of life in the United States. She does not internalize them, but she sees them all—the doctor's office hanging up on her after claiming they can't understand her accent, the times she's been left out of important meetings at work. A-yi is a "forever foreigner" just because of the way she looks and sounds, no matter how long she has lived in this country.

And these, too, are important lessons she has to teach my daughter. Emily herself speaks English without an accent, but this is one of the struggles within her community of Asian American immigrants and so it is her struggle, too.

Reaching Out and Reaching In

Once I saw clearly that my kids were in danger of not identifying themselves as "real Asian" or even Asian at all, I had to act to mitigate that risk. I needed more than my growing friendship with A-yi and its valuable lessons. I needed the fabric of our lives to include some threads of Asian America.

I've heard adoptive parents argue that they don't want to "go overboard with the Asian stuff." They claim that their kids are American too, right? This has now become an offensive comment to me. How could we possibly harm our children with "too much Asia?" This belief is most certainly coming either from an inexperienced parent, as I once was, or someone who is stuck on the idea that being Asian means not being American.

I am not the only adoptive parent who has reached out to the Asian American community for help—that's certain. And many of us have learned that there must be reciprocity; you must bring something to the table to be taken seriously. With the information and confidence I was gaining from learning about our daughter's birth country and being able to talk freely with A-yi about anything, I began to see that as the mom in an Asian American family, I had a role to play in this community—indeed, I owed something to it in return for what it was offering me and my family. We know that we can gain mentors, information, and support, and clearly our children will contribute their own unique opinions and gifts to this community, but what can Caucasian adoptive parents offer the Asian American community? We have to move beyond passively being hosted by these communities to working alongside folks educating others and breaking down walls.

Some Caucasian adoptive parents do not see themselves as part of the Asian American community or experience. Equally, some Asian Americans do not view adoptive parents as having a role within this community. It can be difficult to find a group of people who will support your love for your children and care enough about their well-being to let you in. But when you find such a group, jump in with both feet. And if you are insecure at first, take on a necessary role. Most groups are in great need of "doers." And perhaps the most important piece of advice I can give is this: take any invitation very seriously. I've seen many adoptive parents overlook sincere invitations proffered by the Asian American community and individuals.

One caveat—while I am strongly urging transracial Asian adoptive parents to avail themselves of the Asian American community to carve out a place for their children and their families, I am not suggesting that Caucasians should take the lead in framing issues for Asian Americans. It is a fine line, but one worth walking. It was our decision to adopt transracially. It makes sense that we, not our kids, should be the ones working hard, the ones sometimes feeling uncomfortable. We need to learn the rules of these organizations before we even consider that we have a place there. Some Asian American groups are striving toward identity formation in America and what that means for them. Look for groups that are interested in diversity—don't stay too long in a place that clearly doesn't fit.

Lessons Being Learned

Some adoptive parents I have spoken to about these issues say, "We send our son/daughter to Korean/Chinese school every Saturday," apparently believing that is enough. I couldn't help wondering, is this my role? To drop my kids off on Saturdays so they can "learn how" to be Korean or Chinese? How would this help *me* be a better mom? How would I be able to relate to my kids and their needs? Wouldn't this create a wedge in our family? Wouldn't teaching my child that she can't be Korean or Chinese at home, only on Saturdays, further exacerbate the "duality" of her identity?

I realized that many of the goals and aspirations that we had as a family matched almost identically those of other Asian American families. How do I teach my child about his origins without making him feel more different? How do I ensure that my child values Asian America and sees its relevance? How much culture is too much? How much is enough? Should he/she/we learn to speak the language? What is "authentic Asian"? Will my kids ever be able to claim that? These questions can be hard and they don't yield easy answers. It is nice to find others struggling with the same issues.

Is Identity a Continuum? Is It Changeable?

Such conversations fueled me into thinking more deeply about how racial identity is formed and what factors play into its formation. What I want at the deepest level is for my kids to formulate a healthy and robust Asian American image and self-esteem. I want to work on issues that affect my family, like discrimination and racism. I'm not Asian, but I have the ability to empathize, listen, and learn. With a little forethought, a lot of listening to the true experts, and plenty of love, our confidence as an Asian American family grows.

I feel a responsibility to claim a spot within the Asian American community in order to educate myself properly and to be a good mom in this Asian American family. Maybe I am simply a "placeholder" for my children until they mature into their own places within this community, but I believe there is a role for me. When we adopted our two children and began this new family, we changed forever our present and our future. Adoption has been our crucible, and the application of enough heat (putting myself out there in the Asian American community) created a change in the chemistry of our lives and identities as a family. For that, I am humbly grateful.

19

THE LONG HOMECOMING

Being Chinese and American in Michigan

Katherine M. Lee

I was born in Hong Kong. My father left to come to Detroit in 1951 before
I was born. He left behind a beautiful young wife, pregnant with me then,
and a sweet two-year-old, my sister. My father worked hard for long hours,
enduring many lonely nights, so he could save enough money to bring us to
America for a better future. That was his promise to my mother.

My father was a man of his word. As soon as he saved enough money,
he applied for visas for his family to come to America. There was an error
somehow, however: U.S. immigration authorities did not believe that we were
my father's true family. My father hired lawyer after lawyer and haunted the
immigration office in Detroit week after week, month after month, and year
after year, but still he was not able to cut through all the red tape and win
approval for our immigration. My father was heartbroken, anxious, and very
lonely. But he did not give up.

For fifteen years, my mother raised us all by herself. She worried all the
time. Would my father give up and forget about us? Would he stop sending
money home, as some of her friends' husbands had? What if my sister or I
died? How would she be able to face my father? In those days, my mother's
life held no peace.

Although I had never met my father, growing up thousands of miles away
from him, he earned my respect. I can still remember that during the almost
fifteen years we were separated, every Tuesday—you could bet your life on

it—there would be a letter in the mailbox from my father to my mother. And every month, he sent a check to cover all our expenses. My father also wrote letters to my sister and me. Trying to teach us as he would have if we'd been together as a family, he wrote to us about honesty, integrity, humility, and kindness. Above all, he taught us to use our good fortune to help those in need. I respected my father.

His persistence finally paid off and our visas were approved. I remember very well the day we arrived in America. Newspaper reporters and TV crews were waiting at the airport to interview us. They especially wanted to meet my father, this man who had persevered for so long, a man who had kept his promise to his family, never giving up until he had brought us to America. We were headline news for two days; on August 30, 1967, the *Detroit News* announced, "Family Reunited as 16-Year Quest Ends."

My father's friends and their families greeted us. There were so many of them. My father was very well respected and well liked in the Chinese community. I later learned that he was a very generous man. Lacking his own family for all those years, he treated his friends' families as his. He would buy them gifts, assist in running errands, and sometimes even help pay for their groceries. He would sacrifice sleep to take his friends' family members to the doctor because most of them did not speak English. I was so proud of my father.

I remember one of my favorite times was when my dad came home from work. We'd all sit together at the dining room table, eating snacks that he prepared for us. He would tell us stories and jokes. Often he'd relate the challenges the old-time immigrants encountered in the course of their daily lives in America. One such story we called "Charlie Goes to Boston."

Back in the 1920s, a newly arrived Chinese immigrant with very limited English was trying to buy a train ticket to Detroit, the city he had chosen for his new life in America. He went to the ticket counter and said, "Ticket to Detroit" with his heavy Chinese accent. Well, the ticket agent did not understand him and kept asking, "Where do you want to go, Charlie?" (For some reason, at that time some Caucasians called all Chinese men "Charlie.") After repeating "Ticket to Detroit" many times and not being understood, the Chinese man thought perhaps the problem was his pronunciation of the word "Detroit." It is very difficult for Chinese to roll their tongue to pronounce the sound "R" makes. To test his theory of what was causing the trouble, the Chinese man substituted the name of another city (one with no R in it) and asked the ticket agent: "Can you understand 'Ticket to Boston'?" Well, that was just the first step of the Chinese man's plan to communicate his desire for a ticket to Detroit, but it was as far as he got. The ticket agent was so happy to finally understand that he said, "Okay, Charlie goes to Boston!" and promptly gave him a ticket to that city. So the Chinese man ended up going to Boston and settled there instead.

As for me, I was in the right city—Detroit—but I knew less than "Charlie" had, as I didn't speak English at all. On my first day of school, I didn't know what was going on. Some of the students were saying phrases and telling me to repeat after them, but when they started laughing, I knew they must be saying bad words. I didn't repeat after them.

After a week of settling into our new home in Detroit's Virginia Park, I started to work at my father's restaurant. In those days the children in Chinese families did not have to be told that they were expected to help out with the family business—it was naturally understood. I was lucky in that I had to work only on weekends during the school year, as my father already had more than a hundred employees at his restaurant, but it was every weekend! I never had a weekend off. Friday was the toughest day for me. Every Friday morning I'd get up at 6:00 a.m. for school, and as soon as school let out, I had to go straight to work. My father's restaurant was open from 4:00 p.m. until 3:00 a.m., and I worked that whole shift. By the time I got off, I had been up more than twenty hours. It was even worse after we moved to our new home in Madison Heights, because then I had a longer drive to work, twenty minutes. I was so tired that I often nearly fell asleep driving home after Friday shifts. So do you know what I did? I would drive with my right hand on the wheel, my left hand covering my left eye to let it rest. Then I would switch, driving with my left hand so my right eye could rest.

High school was no problem for me. I attended Cass Tech High School in Detroit, as most young Asians did in those days. Cass Tech was considered the best high school in Metro Detroit at the time, and if you were Asian, you were expected to attend it because you should be an all-A student. Asians students were regarded as the "smartest and best behaved students" then. Well, it was easy for me to get all As in high school since I already knew most of the material—the school system in Hong Kong was much more advanced than America's. But after graduation when I attended Wayne State University, I started to feel the stress. Schoolwork became more difficult, so I had to study again as I used to when I was in Hong Kong, memorizing word for word what I read in the textbook.

I got into trouble doing that. One time, my professor called me into his office after an exam. He told me that I'd gotten a perfect score on my exam but he could not give me an A because, he said, I must have cheated. Somehow I must have copied from the textbook because my answers matched it perfectly. I was so shocked and upset I didn't know what to say. I cried and told him, "Professor, I studied very hard for the exam. I did my best to memorize word for word from the textbook, and I answered every question correctly. What did I do wrong?" My professor didn't believe anyone could do that, but that was how I did my exams in Hong Kong! So finally, he gave me the exam again, this time watching me take it. I answered all the questions the same way. He finally believed me and gave me my A.

After I graduated from Wayne State, I found I had the entrepreneurial spirit that my father had instilled in me. I didn't want to work for anyone, so I used the money I had saved working at my father's restaurant all those years and opened my own Chinese restaurant. My mother had taught me how to save money while we were living in Hong Kong. She was very frugal because of her constant fear that one day my dad would stop sending money to us, so she put away whatever she could—and it added up to a lot. Perhaps I took it even farther than she had. I would spend only a very small percentage of my paycheck; the rest went straight into my savings account. I had earlier used my savings to buy a brand-new car and I paid for my own university education. My father offered to pay for college, but I told him to save the money for his old age. Now I used the rest of my savings to launch my restaurant.

I was very busy working and building my wealth every day. I was blessed with a little luck and some great opportunities. I diversified into many businesses after the success of my restaurant: investment banking, genetic pig farms, high-tech alternative medicines, worldwide business consulting services, and many more. In the course of business, I spent nearly two hundred days a year traveling all over the United States and overseas.

It was not until one day, that I knew, even with all that money, that I was not happy. I realized then that money was not the ultimate source of happiness. I started my search to discover what life is all about. Through trial and error, I found my joy: volunteering in my community. I learned that when you give, you receive even more in return. I am truly excited by my life now.

I have been and remain very active with several nonprofit organizations in Michigan. I was president of the Council of Asian Pacific Americans, whose mission it is to unite Michigan's Asian Pacific Americans and the community at large through culture, education, and community service. I joined the Asian Pacific American Chamber of Commerce, which promotes the growth of Asian businesses in America, and became a board member of the Association of Chinese Americans and the Detroit chapter of the Organization of Chinese Americans. Last but not least, I helped coordinate a very big and worthy project to initiate an Asian Pacific Town here in Michigan. Our goal is to create a unified environment to preserve and promote Asian-Pacific cultures and heritage for the next generation.

It has been my privilege to share my stories with you. When we learn and understand each other, we have a better, deeper relationship. With your help, we can bring all people closer together and make this world a better place for our children.

20

MY FAMILY'S EXPERIENCE OF THE JAPANESE AMERICAN INTERNMENT CAMPS

Dylan Sugiyama

To my father, Curt Sugiyama, and to my aunts, Mickey Murata and Nen Mishima, who are this essay's inspiration and its true authors.

When I was finally old enough to understand what my relatives were referring to when they talked about "the camp," I asked my father what living in a concentration camp was like. He was only a child during his time there, so his memories were limited. But he remembered the suffocating heat of the desert, chasing lizards with his friends, and how excited he was when he was allowed to go into town one day to get ice cream, a treat he was denied at the camp. It was only years later that I learned from my aunt the rest of the ice cream story. Maybe he truly didn't remember that part, or maybe my father, who doesn't like to dwell on unpleasant things, just didn't want to tell his son about what was undoubtedly a humiliating and bewildering experience for a seven-year-old boy. I guess I never had the nerve to ask because I knew it would embarrass him.

Late in life, Aunt Mickey began writing her reminiscences. Not surprisingly, given the emotional impact of the experience, many of those stories were about life at the camp. In one of these stories, "The Trip to Mesa," she wrote that after about a year of camp life, restrictions were eased somewhat and some inmates were given permission to go to nearby towns in trucks provided by the army. My Aunt Nen and her friend, both thirteen, went to Mesa, Arizona, taking my father with them. My father wanted ice cream, so Nen and her friend took him to an ice cream parlor. Nen heard some of the customers make comments about "Jap kids" when they went in, but they assumed there would be no trouble so they left my father waiting patiently at the counter to be served while they went to explore the town. When they returned about an hour later, they found my father still waiting to be served in the nearly empty ice cream parlor. Even though my dad never got that ice cream, he still remembers vividly how badly he wanted it. And I am never able to completely forget that image of my father waiting in vain for that stupid ice cream cone, and of the ignorant and callous adults who refused to give it to him. I think that never-served ice cream is a big part of the reason I went to work for the Michigan Department of Civil Rights.

Reading my aunt's stories was a revelation to me. It allowed me to begin to understand what had happened to my family. When my relatives talk about "the camp," the conversations are lighthearted and joking, but I still hear the pain, humiliation, and indignation in their voices. It's as if they still can't believe, over seventy years later, that it really happened to them. But while these discussions are long on emotion, they are always short on detail. That's only to be expected, I guess. My father and aunts and uncle were kids when they were sent to the camp, so their memories are incomplete. My grand-mother died before I was born and my grandfather died when I was very young, so I never had a chance to ask them about their experiences.

This essay is about the internment of Japanese Americans during World War II generally, but throughout I will intersperse personal memories from my family.

The Japanese attacked Pearl Harbor on December 7, 1941. Almost imme-diately after, there was a major backlash against Japanese Americans by the American public and by the U.S. government. This built on existing racism and resentment of Japanese Americans and Asians in general. Japanese Americans were suspected of being spies and saboteurs, or at least of poten-tial disloyalty. The U.S. government created an "exclusion zone" for Japa-nese Americans covering California, Oregon, and Washington. A curfew was imposed for people of Japanese descent in the exclusion zone from 8:00 p.m. to 6:00 a.m. Japanese Americans could not travel more than five miles from their homes except for work or school. Their bank accounts were frozen, and they were required to surrender their cameras, binoculars, short-wave radios, and any weapons they owned. The state of California barred Japanese Americans from all civil service jobs.

My great-grandparents had come to Hawaii from Japan. My grandparents were citizens, born in the United States. After their marriage, my grandparents moved to California, where my father was born. My father speaks only rudimentary Japanese and has never been to Japan. At the time of the attack on Pearl Harbor, the family was living in southern California in the town of Guadalupe, which had a large Japanese American population at the time. My grandfather was a mechanic.

One of my grandparents' neighbors was taken away by the FBI soon after Pearl Harbor, presumably suspected of being a spy, and was never heard from again. The FBI interviewed my grandfather but he was not detained at the time. Before the agents came to the house my grandparents took down pictures of the Japanese emperor from the wall and hid their Japanese-language books so they wouldn't be seen as disloyal.

On February 19, 1942, President Franklin Delano Roosevelt signed Executive Order 9066 authorizing the internment of approximately 120,000 people of Japanese descent on the West Coast. Of these, approximately two-thirds were U.S. citizens and over half were children. The executive order did not specify the exact criteria of who should be interned, but the army officials who administered it decided that it applied to anyone at least one-sixteenth Japanese. Under this policy, I would have been interned even though I'm only half Japanese. My kids would have been interned even though they are only one-quarter Japanese. Assuming my daughters don't marry Japanese American men, their kids would have been interned even though they would only be one-eighth Japanese, and even my great-grandchildren would be interned. Japanese American children living in orphanages were interned, and even Japanese American children adopted by white parents or living in white foster families were sent to the camps.

The stated motivations for the executive order were military necessity and national security. But the U.S. Army, the FBI, naval Intelligence, and the Federal Communications Commission all issued reports stating that there was no evidence to support the need for mass internment of all Japanese Americans on the West Coast. There were no reported instances of espionage or sabotage by Japanese Americans either before or during World War II. The ten people convicted of spying for Japan during the war were all Caucasian.

The members of my family were relatively fortunate in that they had about a month to prepare after learning they would be sent to a concentration camp. Many families had only forty-eight hours' notice to try to put their affairs in order. But regardless of how much warning they had, everyone knew that Japanese Americans had to dispose of all their property, so people offered to buy items for a fraction of what they were worth, knowing that the internees would have no choice but to accept. My grandparents sold virtually all of their belongings for far less than their value. My father had to sell his bike, which he had only just received for his birthday. Inmates were allowed to take with them only what they could carry, so my grandmother sewed duffle bags, four feet on a side, for family member to bring. Everything else had to be sold or left behind. Japanese Americans' property losses are estimated at $4 billion to $5 billion.

Before the war, many West Coast Japanese Americans had been farmers, producing approximately half the fresh produce grown in California. This was seen as part of the motivation for the internment. Land speculators and the agricultural industry pressured the government to intern Japanese Americans—and then bought valuable land at bargain-basement prices.

Although Executive Order 9066 does not specifically refer to people of Japanese ancestry, only to "enemy aliens," it was always the intention that mass internment would apply only to Japanese Americans. The United States was also at war with Germany and Italy. A small number of Germans and Italians were interned during the war, but virtually none were U.S. citizens, and to justify internment the government had to articulate how each individual was a threat to national security. It was not a wholesale internment based simply on race or national origin, as it was for the Japanese. What is less well known is that approximately twenty thousand persons of Japanese descent were interned in Canada, and that several thousand Latino Japanese from Mexico, Central America, and South America, particularly Peru, were sent to the United States for internment.

When their evacuation dates arrived, Japanese Americans were supposed to present themselves for internment. They had not been told where they were going or for how long, so they had no idea what to pack. Most brought the clothes they'd worn in California, which were unsuitable for the climates to which many were sent. My grandmother brought her wedding silverware, but it was confiscated by the authorities on the grounds that the knives and forks could be used as weapons. The inmates were initially sent to "assembly centers," mostly located at fairgrounds and racetracks, while permanent camps were hastily constructed. My family was relatively fortunate to be sent to a fairground in Tulare, California, because there internees were able to live in communal barracks. The inmates sent to racetracks had it much worse—each family was assigned to a horse stable. The stables had not been properly cleaned and were full of horse manure and flies. The internees stayed at the assembly centers for three to six months. Aunt Nen would write letters to her classmates in Guadalupe so she could feel like she was still part of that life. That lasted only until her best friend wrote to tell her that her father wouldn't let her write to "that Jap girl" anymore.

Once the camps were constructed, the inmates were sent to them by train. There were ten camps in seven states: Arizona, California, Colorado, Idaho, Utah, Wyoming, and Arkansas. One camp, Tule Lake, was designated as a prison for those who were deemed the most serious threats to national security or who were community leaders such as teachers and Buddhist priests. All the camps were in barren, remote areas. My family was sent to the Gila River Camp in Arizona, about fifty miles southeast of Phoenix, in the middle of the desert. It was located on the Gila River Indian Reservation over the strong objections of the tribal government. The tribe received no compensation for the use of its land. The peak population of the camp was around thirteen thousand.

My relatives most often talk about the heat, the sandstorms, the water shortages, and the snakes and scorpions. Their camp, like others, was surrounded by barbed wire and had guard towers with armed sentries. There were several instances of inmates being shot and killed while allegedly trying to escape. Inmates lived in tar-paper-covered barracks, with one small room assigned to each family. There were no bathrooms or cooking facilities in the barracks. Metal cots were the only furnishings. What was particularly degrading for the inmates, especially the women, was that showers and toilets were in communal rooms without partitions. This was humiliating for Japanese people, who have very strong notions about privacy and personal dignity. The fact that this situation was never improved over the duration of the internment is an indication of how culturally insensitive the camp authorities were.

The food at the camp was terrible. The camps were generally given a food budget of 45¢ a day per person, ensuring that provisions were of the lowest quality. Due to the remote locations of the camps, food was often rotten by the time it reached them, but it was served anyway. Another serious problem was the lack of medical personnel and facilities. Many inmates died of relatively minor ailments because they lacked adequate medical care. My relatives spent three and a half years living in these conditions.

One of the most controversial aspects of the internment was the government's requirement, instituted in 1943, that every inmate over the age of seventeen sign an oath of allegiance. It is the only time in our country's history that citizens have been required to sign such an oath—and this while the U.S. government was denying them their most basic constitutional rights by holding them in concentration camps. Inmates were asked if they would swear "unqualified allegiance" to the United States and forswear any loyalty or obedience to the Japanese emperor. This portion of the oath was particularly difficult for the issei, or first-generation, inmates. They were not allowed to become U.S. citizens because the racist immigration laws of the time permitted citizenship only to Asians born in the United States. If the issei answered yes to this question, then they were renouncing their Japanese citizenship—and would therefore become stateless. Inmates who were U.S. citizens were also asked if they would be willing to serve in the U.S. military. Any inmate who answered no to either question was considered disloyal and sent to the Tule Lake prison camp.

Approximately eight thousand inmates asked to be sent to Japan after the loyalty oath was administered, including many who renounced their U.S. citizenship in disgust at the way they had been treated. Some U.S. citizens answered yes to the loyalty question but stated that they would not be willing to serve in the military unless the U.S. government released them and their families from the camps and honored their constitutional rights. As a result, 315 internees were released from the camps only to be imprisoned for draft law violations, serving an average of two years in federal prison.

However, the vast majority of inmates, including my family, answered yes to both questions. Approximately thirty thousand Japanese Americans served in the U.S. armed forces during World War II, mostly in segregated units. One such unit, the 442nd Regimental Combat Team, is the most highly decorated military unit in U.S. history. More than 40 percent of the Japanese American soldiers who fought in that unit were killed in combat.

The draft resisters weren't the only ones who protested against the internment. There were many other dissenters, thus refuting the common impression that Japanese Americans meekly and passively accepted their internment. There were numerous protests and even riots in the camps. A few individuals defied the internment and fought for their rights in the courts. Four Japanese Americans had their cases heard by the U.S. Supreme Court. The most famous cases were those of Gordon Hirabayashi and Fred Korematsu. Hirabayashi was arrested and convicted for violating the pre-internment curfew imposed on Japanese Americans, and Korematsu was convicted for failing to comply with the evacuation order of all Japanese

Americans from the West Coast. Both men appealed their convictions all the way to the Supreme Court, arguing that the U.S. government was violating the Fifth Amendment by depriving Japanese Americans of their liberty and property without due process of law. The court acknowledged that the internment policy was subject to "strict scrutiny" (courts' most stringent test) since it was a legal restriction that curtailed the rights of a single racial group. However, the court upheld the convictions on the grounds of a "pressing public necessity," stating that the internment was a reasonable exercise of the government's war power. These cases were two of the very few in which a classification based on race survived strict scrutiny. In 1988, the convictions of Hirabayashi and Korematsu were overturned after newly uncovered evidence from the National Archives showed that the government withheld from the Supreme Court reports that called into question the government's justification for the internment.

Further undermining the government's stated motivation was the fact that the evacuation order was rescinded on January 2, 1945, while war was still raging. If interning Japanese Americans was necessary to prevent espionage and sabotage, why were they released during the war?

After the executive order was lifted, my grandfather had to start over from scratch. My family had no money, no home, no job, and virtually no belongings. So my grandfather left camp first to try to establish the foundations of a new life, while my grandmother, father, and aunts and uncle remained at Gila River. My grandfather initially went to Montana to work on the railroad, but later he heard from a mechanic friend that there were lots of jobs available in the auto industry in Detroit. So he came to Michigan and got a job on the assembly line. My father and the others joined him soon after. They struggled from then on. My grandfather was never able to advance very far in the company and never able to realize his dream of running his own business. Nor did they ever have their own home again. My father grew up in a two-bedroom apartment above a bakery near downtown Detroit. The effects of internment lasted long after the camps were closed.

In the 1960s, Japanese American activists, inspired by the civil rights movement, commenced a redress movement calling for an official apology and reparations from the government for the internment. Thanks to their efforts, in 1976 President Gerald Ford proclaimed that the internment of Japanese Americans was wrong. In 1980, President Jimmy Carter established a commission to investigate the matter and make suggestions. In 1983, the commission issued an official report stating that the internment was unjust and motivated by racism. In 1988, President Ronald Reagan signed the Civil Liberties Act of 1988, which resulted in an official apology to internees and reparations in the amount of $20,000 to every surviving internee. Because of the long delay, over 40 percent of the internees had already died by the time reparations were paid. A few internees refused the reparations as inadequate to compensate them for all they had lost during internment, but most, including my family, accepted the money. In truth, it was the apology, not the money, that mattered most.

In 1990, Aunt Nen organized a reunion at the Gila River Camp. About two hundred former internees attended. My father moderated a discussion of people's feelings about their internment. The emotion most often voiced was relief that the U.S. government had finally apologized and acknowledged that what it had done was wrong and that there really had been no reason to suspect Japanese Americans of being disloyal. I think the most painful part of the internment experience for many people was the sense of humiliation, disgrace, and loss of face caused by the government in effect calling into question their loyalty and patriotism. The apology helped to alleviate that pain, but the wound is still raw.

I think my father's—and many other former internees'—most fervent hope is that no other group of people will ever suffer as they did. That hope is what inspired me to write this, to raise awareness so that such an injustice never happens again. The significance of the Japanese American internment did not end with World War II or with the government's official apology. It has implications for the issue of reparations being paid to African Americans. It has implications for concerns surrounding the racial and ethnic profiling of Arab Americans and Muslims that occurred after 9/11. I hope that we will all remember the wrong that was done in the Japanese American concentration camps. For my father's sake.

21

GROWING UP HAPA IN ANN ARBOR

Lynet Uttal

Ann Arbor, Michigan. 1967. "Red China! Red China! Red China!" My second-grade classmates are chasing me around the playground during recess screaming these words at me. I veer right off the playground and head home, running as fast as my feet will carry my eight-year-old body away from school.

My mother is concerned by my unexpected return when I arrive home in the middle of the day. "What's wrong?" she asks me, with worry on her face, bending down toward me. Sobbing, I explain that the kids at school are calling me "Red China." I am expecting sympathy but instead my mother straightens up and says dismissively, "Oh, they are just ignorant. We are Japanese, not Chinese. And you are an American." She is referring to the fact that she is Japanese, but my father is an American of Russian Jewish heritage, and she doesn't really see me as being Japanese.

And that's it. She doesn't want to talk about it anymore. I don't get any sympathy or advice about how to deal with this playground bullying. But I wonder, Why are my classmates teasing me? Is it because I look Asian? Is it because I lived in Japan last year? Back at school, I don't complain to my teacher about what happened because the message from my mother was to not do so. Let it go.

My experience in Michigan was probably not typical of what it was like to grow up Asian American in the Midwest during the 1960s and 1970s because I was a biracial Asian American. As I grew older, my looking Asian was replaced with looking Greek, Mexican, First Nation, Hawaiian ("local"), or generic Latina, depending on what region of the country (world) I was in. My Asianness rarely became an issue again in this overtly racist way. However, sometimes racism and race noticing came up in more subtle ways throughout middle school, high school, graduate school, and even now, when I am a full professor at a major university in the Midwest. "Race noticing" is when one is identified as not-white, but not understood within the context of a sociopolitical history such as blacks, Latinos, or American Indians have.

What was typical in my experience and that of other Asian Americans in the Midwest before the 1980s was that although we were seen as different, we were not racialized as members of a group that had experienced oppression and discrimination. We were sometimes explicitly labeled as different, but it was never a difference that deserved much public discussion, like the one that surrounded being black. No one was going to be my advocate or tell those kids who teased me that what they were doing was racist and wrong. As nonblack, nonwhite Americans, we were excluded from the public notice that was given to blacks as society developed a new social consciousness of what it meant to be black in the United States. In the eyes of most Michiganders, Japanese, Chinese, and Korean people were indistinguishable members of an invisible racial group. Mixed-race Asian Americans like myself were even less noticeable. We carried our cultural identities hidden beneath our skins, often being mistaken for another ethnicity.

Replacing the overt racism of little kids, a more subtle form was expressed in high school. The Chinese American boys with Chinese names from their immigrant parents were othered as slightly strange and not fully masculine. The Japanese American girl was the all-American cheerleader, except she also took all the college-prep classes so her white fellow cheerleaders saw her as not quite one of them. With her long, straight black hair and rounded body, she was not "Barbie" enough to be the squad leader or to date the quarterback of the football team. She could get close, but her experience was one of partial inclusion. When she visited her white friends' homes, their mothers wondered about the foreigner at their table—should they serve rice and did she need chopsticks to eat with? These subtle messages marked Asian Americans as different and foreign, even though most of us were third-generation Americans and had been born in the United States. All of us knew how to eat with forks, spoons, and knives.

There was no space to think about ourselves as "Japanese American" because our parents wanted us to be simply "American." The internment camps encouraged many Japanese American parents to push for assimilation at a time when black Americans were naming their oppressions, asserting their cultures, and standing taller with black pride. Most of the time Asian American parents identified with whites, not blacks, on race issues. Close your eyes and listen to my Asian American classmates and their parents talk, and you would hear exactly what the whites were saying about blacks, dashikis, afros, affirmative action, and so on.

My mother sent me mixed messages. At home, she told my two sisters and I that we were American, not Japanese. As a kid, I identified as being Japanese rather than Japanese American or Asian American because although my mother had been born in the United States, because of World War II she lived in Japan from the ages of nine to twenty-three, only returning to the United States in 1953. In many ways, she was a new immigrant.

Yet in the face of the public denial of our race, at home we lived our ethnicity. My mother fed us Japanese food and taught us to act humble and to be hyperaware of others. We worked hard to achieve As and were questioned about why they were not A+s. The sound of Japanese was in our home because my mother regularly invited Japanese women to our home and they talked in Japanese as if they were still in Japan. Being Japanese meant being more gentle and subtle in one's expressions and movements around others, eating more rice than my friends' families did, and taking *nori* (seaweed) and *an-mochi* (pounded rice with a sweet bean filling) treats to school for Culture Day. We had cultural knowledge about ourselves, but it stopped there.

Being Japanese also meant having a mother who asked many questions about what we were doing as teenagers because she really didn't know or understand what was going on in U.S. society. She often asked for explanations and when she learned about how things worked in the United States she often would challenge the values that were being expressed by my friends and their families.

There were no messages that Asian Americans of any ilk existed. To grow up Asian American in the Midwest was to be a noticeable, racialized person, yet without any social or political history. Our group story was unknown. In the Midwest, race was articulated and politicized as only two categories—black and white. We really should have been talking about blacks and non-blacks instead of whites and nonwhites. Although the civil rights movement was alive in Ann Arbor, Michigan, in 1977, it was about blacks. Not Asian Americans. Not Latinos. Not immigrants.

As Asian Americans, most of us ignored that we were also a racialized group that historically had suffered from underrepresentation, historical injustices, legal exclusions, and racial prejudice in U.S. history. In the Midwest, no one knew that Japanese Americans had been interned during World War II and had had all their property stolen from them. In the Midwest, no one knew that Japanese on the West Coast were not allowed to be citizens or to own property for a long time. No one could tell that Japanese and Chinese people were from different ethnic groups.

It was not until the 1980s that we began to develop a sociopolitical historical consciousness. When Americans were buying Japanese cars, Vincent Chin, a Chinese American, was just as good as a real Japanese to be the target of American autoworkers' anger at Japan for weakening the U.S. auto industry. His attackers also didn't know that Japanese were not the same as Japanese Americans when they murdered him.

Vincent Jen Chin's murder may have sparked the beginning of a panethnic Asian American movement in the United States, but not in the Midwest, where it actually happened. I lived in Michigan until 1980 and I don't ever remember Asian Americans having a political agenda. If there was a Japanese American Citizens League in Ann Arbor, I didn't know about it.

Growing up Asian American in the Midwest, we didn't think we were any different from whites; we just looked different. Then, it was difference, not racism. Or was it? Recently, my mother said to me, "We experienced racism; we just didn't know it at the time." Growing up I didn't think I was the target of racism, even when they chased me around the playground and called me Red China. I never thought of the question "What are you?" as racist either. But if my parents had racially socialized me to understand and cope with racism, as black parents were doing, would I have developed more of a sense of belonging to a group and been more resilient against racism? Probably my journey would have been filled with public political struggles rather than private painful experiences if we had dialogued more openly about race and racism in the Asian American community in the Midwest.

"Who am I as a member of a racialized group?" was not answered in the Midwest but through my family's regular visits to Hawaii, where my mother's relatives lived. My cousins, whose Japanese American mother had married a Puerto Rican, were from two cultures, like me. My other cousins, who were Japanese, Hawaiian, and Irish, had grown up in a society where being Japanese was common and normal. They had a lot of cultural pride and history to talk about. They switched between chopsticks and forks depending on what was being eaten, and when they experienced racism, they had the tools of being a member of an ethnic community to cope with it. I wondered how it affects your consciousness to grow up in a place where a whole part of you is not rendered invisible by the larger society, as compared to where I grew up in the Midwest, where one's racial group was not acknowledged or learned about in school.

During my high school years, the apparent economic and educational success of third- and fourth-generation Asian Americans invoked the concept of the "model minority," suggesting that Asian Americans had made it in U.S. society and that we were equal to whites in all respects. Yet sociologist Deborah Woo statistically proved that Asian Americans experience racism: it takes Asian Americans more education to achieve the same job level and pay as whites, and Asian American women were more likely to be working in the back room instead of up front in the public's eye.[1]

Changes in the immigration laws after 1965 brought increased numbers of Chinese and Korean immigrants to the United States, and after 1975 more Southeast Asian refugees from the Vietnam War arrived. In the public eye, being Asian American would be reconfigured from "invisible" to "perpetual foreigner" by this new influx of Asian immigrants.

Yet even today (2014) in Wisconsin, the race dialogue is still about black and white and ignores the racialized trials of Asian Americans. Asian American students still report incidents of overt racism, while black and Latino students more often report struggling with more subtle forms of racism. At the University of Wisconsin–Madison, Asian American students tell me that when they walk down State Street, people call out "Chink!" and yell, "Go back to where you came from!" As a biracial Japanese American professor in the Midwest, I know that my comments about race will be not taken as seriously as when a black professor speaks if the topic is about race.

Today, raising my triracial children in Wisconsin, where things are not much different than they were in Michigan in the 1960s, I remind them that they have roots in cultures and histories that are not just different but have experienced both overt and subtle racism, just as black Americans and Latino immigrants have. I racially socialize my children to be aware of the group histories in the United States that shape them and to have a sense of their racial ethnic identity. We talk about what it means to be different (sort of) and partially racialized by affirmative action policies. I take them to Hawaii and California so they can understand how race is socially constructed depending on the region of the country one lives in and so that they can feel a sense of place for themselves as multiracial Asian Americans.

The Midwest has yet to embrace Asian Americans as a racial group. That is despite numerous examples of Asian Americans' historical experiences with racism (for example, internment, antimiscegenation laws) and continuing racialized misconceptions such as the model minority myth and subtle racist exclusions due to "looking different." When we finally acknowledge the racialized experiences of Asian Americans, our understanding of how race shapes social life in the United States will be better understood. It is not a simple black-white model or a triracialized model of white-honorary white-black,[2] but something even more complex that takes into account how not being racialized can also operate as a form of racism.

Notes

1. D. Woo, "The Socioeconomic Status of Asian American Women in the Labor Force," *Sociological Perspectives* 28, no. 3 (1985): 307–38.
2. E. Bonilla-Silva, "We Are All Americans: The Latin Americanization of Racial Stratification in the USA," In *Race and Ethnicity in Society,* ed. E. Higginbotham and M. Anderson (Belmont, CA: Thomson Wadsworth, 2006), 491–25.

22

THE APOLOGY

Catherine Chung

My whole class is running like crazy, racing from the playground to the bench outside our school where we line up after recess every day. Until now, I've always run as part of the pack. But this time, my feet pounding the pavement, I know I've got a chance—that today's the day I'll find out just how fast I am. So I pump my legs in a burst of speed and surge ahead, and suddenly I'm at the head of the crowd, pulling away from everyone. Only Lisa—a girl I like and want to be friends with—is close. She's exactly an arm's length behind me, and I'm happy it's her, that this race is between us. The whole class shouts as we spring forward, and I feel good. It's a perfect day: the air cool in my lungs and the sidewalk sparkles beneath my feet. We're almost to the school; we're getting closer and closer and Lisa is gaining on me, but she won't pass me—today I'm the fastest kid in the third grade. I'm untouchable. I look back for a moment and see that she knows it too; she can't touch me. But then she reaches out and does. Her hand is on my back, firm between my shoulder blades, and she pushes me, hard. I fly forward—too startled to scream, no time even to think—and I'm falling. The brick wall of the school is in front of me, and I can't stop. I throw out my hands, but it's too late and too close, and my face hits the wall. And then I'm on the ground looking at the sky.

I don't know where I am. There are shoes. There's the ground. There's the sky, and voices. I sit up, touch my face, and when I bring my hands down again so much blood is spilling into them it overflows their cupped edges. In the blood there are bits of teeth and wire from the braces I have only had for a few weeks. I am eight years old, no longer a baby, and in my head I hear a

252

voice speaking just to me: "Don't cry." The voice is authoritative enough that I want to do as it says. But then I look down at my bloody hands again, and at the blood all over the ground, then up into the faces of my classmates, who are backing away from me, and I start to scream.

A door opens, and a teacher comes out and takes me by the arm. I follow her, dripping blood, wailing, vaguely aware of the scene I am causing. The teacher leads me to the principal's office, where the secretary tells me to sit. After a while I calm down, bleeding slowly into a wad of Kleenex. A long time goes by before the secretary calls my mother. "Your daughter was in an accident." By then I am quiet; the bleeding has stopped. I wait. I can't feel my teeth with my tongue: I will find out later that they were knocked up into my head from the force of hitting the wall. The broken wires from my braces hang from inside my gums. I am numb and dizzy with what will turn out to be a concussion. When my mother arrives, she takes me outside and kneels before me in the parking lot, asking what happened. Until now, no one has asked that question. But now I can't answer—I am so freaked out and exhausted and relieved my mother is there that I collapse in her arms, weeping.

The day Lisa Prentiss pushed me into the brick wall, I'd attended Edgewood Elementary for less than a year. It was 1987, and my family had just moved to a small town in Michigan. Michigan was the fourth state I'd lived in, Edgewood the fourth school I'd attended, and I was used to being the new girl, to feeling things out and finding my place. But there were things about this new school that made me want to return to where we'd lived last in New Jersey and never come back. The kids made fun of me—they said my eyes were slanted, my face was flat, that I had no nose—and I knew they thought everything about me was wrong. At first I took the hostility for a kind of hazing ritual, a phase that might soon pass, until one day a boy asked out loud in class—his voice laced with sarcasm—if *anyone* liked me, and no one—absolutely no one—raised their hand. That was the day I realized the trouble I was in. The day I hit the brick wall was the day I internalized it.

I always hesitate trying to explain what happened at Edgewood and why it was so hard for me there. Maybe the other kids disliked me because I was obnoxious or annoying or had a horrible personality. Maybe I was a hideous freak. I believed all these things to varying degrees as I was growing up. It didn't occur to me until years later that things might have been different if I hadn't been a Korean American girl in an otherwise all-white class at a time when Michigan was still deep in anti-Asian sentiment related to the auto crisis. I don't think my ethnicity was necessarily the reason I was picked on, but

I do think it made it possible for things to happen the way they did. The social dynamics within a school mimic, to some extent, the dynamics of the society around it. It's no coincidence that the kids who are picked on relentlessly, mercilessly are often poor, minorities, abused at home, new in town, or gay. Who is being tormented in school reflects who is being harassed outside.

Five years before we moved to Michigan, Vincent Chin had been beaten to death in Detroit by two recently laid-off autoworkers. Their excuse was that they had thought he was Japanese—as if that would have made it all right—and the amazing thing is that they served no jail time; they were given community service and let off with a $3,000 fine. This was the Michigan I came to live in. But as a kid, I didn't think about these things. I didn't care about context—my school was the whole world.

Lisa called me the evening of the accident to see how I was, and I remember feeling grateful for her concern. Maybe she was my friend now, I thought. I have always remembered it as the phone call in which she apologized, and it's only now, as I write these words, that I realize she never actually said she was sorry. The school never followed up on the incident: no grownup ever addressed what Lisa had done. And it strikes me now that if I'd always considered that conversation with Lisa an apology, I also always called what happened an accident. It seemed unfair to call it anything else. She had pushed me on purpose, but she couldn't have known the result, how terribly she would hurt me. By calling it an accident, I wanted to make clear that I knew she never intended to harm me. When I returned to school and my classmates told me that Lisa had been so upset about the incident she'd left school early, I remember feeling sorry for her. When the other children talked about how hard—psychologically—the accident had been on her, I almost believed she was the one who'd been hurt.

I wish now that I'd never called what happened an accident. I wish I'd made more of a fuss. I wish I had told the truth: she pushed me into a wall because I was beating her in a race, and there were terrible consequences that she did not intend. When asked, I've always insisted that the incident wasn't racially motivated. And I'm certain that's true. But at the same time, what I've always left unspoken is that I doubt Lisa would have done such a thing to anyone else. I suspect that if I had been anyone else, the school would have called my parents more quickly and the matter would have been followed up on. Lisa might have been made to apologize. And then perhaps she would never have been able to tell the lie she told our classmates years later: that she hadn't pushed me at all—that what they had seen was her attempt to reach out and hold me back. To save me from running, on my own, headfirst into the wall.

That lie makes me angrier than the incident itself. And part of my anger is directed at myself. By calling what happened an accident, by scrubbing the story free of blame, I feel that I prepared the way for Lisa's lie, made it possible and somehow true.

Her one careless act resulted in injuries requiring multiple root canals, crowns, surgeries, and bone grafts, and the likelihood is I will need more. These procedures cost my parents thousands of dollars during my childhood and in adulthood further operations have put me in debt. These are things Lisa never had to know.

But worse than the continuing cost and the chronic pain was the damage done to my sense of self. During those early years in Michigan after the incident, I grew fearful. I felt unsafe. I felt like a victim, helpless and unlikable, and in some small but terrible ways, I began to hate myself. Admitting this still makes me feel vulnerable, as if I'm laying bare a wound that should stay covered up.

Everything changed again in fifth grade, when I was transferred to a newly built school. There was another child of color in my class, and for whatever reason, I was no longer the pariah I'd been. I made friends. But I remained skittish, afraid of too much attention. Even now, I miss the girl I was before: the one who ran full speed and didn't feel afraid, but free.

Someone asked me recently how I'd come to terms with the bullying I faced and with my own Asian Americanness. How had I found closure and become who I am? The answer is this: my Asian Americanness, my own identity, was never the problem. Some people look for someone to pick on, and I happened to be a convenient target. But the problem, at its core, was theirs. I moved on by deciding to stop allowing my identity to be defined by the perspective of someone else's bigotry. I decided to reject the idea that I was the problem. When it became possible, I stepped out of the world those people had made, and I found I was no longer alone.

When I hear stories about bullying in schools, I feel a chill of recognition, and then I feel lucky that my experience wasn't worse. It seems to me that it's harder nowadays. Sometimes the parents of the bullied children are blamed. Why don't they put a stop to it? people ask. Why don't they stand up for their kids? But I never told my parents I was being bullied. I lied. This was partly to protect them, partly to protect myself. I knew with absolute conviction that there is nothing more unforgivable than being a snitch, and the last thing I needed was to be a tattletale on top of a loser. I am willing to concede now that I might have been wrong; perhaps I should have spoken up. Still, the times my parents did complain to the school about how my brother or I were treated, they got the stock answer that kids will be kids. And when I found out they'd complained, I was mortified and begged them not to do it again.

We want to believe that we can protect our children. But the stories in the news about bullied children reveal a similar pattern: the parents do complain and advocate for their kids; they go to administrators, the school board, the parents of the bullies. Nothing changes, and their child continues to suffer. In the face of such indifference, one person isn't enough. Neither are two. The real question is: Where is everyone else? Where are the teachers, the principals, the other parents, the guy at the corner shop who watches the same kid being taunted each day? It cannot fall solely on the bullied child and his or her family to fix the situation. It takes people at the school watching for it—and intervening when they see it. It takes a whole group of people willing to stand by the bullied child and to say, no, this will not happen here. It takes all of us.

23

CARS, PREJUDICE, AND GOD

Kyo Takahashi

I have been fascinated with cars for a long time. No, I've never dreamed of owning a luxurious automobile or a high-performance sports model. For me the allure is drawing beautiful cars of any type, even an economy vehicle or a monstrous industrial bulldozer. It never mattered. I wanted an artistic career that involved cars. That's how I ended up in Detroit, the automotive capital of the world.

I was born in Tokyo in 1929 and raised in Yokohama. When the Imperial Japanese Navy attacked Pearl Harbor on December 7, 1941, I was a sixth grader. We were conditioned to hate Americans. We were told this was a holy war and that Japan was a holy country, because our emperor was a direct descendant of the God who founded the country twenty-six hundred years ago, or 660 BC. The people of Japan were descendants of God's family.

We also learned that Japan had a destiny to be the leader of all Asian countries. Japanese troops had already been fighting in China to achieve that purpose since 1937. We hated the Chinese as our enemies. Our society, during the war, also discriminated against the Koreans, including those who lived in Japan, and their sons and daughters. Even though many of them had been born in Japan, spoke Japanese as a native language, acted Japanese, and looked Japanese, they were never treated as Japanese, and they never received Japanese civil rights.

When I heard the news of Pearl Harbor on the radio, I was scared; my first impression was that we were little guys who had stepped on a giant's foot. After Japan won a series of battles with U.S. naval forces in the southwest

Pacific, however, my fear diminished. But six months following Pearl Harbor, after the battle of Midway, the war situation in the Pacific reversed. The Japanese began to lose battle after battle. Thousands of soldiers, both Japanese and Americans, were killed as the fighting went on. Our hatred against Americans rapidly escalated and solidified. Japanese war leaders convinced us: "We are the country blessed by God. We will never be defeated. God will save us, and we will win eventually." From the bottom of my heart, I believed this. Or I chose to believe it.

In 1944, when I was a third grader at middle school, equivalent to the American ninth grade, the war situation worsened. The Japanese military desperately needed more manpower. I volunteered for the Imperial Japanese Navy Air Force. I was fourteen years old. Training was strict and severe, and the discipline was fierce. I was able to take that pressure because my determination was absolute. I had decided to devote my life to my country as a patriot. You might call it the devotion to the suicide mission. I had no fear of dying. I believed in God and in a holy heaven after death. I had been taught, "Your personal life is not as heavy as single hair. However, if you devote your life to your country, your honor will live forever." I thought my life was worthless unless I died for the emperor, the living God, and our holy country.

From the beginning of 1945, American bombers flew over our skies freely, destroying many cities and killing thousands. Tokyo was totally destroyed on March 10, killing more than one hundred thousand people. My hometown of Yokohama was destroyed on May 29. My house burned down, but luckily my family survived. The base where I was stationed was bombed in June. I wasn't killed because I was working away from the base. On August 6, the first atomic bomb was dropped, on Hiroshima. Three days later, the second A-bomb destroyed Nagasaki. Six days later, on August 15, Emperor Hirohito announced Japan's unconditional surrender. We were thrown into confusion.

Soon after the surrender, I was discharged from military duty along with many other young soldiers. From then on, my life completely changed. The first thought that came to my mind was "I don't have to die for my country anymore. I'm alive, and I will live well from now on. My life will no longer be lighter than a single hair. My life is as precious as everyone else's." My previously firm beliefs were shaken: "God didn't save us. Where is our God?" Along with a disappearing God, my loyalty toward authorities had diminished. When, a few months after Japan's surrender, the emperor publicly admitted that he wasn't the living God but only a human being, I was disillusioned. I felt I had been betrayed.

Sometime during my early days in the States, Warren Weith, a beloved writer, encouraged me to reveal my experiences in Japan during the war. I hesitated at first, afraid to let everybody know I had been an enemy of Americans in the past, but he assured me, saying, "The victor is always generous to the loser." My account was recorded on tape, and Weith edited it and sent it to a magazine, *Private Pilot*, which published it in 1970. It was a great relief for me to reveal my "secret" publicly.

But at the time, I only knew that I couldn't trust or depend on anybody but myself. My future was uncertain. I had absolutely no idea where I would go and what I would do. In any case, when I returned to my ruined hometown, our immediate concern was food. Like everyone else, I was constantly hungry.

I wasn't the only person in the community whose life had hit bottom. Family, neighbors, teachers, friends, monks, politicians—everybody's life had been changed. We lived in poverty. The occupation troops were marching in. GIs—whom I would have fought as the enemy—were everywhere. I was aware that the Americans were materially far wealthier and physically much better built than the Japanese. I felt that I understood the reason Japan had been completely defeated.

Day after day, our struggle was to get housing, food, clothes, and other necessities. With few choices available, I was working part-time as a janitor at the barracks of the occupation army. There I picked up magazines and books the GIS had left lying about, brought them home, and browsed through their colorful illustrations with amazement. Seeing those skillful drawings, I saw for the first time a possibility for my future. I wanted to become that kind of artist—a commercial illustrator. But to become an artist I had to go to school. I had no money for tuition and my father, preoccupied, struggling to obtain our daily basic needs, would be unable to help me.

Nonetheless, I applied to the National Art University in Tokyo, the oldest and most prestigious art school in Japan. I passed the examination and was accepted. From my freshman year on, I paid my school expenses by taking any job that required some artistic skill. I completed my five-year academic course, but I learned almost nothing from the school—I acquired my professional artistic skills at my part-time jobs. In 1952, when I was still an undergraduate, I was hired as an artist/designer by a small but aggressive advertising agency in Tokyo.

One day my boss asked if I was interested in drawing a car. I didn't hesitate to accept the assignment, although he warned me that drawing cars isn't easy. I didn't reply to his remark, but in my mind I was determined to do good work. The subject of my assignment was the Austin, the first British car that Nissan Motor Company imported. Nissan secretly analyzed the British car and later re-created it as its own Bluebird model.

It took me about a week to complete the assigned poster. I submitted it nervously. The client approved my car illustration but wasn't happy with the person I had drawn leaning against the car. I revised the figure again and again without any satisfactory improvement, and eventually time ran out. The client reluctantly accepted the poster, but I've never forgotten that embarrassing experience. Still, it fueled my growing fascination with cars, and I began focusing on automobile drawings.

I knew I needed to acquire additional skills to draw cars and people, and after several years of searching I concluded the most suitable school for that purpose was the Art Center College of Design in Los Angeles. To fulfill my objective, I had to abandon my career of ten years and give up my status and reputation as a professional. That did not stop me. I was willing to start from scratch rather than constantly suffer my own dissatisfaction with my artwork.

I wasn't financially ready to take this step, but my wife encouraged me: "Better act now, when you know it's the right time." We left Tokyo for Los Angeles on New Year's of 1963, and I enrolled in the Art Center College of Design.

As aliens, we encountered several obstacles. My wife and I both had some knowledge of English because instruction in reading and writing the language had been required in our school curriculum, but we soon found that acquiring listening and speaking skills was another matter entirely. Some American customs were puzzling to us at first—for example, in Japan great emphasis is placed on respect and seniority, but Americans operate more freely, in most cases moving quickly to a first-name basis regardless of seniority.

We had some difficulty renting a room in the Hollywood area. The Art Center College of Design had provided a list of available housing, but each time we went to inquire we were told the apartment was "taken." Whether this was the result of discrimination or bad luck I didn't know then and don't now. Luckily, we became acquainted with a Japanese American family who kindly offered us temporary shelter.

We learned that our new friends had been among the 120,000 people of Japanese descent from Washington, Oregon, and California interned during the war. The more I heard of their story, the greater was my astonishment, and the more I was ashamed of my ignorance. Remembering how I had hated my stereotyped Americans, I felt I could understand the anti-Japanese sentiment that had motivated the incarceration even while I deplored what these Japanese Americans had suffered. It took me over ten years to clarify both the facts of what had happened and my feelings about them. I eventually wrote a book, *Japanese of No Return* (in Japanese for a Japanese audience) for those who had been as ignorant of the internment as I had been. This unknown part of American history opened my eyes and mind. I became aware that all Americans were not created equal; they were people of different races, sexes, classes, and personalities. It was a related eye-opening experience to find that my new schoolmates were of different races, ages, and sexes. Such a situation had not existed in Japan.

Within a year, our savings were depleted, and my wife and I were in tight financial straits. As a full-time student family, we were able to obtain working permits from the local Immigration Service office. I took any job I could find—busboy, kitchen helper, janitor—anything that wouldn't conflict with my class schedule. My wife worked in a clothing factory. I studied very hard and never missed a class. My desire to learn was intense, and the teachers were knowledgeable and skillful. As dry sand soaks up water, I absorbed all they had to offer. Acquiring the necessary skills to accomplish my dream was my greatest joy, no matter how hard I had to study and work.

By late spring of 1965, I had completed all the requirements. Upon my graduation, E. A. "Tink" Adams, founder and dean of the school, encouraged us foreign students to experience "real" work in the United States before we went back to our own countries. I took his advice seriously. Besides, I was eager to work at an American company and didn't really want to go back to Japan. I prepared my portfolio to target advertising agencies that handled automotive clients.

My job hunt wasn't difficult. Although I liked living in Southern California, I'd been advised to relocate to New York, where 75 percent of the total U.S. advertising budget was handled. Within a week after we arrived in New York, I was hired by J. Walter Thompson Company, the largest advertising agency in the world at that time. One of the company's prime accounts was Ford Motor Company, for which an exclusive creative team had been formed. I was assigned to join the team, assisting Dick Tarczynski, one of the art directors. A few people whispered to me that Dick was a difficult man to work with—demanding, supersensitive, and fussy. I soon realized it was true. But I also understood why: his client was demanding, supersensitive, and fussy. It was my challenge to satisfy him in order to satisfy the client. The bottom line was that Ford Motor Company was a primary source of our company's income.

At advertising agencies, art directors work closely with copywriters to create provocative, attention-grabbing, and informative advertising ideas for magazines, newspapers, catalogues, and TV commercials. In the development stage, I had to draw pictures, graphics, and headlines, because in this part of the process no other materials, such as photos, were available. The layout had to look as real as a printed ad page so the client could clearly visualize the final result. We called this "comp," for comprehensive. The comp would serve as a guideline for the photographers' early preproduction work.

Tarczynski and I worked together on one project after another, and we worked hard. We trusted each other and got along very well. Working with Dick was rewarding. He valued my contribution and proudly bragged about me to his boss and colleagues. One day, I timidly asked, "May I take next weekend off?" He replied teasingly, "No!" But then he said, "Yes. I was thinking the same thing." Later our team would laugh about that moment.

A year after I began working at J. Walter Thompson, I received notice from the Immigration Service that my extended student visa was expiring and that because my "practical training" seemed satisfactory, I should go back to Japan. I showed the notice to my boss. Right away Tarczynski said, "If you'd like to keep working with us, we can do something." I said simply, "Yes." Tarczynski, team head Andrew Nelson, and the company's staff attorney gathered all the necessary documents and submitted the petition to the Immigration Service to keep my position "permanent." Ten months later, my wife and I obtained green cards allowing us to stay.

As soon as my status became stable, I concentrated on my interest in cars. I learned everything I could about the automobile industry, the history of the automobile, auto racing, and trends in automobile development. The 1960s were a big growth period for American autos. The top-ranked import was Volkswagen. There were many VW enthusiasts. That trend was accepted by American society, and the industry, because VW was "German made." Besides, its market share wasn't a serious threat to the Big Three: General Motors, Ford, and Chrysler.

Meanwhile, the Big Three's cars had grown larger every year. By the beginning of 1970, cars classified as "intermediate" had become as large as cars previously designated full-size. Naturally, "full-size" had correspondingly grown even bigger. Engine horsepower increased as well. Size and power were at the center of advertising strategies in the competitive auto market.

At the same period, I was involved in promoting an American Petroleum Institute project to increase gasoline consumption. Their successful campaign encouraged consumers to plan a "Weekend Trip—drive more and burn more gasoline." No one ever imagined the "oil crisis" in those days.

Unexpectedly, the Japanese companies Toyota and Nissan gradually started taking more market share. The Big Three were still optimistic about their competitive edge with the emerging Japanese cars. Executives at the management level still believed "Made in Japan" was a synonym for "inferior quality." That was indeed true when it referred to early 1960s Japanese merchandise. I remember a student at the Art Center College of Design who, wanting to be different, purchased a Toyota Toyopet and flamboyantly drove it around. His only trouble was its engine. The car accelerated so poorly that it could hardly merge onto the freeway. His friend often teased him: "Look at the name of your car—Toy o' Pet! That represents its quality." But "Made in Japan" gradually began to mean a quality product. Japanese-made transistor radios and cameras quietly but steadily contributed to this trend.

The new year of American automobiles comes every fall, when brand-new styles and features are unveiled. Preceding that exciting time of year for automakers and consumers alike, however, are months of groundwork. Advertising agencies started to prepare for the new car campaigns as early as seven months ahead of the announcement of the new models. Usually, the proposed marketing plans are approved in the spring. Meanwhile, the prototypes are built. Art directors and producers are deployed to take pictures as soon as the prototypes are ready. This became our traditional preparatory advertising campaign, tied to magazines, newspapers, and TV commercials.

As American cars grew larger, photographs began taking precedence over traditional illustrations. Car illustrators were gradually becoming obsolete. But this trend didn't affect me because my car illustrations were for presentation rather than reproduction. I illustrated cars for conceptual page layouts, printed mass media, and TV commercial storyboards that were then presented to our client as the proposed marketing strategies.

In the early summer of 1967, I flew to Detroit to assist Tarczynski as he supervised Warren Winstanley, the veteran automotive photographer. Winstanley was shooting a brand-new line of Ford intermediates called Torinos. He believed the best outdoor lighting was at dawn, so we went out to the location and set up the car and camera before sunrise. Then we waited for the precise moment to take the photos. We also shot the car in Winstanley's studio, working till late at night. We seldom made it back to our motel rooms; we slept on a couch in the studio, when we could. We ate takeout fast food three times a day. It took us a week to finish shooting and by that time we were exhausted.

The unforgettable Detroit riot happened right after we got back to New York. Fortunately, Winstanley's studio was located on the east side and was not much affected.

Soon every one of our campaign projects was under control. The new car announcements spread all over the nation. I decided to buy a Ford Torino because of my involvement and as an expression of loyalty to our client. In early fall of 1967, I shopped around the Ford dealerships in town and found a Torino with all the options I wanted. As soon as the salesman took my order, the UAW chose Ford as the target of the year and went on strike. The strike lasted several months. Finally, Ford accepted the UAW's demands. As a result, the wage of workers at Ford Motor Company far exceeded that of the average American worker.

I had anticipated the arrival of my Ford Torino, but when it was delivered in late January 1968 it was a disappointment. I found several screws left on its floor. Several accessories didn't work properly. The gearshift malfunctioned. I concluded the car was a lemon. Workers on the Ford assembly line had performed their jobs poorly in spite of their high wages.

From time to time, I returned to Detroit to supervise photographers—Winstanley and others. On several occasions, I worked with George Kawamoto, who was a kibei nisei, meaning a second-generation Japanese American who had been educated in Japan. He was also a graduate of the University of Southern California. Kawamoto was the most organized and efficient photographer I had ever known. He had a studio and a condo in downtown Detroit. Unlike Winstanley, Kawamoto preferred shooting cars toward dusk. He theorized that evening light is as beautiful as morning light and lasts much longer. That gave him plenty of daytime hours to set up the car and equipment. Kawamoto was also an excellent businessman. He made a fortune investing in real estate and other businesses. At one time, he was a board member of the Michigan International Speedway.

In 1970, a cigarette company, Liggett & Myers, came into my life as a result of its interest in racing cars. Before the FDA ruled that after 1971 cigarette commercials could no longer be aired on television, cigarette manufacturers spent billions of dollars on their TV commercials. After the TV ban, some transferred their advertising budget to auto races: racing cars bearing cigarette logos on the TV screen served as efficiently as commercials. Liggett & Myers purchased Formula One cars and hired Jackie Stewart, the well-known British racing driver. The company held a competition to find a graphic designer to create the logo and body paint. I thought it would be a once-in-a-lifetime opportunity to achieve recognition for my creative designs.

I competed with more than a dozen ambitious contenders, and my design was chosen.

On top of the prize money, I was invited, along with my wife and two-year-old daughter, to the first race of the season in Riverside, California. That was one of the most glorious times in my life. We thoroughly enjoyed the trip, receiving VIP treatment and a side excursion to Los Angeles. The experience was so enjoyable that we decided to escape from New York and live in the sun and warmth of Southern California. Six months later, I quit my job and we moved.

I freelanced in Los Angeles for a while, but things didn't go as well as I had expected. I had been too optimistic. One day in the spring of 1972, Joe Feke and Sean Fitzpatrick, creative directors from J. Walter Thompson's Los Angeles branch, called me to offer an art director position. I couldn't turn it down; the package they proposed was too attractive.

My new assignment was to work for all the Ford dealers in the western region. In the early 1970s, the American auto industry wasn't doing as well as it had in the past. Sales were declining because of the emerging Japanese brands and other imports. Volkswagen, the top-ranking imported compact, had to yield its longtime market position to Toyota and Nissan. The buyers of Japanese cars were not necessarily low-income consumers. Some bought them initially as second or third cars but soon came to recognize the cars' maneuverability, better quality, gas economy, reasonable prices, and meticulous finishing touches.

As Japanese car sales rose, Ford had to do something to compete. The company created subcompact and compact cars: Maverick, then the slightly smaller Pinto. We examined them when they were first released and delivered to dealers. Working with Ford products and being a Ford owner, I hoped Ford was making better cars than the Japanese. Unfortunately, I had already found my Torino a lemon, and the Maverick and Pinto were also disappointing. Ford cut many corners to reduce production costs and compete with the imports. For instance, the cars' glove compartment had no lid. They had cheap upholstery and a sloppy finish. Honestly, my evaluation of the Maverick and Pinto was "Failure!" Thus, I found myself in a dilemma. I tried to convince myself that it was not a war between Japan and America but merely competition between Ford and another brand. Though I had doubts about the quality of the company's cars, I kept working hard illustrating and loudly shouting about the "beautiful and superior" Ford products.

All of a sudden, in 1975, the gasoline shortage, or oil shock, struck. The American myth that "oil is inexhaustible" collapsed. We began to see long lines at gas stations everywhere. The freeway speed limit was lowered to fifty-five miles per hour to save gas. Gas economy became of paramount importance in automobile choice. Naturally, Japanese car sales skyrocketed. Henry Ford II and Lee Iacocca publicly blamed Japanese auto manufacturers for "unfair trading practices," or "dumping," a charge that was never proven. The increase in Japanese car sales was a surprise to Japanese carmakers as well. Their cars had for years been tailored to meet conditions of the Japanese market. Japanese consumers paid three times more for gasoline than their American counterparts. Of course the auto industry had to produce fuel-efficient automobiles with a smaller body and engine, plus a more fuel-efficient combustion system. When the energy crisis hit, Japanese automakers were ready with fuel-efficient car designs.

After six years at J. Walter Thompson, Los Angeles, in 1977 I had an opportunity to take an art consultant position at McCann-Erickson in Tokyo. I accepted somewhat reluctantly because I enjoyed living in Southern California, although Japan bashing annoyed me.

Japan was surprisingly different in many ways from the country I had left fourteen years earlier. The economic boom had reached its peak. Many families owned cars. Expressways stretched from north to south. The bullet train could carry passengers from Tokyo to Osaka in three hours, as fast as air travel. The stores were overflowing with food, goods, and publications. It seemed unimaginable that Tokyo and other major Japanese cities had been bombed to ruins by the United States thirty-two years earlier.

One of my tasks at my new job was liaising with GM Overseas Distribution Corporation and a few Japanese dealers who were selling GM cars. In Japan, dealers could afford their own advertising and could promote merchandise their own way. GM did not have power to control them, but exerted tremendous pressure from the main office in Detroit. GM's main complaint was the dealers' miserable sales volume—fourteen hundred vehicles per quarter. That wasn't acceptable for the world's largest automobile manufacturer. But GM was arrogant and ignorant about the Japanese car market.

First of all, a full-size Cadillac, Buick, or Pontiac was too large to maneuver in narrow Japanese streets. In response, GM created X-cars—the Chevy Citation and Buick Skylark—but these were still larger than full-size Japanese cars. Second, in Japan you drive on the left side of the road, so the steering position is on the right. GM produced only left-hand-drive cars. Third, larger engines consume more gasoline. The Japanese, paying three times more per gallon than American drivers, called American cars "gas guzzlers." Last, the manufacturer's suggested retail prices were already five times higher than Japanese luxury cars; adding shipping costs and surcharge, the final price was unrealistically high. Therefore the typical Japanese consumer was not a potential buyer of American-made cars. Only rich and famous entertainers or gangsters wanted to own one.

Again, the Big Three blamed Japan's limited import policy for their failure to penetrate the market. However, if there had been no restrictions, the sales volume of American cars would have been the same. The majority of Japanese auto buyers were simply happy to stick with their domestic cars.

After almost five years of fruitless effort, in 1982 I came back to New York for personal reasons. My timing was poor. The United States was in the middle of a recession. Headlines in the *New York Times* and weekly magazines all spoke of the economic slump. Cars didn't move out of showrooms. Many workers, both blue collar and white collar, were laid off. Fortunately, my old friends and colleagues helped me get occasional part-time freelance work.

About a year later, there was an opening at my old employer, J. Walter Thompson. I took it, joining my restructured creative team. My old boss, Dick Tarczynski, was still there. He welcomed me, and I was so grateful. I somehow felt like I had gone back to the good old days. There were drastic changes affecting the team, however. All the car accounts had shifted to the Detroit branch office, leaving only the truck division in New York. I didn't mind drawing trucks as long as I was still part of the automobile industry.

One day in 1982, I heard some terrible news. Two autoworkers, drunk in a bar, were complaining about Japanese automakers, blaming them for their job loss. Unfortunately, Vincent Chin, a Chinese American, happened to come into the bar. The autoworkers cursed him, an argument ensued, and in the end the angry autoworkers beat Chin to death. When they were arrested, one said, "I thought he was Japanese," as if that were an excuse for murder. I was shocked and upset.

A lesser but still distressing incident involved UAW members. Some members drove their Japanese-made cars to attend a union meeting. Anti-import extremists smashed these cars in the parking lot.

Shortly after Vincent Chin's tragic death, I got a call from Sean Fitzpatrick, who had been a creative director at J. Walter Thompson, Los
Angeles, when I had worked there. He had climbed the corporate ladder
since then and was recruiting a creative team for Campbell-Ewald in Warren, Michigan. He asked if my wife, daughter, and I would consider relo-
cating. I didn't want to refuse his generous offer. The matter of Vincent
Chin, however, concerned me. I asked Sean, "People in Detroit hate Japanese, don't they?" Sean denied it. "No, not at all. There are some crazy
people everywhere." I took the position.

That was the summer of 1984. At my new office at Campbell-Ewald, my
assigned account was GM's Chevrolet Division, the old competitor of Ford. By
that time, the auto industry's competitive structures had changed discreetly.
GM and Toyota had established a joint venture in northern California to build
the popular Toyota Corolla under a Chevrolet brand name. The new division
was called Geo and was selling Japanese cars, such as the Toyota Prism, Isuzu
Spectrum, Suzuki Tracker, and Metro, under the Geo brand. Ford wasn't an
exception; the company eventually absorbed a Mazda plant in Flat Rock,
Michigan. Chrysler dealt with Mitsubishi, a major supplier of its engine com-
ponents. Moreover, some American cars and trucks were now being built in
Canada and Mexico.

My drawing skill was still a valuable asset to me and my company. Over
the course of my career, I had made thousands of drawings and sketches
of cars and trucks. These illustrations sold our ideas to clients and gave a
precise guide for producers and photographers. Sometimes I bragged that
I could draw better and faster than the computer. Why, then, did I promote the new technology? Let's look at that. Computers are better and
faster for some tasks, like word processing, manipulation of graphics, and
designing page layout. Consequently, they were an asset to my company.
We were able to expand our plans much further and we established preproduction facilities capable of preparing ready-to-print materials. This saved
time and expenses in the long run. This new system, however, put many of
our suppliers—art-preparation studios, typographers, engravers, and print
shops—out of business. I felt bad for them, but what could I do? This world
is constantly changing, especially in terms of technology.

During my ten years of service at Campbell-Ewald, there were several
major changes in my life. My wife died after a long illness. When I bought a
cemetery plot in Southfield, Michigan, I ordered two headstones, one for her
and one for myself. I became an American citizen. My daughter graduated

from art school and moved to the West Coast. In 1994, I knew it was time to step back and take a look at my life. I retired from my full-time job but I did not retire from life. I still have dreams and work to pursue.

Since 1963 (my earliest awareness of the Japanese American roundup during World War II) I had been writing a book, *Japanese of No Return,* about Japanese immigrants in North America, focusing on their struggles and suffering from prejudice. It's based on documentary history and some interviews with isseis and niseis. In this book, I included many pioneers' stories, including that of Tadae Shimoura, a prominent machine engineer, who came to the States in early 1900 looking for opportunity. First he went to a factory in Pennsylvania, where he was advised to come to Henry Ford's company in Detroit. Luckily, Tadae accidentally bumped into Ford himself, who hired him at once.

Later, a friend and member of the Japanese American Citizens League (JACL) who read my book noticed Tadae Shimoura's story. He told Toshiko Shimoura, the widow of Tadae's son, who happened to be a leading member of JACL. I finally met Toshiko at a JACL gathering. Since then, we've become good friends. Incidentally, Toshiko's oldest son, James, was involved as a lawyer in the Vincent Chin case. If one good thing came out of that tragedy, it is that the entire Asian community pulled together.

After my book's first publication in 1991, I discovered through several readers' responses that not all Americans were prejudiced against Asians during the internment period. This new information led me to revise the book. When in 1942, a few months after the Pearl Harbor attack, President Franklin Roosevelt signed Executive Order 9066 to remove Japanese immigrants and their descendants from the West Coast, the Quaker organization American Friends Service Committee (AFSC), protested the government's action, claiming it was unconstitutional. The AFSC protest had no effect on the government's policy. However, the organization continued to support Japanese internees. It tapped many colleges and universities to open their doors to young Japanese American internees to give them the opportunity to receive a higher education. Many institutions refused, but some agreed. Swarthmore College in Pennsylvania was one that opened its door wide, accepting many young Japanese internees.

When Japan was defeated in 1945, I denied the existence of the god that had been shoved down my throat. But when I learned of AFSC's action, I was moved. I felt that it was a blessing from God. I began to attend Quaker meetings regularly, meeting many inspiring Friends. A few years later, I officially became a member of the Religious Society of Friends while still retaining my family religion, Buddhism. Through Quaker activities, I met my Quaker wife, and we are happily married. Nowadays, I am convinced that God exists within my and everybody's soul, but I still firmly reject the gods of mythology or fairy tales.

I believe that no human being has prejudice at the time of birth. In my opinion, prejudice, hatred, and lack of understanding are taught. That results in the type of twisted mind that creates discrimination and war. I believe that God will bless people who have no prejudice or hatred.

Love and peace.

24

A JOURNEY BEGINS ON APRIL 30, 1975

Being Vietnamese American in Michigan

Mimi Doan-Trang Nguyen

"A journey of a thousand miles begins with a single step," and the path of my journey to America began with a series of unfortunate events beginning on April 30, 1975. The significance of this date in Vietnamese history was when South Vietnam collapsed at the hands of the Communists, who took over the capital city of Saigon. On that date, the Americans also withdrew from the region. For a few weeks before April 30, about 130,000 South Vietnamese citizens had been leaving their country by whatever means they could find. They suddenly had to leave their beloved country for freedom and liberty. People escaped in large numbers because they did not want to live under a Communist regime. Since many of the Vietnamese refugees who fled during this period had American friends or used to work with Americans, the United States of America became a natural destination. Those who were fortunate to be part of the U.S. airlifts were taken to Guam or the Philippines. From there, they were taken practically overnight to refugee resettlement centers established in California, Arkansas, and many other states.

Others left in the late 1970s and early 1980s. The refugees who cast off in boats became the "Boat People" who landed in refugee camps in Indonesia, Thailand, or the Philippines. They waited for resettlement to the United States, Canada, Europe, Australia, or wherever else they would be accepted. The number of Vietnamese refugees increased dramatically during this period. In some months, it was estimated, more than fifty thousand people left the country. The number is probably higher, since an estimated one-third died in passage. Some escaped South Vietnam by land, traveling north to China or west to Cambodia, and ended up in Thailand's border camps.

To escape South Vietnam entailed a long and hazardous journey. But to remain was just as dangerous for many people. When the new Communist regime took over the country, it rounded up former political officials and military personnel tied to the South Vietnamese government and sent them to Communist reeducation camps. There they were indoctrinated in Communist ideology and forced into hard labor. Most were imprisoned for four to eight years, some for as long as seventeen. My father, who had been a captain in the South Vietnamese military, was held for eight years. Those were miserable years for my family, as for many others.

There were many international efforts to help the Vietnamese people still suffering in Asia. Spurred by the outcry over the horrors encountered by the Boat People, the United Nations Commissioner for Refugees and other organizations coordinated with the Communist government to create the Orderly Departure Program in late 1970 and early 1980, which allowed people to leave Vietnam legally for family reunification. Then, in 1987, the U.S. Congress passed the Amerasian Homecoming Act, an effort to resettle the children of American servicemen and Vietnamese women. The act allowed over seventy thousand Amerasians and their family members to immigrate to the United States. Amerasian children faced severe social and economic discrimination in Vietnam.

Finally, in 1990, another initiative was progressing, the Special Release Re-education Center Detainee Resettlement Program (known as the Humanitarian Operator, or H.O., Program), the first group of former South Vietnamese political and reeducation camp prisoners was admitted to the United States. This was the first great positive news for my family because we were qualified to enter the country under this program. Our opportunity for a new start was at hand. We had heard many stories of the grandeur of this land of opportunity called America. My family and I arrived from central Vietnam's Hue City as a result of the H.O. Program in 1993. As this new flow of Vietnamese immigrants began, U.S. government resettlement programs attempted to spread out the refugees geographically, for two reasons: first, it was assumed that this approach would help refugees assimilate more quickly, and second, no single area would be burdened with a sudden large influx of refugees. My family's sponsor was in Michigan, so we were sent to Lansing, where only a few thousand Vietnamese residents lived at the time, although later the

Vietnamese population in Michigan grew: they numbered 16,787 in the 2010 census, a 23 percent increase over the previous ten years.

The beginning of our story in America was a humbling experience. My parents had majored in English in college and had a limited understanding of American culture, but my five siblings and I did not know anything about the society—the food, the culture, or the language. We were worried about obtaining an education and becoming a part of American society.

I vividly recall enrolling at Eastern High School at the age of twenty. I was placed in the eleventh grade, my nineteen-year-old sister in the tenth, and my seventeen-year-old sister in the ninth. For the first few months, we often felt bewildered and overwhelmed. Sitting in the front row of class my first day, I felt lonely and frightened as I stared at the plain white wall and the large, dusty blackboard in front of me. The students and teachers in the school made me nervous. I had never been around so many Americans. My English was extremely limited so I was not able to communicate with anyone. Basically, I could only say such things as "How are you?" "Yes," and "I don't know." I understood only very simple sentences. Of the six classes I was enrolled in, I found that English was the most challenging but the most beneficial.

I was lucky to have an understanding and adept English teacher, Mrs. Ovenhouse. At first, when she asked me to do something, I could not under-stand her. Realizing this, she would smile sympathetically and encouragingly at me before rephrasing her request more simply. Mrs. Ovenhouse had the special skills and patience that quickly helped foreign students like me learn English efficiently. In essence, I had to learn how to communicate my internal thoughts and feelings more adequately. As a result of this advice, every day going forward from that moment, I practiced English, listening carefully to people speaking around me and to people on television. Gradually, my Eng-lish improved as I developed skills in both speaking and comprehension, but my first attempts caused me a great deal of anxiety and sometimes embar-rassment. One of the most excruciatingly painful subjects for me was my written work, which seemed always to clash with my Vietnamese grammar. It could take me an entire day to write two paragraphs, as I had to translate each Vietnamese thought into an American sentence. I often felt frustrated as I laboriously composed my sentences, diligently searching through my tattered Vietnamese–English dictionary attempting to find the correct English words.

My speaking skills were another problem. My tongue was often uncoop-erative as I struggled with unfamiliar sounds. The puzzled expressions on peo-ple's faces made me realize that Americans were having trouble understanding me. Fortunately, Mrs. Ovenhouse offered to work with me and my two sisters after school. We began meeting each day, and as we worked together, she frequently commented that she was extremely proud and amazed by our quick progress. These study sessions were always so pleasant because Mrs. Ovenhouse never ridiculed us. Instead, we laughed together like friends, even over errors. She often said that a person who is studying a foreign language must have a good sense of humor.

Throughout my senior year, I gradually developed more confidence, and I finally began to communicate with people more easily than I had believed possible. After two years at Eastern High School, I started to find myself initiating conversations and even thinking in English. My growing confidence and ability provided me with a newfound interest in succeeding in my other classes as well.

I was extremely proud when I graduated with honors in 1994. I enrolled at Michigan State University and graduated from there, also with honors, with a bachelor's degree in electrical engineering. In 1999, I was hired to work at General Motors in Warren, Michigan, as an engineer. While working there, my educational goals were formed with more than the classroom in mind; I wanted to broaden my knowledge and expand my perspective. As a result, I pursued a graduate program offered by the University of Phoenix and graduated with honors in business administration. I shall always be grateful to Mrs. Ovenhouse, for without her contribution, I would probably still be struggling with my second language.

The major goals of many Vietnamese people are going to school, learning English, earning a university degree, and getting a good job, and many in Michigan have successfully achieved these objectives. They are lawyers, doctors, engineers, or business owners. An example is the Bui family, who came to Michigan in 1975. Though the family was penniless and spoke little English, the parents struggled to build a new life for their children. The father put all seven children through college and grad school by working on a manufacturing assembly line. My own parents helped six of us complete college by working any type of job they could find. And Mrs. Vu not only managed to put all her children through college but herself graduated as a pharmacist at the age of fifty-two.

Most Vietnamese American parents are willing to sacrifice everything to ensure their children receive a good education, for it is their top priority. They want and expect their children to do well. Thus, you can imagine the elation my parents felt when their two youngest children graduated from high school as valedictorians of their respective classes. The happiest days of their lives were when they saw their children graduate from college. I saw how proud my parents were of me and my siblings at our graduation ceremonies, and that's something I will never forget.

As we shift the focus onto those Vietnamese Americans who may not have the opportunity to obtain a higher education, we see that they can still achieve success via ownership of a variety of businesses. Vietnamese American businesses have increased in number considerably, ranging from restaurants to nail salons. The latter business has become increasingly prevalent. If you walk into almost any nail shop in your local strip mall, chances are it is owned by a Vietnamese American or staffed by a Vietnamese American manicurist. Originally such shops, often family owned and operated, provided only manicures and pedicures, but now they offer waxing, spa treatments, and facials. The high-tech spa equipment, incidentally, was designed by Vietnamese Americans.

I believe a large number of Vietnamese really drive themselves to achieve success, but of course, not every Vietnamese American has been successful. Sadly, some of our youth have been involved in gang shootings and other illegal activities. For example, in one household of recent immigrants, the father worked delivering newspapers, providing for his family. Although the two younger children did well in school, their older brother is now in custody, threatened with deportation for illegal activities. I am pretty sure that those parents taught, loved, and supported all of their children equally. However, on the streets, peer groups can exert a lot of influence on children, and how they turn out can depend greatly on that pressure.

As young Vietnamese Americans become increasingly Americanized, members of the older generation tend to cling to their old, familiar values and traditions. This can be especially frustrating for the young. Young people are constantly being enticed by America's consumerism mentality: the top brands, the trends, the luxuries. We live in a world in which acquisition is the norm, yet our parents tell us it is ridiculous and wasteful to want anything that is not absolutely necessary for living. The older generation truly believes that we should always save for a rainy day.

At family gatherings or parties, it is not uncommon to see Vietnamese Americans urging their guests in a buffet line to help themselves to big chunks of meat, large shrimp, noodles, a large bowl of *pho* and, of course, delicious *goi cuon* (Vietnamese spring rolls). What is a spring roll? It is a wrapped rice paper roll with various fillings. The traditional version is filled with rice noodles, mint, basil, bean sprouts, lettuce, and slices of pork and shrimp and is often dipped in hoisin sauce with chili and peanut butter. I have seen these rolls with tofu, duck, chicken, and many types of vegetables, all equally appetizing. Best of all, adults and children alike can enjoy it since it is a delightful finger food and fits within the diets of even the most health-conscious consumers. What is pho? It is a soup with rice noodles, slices of beef, bean sprouts, basil, onion, cilantro, lime, and hoisin sauce. It is very delicious and healthy to eat. Actually, goi cuon and pho are considered common, simple foods in the Vietnamese diet, but both have become popular in the United States as well. From international food fairs to five-star restaurants, our goi cuon and pho are the hippest items on the menu and do not show any signs of losing their popularity.

Let's discuss Vietnamese culture etiquette. At most Vietnamese gatherings, when it comes time for the hosts to prepare their own plates, they will usually take only a small amount and bypass the best foods. If asked why no meat or shrimp or noodles, the host will generally say, "Oh, I am not that hungry. I really like rice." In reality, the person is undoubtedly craving the meat and shrimp but thinks it would be rude to take them, believing that they should be left for the guests. In my family, men will take less food and claim they are full before they really are because they want to make sure there is enough food for the others. This might even occur when there is more than enough food for everyone to have seconds and thirds.

Another traditional custom in my family: the adults usually sit at one table and the children at another. If there are not enough places at the adult table for all, some of the women quickly announce that they want to sit at the youngsters' table so they can get up more easily. In reality, the women would prefer to sit at the adult table and engage in mature conversation, but they would never admit this. Instead, they take their plates and eat quickly so that they can get started on washing the dishes.

As a child, I never paid attention to these deliberate acts of self-denial, but I notice them now. Undoubtedly, this is because as a young adult I am feeling the pressure and expectation to engage in such a selfless approach myself. Why this is a part of our culture perplexes me. However, when I reflect on it, I conclude that Vietnamese people are used to struggling. Many came to the United States as refugees of war and had to live on very little while providing a home and food for large families. They had to learn not to waste anything and not to spend money except on absolute necessities. Vietnamese Americans are frugal, yes, but as a group we are very generous and giving as well as resourceful, inventive, and creative.

Growing up in a Vietnamese family means responsibility, duty, and respect for your family. Vietnamese families are extremely close-knit, which is a blessing. Yet at the same time, this can also be detrimental. At times it can cause Vietnamese American adults who grew up in the United States to feel a bit oppressed by the expectations of their parents. For example, they are expected to assemble as a family as often as possible, which can be problematic if they live in other communities. Nevertheless, these adult children seem willing to sacrifice some of their own independence and freedom for their parents' happiness.

Additional differences are evolving between the generations. Members of the older generation tend not to be demonstrative. They don't tell their children they love them. Instead, they show their love, and their children feel it; for example, moms will prepare their children's favorite foods. However, today younger Vietnamese Americans seem to be adopting the American approach. They are being openly affectionate with their children, hugging and telling them that they love them, while the children are reciprocating. Interestingly, I've noticed that my own father is changing in this regard. When he wants to express his emotions in words, he does so in English rather than in Vietnamese; for instance, I heard him tell my youngest sister "I am proud of you!" at her college graduation.

The Vietnamese American community is struggling with a major language issue. The older generation speaks Vietnamese, while the younger generation wants to use English. Of course, for older people, learning English is much more difficult than it is for younger ones. A huge problem occurs when an adult speaks little English and a young person speaks little Vietnamese. We want to preserve our language and customs, and at the same time we want to be able to function well in the broader American society. As a result, Vietnamese churches and temples are offering classes to teach young kids to read and write in Vietnamese and instruction in English for adults.

Vietnamese American cultural events are thriving in Michigan communities. Among them are Tet, or the Lunar New Year (also known as the Spring Festival), and Vietnamese weddings. Both are times for Vietnamese Americans to dress up, get together, showcase their children, chat, celebrate, and make new friends.

Vietnamese Americans of my generation are becoming more actively involved in their communities as a whole, including the schools. I believe we are beginning to feel that we are truly Americans. For myself, I am working hard to craft my own identity and live as an American, taking advantage of the possibilities of life in America, while at the same time respecting my own heritage.

25

A STRANGE LAND

Elaine Lok

I'm not exactly a person with close ties to my family. In fact, I've never been intimate with any of my relatives. So it's quite ironic that I chose vintage family photos as a basis for this project—a project that, in the end, is the only avenue of profound communication between them and me.

Of course, a language barrier has always existed. I'm one of the few people in my family who does not speak Cantonese. Perhaps it's because my parents were hardly ever around when I was growing up, and when they were, they certainly weren't making polite conversation with me. Or perhaps it was my reluctance to learn anything associated with the Chinese culture for fear of being further ridiculed by the kids in my Westland, Michigan, neighborhood and school.

But after spending my childhood alienating myself from the culture, I find that I am sprinting back to know it, embrace it, love it. It took the first quarter century of my life to realize that I can't run away from being "different." I know now that it is perfectly natural to fit in so unnaturally with the rest of the world. That's called "flavor," even though some people perceive it as a license to put others down.

Growing up in a home where girls were expected to follow custom and orders blindly, I strove my entire life to squeeze myself out of that box of subservience and passivity, further stretching the rift between the white me that I wanted the rest of the world to see and the seemingly nonexistent yellow me that my family wanted.

In choosing to pursue this genealogical project, I was deeply influenced by my paternal grandfather's story—or, rather, lack of story. What I do know about him is this: he emigrated from southern China to Canada so he could work as a miner and save money to bring his second wife (my grandmother) and his son from a previous marriage to the United States. He returned to China only once every four years; consequently, my father and his two sisters are all four years apart in age. My grandfather never achieved his goal; he eventually died alone in Vancouver in the 1950s.

Shortly before her death, my grandmother told my father she couldn't remember what her husband had looked or sounded like. My father has virtually no memories of him. The one known photograph of my grandfather was destroyed in a move in the 1960s.

My feeling of never knowing what came before my lifetime has pushed me toward this series of images. They convey feelings of mystery and a sense of being forced to leave our identities in the gutter. I feel that these manipulated portraits are a step toward materializing a memory, making the intangible concrete, giving meaning to the people I am closest to, despite the fact that we are merely strangers in a pod.

26

DAY REMEMBERED

Ti-Hua Chang

Days pass into months, months into years so quickly. That is what my older friends tell me; that is what I have come to learn myself as I age. One day can be like any other, all so similar we cannot remember them as distinct entities. Days are forgotten unless something happens to cause you to remember.

Consider September 20, 1987. It was an ordinary day in terms of world and national events, not sufficiently noteworthy to elicit memories. I remember it, though. At least three hours of it. It was a Sunday, and it was the day I bid good-bye to Mrs. Lily Chin.

I drove to Detroit's Metropolitan Airport to see her off. I was slightly late and I spotted her already at the ticket counter, a group of friends surrounding her. She was having problems buying a one-way ticket from an airline accustomed to round trips. I wondered if I would ever see her again, so I concentrated on straightening out the trouble and tying cords around her vinyl luggage. I concentrated on her departure to forget her leaving.

It was a long walk to the plane. We were all silent except Mrs. Chin's sister, who was weeping. My friend was leaving America after thirty-nine years because she felt her adopted country had abandoned her; the United States would not give justice to Asians. She was leaving because two white men had killed her son, Vincent Chin. Two white men had beat him to death with a baseball bat just because he was Asian. And these killers were free.

Lily Chin last talked with her son on June 19, 1982, another ordinary day. A few hours later, twenty-seven-year-old Vincent went to the Fancy Pants Lounge, a strip joint in Highland Park, Michigan. It was his bachelor party.

He was planning to marry Vicki Wong from suburban Mount Clemens. He worked two jobs, as a draftsman and waiter, to earn enough money to marry and buy a house suitable for his bride-to-be and his mother. He was studying engineering at the nearby Institute of Technology.

Vincent, described as gregarious and easygoing, was having a good time with his friends when he and two other patrons—Ronald Ebens, forty-three, a Chrysler foreman, and his stepson, Michael Nitz, twenty-three, a laid-off auto-worker—began to argue. A dancer at the Fancy Pants testified that she over-heard Ebens curse Chin: "It's because of you little motherfuckers that we're out of work." It was not the first time the Japanese had been held responsible for the recession, and it was not the first time Chin had been mistaken for Japa-nese. The three men exchanged punches, and they were ejected from the club.

The fight resumed outside the bar. Ultimately Chin ran; Ebens and Nitz, the former now armed with a baseball bat, chased him. Twenty minutes later, Ebens and Nitz caught him outside a McDonald's. Highland Park police offi-cer Michael Gardenhire II, who witnessed the scene, testified at the prelimi-nary examination that he saw Ebens take four full swings at Chin with the bat while Nitz held Chin on the ground. According to one of Chin's compan-ions that night, Jimmy Choi, Vincent—with blood pouring from his ears—pointed at Ebens and uttered his final words: "It isn't fair."

The "justice" that followed was even less fair. Through plea-bargaining, Chin's assailants obtained the reduced charge of manslaughter. Despite the violence of the crime and the fact that manslaughter is punishable by up to fifteen years in prison, Judge Charles Kaufman of Wayne County Circuit Court sentenced Ebens and Nitz to three years' probation and levied $3,780 in fines and court costs. Neither killer has served even one full day in prison.

The Vincent Chin case mobilized Asian Americans throughout the United States. The resulting protests and publicity prompted the filing of fed-eral charges against Ebens and Nitz for a racist violation of Chin's civil rights. In June 1984, a racially mixed Detroit-area jury found Ebens guilty, Nitz not guilty. Ebens was sentenced to twenty-five years in jail but was allowed to remain free on bond. On appeal, the U.S. Sixth Circuit Court overturned the jury decision, ruling that Ebens did not receive a fair trial because of three legal technicalities. Ironically, it noted that there was more than sufficient evidence to prove his guilt. On May 1, 1987, another ordinary day, a second trial in Cincinnati ended with a predominantly white jury finding Ebens not guilty. In a published report, Ebens later admitted starting the fight—verbally and physically—a key factor in his acquittal.

So now you know why I remember September 20, 1987. I had met Mrs. Chin because of her son's death, and now she was as close to me as if she were family. I remember the tears on the faces of the dozen of us who came to say good-bye to her. I can see the wool sweaters she knitted for those who worked for justice for her son. I can picture in my mind the hugs she gave that day, soft except for the clasping grip of her hands. I even recall noticing that she grasped to her breast the hardest those who had stayed with her the longest at the trial in Cincinnati. And the strong women and men gathered at the airport, who had never before, throughout the long fight for justice, faltered in their stoicism, let their eyes flow with the waters of their emotions. As Mrs. Chin sobbed quietly, I kept thinking of her words after justice failed in Cincinnati: "I can fight if I know even a little chance of win. But no more chance."

As I watched Lily Chin's plane take off that day, I remember thinking inside, "Good-bye, please take care. Please come back again." That was in the afternoon. I cannot tell you what else happened on September 20, 1987.

I have a photograph taken that day at the airport. Not for my own memory's sake but to show one day to my children and grandchildren and say, "This was Mrs. Lily Chin. She was a very courageous woman. She fought for her son and all of us. She was a person who made a difference."

Lily Chin returned to Michigan in 2001 for cancer treatments. She died in a Farmington Hills, Michigan, hospital on June 9, 2002. She was eighty-two.

PART V

Contemporary Prospects and Voices of the Future

Christine Chen

This final part does two jobs. First, it looks at two contemporary sites that can help build a different Asian American future in Michigan: higher education and political involvement. Second, it listens to voices that represent the future of Michigan and its Asian American populations. Dr. Leslie E. Wong writes his assessment of Asian Americans in higher education from his vantage as former president of Northern Michigan University and current president of San Francisco State University. Sook Wilkinson, the coeditor of this volume, explores how Asian Americans have become involved in the political process in Michigan. After these assessments, the section ends with voices from the future of Asian America in Michigan. Those voices belong to five young Asian Americans in the state: two Korean American adoptees (Kira A. Donnell and Rachel Hyerim Sisco), a Hmong American (Sheila Xiong), an East Indian in Lansing (Samir Singh), and a Chinese American who was a high school student at the time she wrote her contribution (Emily Hsiao). Before we hear about contemporary prospects and the Asian American future, we get insights into both from Christine Chen, an Asian American community activist who hails from the Midwest. (Victor Jew, ed.)

As an Asian American activist who grew up in the Midwest, I know that the future needs to be achieved, not just awaited. I have been organizing within the Asian American community for more than twenty years, since I was a university student. Many in this new generation are also gaining their experience early on. These young leaders are finding their voices and expressing them in a variety of ways: via the Internet and technology, through traditional storytelling, or by creating their own performance space by means of the spoken word.

Back in the 1980s, when I was growing up in Columbus, Ohio, there was no consciousness of a pan-Asian identity or community. In trying to define the Midwest Asian American identity, you have to look at Asian Americans on the West Coast, where there is a long history and a large population. On the East Coast, Asian Americans were defined by how well they adapted to immigrant communities established before their arrival. Defining an Asian American self in the South is about figuring out where one fits into the context of black and white social paradigms. I developed my identity in "Middle America," where these issues intersect in one region.

I considered myself as American as apple pie: I went to football games, was involved with student government and other student organizations, went to homecoming and prom. At the same time, I, like many others, considered myself within my own ethnicity, viewing myself as Chinese American. However, I did so without any understanding of Asian American history. Only in my college years did I come to understand what was brewing in the Midwest and how many of us would be impacted by various events.

Michigan has been the backdrop for the development of Asian American identity. The murder of Vincent Chin was a catalyst for community coalition, bringing together those who understood the incident was based on discrimination and racism directed toward the whole Asian American population.

In addition, because Asian Americans in the Midwest are few in number, many understood the need to work in coalitions as a pan-Asian ethnic community. Asian Americans in the Midwest learned early on that giving voice to the community meant building diverse alliances.

This activism and community building impacted the younger generation with the formation of the Midwest Asian American Students Union (MAASU). This network was created to promote political unity among Asian American students in the Midwest and to support the growth of student-based organizations and resources for programming and for Asian American studies. MAASU also provided emotional support and a safe space for students exploring their identities as Asian Americans in the Midwest. Students at Michigan State University and the University of Michigan were critical leaders in nurturing a network that still exists today.

For far too long the rich and diverse stories of Asian Americans have been neglected. The narratives that follow provide snapshots of how different individuals have been influenced and impacted by their environment and experiences. Just as important is the insight that issues of identity continue to be at the heart of our stories. In the past twenty-five years, we have made strides in strengthening the community's voice but, as you will hear in the voices of these pages, the struggles, joys, and frustrations are more similar than different across the generations.

As the Asian American community grows and becomes more sophisticated, a foundational requirement will be a clear identity as a collective. By developing our identity both as individuals and as a collective community, we gain a stronger voice and become advocates for our own inclusion, for equal participation, and for fair opportunities. It is through these pages we can begin to understand the complex experiences of this new generation of leaders and see our bright future.

27

ASIAN PACIFIC AMERICANS IN HIGHER EDUCATION IN MICHIGAN

Leslie E. Wong and Brianna Reckeweg

The Complex Puzzle of Asian Pacific American Communities

To address Asian Pacific American experiences in higher education in Michigan, one must first understand the context of Asian Pacific Americans (APA) in society at the national level. To achieve this understanding is to confront a complex and multilayered puzzle. One layer involves ethnicities and so-called hyphenated identities, such as Japanese American, Chinese American, Hmong American and Filipino American. Another layer is multigenerational; for example, third- and fourth-generation Chinese Americans are found in many urban communities, not only in the West but across the country. A further layer involves time of entry into the United States. Yet another deals with identity construction from mixed-heritage backgrounds. And an additional layer exists within adoption trends. The complexity of this puzzle makes it difficult to understand the social, familial, economic, and educational situations of the many diverse people who nonetheless seem to fit into the single category APA. But understanding this intricate context, this rich social legacy, helps us to comprehend the significant disparity between educational success and leadership, a discrepancy that we are only now acknowledging.

An examination of the larger context of APAs' social and educational attainment versus the paucity of APAs in leadership positions in education is a lesson in erroneous perceptions of educational success. The implications are immense, for this disconnect challenges one of our most fundamental beliefs: that to be educated is to succeed, a mantra that lies at the very heart of the American experience. We hope that understanding how this tenet has been challenged by APAs in the twenty-first century will lead to strategies and interventions to restore our faith in the effectiveness of American higher education.

The dominant image of APAs is of success at all levels of the educational experience. It's true that the presence of APAs in academia has been strong and continues to be a distinctive characteristic of the APA culture. The incidence of APAs in the professional workforce—industry, public service, education, law, medicine, and politics—is considerable. In each case, the central role played by education in this success is not only recognized but touted both within and outside APA communities.

However, some current educational and social trends within the APA community are different from immigrant success patterns of the past or present. In fact, the successes of earlier generations divert one's attention from the issues of poverty and social isolation that plague many sectors of the APA community today. This historical image of success is responsible for the continuing inability of American education and, in some cases, American culture, to assist APA immigrant communities, which occupy a part of the sociopolitical puzzle quite different from the "model minority" stereotype. The rising presence of Asian youth gangs and the near absence of APA males in education, media, athletics, and entertainment are vivid examples of social contradictions long unresolved. APA success has been so highly publicized that it is now expected on so many fronts; thus, confronting employment barriers and workplace prejudices is challenging and frustrating to APA families. Mainstream social scientists are puzzled by the "troubles" within communities believed to be peaceful and law-abiding.

These contradictions are attributable to changing demographics, particularly regarding the APA war refugee population. Such communities are often defined by partially complete families that relocated to America through repatriation and/or postwar relocation. They generally occupied the lower economic strata of their home culture, thus compounding their difficulties with English. While individuals and families within these subcommunities struggle to achieve any form of success, this nation struggles even to notice such glaring disparities within the "new" APA population.

It behooves universities to understand these disparities since higher education remains a preferred avenue of success for APAs, especially within refugee APA communities. APAs will turn to colleges and universities as their first step to social acceptance and economic security. Higher education's poor understanding of this new segment of APAs has led to some startling omissions, if not neglect, in policy and services with regard to language preparation, financial aid, scholarships, eligibility for tutoring, and other programs that poor, resource-deprived APA students require to succeed in universities. The "success stereotype" blinds us to the need for these programs, although providers familiar with the APA community deem them necessary. The belief that these needy students do not need assistance because "everyone knows Asians are bright and high achieving" can stifle the provision of critical services.

Since education remains a visible mainstay of APA values, understanding how APAs perform in college is essential to understanding the evolution of specific APA communities and their position within the broader context. Thus addressing a richer and more complex multicultural picture of APAs in college will also help us to assess whether such educational striving results in the outcomes normally associated with a college diploma. If the data suggest that this axiom does not apply to APAs, then a new set of questions must be engaged to develop appropriate remedies.

There are startlingly few APA public university presidents in the United States, and there are no APAs in senior administrative positions in Michigan colleges or universities. These facts call into question our belief that education is the great equalizer. Understanding and acknowledging this void in APA educational leadership is the motivation for this chapter. The data are clear, and the growing awareness of this "glass ceiling" challenges our most fundamental beliefs that educational achievement is connected to social and personal success. The result could be that we must acknowledge that education opens the door only slightly for APAs. Unraveling the mystery surrounding the absence of APA leadership at the university level is an important first step to improving the APA community and reaffirming one's sense of the rewards resulting from a college degree.

Asian Pacific Americans in Higher Education: The Broad Picture

Recent data on educational attainment reveal the weaknesses of the model minority stereotype. First, one must acknowledge the well-documented success of APAs in higher education, historically and currently. The *Chronicle of Higher Education Almanac* shows that attainment of all professional degrees from the baccalaureate to the PhD is consistently higher among APAs than all other ethnic groups, including whites. The 2013 almanac reports that the baccalaureate graduation rate for Asians across the United States is 72.1 percent, the highest of all groups. The graduation rate for all groups is 59.7 percent, with whites at 63.4 percent.[1]

However, according to many studies, APAs have the lowest high school graduation rate of all major ethnic groups. A 2008 White House study of Asian Pacific Islanders produced these national statistics: 15 percent of the Asian Pacific Islander population had not graduated high school; 28.5 percent held a high school diploma; 28.8 percent had completed some college; 17.5 percent had earned a bachelor's degree; and 10.2 percent held a graduate degree and/or some professional degree.[2] Thus, the segment of the APA population that graduates college is roughly equivalent to the segment that completes high school. A 2014 study of APA educational attainment revealed that 50 percent of the APA community twenty-five years and older held a bachelor's degree or higher.[3] Of these, 20.7 percent held an advanced degree, nearly 10 percent higher than the population in general. However, this same study showed that 12.8 percent of the APA population lived below the poverty rate. Clearly, in times of economic duress, APAs went to college but an even larger number did not. It is as if we expect APAs will be educationally oriented and graduate but we do not ask ourselves the obverse: what is happening to the large segment of the APA population that doesn't go to college? Our perceptions and ultimately our expectations dwell on those who went to college and succeeded. We need to know much more about the equally large segment of the APA population with only a high school education.

This finding is particularly enigmatic because it is not clear whether these data fully reflect the impact of immigrants, though the studies clearly do not include "foreign students." International students attending U.S. colleges and universities are quite different from resident immigrant populations. It is also not clear whether the data include the post-Vietnam resettlement communities (Laotian, Hmong, Cambodian, Malaysia, Philippines, and Myanmar), whose children are attending American high schools in significant numbers but where studies of their educational experience is anecdotal at best.

If one factors in this Southeast Asian influx, the previous demographic picture that highlighted the success of APAs in college changes dramatically. This means that today's colleges and universities will have to face a large APA cohort that is less prepared than other ethnic groups, or at least less prepared than prior APA students to succeed in college. The very fact that APAs have historically been so successful in higher education means that universities nationwide are unprepared to accommodate the needs of large populations of APAs who do not fit the model minority image: they don't speak English, they have no job skills, and they are not academically prepared. The results of this lack of preparedness will prove costly to APA communities and the nation.

The *Chronicle of Higher Education*'s 2005–06 almanac revealed a significant change in APAs' higher education choices. Before fall 1999, APAs more frequently enrolled in public baccalaureate institutions than in community colleges.[4] However, the 2013 almanac tells a different story: enrollment statistics from the fall term of that year show consistently higher matriculation rates at community colleges compared to baccalaureates. APA enrollments at private institutions, both four-year and two-year colleges, though lower in overall numbers than public enrollments, doubled during this time frame.[5]

These data show two contradictory trends. First, the growth of community college enrollments reflects the choice of APAs to attain fundamental citizenship and job-prep skills. Community colleges provide immediate social and economic solutions regarding language and job-preparation skills. The perceived desirability of this is evident not only in the numbers attending community colleges but in the programs APA students choose to pursue there. The goal appears to be an educational service that will quickly facilitate one's success in American society. Second, the increase in private school enrollment shows that APA families are willing to pay the higher price for private education. This reflects a strongly held cultural belief that education is worth sacrifice. Unfortunately, many APAs do not have the financial means to pursue a private education, especially as greater numbers live near or below the poverty line. The influence of financial distress is most evident in the great number of APAs who cannot even complete high school.

This complicated picture is the backdrop to understanding the APA educational context in Michigan as well as in other states facing large influxes of APAs. (The most recent state censuses report that APAs, including immigrants, comprise the second-fastest-growing ethnic population in many states, including Michigan.)

Asian Pacific Americans in Michigan Higher Education

More and more APAs in Michigan are going to college, although the rate of attendance is far lower in the state than nationally. According to the *Chronicle of Higher Education*'s 2013 almanac, APAs represent 4.8 percent of college students nationally but constitute only 2.5 percent of the college student population in Michigan.[6] Of course, one should keep in mind that Michigan's APA population is a smaller proportion of the state's total population than the proportion of Asians within the total U.S. population. Nonetheless, APAs are reported to be the fastest-growing ethnic group in Michigan, and yet their college attendance rate is not commensurate with their numbers. Those who enroll in college succeed, but there is an even larger group that doesn't attend. And this population needs further study.

As reported by the *Chronicle of Higher Education*, in 2003 APA students made up 3.5 percent of the total enrollment at Michigan's higher education institutions (public and private colleges and universities). Of the 605,835 students registered for fall 2003–4, 20,953 were Apas. Ten years later, in 2013, Michigan's APA enrollment had shrunk to 2.5 percent, with 20,494 students, 459 fewer students although the state's APA community was larger.[7]

A closer examination of Michigan's APA college-going population reveals some interesting trends. More APA males than females go to college and they are much more likely to earn advanced degrees. Generally, APA women outnumber APA men up to the baccalaureate level. If there is an educational ceiling for APA women, the baccalaureate degree appears to be it. The reasons for this unexpected pattern are not yet understood.

Discrepancies between Educational Attainment and Educational Career Opportunities

We start from the assumption that education's benefits strike all populations fairly and equally. Education, if perceived as vital to personal and community growth, must also be essential to a host of other social rewards. Therefore, APA participation in higher education should reflect an ever-lengthening stride into mainstream America. That is, higher levels of education should be accompanied not only by economic reward but by greater leadership and stewardship opportunities both within ethnic communities and in the larger public and civic society.

Michigan provides an excellent example of how the social gains expected to accompany rising educational attainment do not occur. Data from the *Chronicle of Higher Education* and the American Association of State Colleges and Universities point to an alarming situation.[8] If one assumes that higher levels of educational attainment will be accompanied by greater employment responsibilities and advancement in the general economy, one would expect to see a correlation within the field of higher education. As more APA graduates hold advanced degrees and attain faculty posts, one should see a corresponding and equitable growth in the number of APA assistant professors, associate professors, professors, department chairs, deans, provosts, and presidents. While this correspondence generally holds true for white males—and to an even greater extent for white females—the case of career advancement in higher education for APAs is a very different and surprising story.

In 2011–12 the National Center for Educational Statistics confirmed the growing ranks of APAs in the academic community nationally.[9] Eight percent of lecturers, 6 percent of instructors, 13 percent of assistant professors, 10 percent of associate professors, and 8 percent of full professors identified as Asian Pacific Americans. This exceeded the benchmark of APAs in the general population (roughly 5.6 percent of the total). Of the major ethnic groups holding full-time faculty appointments, APAs held 9 percent, African Americans 6 percent, and Hispanics 4 percent. This would suggest that, as is the case with other ethnic populations, the percentage of APAs in the administrative educational ranks would be similar. But this is where the breakdown occurs; expectations and reality separate, with consequences we are only beginning to understand.

While the American Council on Education reports an increase in Asian American presidents for all four-year institutions, public and private, from 1994 to 2004, there was a different picture from 2004 to 2013.[10] First, in both public and private institutions, the number of female APA presidents remains low, despite an increase in doctorates awarded to Asian females from 1990 to the present. Remarkably, the number of public baccalaureate institutions led by APA men in 2004 was just four, despite APA males' continued attainment of doctorate degrees and a greater presence in academic ranks.

Quite surprisingly, the overall number of male and female APA presidents did not change throughout the decade to 2013. One should note that more females than males are first-time university presidents, though many of the male APA presidents in 2004–5 have since moved to their second presidency (including this author). It is also true that many of the 2004–5 APA presidents retired or announced upcoming retirement. In only one reported case has a new APA chancellor/president succeeded a retiring APA chancellor/president (the University of Washington's Bothell campus in May 2013). One would not be surprised to see whites, Hispanics, or blacks succeeding one another. That there is only one instance of an Asian succeeding another Asian is not just noteworthy, it is startling.

The leadership of Michigan's public universities is an acute example of omission and neglect. Keep in mind that the state's APA population is growing and more APA students are attending Michigan schools and colleges. With the author's departure from the presidency of Northern Michigan University to San Francisco State University in 2012, there remains only *one* APA president of a Michigan university (a private nonprofit). The Presidents Council of State

Universities in Michigan reports that no Asian Pacific American sits in the president's or vice president's seat in any of the fifteen public four-year universities. The number of APA male presidents at public four-year institutions is declining, despite the fact that parity at academic and administrative ranks leading to a presidency exists, according to Beheruz N. Sethna.[11] Apas populate and serve as department chairs, deans, and associate or assistant vice presidents. That the number of vice presidents and presidents is zero in Michigan is akin to the near-zero level of APA presidents at four-year institutions nationwide. This is in the context of an ever-increasing number of Apas earning doctorates and assuming midlevel administrative positions in colleges and universities. The highly visible presidential appointments of APA women at the University of Houston and the University of Illinois at Urbana-Champaign overshadow the stalled growth of APA presidents, male or female, in general. It is also clear from Sethna's data that APA women choose not to enter senior administrative ranks to the same extent as their white counterparts.[12] The number of white female presidents at four-year campuses actually increased, from 73 in 1994 to 88 in 2003 to 117 in 2004. A decade later, this has not changed. Today's portrait of the typical university president—male, white, sixty-one, with seven years in the position—has not changed in more than twenty-five years. Private campuses and community colleges offer greater presidential opportunities for minorities in all these reporting years, but that so few APA men and women hold top leadership positions in public and private universities is a sad trend, especially in the face of a larger APA college population.

In university and college careers, success for Asian Pacific Americans is evident in all but what is arguably the most important category: presidential leadership. The lack of Asian Pacific Americans leading public and private four-year campuses is of critical importance to APA communities. Educational and civic leadership is often best represented by the presence of campus leadership, which epitomizes the belief that education leads to success. For the APA community, the disconnect between educational attainment and presidential leadership is painful to acknowledge. Michigan's sole APA president leads a private university. California, a state heavily populated with APAs, has only two APA presidents in the California State University system of twenty-three campuses enrolling nearly four hundred thousand students; there is just one APA president in the University of California system. Campuses, especially publicly funded ones, strive to reflect the face of their communities. The gap between rhetoric and reality in Michigan, in California, and across the United

States must be confronted. Closing this gap is a significant challenge facing higher education.

Conclusions

There is considerable good news in the increasing number of Asian Pacific Americans attending and succeeding at colleges in the United States. They represent the fastest-growing population at community colleges and four-year campuses alike. Educational attainment remains a hallmark of the APA community and reinforces the cultural importance of education. These national trends are mirrored in Michigan. The growing APA participation in the realm of Michigan higher education is clear.

But there is a clear absence of APA leadership at the very top of the ladder. The development of leadership skills will become a major challenge for APA communities. And what comes first is recognition that this leadership vacuum exists. Higher education must examine why APAs serve at all levels of academic leadership except the highest, that of president. That APAs make up only 1.4 percent of all presidencies, public and private, only 1.3 percent of provosts, and only 2.2 percent of other administrators not only needs to be understood; it needs to be changed.

Notes

1. *Chronicle of Higher Education, Almanac of Higher Education,* 2013.
2. *The White House Initiative on Asian American and Pacific Islanders,* 2008.
3. C. N. Le, "14 Important Statistics about Asian Americans," *Asian Nation: The Landscape of Asian America* (April 2014).
4. *Chronicle of Higher Education, Almanac of Higher Education,* 2005–6.
5. *Chronicle of Higher Education, Almanac of Higher Education,* 2013.
6. Ibid.
7. Ibid.
8. Ibid.; Beheruz N. Sethna, "A Pipeline Problem? The Progress of Minorities through the Higher Education Pipeline," *Public Purpose,* the magazine of the American Association of State Colleges and Universities, September–October 2005, 19-21.
9. U.S. Department of Education, National Center for Education Statistics, Integrated Postsecondary Education Data System (IPEDS), "Fall Staff Survey"(IPEDS-S:91–99); and IPEDS Winter 2001–02 through Winter 2011–12, Human Resources component, Fall Staff section.
10. American Council on Education, *Raising Voices, Lifting Leaders: Empowering Asian Pacific Islander American Leadership in Higher Education,* May 1, 2013.
11. Sethna, "A Pipeline Problem?"
12. Ibid.

28

POLITICAL ENGAGEMENT OF MICHIGAN ASIAN AMERICANS

Sook Wilkinson

In 2009 the first permanent Michigan Asian Pacific American Affairs Commission (MAPAAC) was established through a legislative process to serve the state and its 292,500 Asian Pacific Americans. This essay tells the story of why and how the commission was created and describes its contribution to the state.

In Michigan, the Asian American population is the fastest-growing ethnic minority, as noted in Kurt Metzger's essay. As well as the growth in population, the confluence of three important trends played a critical role in the creation of the commission: the growth of grassroots pan-Asian nonprofit organizations, Asian American legislators in Michigan state politics, and the success of the MAPAAC's predecessor, the Governor's Advisory Council on Asian Pacific American Affairs.

Growth of Pan-Asian Organizations

The 1982 Vincent Chin case, described elsewhere in this book, became a rallying point for Asian Americans. In Michigan, it led to the creation of American Citizens for Justice (ACJ), the state's first pan-Asian organization. Some years later, Michigan saw the formation of other pan-Asian organizations, such as Asian Pacific American Chamber of Commerce (APACC), Council of Asian Pacific Americans (CAPA), Asian Professionals Organization (APO), and APIAVote Michigan. The proliferation of these organizations became a driving force bringing people of diverse ethnic and cultural backgrounds together to become a more cohesive community with the common purpose of serving the needs of Asian Americans. It became clear that Asian Americans needed a collective political voice.

Election of Asian American Lawmakers

In 2002, for the first time in Michigan, politicians of Asian heritage were elected to serve in both the Michigan House and the Senate.

The first was Senator Hansen Clarke, elected to represent the First District in Detroit. He had served as a state representative in the 1990s. Clarke grew up on the lower east side of Detroit as the only child of a Bangladeshi father and African American mother. He had a difficult childhood but eventually received a scholarship to Cornell and graduated with a degree in painting. At Cornell, he discovered he had an abiding interest in ensuring that vulnerable and disenfranchised people had representation. This led him to Georgetown Law School, then to politics. He became a U.S. congressman in 2010.

The second was Hoon-Yung Hopgood, representing the Twenty-second District in Taylor and its vicinity near the Detroit Metropolitan Airport. Hopgood, adopted at age two from the Republic of Korea by Chris and Rollie Hopgood, two leaders in education in Taylor, became the first Korean American elected to statewide office in Michigan. He was elected three times to represent the district.

Hopgood was a champion for education in the House, also introducing legislation on transportation, energy, and technology, to name a few. It was he who introduced House Bill 6172, which eventually created MAPAAC. He was elected to the Michigan Senate in 2010 to represent District Eight. He has been the primary sponsor of 393 bills and is a member of eight committees: he serves on the Appropriations Committee, where he is minority vice chair of the Agriculture, Department of Environmental Quality, Department of Natural Resources, and the K-12 School Aid and Education Appropriations subcommittees. He also serves as minority vice chair of the Education Committee and the Energy and Technology Committee.

Sam Singh was elected in 2012 to represent Michigan's Sixty-ninth House District, which includes East Lansing, Haslett, Okemos, Williamstown Township, and Locke Township. Singh's story is one of civic engagement. His parents immigrated to Michigan from India in the 1960s for a better life and the opportunity to attain the American dream. From the time Singh was young, his parents taught him the value of giving back to the country that had given them so much. Singh took those lessons to heart, knowing how hard his parents had worked to provide a good life for him and his brother.

Success of Governor's Advisory Council on Asian Pacific American Affairs (ACAPAA)

In 2005, Governor Jennifer Granholm established this advisory council within the Department of Civil Rights by executive order. The purpose of the council was to advise the governor and the Department of Civil Rights on policy matters pertaining to Asian and Pacific Americans in Michigan.

Within four years, the council and its thirty-two members (twenty-nine appointees, two honorary members, and one advisory member) had left their marks in several areas. The most immediate contribution was to connect Asian and Pacific Americans to state government and the governor's office, so that they had a voice in policy and program changes affecting Asian Pacific Americans (APAs) in Michigan and ultimately all Michiganders. Those changes include:

1. 2006: elimination of the CGFNS (*Commission on Graduates of Foreign Nursing Schools*) examination. Two Michigan Filipino Nursing Organizations brought it to the attention of ACAPAA that Michigan required a time-consuming and expensive CGFNS exam in their home countries. They asserted that this examination was redundant because the foreign nurses already had to pass a national nursing exam similar to the CGFNS exam to be eligible for employment in the United States. Through a legislative bill sponsored by then Representative Hopgood and ACAPAA's letter to the governor advocating for its elimination, the examination is no longer required.

2. 2007: institution of cultural sensitivity and customer relations training programs for Department of Energy, Labor, and Economic Growth (DELEG) managers and inspectors. This policy change came about because of complaints from Korean American owners of dry-cleaning businesses about intimidation by a DELEG boiler inspector. ACAPAA invited the director of DELEG, Keith Cooley, to a regular council meeting to discuss the issue. He promised to investigate the problem. The boiler inspector resigned early in the investigatory process and the training program was instituted.

3. 2008: reevaluation of Michigan driver's licenses rules for foreign nationals. In December 2007, Michigan attorney general Mike Cox issued an opinion, "Permanent Residency Requirement for Driver's Licenses," specifying that an applicant must be a lawful permanent

resident to obtain a license. That would have prevented many lawfully present noncitizens from obtaining licenses, including foreign business executives and international students and their families. ACAPAA played a critical role in bringing this issue to the attention of many stakeholders. Through grassroots campaigning, legislative intervention, and a letter to the governor about the negative impacts of such a policy, the state ultimately changed the requirements to make it possible for lawfully present noncitizens to obtain driver's licenses.

Establishment of Michigan Asian Pacific American Affairs Commission

In 2009, Granholm, in Executive Reorganization Order 2009-16, transferred the powers and duties of ACAPAA to MAPAAC, thereby replacing the advisory council with a permanent, legislatively mandated commission. The APA community had long advocated such a permanent entity to ensure that future generations would have continued representation in the state government.

Thanks to the determination and hard work of APA community leaders, elected officials, and ACAPAA appointees, that dream came true in 2009 with the passage of House Bill 6172. MAPAAC brought about the beginning of a new era for Asian Pacific Americans in Michigan. As a permanent entity in state government, a commission is not affected by changing administrations.

But this success was a long time in the making. The first bill to create such a commission was introduced in 1990 by Representative Lynn Jondahl during the administration of Governor James Blanchard. However, the timing was not right. Almost two decades later, in the spring of 2008, Hopgood introduced House Bill 6172 with thirteen other lawmakers to establish a legislatively mandated commission. Clarke introduced the companion Senate Bill 1371.

This time, the confluence of the three factors described above created a tipping point. On June 24, 2008, three community members, Bing Goei of Grand Rapids, Peter Wong of Grosse Pointe, and I of Bloomfield Hills, were invited to testify in Lansing at the hearing for the House Committee on New Economy and Quality of Life, chaired by Representative Ed Clemente, on why the commission was needed and how Michigan would benefit from it. This was a necessary first step before the bill could be voted on by the full House. Support from the House committee was unanimous. Later that day, when the House voted on the bill, it passed with true bipartisan support and spirit: 101-6, with three abstentions.

House Bill 6172 was then sent to the Senate. The senators were on summer break, but when they returned they and Senate Majority Leader Mike Bishop were petitioned by many members of the community to assign the bill to a standing committee. On the last day of the Senate session, the bill passed, 35–1, with overwhelming bipartisan support.

Finally, on January 12, 2009, Governor Granholm signed House Bill 6172 into Public Act 536-2008, establishing an Asian Pacific American Affairs Commission. In June of that year, Granholm appointed twenty-one members to the commission: Lawrence Almeda, Connie Dang, Willie Dechavez, Bing Goei, Mumtaz Haque, Roland Hwang, Tack-Yong Kim, Anand Kumar, Guozhen Lu, Rona Lum, Ananda Prasad, Ernestina DeLos Santos-Mac, Marilyn Schleiff, Ehsan Taqbeem, Jeff Vang, Ramesh Verma, Marie Weng, Les Wong, Peter Wong, Tsu-Yin Wu, and myself, appointed by the governor to serve as its first chairperson. The commission was housed initially within the Michigan Department of Energy, Labor, and Economic Growth, but was later transferred under Governor Rick Snyder to the Michigan Department of Civil Rights.

The commission's main duties and responsibilities are as follows:

1. To stimulate and encourage the study and review of the status of Asian Pacific Americans in Michigan.
2. To develop a unified policy and plan of action to serve the needs of Asian Pacific Americans in the state.
3. To advise the governor, the legislature, and the office concerning the coordination and administration of state programs serving Asian Pacific Americans.
4. To make recommendations to the governor and legislature regarding changes in state programs, statutes, and policies.
5. To advise the governor and legislature of the nature, magnitude, and priorities of the problems of Asian Pacific Americans in Michigan.
6. To review and advise the governor and the legislature on the state's policies concerning Asian Pacific American affairs.
7. To secure appropriate recognition of Asian Pacific American accomplishments and contributions to the state.
8. To review and approve the annual report by the Office of Asian Pacific American Affairs. (Due to budget constraints, this office is not yet established.)

9. To make recommendations to the governor and legislature regarding methods of overcoming discrimination against Asian Pacific Americans in public and private employment and in respect of civil and political rights.

10. To work to ensure equal access to all levels of education for Asian Pacific Americans.

11. To promote methods to ensure equal access to state services for Asian Pacific Americans.

12. To cooperate with and coordinate activities with the commission on Spanish-speaking affairs, the Michigan women's commission, and any other commission that deals with minority or ethnic affairs.

13. To monitor, evaluate, investigate, advocate, and initiate programs for the betterment of Asian Pacific Americans in Michigan.

14. To serve as a reporting agency for incidents of anti-Asian and anti–Pacific Islander American harassment in the state.

15. To promote public awareness of Asian and Pacific Islander cultures.

The first group of gubernatorial-appointed commissioners represented all regions of Michigan and eleven ethnic communities: Bangladeshi, Chinese, Filipino, Hmong, Indian, Indonesian, Japanese, Korean, Pacific, Taiwanese, and Vietnamese. We felt proud and privileged to serve the state of Michigan and our communities. The commission's mission is "to advance the full and equal participation of Asian Pacific Americans in the building of a greater Michigan." The commission is ready to lead to make Michigan a better place to live and work for all Michiganders. Some highlights of MAPAAC's accomplishments are the following:

1. In 2011, cultural competency training was provided for Michigan Department of Human Services/Oakland County Children's Services Administration. In 2008, ACAPAA member Mumtaz Haque shared the case of an Asian Indian family whose two children were taken away and placed in a foster home by Department of Human Services (DHS) caseworkers without following due process. The caseworker, unable to understand cultural nuances, misinterpreted the situation, resulting in the wrongful separation of the children from their family. ACAPAA invited the director of Human Services, Ismael Ahmed, to a council meeting to address the issue. The case, however, went

to court. Almost two years later, the court ruled that the children be returned to their parents. To avoid future cultural misunderstandings, Haque presented two sessions of cultural competency training to the staff at the Department of Human Services/Oakland County Children's Services Administration. The staff was provided with a list of APA organizations and individuals who could help DHS workers understand language or cultural nuances in future. DHS reported that the training sessions were valuable and that further cultural competency training sessions might be needed.

2. In 2011 and 2012, the commission focused on the governor's Global Michigan Initiative to revitalize Michigan's economy by utilizing the talents of Asian Americans. MAPAAC hosted "Paths to Success" panels in business and education. In business, small-business owners voiced the issues faced by APA entrepreneurs. In education, panelists included international students from Michigan universities who provided valuable information and insights about the challenges they face.

3. MAPAAC hosts an annual Asian Pacific American Heritage Month celebration in Lansing at the Capitol Rotunda.

4. MAPAAC cohosts annual Vincent Chin Memorial events with American Citizens for Justice (ACJ).

5. In a January 2012 Troy City Council meeting, a resident being considered for the city planning commission used the term *Chicom* in his public comment. This was tolerated and accepted by the city council without admonition. MAPAAC released a letter to the editor to express the commission's objection to the use of the term, which evokes ethnic hatred from the Korean War era. At the next month's city council meeting, I requested an apology and a comment from Troy's mayor and council for allowing the use of such a term. Michigan Department of Civil Rights director Daniel Krichbaum and Haque, a resident of Troy, also spoke to the issue. Mayor Janice Daniels invited Haque to discuss the issue a day prior to next city council meeting. The mayor promised respect for all ethnic groups (in the second-most diverse city of Michigan) and pledged to maintain decorum during council meetings. Then the council passed a new rule governing meetings: "[P]lease do not use expletives or make derogatory or disparaging comments about any one person or group. If you do so, then there may be immediate consequences, including having the microphone turned off,

being asked to leave the meeting, the deletion of speaker comments for any re-broadcast of the meeting. Speakers should also be careful to avoid saying anything that would subject them to civil liability, such as slander and defamation." The City of Troy also agreed to recognize May as Asian Pacific American Heritage Month.

6. MAPAAC took swift action the day after a racially insensitive ad for U.S. Senate candidate Pete Hoekstra appeared in Michigan on Super Bowl Sunday 2012. MAPAAC issued a press release requesting that Hoekstra stop airing the ad, and participated in a press conference with a coalition of civil rights leaders, led by APIAVote Michigan, urging all political candidates to make a pledge to "Respect America, Respect Michigan" in their campaigns.

7. MAPAAC worked successfully with the governor's office to recognize Fred Korematsu as an Asian American civil rights hero. The first commemoration took place at Troy High School on January 30, 2013. The 2014 Fred Korematsu Day was observed at Huron High School in Ann Arbor.

8. MAPAAC hosted Affordable Care Act townhall meetings reaching more than fifteen hundred people in the Asian American community in 2013.

The political engagement of Michigan Asian Americans is gaining momentum. On the voter side, a non-partisan, non-profit organization, Asian and Pacific Islander American (APIA) Vote Michigan has worked hard to raise the community awareness about the importance of voter registration, civic participation, and voter engagement.

More Asian Americans in Michigan have shown their resolve to run for elected offices at the state and national levels. Mr. Bing Goei ran for the state House seat in 2010 and 2012 as a Republican candidate. He is a successful Grand Rapids businessman tapped by Governor Snyder as the Director for New Americans, a new office created in early 2014. Dr. Syed Taj, a member of the Board of Trustees of Canton, Michigan, was the Democratic nominee for Michigan's 11th congressional district for the United States Congress. Ms. Stephanie Gray Chang is a 2014 Democratic candidate for District 6 that includes southwest and downtown Detroit, a portion of the eastside of Detroit, River Rouge and Ecorse for the Michigan House of Representatives. Dr. Anil Kumar narrowly lost the primary in his bid for Gary Peter's seat in the United States Congress.

29

ARIRANG

Kira A. Donnell

July 11, 2001

Pusan

*I was born on March 1, 1983, a Korean national holiday, at 1:20 a.m.—
the dead of night. Was it raining? Was everyone celebrating deep into
the night? I'm convinced that if I concentrate hard enough, I'll be able to
remember that one glimpse I had of her before being whisked away.*

There is confidential material in my file. Proof that a history, deeply rooted
somewhere here in this rice-paddied soil, exists before my migration to America. But Korea seems determined to keep me an outcast. There are so many
rules, and one is that queries from Korea's banished children have no meaning unless the mothers want to be found. Oh, but it would be so easy if she
would welcome me home. I am waiting for her to reach her hand out to me
because I cannot reach for her. Does her silence mean that she doesn't want
to be contacted? She's had eighteen years. I'm beginning to think that if she
hasn't inquired by now, she never will.

I have returned to my motherland after an eighteen-year exile. And
though I've been waiting for this homecoming, fantasizing about it, for as
long as I can remember, the reality is far more complicated than I'd dreamed.
For the first time in my life, I look like everyone else. My exotic almond eyes
and glossy hair are common and plain. Walking down the narrow streets of

Pusan, I am swallowed up in the crowd. I'm terrified that I'm losing myself somehow in looking like everyone else.

Yet I am a stranger in my native land. Fed on corn and mashed potatoes, my palate finds *kimchee* too strong. Accustomed to the easy drawl of the Midwest, my tongue stumbles awkwardly over the unfamiliar syllables of a simple "hello." My hair is too short for the good luck jade hair stick, and the intricate bow of my *hanbok* is haphazardly kept in place with strategically placed safety pins. I feel like an impostor.

Pusan is the second-largest city in South Korea, situated on the southern coast of the Korean Peninsula. Miles of coastline border the city, and large freighters call to one another as they dock in port. In this city, a woman gave birth to a baby girl and sent her across the sea.

As I walk down the beach at low tide, my mind desperately tries to convince my roving eyes that it's foolish to search the crowds for a familiar cheekbone, eye, or nose. I am not going to find my birth mother. She has disappeared into the folds of a nation still bound by the Confucian edicts of patrilineal blood inheritance. Korea's pride in the purity of its people's blood has kept it strong through centuries of invasion and massacre. But babies who mar the country's venerable roots are not tolerated. How easily Korea erases its bastard mistakes. But whose fault is it, really? A nation is far too large an opponent to stage a personal vendetta against. And how can I blame her, when she has always been my first-star wish? Despite what my therapists tell me, I can't help but feel guilty.

Poet that I am, I've been toting my journal in my back pocket all across this foreign nation. The creased pages hold unrhymed nonsense and poorly spelled Korean phrases. Lately I've been keeping a list of the things I've found washed up on the shore:

- a lightbulb
- onions
- a tomato
- a very dead rat
- even deader fish
- a whole watermelon

It's as if these objects, so similar to what I might find at home on Lake Michigan's shore, are pieces of evidence crucial to figuring out what happened eighteen years ago. Or maybe I'm compensating, filling this spiral-bound with flotsam to mask the fact that I haven't found the real answers yet. The practical part of my mind takes over and I scribble out my list. "Stupid," my conscious scolds. "What did you think you'd find out here? You didn't expect to find her, did you?" Glancing at my watch, I turn to head back to the hotel. I have an appointment with a Korean social worker to go over my adoption file.

David Lim has been working with Korean adoptees for over twenty years. He has short graying hair and deeply grooved smile lines that work quickly to dispel my nervousness. I cannot help wishing a little that he could be a surrogate grandfather: the bridge between who I am now and what I have left behind. With a reassuring smile, he opens my manila folder and scans the first page of angular Korean text.

"Well, Kyung Joo, do you know why you were given up?" Mr. Lim raises his head from the flimsy rice paper to peer at me through his thick wire-rimmed glasses.

I nod. I've pored over the blurry ditto sheets from the adoption agency, trying to find my mother's face in the shadows of smudged ink. A doctor's hasty scrawl on my birth certificate verifies a live birth and there, stapled to the right-hand corner, is my picture: I gaze straight at the camera, unsmiling. I imagine there is a look of accusation behind the tired resignation in those eyes. Sometimes I still see that expression in the mirror. I never know what to make of it.

My birth parents were lovers, unmarried. When my birth mother became pregnant, my birth father ran away. Single motherhood in such a paternity-oriented society is dangerous to both mother and child. Fatherless children in Korea have virtually no identity. The mothers are spurned as debauched and impure. Education, employment, aid—so many things are prohibited. So my birth mother decided adoption was the best option. It is a mere skeleton of a story, with plenty of room for me to wonder whether my birth mother loves me or hates me. Or thinks about me at all.

Mr. Lim flips through the pages, making thoughtful "hmm" sounds every few seconds. I lean over to peer at the sheets, but Mr. Lim pulls them away. "This information is confidential," he says, turning the pages facedown. "Your mother's name, her address."

I frown at him. This is my file. How can my own mother be forbidden to me? I resist the urge to snatch the pages away by sitting on my hands. Violating the strict Korean etiquette will get me nowhere. Irrationally, I try

0

to memorize the faint *Hangul* characters I can see backward through the thin paper.

Mr. Lim, oblivious, continues to leaf through my file. "Ah," he says. "Here is something I can tell you. Your Korean name, Kyung Joo? Your mother chose that."

Though the fact that the name and address of the woman I've been grieving for my entire life is a mere fourteen inches away diminishes the significance of this scrap of information, it is something. That my mother chose my name is unusual. Most unwanted babies are named by the nurses at the hospital or the orphanage nuns. I am named for one of the most beautiful cities on the Korean Peninsula, a far cry from the flat, neutral tones of fields and pastures in a Michigan landscape. The mountains of Gyeongju are studded with blossoming japonica trees that hide ancient Buddhist temples with giant bells and stone statues that gleam as the first sunrays of the day catch the gems imbedded in the forehead of Buddha. My name means bright jewel.

My session with Mr. Lim ends, and I quietly thank him and turn away while my mind tries to sort out the confusion this meeting has generated. Korean adoption policies make it very difficult for adoptees to obtain information about their history or make connections with relatives. Adoptees must wait to inquire until they are eighteen. Information is doled out in such tiny portions that it produces far more questions than answers. Reunions are possible only if both the birth family and the adoptee contact Korean Social Services. This is to protect birth mothers, who often end up getting married and having families without telling anyone they've given up a child. In Korea the stigma of unwed motherhood is such that sometimes it's not safe for birth mothers to tell their loved ones about the child they've given away, even years afterward. Their august ancestry forces them to remain silent.

Returning to the beach, I struggle with my emotions. Frustration wells inside me as I think how physically close I was to that key information I have been searching for my entire life. Another part of me knows that even if I had the information, contacting my birth mother could condemn her.

A child wearing just a diaper runs along the shore on his tiptoes, squealing when the gentle waves lap at his ankles. Nearby, his mother claps her hands and calls to him. I sigh as I watch the child prance to his mother and be swept up into a tickly cuddle.

July 14, 2001

Pusan

Omoni—

Find me, keep me. I'm crying and I don't know how to stop. I hurt. Fill these holes inside me. I have so many questions, and I've fooled myself into thinking that you hold the answers.

I'm here where I began, and I feel so lost. It's so beautiful here, on the ocean; I feel so close to you. Did you walk on the beach while I grew inside you? Did you listen to the monsoon rains tapping on the roof? Are you still here somewhere? Night falls and I am so scared. I need you. I need you to be my light. Hold me and let me know it's okay to be broken for a while. Chase the shadows away and make me whole.

I have slept for two days straight. This utter exhaustion seems to be the way my body has decided to cope with grief. But something inside wonders how I can be mourning for something that maybe wasn't even mine to begin with.

My family buzzes around me. Not Omoni, but Mom, Dad, Erica, Jeff, Drew. The pale tones of their skin, standard enough at home in Michigan, light the room here in an unnatural way. I feel myself retreating from their usually comforting open circle of warmth. I cannot complete their ring when I feel so fractioned.

I leave their worried expressions to scour the beach again. I cannot allow myself to be Kira when Kyung Joo is still so lost. Being Kira means being surrounded by warmth, by laughter. But somehow, in recrossing the Pacific, Kyung Joo has convinced Kira that she, too, will be abandoned, forgotten, denied. To save myself from that hurt, I distance myself, become a lonely island in the gray sea.

How can I exist without Omoni? I have somehow defined myself through her absence, have allowed myself to be nullified. Inside I feel hollow and counterfeit. I can hear the winds howl within me as they snake around my bones—empty, empty. I long for her existence to verify my own.

Today it is overcast and chilly, the air pregnant with rain. There has been talk of a typhoon. The strong salty wind propels me down the shore. Gazing out across the green-gray sea, I see a fish jump, twisting his body around in a loop before crashing back beneath the ponderous waves. It is a golden opportunity, a wish on a fish, and I recite familiar words in my head. *Find me, keep me.* The phrase is so worn that its edges have been rounded smooth, like a tide-tossed stone. It's not even words anymore but just a wisp of color, the faintest of blue, the smallest of sounds. I worry that by now, there's no meaning left behind it. The magic's been used up.

There is a song that every Korean knows by heart. It conjures kinship in a way that even the national anthem cannot. I have seen choirs of Koreans singing the simple melody with poignant wistfulness, swaying back and forth like waves. It is a song of desertion, of loss, of longing. *Arirang.* I hear the words in the cadence of the ocean swells.

Arirang, arirang, arariyo	Walking over the peak at Arirang
Arirang kokearo naumawkanda	you left me behind. You will be tired before you reach one mile.
Na reul pauriko kasineun nimeun	Walking over the peak at Arirang
Simnido motkasaw palpyaungnanda	the sorrows in my heart are as many as the stars in the sky.

It has grown dark. I scan the sky for familiar constellations, patterns that exist both here and across the sea. But the stars are hiding, the clouds obscure their shine. No star-wishing tonight. Squaring my shoulders, I practice smiling, preparing myself for reentry into the commotion of my family. I harden my skin against their hugs. They are so tactile, touching for reassurance, to forge connections. I remind myself not to recoil from their hands like a beaten stray. With one last glance toward the night-blanketed sea, I walk toward the steady lights of the hotel.

July 15, 2001

Pusan

I had a dream about her last night. I can recall vividness in rich greens and pinks. We sailed down a pebble-bottomed stream, she in a white cotton skirt, me resting between her knees, sitting cross-legged in the bottom of the boat. The air smelled of frangipani. Her cool hands on my forehead felt like home—neither Michigan nor Korea but a place I didn't even know existed—and her laughter was high and tinkling, like scattering diamonds.

I remember the feel of the smooth sun-warmed keel beneath my hands and the low creak of contented wood as we let the current carry us. The eddies reached their fingers out to caress our boat. The boat picked up speed as we navigated large boulders, and water sloshed over the sides into my lap. I held my breath through the rapids, pitching to and fro with the little row-boat. As we skated onto smoother waters, I turned around, reaching for her hand. But she had disappeared.

It always happens this way when I dream her. She vanishes, and only then do I realize that I never see her face.

I am leaving this city, returning to the plainness of overcast midwestern skies. I'll remember the horizon, how it looked at daybreak with the gentle fog rolling in. And the beach, the rolling waves. Yet it's not enough. I'm still grasping for something of this place that will make it mine. A sign, to show me that I've come home. Something to tell me where I came from. Something to tell me where to go from here.

The beach has vanished, covered now by swirling gray monsoon, foamy and hissing. I stand at the edge of the cement seawall, shivering in the heavy air. I curl my bare toes around the ledge, shying away from the murky water. I am alone. Even the seagulls have found sweeter shores. I have built a paper boat, have manned it with flower petals, sweet and parchment thin.

My mom comes up behind me. She has followed me. She stands beside me and places a gentle hand on my shoulder. I flinch. Her russet hair billows around her like a halo. "How do you feel?" she asks, peering into my face, her round green eyes vivid against all the gray.

I shrug and turn my head away. I can't bring myself to look in her eyes. I cannot allow myself her solace. Kyung Joo is not ready to let go yet. Kneeling, I release the paper craft into the swirling water. It tilts precariously, rights itself, and heads toward the horizon. My mom gives my shoulder a squeeze as I stare unblinkingly ahead. With one last pat to my shoulder blades, she retreats to the warm comfort of the hotel.

For several long minutes, I stand motionless, watching my little boat pilot the choppy sea. I wish my wish and concentrate, willing the craft to stay afloat. But the paper is thin, and it begins to list, pitching drunkenly. It slowly disintegrates until one final wave pulls it under. I crouch on the cold cement, curling small, so small, into a tight ball. And then all I can do is cry and cry and cry.

30

FIVE SECONDS

Sheila Xiong

I take the last of what is left in the gallon jug of water, which fills my cup half-way. I drink it all in one gulp and sit down. I turn on the TV and flip through the channels quickly, paying no attention to what is on the screen. For some reason, I feel remotely calm, as though I have somehow escaped reality. I have escaped what is inescapable. I pick up the box and read it again: *Proven to be 99 percent accurate.* A feeling of uneasiness begins to devour me.

As a child, I had never felt that my parents would love me less because of something I'd done. But as I got older, it became apparent that their love for me was measured by a ratio: what I was supposed to be versus what I really was. I was supposed to be an obedient girl, never questioning my parents. In actuality, I was a rebel—full of questions, not afraid to do what I wanted when I wanted—all in an effort to understand aspects of my culture I could never quite fully comprehend.

They told me as a child, "You can do whatever you want; the sky has no limits." As soon as I turned eighteen, though, I learned that the sky, for a young Hmong girl, has nothing but limits. "You cannot wear that. You cannot call boys. You cannot go out. You must marry a Hmong man. You *have* to marry Hmong." I felt like I was I obligated to live within confinement.

It was the beginning of a new relationship with my parents, one of constant battle. We were at war, fighting over the contested ground of "marriage." Historically, the age at which Hmong girls marry can be as young as thirteen years old. I was well beyond that. My parents welcomed suitors who pursued me. I refused to have anything to do with them. For months, various suitors

arrived to eat dinner with my family and me. I was infuriated; you could virtually see the flames following me every time I stormed downstairs at din-
nertime. While the men were busy trying to impress my parents with their
credentials, since they were usually much older than I, I was busy secretly
planning ways to disappear from the dinner table and escape back into my
room. I named my plan Operation GMTHOH, that is, Operation Get Me the
Hell outta Here!

Why couldn't my worries be those of the average eighteen-year-old?
Homework, the SAT, finding a date to the prom? But this was the life I was
born into. I wasn't your average teenage girl with average teenage worries. I
was Hmong. Meaning I would be forever tied to a distinctive culture with its
unique traditions and values. I would be forever tied to parents who would
never, under any circumstances, let me forget who I was and where I came
from.

The word *Hmong* means "free." The men, indeed, are free to do whatever
they please. Hmong men can marry more than one wife if they choose. They
can marry a substantially younger woman. They can even marry someone
who is not Hmong (and not feel any guilt about it). None of these options
applied to women.

Growing up, I did whatever I wanted, when I wanted to do it. I broke rules
left and right. I called boys, I sneaked out to hang with friends, and I dated
outside my ethnic background. But I did all this secretly. My parents eventually became aware of my horrible wrongdoings and I was officially labeled a
"bad girl." And nothing could be worse than a bad girl. Who would marry her?

But I have always wanted to know the answer to the million-dollar question: Who decided that a Hmong girl's worth is based on what kind of wife she
would be? It was as if this concept was the national anthem in my culture, and
my parents proudly sang it every day. To make them happy, I had no choice
but to stand up, place my right hand on my heart, and pretend I was singing
harmoniously right alongside them.

I finally muster the courage to get up and go to the bathroom. My hands
are shaking. I feel like I can't breathe. I have just turned twenty-one and have
taken my first pregnancy test. *Please wait five seconds for results.* That's all it
takes, five seconds, to see if I am going to be condemned as a bad girl forever.
Five seconds to know if my parents will disown me. Five seconds before I will
know if my life is going to drastically change.

One. How am I going to tell my parents? What am I going to tell my parents? How will they react? Will they still consider me their daughter? Will

they try to force me to marry the father of the baby? Will they ask for a bride price? How much will they ask? If they don't ask, is that an insult to me? And —will they still love me?

Two. What about my relatives? What about all my aunts, uncles, grand-parents, cousins, and the rest? Am I going to be able to face them? Am I ready to hear the same lecture over and over again? Will I have the courage to stand up for myself while they continually refer to my pregnancy as a "huge mistake?" How much pride can I swallow?

Three. What about the Hmong community that surrounds me? Can I handle the fact that my unplanned pregnancy will be pushed in my face every time I step out in public? Can I deal with hearing, countless times, that I have caused my parents to lose face? Can I handle the gossip, the faint whispers, the looks of disapproval, the repetition of the all-time classic phrase, "That's so and so's daughter" murmured by people I don't even know?

Four. What about the father? My parents will not accept him. He is not Hmong. Will he respect and abide by the traditions of my culture and marry me? Or will he run away from what my culture expects? Away from me?

Five. What about me? What do I want?

As a young girl, I had always felt that being Hmong meant that my cup could never be filled more than halfway, that I would be allowed to do only half the things a man could. That I would always be considered only half of what a man was. Regardless of how hard I tried to fill my own cup, I felt as if I would have to wait for someone, a man, to come along and make my cup—my life—full. This was my reality.

Summoning all the courage I possess, I look at the test results. They are negative.

31

A SEARCH FOR HYERIM

Rachel Hyerim Sisco

Who Is Rachel Jones?

Only a few days ago, an old high school friend stopped me on the University of Michigan diag with the grandiose exclamation, "Well, if it isn't Miss Jones herself!" I was immediately swept up into a flurry of hugs and loving rib-pokes. Had it been someone else, someone who knew that I had abandoned the name Jones six months before, he or she would have been greeted with a feisty retort: "Who the hell are you talking to?" But not wanting to embarrass my friend, I smiled and greeted her more simply: "Oh, hello." I eventually made a point of mentioning the shift of name from Jones to Shin.

"A rose by any other name would smell as sweet" goes the famous line, and yet it is not true for me. The "title dysphoria" I have experienced since I became an adult is a concept that should not come as a surprise to those familiar with the complicated issues involved in adoption. I am a woman furrowing my way along a path that will eventually lead to law school. I have my feet firmly planted on the ground with a determination to create a more pluralistic world for myself. I am a genuinely happy person, but when considering the influence of my adoptive identity, I have never been able to answer the question, "Who is Rachel Jones?"

Having the term *adoptee* permanently attached to the back end of my Asian-self acted like a restraining order, stifling my ability to identify solely as an Asian American. With the limited resources available to me, all I knew of what it meant to be Asian in this world was what I had seen on TV and read in the books my parents lovingly gave me. These books and TV shows depicted

Asians as soft-spoken people with black hair. The men were secretly kung fu masters wielding powers from another dimension, and the women were shy, diminutive figures, always following their husbands around for protection.

When I see these images now, I find myself reverting to feelings I haven't felt since I was ten. Even then, I was alienated from the five or six other Asian children in my school, who had been raised in "real" Asian households. I was the decoy—the one replica hidden within a case of fine celadon vases. Because of my isolation from all things "Asian" during my K-12 years, I thought it was my *name* that was keeping me from fully understanding the significance of the Asian blood that flowed through my veins. "Rachel Elizabeth Jones" had no hint of anything remotely foreign. Consequently, *it* must have been the problem. I loved my family dearly and felt no anger toward them for bestowing upon me this All-American title. However, I knew they would not be able to answer all the tough adoptee questions I so furiously pondered.

During this early period, I was tremendously ignorant of the long history of Asian Americans in this country. Searching for answers, unable to question my family, it eventually dawned on me that the way people choose their identities is strongly influenced by what history has laid before them. Therefore, if I was ever to truly grasp the ways in which "Asian female" or "Asian adoptee" could be defined, I must look to my history books and my schooling. And unbeknown to me, there were people watching, waiting for me to throw a pitch.

The Motivator

The minimal Korean I had learned attending culture camps as a child was not sufficient to allow me to blend into the sea of Asians at the University of Michigan. Starting college is bad enough for anyone—thrown into a whirlwind of lecture notes, exams, pop quizzes, and smelly roommates. But to try to handle identity issues on top of it all was nothing short of exasperating. And perplexing. I had come to this university to immerse myself into a new and diverse environment with the hope of shedding my Asian otherness. So how could it be possible that the Asian community that I was trying to join at this top-notch, affirmative-action-promoting school was showing me the same intolerance I thought I had left behind in my hometown? If I was going to run into this type of roadblock—here, of all places—how was I supposed to connect with someone and start making my identity struggle known?

It was a providential day for me when all my frustrations came spilling out in one great rant in the office of my psych professor Charles F. Behling.

A South Carolinian by birth, he had experienced firsthand growing up in a racially segregated society. As if he had all the time in the world, his genuine interest apparent, he sat there with me while I let out all the aggravation I had pent up inside. When I had finished my emotional tale, Charles placed a hand on my shoulder and suggested I express these issues in the forum of a program he was codirecting: the Program on Intergroup Relations (IGR). In that setting, I could share my predicament with the goal of finding others to connect with. He believed my participation would be beneficial to both his program and my own well-being.

The IGR focused on methods for teaching social justice and multiculturalism. One brilliant technique was "intergroup dialogues," in which students, led by a team of rigorously trained peer facilitators, discussed specified social identities (race, gender, socioeconomic class, and so on).

For the first time, I felt free to explore my own social identities through the power of group discussion. For three semesters, I trained and facilitated alongside more than a hundred other wildly enthusiastic students. Charles was always there to coach me, and he eventually helped me prepare for the 2005 winter semester in which I had the chance to co-facilitate a dialogue for Asian women and men. My co-facilitator and I agreed that we wanted to emphasize the disadvantages *and* the advantages of being Asian American. Through the readings assigned and the discussions planned, we hoped to provide participants with a safe and open arena in which to combat the stereotypes and social constructs that plagued us individually.

Through the dialogue, I was able to find my way deep into the hearts of other people whose Asian "otherness" had been a root of their self-discovery ordeals. A great weight was lifted from me once I realized I was "one of many." That we all had experienced racial slurs and malevolent harassment was strangely comforting. Our struggles became our glue—the one constant among us. And even though I had yet to receive the support of another Asian *adoptee* at the university, I knew I was one step closer to coming to terms with my Asian side.

The Artist and the Mentor

My involvement with IGR exposed me to classes on related topics. That is how I happened upon Asian Pacific Islander American (APIA) Women, headed by Professor Emily Lawsin, an amazing spoken-word artist. My first encounter with Emily was somewhat startling. Though small, she carried herself supreme confidence. "Stunned" and "intimidated" do not begin to describe my feelings when I first raised my hand during attendance. Emily was fierce, strong, and unnervingly articulate. Sure, I had seen Margaret Cho on Comedy Central numerous times, but this was a different kind of self-assurance. Emily demanded, but she did not do it in a loud and angry manner. She was composed and charming—and accessorized with a stare that could bring Rambo to his knees.

It was important to our professor that we be exposed to all forms of art and literature that opened the conversation of the "modern Asian woman." Our three-hour classes were filled with intriguing, wide-ranging discussions: the history of Asian immigration in the United States, current media portrayals of Asian women, the disproportionate amount of domestic violence in APIA communities. It was because of her class that I decided to attend law school, hoping to pursue a career that allowed me to assist battered women of color.

We read several memoirs by Asian American women, both famous and local. All of us were moved by these works, as was Emily's intention. She believed that the history and identity of the Asian American woman was best learned and appreciated through individuals' memories of their experiences. Thus she proposed that our final thesis papers document the life and times of an Asian American woman of our choice. The purpose was to research how our subject's life contributed to the history of all APIA women. It was my great fortune that this final assignment led me to Dr. Sook Wilkinson.

Sook invited me into her home and led me through an incredible retelling of her life and her efforts to define herself against cultural expectations. Sook had grown up in war-torn Korea and attended Ewah Women's University, despite her struggles as a child. She eventually came to America and took an incredible job with the Peace Corps. I was awestruck by her stories, about which we laughed and cried for hours.

For me, Sook's most intriguing story was about her interest in international adoption. She had spent many years working with young adopted Asians, coming to greatly appreciate their unique circumstances. Her experiences inspired her to attain a PhD in psychology. Hearing this story reinvigorated my interest in my own adoptee identity. Somewhere in the course of Emily's class, I had almost forgotten about the adoptee in me, concentrating only on my social identity as an Asian American female, but now I was ready to be reintroduced. Thanks to the inspirational lessons and stories I had taken from both Sook and Emily, recognizing and valuing my "APIA female" identity was no longer an issue. I now had two very influential role models supporting me, and I knew that I could use that support to find what I needed to help me uncover a paradigm for my adopted self.

KAAN-frontation

During the time that I was working on these dialogues, interviews, and classes, my involvement with the Korean American Adoptive Family Network (KAAN) began to blossom and provide even more opportunities for me to seek out the stories of adoptees of all generations. I first attended a KAAN conference the summer before my senior year of high school. Over two hundred people were there, and it was overwhelming to see so many adoptees in one place, and all for the same reason: community. This was a community that I had never heard of before, and I could not wait to get involved. The KAAN conference was immeasurably beneficial, fueling my soul and my need for self-definition. Participating in the conference led me to a new vocabulary—and through that, new ways of seeing. Simply substituting "waiting child" for "unwanted child" made a tremendous difference to me. KAAN was a place where I could immerse myself among hundreds of other adoptees, both experts and clueless souls like myself. There was no hiding from the adoptee in me when I was among these people.

Even with taking on the task of helping plan for the 2005 KAAN conference in Detroit and reinserting myself in this community, I knew that it would take an act much bolder than attending a gathering to help me resolve my personal identity issues. I wholeheartedly recommend conferences as a great starting point for identity searches. But naturally, they can never provide all the answers. For my part, I knew I needed a way to fully express my newly formed identity, beliefs, and emotions to the whole world. I wanted to show everyone that after all the papers I had written, all the people I had met, I was finally ready to unveil my pride as an adopted Asian American person. I wanted the action to be grand, both in scale and in significance. It had to be remembered by my peers, mentors, and loved ones. And so on April 28, 2005, after much consideration and courage-mustering, I went to the Ingham County Probate Court and reclaimed my Korean birth name.

The Final Statement

April 28, 2005: the date Rachel Hyerim Shin entered the world. To me, the reclamation of my Korean name was a symbol of finally having reached a place where I feel comfortable saying, "Yes, I'm Asian, American, *and* adopted." And now, I also have a clear sense of what those three words denote when put together.

There are many adopted Asians out there still trying to find their identities by rejecting their unique social status rather than by embracing it. In doing so, they miss the opportunity to be part of an incredible community. Adoptees like me, when brought together, have the potential to become a very influential force. By the nature of our experiences—how we came into this world and survived the tribulations of new environments—we have grown to be incredibly resilient and aware of our surroundings in ways that no other social group can claim. We literally have the best of both worlds working for us.

I now realize why I always used to see the word *adopted* as a pesky add-on. Deep inside me, I was just using that idea to avoid ruffling any feathers in society. I was afraid to confront the preconceived characteristics, placed on me by the dominant society, that classified me as Asian. But now I see that in reality, there are no feathers to disturb. Embracing this new and traditionally underdeveloped identity allows me the freedom to define it as I wish. The fact that the "adopted" label is not always recognized in mainstream society is no longer a curse to me. But I recognize that many other people, bound to their socially constructed roles, have yet to reach this self-determined identity.

If you find that role models are lacking in your life, encourage yourself to become your own role model, and perhaps someday you will become one to a person in need of inspiration. My family, Charles, Emily, Sook, and the many people at KAAN saw something in me that they felt was too valuable to overlook. And I think that I, after all this time, finally see it too.

32

POLITICS RUNS IN THE FAMILY

Samir Singh

It wasn't a big surprise when I told my parents that I was going to run for a seat on the East Lansing City Council during my senior year at Michigan State University. My family has a history of being involved in politics in India. My grandfather served as the high commissioner to Fiji, Tonga, and Nauru for India, and my uncle served as a member of the Indian parliament and a deputy secretary for railroad transportation. Public service runs in my family, so my parents encouraged me to pursue the city council election as a way for me to give back to my community.

Commitment to Give Back

Though I didn't have experience in public service, my family and my education provided me with the backdrop for my career choices in both nonprofit organizations and politics. One of my most vivid memories of my first visit to India is of the poverty. In the United States, we do a good job of hiding our poverty; many Americans go through their entire lives never coming face-to-face with it. But in India poverty is all around you. As I was traveling with my grandfather in a chauffeured car, a boy knocked on the window begging for change. I remember the strange new feelings that rushed forward. I asked my grandfather why there were so many poor people. He started to explain, but I interrupted him. Why didn't somebody do something about it? I demanded. His simple response is still seared in my mind: "What will you do about it?" I didn't have an answer, but it was the first time I understood I had a responsibility to other people and that poverty wasn't just a problem for someone else to solve.

As I was growing up, there was an understanding in my family that each of us was responsible for being informed about the issues facing our country and community. Simple family traditions grounded that belief. Every day we were required to read the newspaper and, after dinner, to watch the evening news. Learning about issues and politics was something I took for granted. I didn't know how rare that was among my peers until I went to high school and found myself in a government or history class debating the issues. Only a handful of students were informed enough to be able to participate.

My experiences in both high school and college facilitated a better understanding of community and service learning. Churchill High in Livonia encouraged students to participate in volunteerism. To be part of the academic honor society, it was mandatory to perform community service with local nonprofits. I took that experience to college and became very involved with the Service Learning Center at Michigan State University. One of my first projects was working with a national initiative then just beginning on MSU's campus, Into the Streets. The program took college students into the community to analyze the issues facing it and then match the problems to community groups and nonprofit organizations that could work on solutions.

My task was to organize a community cleanup. We worked with the neighborhood association and the children in the neighborhood to design a park. When we needed resources, we approached the mayor's office in Lansing and found that he was open to our requests. Since it was the program's first year, we wanted it to have visibility. We persuaded the president of Michigan State, John DiBiaggio, to become personally involved with the park project. By the time of the event, we had over a thousand volunteers working on twenty different projects throughout the cities of Lansing and East Lansing. Our neighborhood park project had two hundred volunteers, and we were able to turn an abandoned lot into a community park. The experience taught me the keys of community organizing and the power of asking the right people to be part of transforming the community.

As I continued through college, I spent more of my free time working with nonprofit organizations. I started to focus on how I could make an impact on my local community and government. I challenged a local East Lansing City Council member, Zolton Ferency, to lessen the divide between MSU and the city. His reply was eerily familiar to the response my grandfather had given me fourteen years earlier. He turned the question around and asked me what I was doing to bridge the gap between the two. I took him up on his challenge and was appointed a few weeks later to serve on the city's transportation commission, which eventually led to my desire to serve on the city council.

Decision to Run in 1993

Though the city of East Lansing is today a progressive college town, for much of its early history, the city was a closed community that was not welcoming to minorities. It wasn't until the late 1960s that East Lansing finally passed an ordinance that opened the community to minority residents. Only one person of color had served on the city council, and that individual had been appointed to an open seat but didn't win reelection. I was cautioned by many in the community to be aware of this background as I embarked on my campaign. Well-meaning people told me that my ethnic-sounding name would be an obstacle when it appeared on the ballot. I was advised to shave my beard because it made me look intimidating. And I was informed that certain neighborhoods would not be open to me because I was a minority. My bull-headed personality served me well as I ignored all this advice, refusing to dwell on my ethnicity in my campaign. There wasn't anything I could do to change my name on the ballot; it was the name my parents had given me. I liked my facial hair and believed people were going to vote based on my ideas, not my appearance. As for those neighborhoods that were supposedly "not open," I walked them more than once in the campaign.

But the 1993 election for the East Lansing City Council was no simple event. The city was debating a controversial extension of domestic partner benefits for city employees, and the city manager was under attack for his decision not to allow employees to show support for soldiers in the first Gulf War. There were only two open seats, but eleven candidates filed to run in the August primary. The four candidates receiving the most votes would move on to the November election. I was naïve enough to think my ideas and the student vote would sweep me into the council. That naïveté, combined with my inexperience, pretty much guaranteed my loss.

But more was at play than my own mistakes. I was not taken seriously as a candidate. The East Lansing Chamber of Commerce didn't invite me to interview for its endorsement. Similarly, Concerned Citizens for East Lansing didn't ask me to its "meet the candidates forum" at a community member's home. There was nothing I could do about the chamber's endorsement process, but I knew I needed to make sure the Concerned Citizens of East Lansing regarded me as a viable candidate, so I stormed the meeting.

I vividly remember the look of surprise on the host's face when I came through the door, introducing myself and stating that I assumed my invitation had been lost in the mail. I don't know to this day who was more uncomfortable—the members of Concerned Citizens or me—as I walked from person to person introducing myself and my platform. I think all of us recognized, that day, that I was going to be a part of the East Lansing community for years to come.

I finished in tenth place; the only reason I didn't finish in eleventh was because the last-place candidate was a student who worked even less smartly than I did. One candidate who finished in the top four, Mark Meadows, asked me to join his campaign for the November election because we shared many platform issues. Thus I had the opportunity to learn how a real campaign worked. We executed Meadows's campaign plan well over the next four months, but he fell short on election night. Though my first foray into politics was a failure, it gave me the desire to run a campaign I could be proud of—and the understanding of how to do it. My defeat was a learning opportunity that served as a springboard for my second campaign, in 1995.

Wiser the Second Time Around

Between the 1993 and 1995 elections, I graduated from Michigan State with a history degree and took a job with the Michigan Nonprofit Association. I began to focus on statewide public policy, advocacy, and training for Michigan's volunteer and nonprofit organizations. Each of these skill sets would be good experience for my eventual work with the city of East Lansing.

In the spring of 1995, I decided to run for the city council again. Three seats were opening up, which meant that the top six candidates would go to the November election. I determined to run a more professional campaign. I drew up my strategy, organized my campaign committee, and persuaded one of my best friends, Thor Sandell, to manage the campaign. I made inroads with neighborhood activists and established an alliance with two older candidates. I had learned since 1993 that there is a science to door-to-door canvassing; one can target households using political demographics. I focused on the most likely voters and made sure my message featured a broad, community-based agenda. The strategy was successful, and I finished in the top five in the primary. In the November election, I am proud to say, I finished in the top three. On November 13, 1995, I was sworn in as one of the youngest-ever members of the East Lansing City Council—and the first Asian American. I was pleased to find out that I had been right—my appearance and skin color were no barriers to election.

Mayor of an International Community

After serving ten years on the city council, I was elected mayor by my peers. I became the youngest and first person of color to serve in that position. The city of East Lansing has a sizable international and ethnic community, and my ethnicity has helped revive the concept of East Lansing as an international community. Shortly after I took office, the mayor of Lansing and I were asked by the Lansing Sister Cities Commission to lead a delegation to South Korea. It was the first time that East Lansing and Lansing had collaborated on a visit to another country to pursue economic and cultural ties. It has become an important part of my platform to use the ties of the university and the community to create a center for international economic development here in mid-Michigan.

Pressure to Succeed

It didn't occur to me until a few years after my first successful bid for election that I was not only a city council member but also a representative of the Indian American community. Journalists would ask me to comment on issues facing Indian Americans or to weigh in on U.S.-Indian relations. Indian students would contact me for help or advice. Those who were interested in politics or nonprofit organizations would ask me to explain to their parents that these were viable, even respectable, career options.

At first I was surprised by the attention and sometimes a little annoyed that I was expected to do favors for strangers. But as I matured as a council member, I also matured in my role as an Indian American in politics. I began to understand more fully what my mother had taught me when I was younger: because we are from a different culture, we have an obligation to teach others about that culture. Over time, I became more comfortable with the extra meetings and phone calls. It was my responsibility to my community, not a burden.

These experiences led me to reflect deeply on my role in the Indian American community. It was just two generations ago that my grandfather struggled to end British rule of India and democratize the country. It was just a little over forty years ago that my father immigrated to the United States and grappled with adapting to a new culture, new traditions, and new opportunities. Then my family made sacrifices to provide opportunities for my younger brother and me, the next generation.

These reflections prompted more questions. What will be my legacy? Will I rise to the challenges that come my way? I am introduced at Indian functions as the individual who might become the first Indian American governor or U.S. senator. Though I am pleased by this vote of confidence, it also creates a great weight on my shoulders. As I consider my future, whether to continue in politics or pursue a career in the nonprofit sector, I feel the pressure, unintentional though it may be, of meeting the expectations of the Indian community. But this pressure is part of the reality of being one of a handful of elected Indian Americans in Michigan, and that is a role I am honored to take seriously.

33

UNCONSCIOUS AND UNRECOGNIZED

Emily Hsiao

I was born in Ann Arbor, Michigan, and I have attended the Ann Arbor Public Schools all my life. We like to think of ourselves as diverse in our schools. After all, Ann Arbor has the reputation of a progressive city. It is the home of the University of Michigan, which boasts a large number of international students. In such a diverse community, one assumes, we would be tolerant of all races. And indeed, until I attended high school, I never heard any degrading racial comments in real life, only in movies and books. I never experienced any difficulty because of my race or ethnicity. Unfortunately, when I started high school, I realized the extent of my naïveté.

During my freshman year, I started to hear stereotypes, teasing, and racist talk toward Asian Americans. I observed how such discrimination crept into the classroom and affected our studies. I came to understand just how much wrongdoing occurs against Asian Americans in our schools, including "model minority" stereotyping, general stereotyping, and racial slurs. This issue cries out for attention, yet it is not being heard. It needs to be confronted immediately.

The Model Minority Stereotype

Racism follows a complicated cycle that is instigated by stereotypes. For Asian Americans, the most common stereotype affecting students is the "model minority" myth. It is the belief that all Asian Americans are of high intelligence, specifically in math, science, and music. However, many Asian Americans don't fit the stereotype. They might struggle in math or excel in English.

The stereotype also presumes that all Asians are hardworking academically, and do little outside of academic preparation.

From these stereotypes, derogatory terms such as "Asian failing," "Twinkie," and "You're so Asian" are generated. "Asian failing" refers to the idea that getting a less than perfect grade, such as a mere A-, is "failure" to an Asian. "Twinkie" means kids who are "yellow on the outside" but "white on the inside"—in other words, people who look Asian but are stereotypically white: athletic, outgoing, and/or apathetic about grades. "You're so Asian" belittles students for doing supposedly "Asian" things, such as studying for a test, practicing a musical instrument for hours on end, or incessantly striving for excellence.

One might think a positive stereotype would benefit the Asian American community, but it does not have that effect. In my experience, high school students offer examples of how positive stereotypes are, in fact, negative. Because of the model minority stereotype, Asian American students feel pressured to take the most advanced classes, especially in math and science. Some who are clearly not ready for accelerated courses take them anyway to avoid being labeled "stupid Asians" and as a result get mediocre or failing grades. Statistically, however, they add to the number of Asian Americans in accelerated courses—people then repeat the stereotype, and the cycle continues. College admissions officers routinely expect Asian American students to take all accelerated courses. If, on the other hand, a Caucasian were in all accelerated courses, the officers may have been impressed. But because they believe accelerated courses are an Asian American standard, it is harder for Asian Americans to exceed already high expectations. Unconsciously, the officers are affected by the model minority stereotype, to the detriment of Asian American applicants.

How Stereotypes Can Affect the Teacher-Student Relationship

Imagine a teacher evaluating two math tests. One is the work of an Asian American student, the other a non-Asian. The teacher will tend to be more lenient grading the non-Asian, giving partial credit here and there for effort, and stricter grading the Asian American, taking off points for a small calculation mistake. This discrepancy is caused by the stereotype, which prompts the teacher to expect the Asian American to do better in the first place. With a higher bar set, it is more difficult for the Asian American to get an A.

Now, picture a classroom where a teacher is asking a question. Two students raise their hands: one Asian American, the other non-Asian. The non-Asian is more likely to be called on because the teacher, prompted by the model minority stereotype, presumes that the Asian American already knows the correct answer and has no need for further coaching. Thus, the non-Asian has a better chance at learning the material.

In a reverse situation, where students are asking questions, the non-Asian is again more likely to be called on, as the teacher believes the Asian American already knows the material. Therefore, the Asian American is less likely to be able to ask his or her question before the bell rings.

The model minority stereotype is not the only one that shapes teacher-student relationships. Asian Americans lead a scripted life, considered meek followers, the ones obeying orders instead of giving them. Related general stereotypes of Asian Americans are that they are "nice," "quiet," "polite," and "without a voice." My teacher recently told me that he didn't think his field-trip chaperone, being Asian, knew quite what to do when a student was being talkative and disrespectful because such behavior wouldn't arise among Asians; he felt sure the chaperone was "afraid of being impolite or rude to the student and did not wish to speak out." My brother quoted a teacher who said her nephew was not good at soccer because he was Asian American and thus athletically challenged. A teacher looking for someone to play the piano at an event automatically asked my Asian American classmate—who, much to the teacher's surprise, did not know how to.

Racial Slurs Are Censured Unequally

Stereotyping is not the only type of discrimination against Asian Americans in our schools. Derogatory terms such as "Chink" and "Jap" are regularly spoken. Students whose first language is not English are picked on because of their accents. What is most shocking and confounding, however, is that the use of these slurs seems to go unnoticed. Teachers rarely reprimand or even mildly reprove students who say "Chink" or "Jap." If one student were to call another "nigger," he or she would be chastised. In English class, we discussed whether we should say the word *nigger* out loud while reading *Huckleberry Finn*. I asked why we had never had this conversation regarding *Jap* or *Chink* while reading about the Japanese internment camps. Why sensitivity toward one term but not analogous ones? *Nigger* is a racial label that stems from historical atrocities, just like derogatory racial words coming from the Chinese Exclusion Act of 1880 or the Japanese internment camps of World War II. Teachers must recognize the hurtful implications of all such expressions.

Discrimination against African Americans is always taken seriously in the public school system. However, people do not seem aware that discrimination against Asian Americans is also having an adverse effect on our educational environment. Diversity is more than just a black and white issue.

People often pass off these derogatory terms as jokes, but the jokes do not seem quite as funny as they were intended to be. Do the people who use these terms forget the sad history that spawned them? Do the people who accept being called by these names consider that their own position is lesser? Jokes can become stereotypical beliefs, their repetition inducing us, often subconsciously, to accept them as true. Even Asian Americans are beginning to joke about these hackneyed labels. If an Asian American says he is "failing" a class, another Asian American will immediately ask, "Failing? Or Asian failing?"

It's Time for Action!

Discrimination against Asian Americans must be recognized for the unacceptable prejudice it is. The issue has been treated lightly for too long. Only when we reach a state of equilibrium in which all races are treated equally can we truly call our communities diverse.

Fortunately, this discrimination is not insuperable. We need to educate the public about the problem and how it affects our schools as well as our society. Even one person can change things. Students can urge administrators to provide education in schools while educating peers themselves. Fliers can be posted, and seminars and assemblies can be held to educate students, teachers, and administrators. Only through knowledge, understanding, and a little personal soul-searching can people truly grasp how stereotypes and racial slurs hurt students and create unfairness in our schools.

In the past, the challenge was to convince others to agree that racism is wrong. Today, the challenge is to convince others that such agreement is not enough. Racism is almost a reflex. It is an unconscious judgment one makes at first sight. Does such a judgment preclude the true potential of Asian American children? An Asian American child may aspire to become a member of Congress, only to be put at a disadvantage because others hear an accent that is not there, or see a meek follower where there is a leader. Too few of us fight discrimination, though all of us see it and many of us experience it. I comprehended the reality and extent of discrimination against Asian Americans when I began high school. I have read and written about the topic. I have spoken out, challenging my peers and my teachers. However, this is just a beginning. It is only a small effort toward creating a future without minority discrimination, a future where teachers will not grade, make assumptions, or overlook people based on race. This future is attainable, but only through public awareness and action. We have an obligation to do more than just shrug at racism, more than just complain about it. Defeating racism is in our power. We have both the right and the responsibility to do it.

AFTERWORD

Bich Minh Nguyen

My story echoes many in these pages. On April 29, 1975, when I was eight months old, my family fled Saigon as refugees and eventually ended up in Grand Rapids, Michigan. I grew up in a predominantly white area where the standards of beauty, normality, and acceptance were represented by the blonde, blue-eyed classmates I admired—and knew I could never become. Even as a kid I had a sense that no matter how American I tried to be in what I wore, what I ate, and what I watched on television, I would always be viewed as a kind of foreigner, never American enough. This double-consciousness, this hyper-awareness of self, defines my childhood experiences. It defines, too, many of the illuminating essays in this collection, from Chelsea Zuzind-lak's "Tell 'Em You're From Detroit" to Min Hyoung Song's "Genealogy of a Detroit Childhood," to Lawrence G. Almeda's "Growing Up in Michigan" to Lynet Uttal's "Growing Up Hapa in Ann Arbor," to Catherine Chung's "The Apology" to Sheila Xiong's "Five Seconds." *Asian Americans in Michigan* provides a context, historical and current, for so many experiences I had but couldn't name or explain.

In his foreword, Frank Wu says that he wished he'd had this book when he was growing up in Michigan. I wish the same. I wish I could go back in time and explain to my younger self what was happening, not just in the dynamics of my family or elementary school but also in the world around me. Like many of the writers in this collection, I remember June 1982, when Vincent Chin was murdered. I had just finished second grade and I remember the talk and hush and tension of the grown-ups—my parents, uncles, grandmother; I knew I wasn't supposed to ask questions. It was common, at that time, to hear anti-Japanese sentiment in casual conversation, people talking about "those

Japanese" taking over our country with their Toyotas and yen. It wasn't until I got to college that I began to learn the details of Chin's murder, the injustice that followed, and the contexts of racism and xenophobia.

Indeed, I had no real concept of identity, racial or otherwise, until I left Grand Rapids to attend the University of Michigan. All I knew were moments: the kids who made fun of my grandmother's Vietnamese; the clerk at the hardware store who walked away from my father instead of helping him; the neighbors who let us know that the food we ate was weird, smelly, and gross; the list could go on and on, including many detailed in the pages of this anthology, like the boy who is called names or the girl who is pushed into a wall. What do we do with these moments? How do they shape us, change us, drive us?

If there's one element that marks the varied and complicated experience of Asian Americans in Michigan, it may be the understanding of isolation. From the first Chinese settler in 1872 to the present-day children and grandchildren of immigrants, the particular feeling of self-consciousness—How are people seeing me? Are they staring at me? Do they think I'm a foreigner? Should I brace myself for comments?—surely must be familiar and ongoing.

When you grow up in isolation, daily reminded that you are an aberration or something like a foreign object, you learn to deal with it. You reconcile yourself to the feeling; you anticipate it, planning the routes of your day. You have experienced so many levels of racism, from the direct taunts to the subtle micro-aggressions, the questions, the condescensions, the assumptions, that you almost think you are inured to it. But you never are. Each one surprises you, takes you back, makes something in you feel like you are starting over again and again.

Asian Americans in Michigan provides a framework for remembered experience as well as a way to understand a crucial yet often overlooked part of Asian American history. Too many people refer to the Midwest as flyover territory. For Asian Americans, the dismissal, the forgetting, can become compounded. While the experience of Asian Americans on the coasts is well documented, those of us in or from the middle of the country may sometimes wonder if our experiences matter. We wonder how we ended up where we did, and what we can claim as our own.

My family arrived in Grand Rapids by way of the refugee camp at Fort Chaffee in Arkansas. There, we were offered three options for resettlement: California, Wyoming, and Michigan. The story goes that we went with Michigan because of the University of Michigan; it was known to my grandmother, and she wanted her family to be near to that possibility. And so there we moved, and there much of my family has stayed. I grew up with Vernors soft drinks and Lays potato chips. I grew up with a sharp awareness of the seasons, with a deep understanding of lake effect. I grew up with 80s shows and music, with junk food crowding out my grandmother's cooking. I grew up thinking my world would have to bifurcate itself into Asian and white. The consequences of this duality, this constant questioning of identity, has a permanent effect; to this day I'm still sorting through it. Perhaps, for many Asian Americans in the Midwest, the past is never static, never far from us. Perhaps it is also a long lesson in the power, the devastation, and the delights of negative capability. For me, every taunt on the playground is matched by slumber parties with friends, playing board games, riding bicycles, and chasing down the ice-cream truck. There was then and is now still a constant balance of selves—identity always in the making.

Growing up, I never knew what to do with my self-consciousness because I had no way to understand what it signified. Reading *Asian Americans in Michigan* is retroactive perspective, retroactive understanding. To be able to access this background, and to see such a rich and varied history, and to experience the wonder of trajectory—the deepening and changing of what Asian American identity means—is a comfort. My wish now is for all of us, Asians and Asian Americans, Michiganders, Americans, to know this context and history too.

APPENDIX

Milestones of Asian Americans in the United States

1587	Landing of Filipinos in California from Spanish galleon *Nuestra Señora de Esperanza*.
1830s	Chinese laborers begin working on sugar plantations in Hawaii.
1837	Michigan is admitted to the Union as the twenty-sixth state.
1848	California gold rush brings twenty thousand Chinese to San Francisco.
1854	The California State Supreme Court in *People v. Hall* rules that a Chinese cannot testify against whites in California courts.
1863	Construction of the Central Pacific Railroad begins, using the labor of thousands of Chinese.
1872	University of Michigan accepts its first Asian American student, Saisuke Taigai, who is of Japanese descent.
1882	Congress passes the Chinese Laborer Suspension bill, often considered the first Chinese exclusion law. It laid the groundwork for the Chinese exclusion regime, a system of statutes, judicial decisions, and administrative acts that severely constricted Chinese immigration to the United States. This was the first time Congress restricted and regulated immigration on the basis of race, ethnicity, and national origin. The law was to be in effect for ten years and then be reviewed by Congress. It was renewed in 1892 (see below).
1886	U.S. Supreme Court rules in *Yick Wo v. Hopkins* that a state law that has unequal impact on different people violates the Fourteenth Amendment's equal protection clause. The Court decided this when it examined an ordinance in San Francisco that fell harshly on Chinese San Franciscans and barely concealed its discriminatory and hostile purposes.
1892	With the Geary Act, Congress extends the Chinese Laborer Suspension bill for another ten years, and also extends the reach of the Chinese exclusion system to all Chinese regardless of if they are laborers or not. All Chinese immigrants are required to carry registration certificates in the United States.

1894	Swami Vivekananda, an Indian monk and emissary to the Parliament of World Religions, visits Detroit.
1896	Four Chinese Detroiters (Wong Wing, Lee Poy, Lee Yon Tong, and Chan Wah Dong) challenge the punitive incarceration measures of the Geary Act. Their case goes to the United States Supreme Court where they lost, but not without eliciting some reservations about the punitive Exclusion system from one U.S. Supreme Court justice.
1898	The U.S. Supreme Court in *Wong Ark Kim v. U.S.* rules that Chinese born in the United States are citizens due to their birth, a conclusion that the Court drew from the Fourteenth Amendment's provision that "all persons born or naturalized" are citizens. Thus, Chinese born in the United States could not be stripped of their citizenship.
1900	Three Filipino students arrive in Ann Arbor to study at University of Michigan.
1902	Chinese Exclusion Act extended for another ten years.
1903	102 pioneer immigrants arrive in Hawaii from Korea.
1904	Chinese Exclusion Act extended indefinitely.
1910	Arthur K. Ozawa graduates from the University of Michigan, passes the bar exam, and is the first Asian American to practice law in Michigan.
	Detroit's Chinatown forms at Michigan Avenue and Third Avenue.
1918	Asian American servicemen of World War I are awarded citizenship.
1922	Cable Act revokes the citizenship of any U.S. woman who marries an "alien ineligible for U.S. citizenship," a category that came to apply exclusively to Asians.
	The U.S. Supreme Court rules in *Ozawa v. United States* that Japanese immigrants are ineligible for citizenship.
1923	U.S. Supreme Court rules in *U.S. v. Bhagat Singh Thind* that Indians are ineligible for citizenship.
1924	National Origins Act halts the immigration of all Asian laborers except Filipinos.
1925	John Mohammad Ali of Detroit loses his fight to retain his U.S. Citizenship in the United States District Court, Eastern District of Michigan. The judge followed the rule laid down by the United States Supreme Court in *U.S. v. Bhagat Singh Thind.*
1934	Tydings-McDuffle Act prohibits Filipino immigration.
1936	Cable Act of 1922 rescinded.
1941	Two thousand Japanese American community leaders along the Pacific Coast sent to Department of Justice internment camps as United States enters World War II.

1941	Grace Lee Boggs, an activist of Chinese descent, begins her sixty-year work for progressive social change in Detroit.
1942	Executive Order 9066 is signed by President Franklin D. Roosevelt. It delegated authority to the U.S. War Department to establish zones from which some persons could be excluded. This delegation empowered the U.S. Army to forcibly remove 120,000 Japanese Americans from the West Coast of the United States. The removed Japanese Americans first went to "assembly centers" administered by the army under the Wartime Civil Control Administration; then they went to internment camps administered by the civilian entity the War Relocation Authority.
1943	Magnuson Act repeals Chinese Exclusion Act of 1882.
1944	In December, the U.S. Supreme Court handed down two decisions that dealt with the wartime Japanese American situation. First, in *Korematsu v. U.S.*, the Court decided that the initial exclusion orders that removed Japanese Americans were constitutional as an exercise of national wartime power. Second, in the case of *Ex Parte Endo*, the Court ruled that an admittedly loyal American citizen could not be held in a relocation camp against her will (Mitsuye Endo, a Japanese American woman, pursued this case).
1946	Luce-Cellar Act allows citizenship for Asian Indians and Filipinos.
1952	Immigration and Nationality Act allows all Asian Americans the right to become citizens and vote.
1955	Harry Holt adopts eight Korean War orphans, establishing international adoptions between Korea and the United States.
1956	Dr. Dalip Singh Saund of California becomes the first Asian American in Congress.
1962	Minoru Yamasaki, an architect in Troy, Michigan, is chosen to design the World Trade Center.
1964	Patsy Mink of Hawaii becomes the first Asian American woman in Congress.
1965	Immigration and Nationality Act removes the "national origins" provisions of the 1920s that aimed to tilt immigration in favor of Great Britain and northern European countries. Removing these provisions and replacing them with new preferences that emphasized family reunification and professional employee recruitment contributed to new Asian-derived immigration flows after the 1960s.
1968	Student protests establish Asian American studies programs at San Francisco State University and the University of California, Berkeley.
1975	Over 130,000 refugees from Vietnam, Cambodia, and Laos immigrate to the United States to escape Communist governments after U.S.-supported governments and allies collapse in April. In Decemnber, the first large contingent of Hmong refugees arrives.

1976	Executive Order 9066, which authorized the relocation of thousands of Japanese Americans to internment camps, is rescinded by President Gerald Ford, a Michigan native.
	Dr. Samuel Ting, a Chinese American born in Michigan, is awarded the Nobel Prize in physics.
1979	The resumption of diplomatic relations between China and the United States allows for reunification of Chinese American families.
1980s	Bangladeshi families move from Queens, New York, to Hamtramck, Michigan, in response to rising housing prices in Queens; "Little Bengal" forms.
1982	Vincent Chin, a Chinese American, is clubbed to death with a baseball bat by two white autoworkers in Detroit. The murderers agreed to a plea bargain because they were caught in the act by two off-duty Detroit policemen. They withstood attempts to bring federal charges against them of having violated Vincent Chin's federal civil rights. They did not serve a single day in prison.
	The American Citizens for Justice, the first pan-Asian organization in Michigan, is established after the death of Vincent Chin.
1984	Michigan Governor James Blanchard forms the first Governor's Advisory Commission on Asian American Affairs, which functions from 1984 to 1990.
1985	Ellison Onizuka becomes the first Asian Pacific American in space. He died in the *Challenger* tragedy in 1986.
1987	First formal signing of APIA Heritage Week at the White House.
1988	Civil Liberties Act gives descendants of citizens held in internment camps an official apology and $20,000 in reparations.
	Congress passes Amerasian Homecoming Act, which allows twenty-five thousand Amerasians and seventy-five thousand immediate relatives from Vietnam to immigrate.
1989	APIA studies program established at University of Michigan.
1990	Hansen Clarke, a politician of Pakistani and African American heritage, elected to Michigan House of Representatives.
1992	Rodney King verdict results in riots and looting in Los Angeles's Koreatown, known as *Sa-I-Gu* (April 29) by Korean Americans.
1993	Consulate General of Japan opens in Detroit.
1996	Gary Locke wins election in Washington, becoming first Asian American governor.
1999	President Clinton signs an executive order establishing the president's Advisory Commission of Asian Americans and Pacific Islanders.
2000	Asian Pacific American Chamber of Commerce established in Auburn Hills, Michigan.

2000	Child Citizen Act allows foreign-born adoptees automatic U.S. citizenship upon arrival.
	Council of Asian Pacific Americans founded in Michigan.
	Dr. Michael Rao appointed president of Central Michigan University.
	Norman Y. Mineta confirmed as U.S. Secretary of Commerce, making him the first Asian American cabinet member in U.S. history.
2001	Governor Jennifer Granholm appoints Teri Takai as director of the Department of Information and Technology, Michigan's first woman and Asian American cabinet member.
	Norman Mineta confirmed as U.S. Secretary of Transportation.
	Elaine Chao confirmed as U.S. Secretary of Labor, making her the first Asian American woman cabinet member in U.S. history.
2002	Hoon-Yung Hopgood elected state representative of Michigan's Twenty-second District, becoming the first Korean American to hold statewide office in Michigan.
2004	Asian American studies program established at Michigan State University.
	Dr. Les Wong appointed president of Northern Michigan University.
	Dr. Frank Wu appointed dean of Wayne State University's School of Law.
	Detroit Asian Youth (DAY) Project established to develop leadership skills and cultural awareness in Detroit's ethnic youth.
2005	Michigan governor Jennifer Granholm establishes the Advisory Council on Asian Pacific American Affairs. Dr. Sook Wilkinson is appointed as its chairwoman.
	U.S. Senate passes a resolution recognizing the one hundredth anniversary of Korean immigration to the United States. January 13 is proclaimed as Korean American Day.
2006	APIAVote MI is organized to encourage voter registration and voting among Michigan Asian Americans.
2007	Governor Jennifer Granholm appoints Judge Shalina D. Kumar, Michigan's first Asian American judge, to the Oakland County Circuit Court.
	Bobby Jindal elected governor of Louisiana, the nation's first Indian American governor.
2008	Rep. Hoon-Yung Hopgood introduced HB 6172 to create Asian Pacific American Affairs Commission, which was adopted both in the Michigan House and the Senate.
2009	Governor Granholm signed HB 6172 and issued an executive order creating the Michigan Asian Pacific American Affairs Commission. Dr. Sook Wilkinson was appointed as its first chairwoman.

2010	The U.S. Census reported that persons self-identified as Asian made up 14.7 million of the U.S. population, which had a total of 308.7 million as of April 1. Contrasted with the U.S. Census for 2000, the 2010 figures showed that the Asian-derived population grew faster than any other ethnic group, increasing by 43 percent over that ten-year period.
2012	Drawing upon the U.S. Census for 2010, the Asian American Center for Advancing Justice (a consortium of community and advocacy organizations) published a report on Asian Americans in the Midwest. *A Community of Contrasts: Asian Americans, Native Hawaiians, and Pacific Islanders in the Midwest* reported that there were nineteen different Asian communities and six Native Hawaiian and Pacific Islander communities in the Midwest.
	Sam Singh was elected state representative of Michigan's Sixty-ninth District, becoming the first Indian American to hold statewide office in Michigan.
2013	In October, a diverse group of Asian American evangelical Protestant Christians wrote, signed, and circulated an "Open Letter to the Evangelical Church." Under the name Asian Americans United, they asked for dialogue among evangelicals in the United States to address racial stereotyping against Asians, cultural insensitivity, and routes toward reconciliation. Signed by seven hundred people, including faculty at theological seminaries and divinity schools as well as staff persons at evangelical organizations, the "Open Letter" possibly represents the first time evangelical Asian Americans had advocated so prominently for Asian American equity within evangelical settings.

SUGGESTIONS FOR
FURTHER READING

Victor Jew

This short list of further reading is for those wishing to explore themes raised by the essays in *Asian Americans in Michigan*. I selected a few telling titles from the ever-growing body of scholarship associated with Asian American studies. I was especially keen to find books that address the core question raised by this volume of Michigander reflections: How do we understand Asian American communities in the U.S. heartland?

General Works on Asian America and Pacific Islander Studies

Dhingra, Pawan, and Robyn Magalit Rodriguez. *Asian America: Sociological and Interdisciplinary Perspectives*. 2014.

Kim, Elaine. *Asian American Literature: An Introduction to the Writings and Their Social Context*. 1982.

Lai, Eric, and Dennis Arguelles, eds. *The New Face of Asian Pacific America: Numbers, Diversity, and Change in the 21st Century*. 2003.

Le, C. N. "14 Important Statistics about Asian Americans." *Asian Nation: The Landscape of Asian America*. April 2014.

Sang-Hee Lee, Shelley. *A New History of Asian America*. 2013.

Sucheng, Chan. *Asian America: An Interpretative History*. 1991.

Takaki, Ronald. *Strangers from a Different Shore*. 1989, 1998.

Yu-wen Shen Wu, Jean, and Thomas C. Chen, eds. *Asian American Studies Now: A Critical Reader*. 2010.

Zhou, Min, and J. V. Gatewood, eds. *Contemporary Asian America: A Multidisciplinary Reader*. 2nd ed. 2007.

Asian American Communities
Asian American Panethnicity

Espiritu, Yen Le. *Asian American Pan Ethnicity: Bridging Institutions and Identities*. 1994.
Maeda, Daryl J. *Chains of Babylon: The Rise of Asian America*. 2009.
Trinh Vo, Linda. *Mobilizing an Asian American Community*. 2004.
Wu, Frank H. *Yellow: Race in America beyond Black and White*. 2002.

Chinese America

Chan, Sucheng, ed. *Chinese American Transnationalism: The Flow of People, Resources, and Ideas between China and America during the Exclusion Era*. 2006.
———. *Entry Denied: Exclusion and the Chinese Community in America, 1882–1943*. 1991.
Lee, Erika. *At America's Gates: Chinese Immigration during the Exclusion Era, 1882–1943*. 2004.
Ling, Huping. *Chinese Chicago: Race, Transnational Migration, and Community since 1870*. 2012.
———. *Chinese St. Louis: From Enclave to Cultural Community*. 2004.
Shah, Nayan. *Contagious Divides: Epidemics and Race in San Francisco's Chinatown*. 2001.
Wong, K. Scott. *Americans First: Chinese Americans and the Second World War*. 2008.

Japanese America

Daniels, Roger. *Prisoners without Trial: Japanese Americans in World War II*. 2004.
Kurashige, Lon. *Made in Little Tokyo: Politics of Ethnic Identity and Festival in Southern California, 1934–1994*. 1994.
Matsumoto, Valerie. *City Girls: The Nisei Social World in Los Angeles: 1920–1950*. 2014.
United States. Commission on Wartime Relocation and Internment of Civilians. *Personal Justice Denied: Report of the Commission on Wartime Relocation and Internment of Civilians*. 1983.

Korean America

Abelmann, Nancy. *The Intimate University: Korean American Students and the Problems of Segregation*. 2009.
Abelmann, Nancy, and John Lie. *Blue Dreams: Korean Americans and the Los Angeles Riots*. 1995.
Kim, Elaine H., and Laura Hyun Yi Kang, eds. *Echoes upon Echoes: New Korean American Writings*. 2002.
Kim, Elaine H., and Eui-Young Yu, eds. *East to America: Korean American Life Stories*. 1996.
Kim, Nadia. *Imperial Citizens: Koreans and Race from Seoul to LA*. 2008.

Filipino America

Bonus, Rick. *Locating Filipino Americans: Ethnicity and the Cultural Politics of Space*. 2000.
Choy, Catherine Ceniza. *Empire of Care: Nursing and Migration in Filipino American History*. 2003
Espiritu, Yen Le. *Filipino American Lives*. 1995.

Asian Indian America

Dave, Shilpa. *Indian Accents: Brown Voice and Racial Performance in American Television and Film.* 2013.
Prashad, Vijay. *The Karma of Brown Folk.* 2000.
Rangaswamy, Padma. *Namasté America: Indian Immigrants in an American Metropolis.* 2000.
Rudrappa, Sharmila. *Ethnic Routes to Becoming American: Indian Immigrants and the Cultures of Citizenship.* 2004.

Vietnamese America

Chan, Sucheng, ed. *The Vietnamese American 1.5 generation: Stories of War, Revolution, Flight, and New Beginnings.* 2006.
Do, Hien Duc. *The Vietnamese Americans.* 1999.
Lieu, Nhi T. *The American Dream in Vietnamese.* 2011.

Hmong America

Chan, Sucheng, ed. *Hmong Means Free: Life in Laos and America.* 1994.
Her, Vincent K., and Mary Louise Buley-Meissner, eds. *Hmong and American: From Refugees to Citizens.* 2012.
Lee, Stacey. *Up against Whiteness: Race, School, and Immigrant Youth.* 2005.
Moua, Mai Neng. *Bamboo among the Oaks: Contemporary Writing by Hmong Americans.* 2002.
Vang, Chia Youyee. *Hmong America: Reconstructing Community in Diaspora.* 2010.

Cambodian America

Chan, Sucheng, ed. *Survivors: Cambodian Refugees in the United States.* 2004.
Hein, Jeremy. *Ethnic Origins: The Adaptation of Cambodian and Hmong Refugees in Four American Cities.* 2006.
Ong, Aihwa. *Buddha Is Hiding: Refugees, Citizenship, the New America.* 2003.

The Midwest: Site of Asian American Memories and Imagination

Boggs, Grace Lee. *Living for Change: An Autobiography.* 1998.
Boggs, Grace Lee, with Scott Kurashige. *The Next American Revolution: Sustainable Activism for the Twenty-first Century.* 2011, 2012.
Furiya, Linda. *Bento Box in the Heartland: My Japanese Girlhood in WhiteBread America; A Food Memoir.* 2006.
Moua, Mai Neng. *Bamboo among the Oaks: Contemporary Writing by Hmong Americans.* 2002.
Nguyen, Bich Minh. *Pioneer Girl: A Novel.* 2014.
———. *Short Girls.* 2009.
———. *Stealing Buddha's Dinner.* 2007.
Telemaque, Eleanor Wong. *It's Crazy to Stay Chinese in Minnesota.* 1978, 2000.
———. *The Sammy Wong Files.* 2010.
Yang, Kao Kalia. *The Late Homecomer: A Hmong Family Memoir.* 2008.

CONTRIBUTORS

LAWRENCE G. (L. G.) ALMEDA is a shareholder at Brinks Hofer Gilson & Lione, a national law firm specializing in intellectual property. L. G. served on the Governor's Advisory Council on Asian Pacific American Affairs and on the United States Commission on Civil Rights' State Advisory Committee. He holds leadership roles in state and national bar associations.

GRACE LEE BOGGS is an activist, writer, and speaker whose more than seventy years of political involvement encompass the major U.S. social movements of the twentieth century. She received her BA from Barnard College in 1935 and her PhD from Bryn Mawr College in 1940. She is the author of an autobiography, *Living for Change* (1998) and *The Next American Revolution: Sustainable Activism for the Twenty-first Century* (2011). *Living for Change* is being well received in China.

TAI CHAN is president of Acacia168, a global environmental consultant firm. He received his PhD in environmental health sciences from New York University before joining General Motors as a research engineer. He was later program manager of occupational health and safety research and executive secretary on the GM-China Technology Advisory Board in 1993–95. He was president of both the American Association of Aerosol Research the Detroit Chinese Engineers Association. Since 2009, he has been visiting scholar at Tsinghua University in Beijing and visiting professor at Hong Kong University of Science and Technology.

TI-HUA CHANG, an award-wining television journalist, was the crime reporter for WJBK-TV in Detroit from 1984 to 1989. He exposed malfeasance in the Detroit Police Department, leading to the arrest of Police Chief William Hart for stealing forfeiture monies confiscated from drug dealers to pay his mistress's rent. In 1996, he won the prestigious Peabody Award for a series of reports on accused drug-dealing murderers. He received an Edward R. Murrow Award in 2005 for a piece exposing police officers' use of a helicopter and high-tech infrared equipment to spy on private citizens. Chang is especially proud of uncovering four witnesses who helped reopen the case of the 1963 murder of civil rights activist Medgar Evers. He is a member of American Citizens for Justice. Chang currently lives in his hometown of New York City. He is married and has two children.

CHRISTINE CHEN is a well-known activist. Her track record in building coalitions and working at the grassroots and national levels established her as one of the strongest voices in the Asian Pacific Islander American (APIA) community. Profiled by *Newsweek* magazine in 2001 as one of fifteen women who will shape America's new century, she serves as executive director of APIA-Vote. Her role as a trusted coalition builder allows her to effectively build relationships with key political offices, including the Congressional Asian Pacific American Caucus, federal agencies, and the administration.

CATHERINE CHUNG grew up in Okemos, Michigan, among other places. She is the author of *Forgotten Country* and an assistant professor at Adelphi University. She received her undergraduate degree in mathematics from the University of Chicago and her MFA in creative writing from Cornell University. She is fiction editor at *Guernica Magazine* and has been a Granta New Voice and a fellow at the MacDowell Colony, the Camargo Foundation, and Yaddo. Her work has appeared in the *New York Times,* the *Rumpus,* and *Quarterly West,* among other publications. She lives in New York City.

KIRA A. DONNELL grew up in Grand Rapids, Michigan, and resides in San Francisco. She holds a BA in English from the University of Michigan, an MA in Asian American studies from San Francisco State University, and an MA in ethnic studies from the University of California, Berkeley. She is currently a doctoral student in the University of California, Berkeley's ethnic studies program, where her research focuses on cultural productions by Korean adoptees and birth mothers. In 2010 she reunited with her birth mother after twenty-seven years apart, and she continues to forge a relationship with her newfound Korean family.

JOSEPH A. GALURA teaches at the University of Michigan in the School of Social Work and the College of Literature, Science, and the Arts. He is president of the Filipino American Historical Society, Michigan chapter, and author of several articles and books related to service learning, multicultural education, and diversity.

KUL B. GAURI is a retired dean of Macomb Community College. He served on the American Citizens for Justice board, the Macomb County Interfaith Volunteer Caregivers board, the Troy, Michigan, Library Advisory board (of which he was president), and the Elder Advisors to the Institute of Gerontology board of Wayne State University. He received his PhD from Case Western Reserve University.

JEN HILZINGER is an educational advocate and volunteer working on issues of social justice. She and her husband, Glen, both born and raised in Michigan, have three children. One was adopted from China and one from Korea. The Hilzinger family (which includes a dog and a cat) lives in a suburban Detroit community.

EMILY HSIAO, who identifies as Taiwanese American, has fond memories of growing up in her hometown of Ann Arbor, Michigan. She wrote her contribution at age fourteen. She graduated magna cum laude from the Huntsman Program in International Studies and Business at the University of Pennsylvania, receiving a BA from the College of Arts and Sciences and a BS from the Wharton School. She is a Coca-Cola Scholar, Toyota Community Scholar, Lipman Fellow, and FLAS Foundation Scholar. She currently works in Tokyo as a management consultant. In her spare time, Emily can be found volunteering or singing—and, on Saturdays, watching University of Michigan football.

VICTOR JEW grew up in Los Angeles, California, an unexpected preparation for living in the U.S. Midwest (a number of writers have commented on the resonance Southern California has with midwestern locales). Receiving his BA in history from the University of California–Los Angeles, he ventured to the heartland to earn his doctorate in U.S. history from the University of Wisconsin–Madison, where he currently teaches in the Asian American Studies Program. Earlier, he taught at institutions such as Cornell University and Michigan State University, where he offered that campus's first course in Asian American history. He has written on anti-Asian violence in the nineteenth century (Milwaukee in 1889 and Los Angeles in 1871), and he is working on a history of Asian American communities in the Midwest from 1870 to the present.

BARBARA W. KIM is professor in the Department of Asian and Asian American Studies at California State University, Long Beach. Her research areas include health care access and retirement planning for Korean Americans, Asian American families, and aging. She is the coauthor (with Grace J. Yoo) of *Caring across Generations: The Linked Lives of Korean American Families* (2014), which focuses on intergenerational relationships between Korean immigrants and their adult children, the so-called 1.5 and second generations. Kim's 2001 PhD dissertation at the University of Michigan was "Race, Space, and Identity: Examining Asian American Racial and Ethnic Formations in the Midwest."

TUKYUL ANDREW KIM is pastor emeritus of the Korean Presbyterian Church of Metro Detroit in Southfield, Michigan. Born and raised in Korea, he was a professor of religious education at Yonsei University in Seoul. Reverend Kim was called to serve the Korean immigrant congregation in Metropolitan Detroit. He has authored books on Christian education and pastoral ministry.

KOOK-WHA KOH obtained her PhD in chemical engineering from the University of Iowa. She founded Chrysan Industries in Plymouth, Michigan, with her husband, Kwang, in 1977; the company manufactures industrial lubricants for the automotive industry. She officially retired from Chrysan in 2006 but remains vice chairman of the board. She is active in local professional societies, including the Society of Tribology and Lubrication Engineers, and enjoys traveling. She is the author of *Across the 38th Parallel*, an autobiography published in 2005, and *Hopping Seven Continents*, cowritten with her husband, published in 2013. She and her husband live in Northville, Michigan.

SACHI KOTO, a third-generation Japanese American, served as a news anchor for CNN Headline News at the network's world headquarters in her hometown of Atlanta. After more than sixteen years with CNN, in 2005 Koto launched a public relations and communications firm, Sachi Koto Communications, Inc., in Atlanta.

EMILY P. LAWSIN teaches Asian/Pacific Islander American studies in American culture and women's studies at the University of Michigan. An oral historian and spoken-word performance poet originally from Seattle, Washington, she is a trustee of the Filipino American National Historical Society and cofounder of the Detroit Asian Youth Project and the Filipino Youth Initiative class at Paaralang Pilipino. She is the author with Joseph A. Galura of *Filipino Women in Detroit, 1945-1955*.

KATHERINE M. LEE is a respected businesswoman, an accomplished entrepreneur, a recognized community leader, a dedicated proponent of alternative medicine, a wife, and the mother of two sons. Lee brings to everything she touches a spirit of dedication and contagious enthusiasm that inspires everyone around her to find their own path to excellence.

ELAINE LOK is a native of the Metro Detroit area. She has been working in ophthalmic photography since 2007, performing diagnostic imaging for doctors. A desire to find the perfect blend of science and art has cultivated her passion for this specialized medical photography field. Elaine resides in Nashville, Tennessee. To see her current projects, visit http://elokphoto.com.

DURRIYA MEER, Psy.D., has been a psychologist at Counseling and Psychological Services at the University of Michigan since 2003. She is from Bangladesh and completed her higher education in India and the United States. She describes herself as a "mosaic," influenced by the cultures and subcultures of the countries she has lived in and visited. She takes pride in her nontraditional identity, and this perspective impacts the work she does with survivors of violence, Asian/Asian American students, international students, and underprivileged students, in which the focus is on helping people to accept and empower themselves.

KURT R. METZGER is the director emeritus of Data Driven Detroit. D3's mission is to provide accessible, high-quality information and analysis to drive informed decision making. Kurt is regularly sought out by local media and regional, state, and national organizations to speak on demographic trends. He previously worked for the U.S. Census Bureau, Wayne State University's Center for Urban Studies, and the United Way. He is dedicated to assisting community groups throughout Detroit and the region to understand and use data to advocate for themselves and to assist philanthropy, nonprofits, corporations, and government to create a better quality of life in southeast Michigan.

BICH MINH NGUYEN received an MFA in creative writing from the University of Michigan and has taught fiction and creative nonfiction in the MFA Program at Purdue University and the MFA in Writing Program at the University of San Francisco. She is the author of three books, all with Viking Penguin. *Short Girls*, a novel, was an American Book Award winner in fiction and a *Library Journal* best book of the year. *Stealing Buddha's Dinner*, a memoir, received the PEN/Jerard Award from the PEN American Center and was a Chicago Tribune Best Book of the Year. *Stealing Buddha's Dinner* has been featured as a common read selection within numerous communities and universities including the Michigan Humanities Council's Great Michigan Read for 2009–2010. Her most recent novel is *Pioneer Girl*. She and her family live in the San Francisco Bay Area, where is she presently working on a series of essays.

MIMI DOAN-TRANG NGUYEN was born in Hue, Vietnam. After her father was released from eight years of imprisonment at a Communist reeducation camp, she and her family arrived in Michigan in 1993. In 1999 she graduated with honors from Michigan State University in electrical engineering and pursued a career in the automotive industry with General Motors, where she is currently the lead electrical system engineer. She continued her education and received an MBA in 2008. A compassionate community volunteer, she is married and has two children, Isabelle and Nathan.

BRIANNA RECKEWEG earned a BA in sociology and English from Michigan State University before studying poetry and working as a teaching assistant at Northern Michigan University, where she earned an MA in creative writing. Her work has been published in *Gulf Coast, Paradigm,* and *42 Opus*. Currently, she is raising her daughter, Helen, but hopes to continue her creative pursuits again when her daughter enters kindergarten. She enjoys running and cooking.

ASAE SHICHI was born in Tokyo. After graduating from Tokyo Woman's Christian University, she came to the United States to study at Union Theological Seminary and Columbia University's Teachers College in New York on a Fulbright Scholarship. She also studied leadership training at the University of California, Berkeley. After coming to Michigan, she taught Japanese at area universities: Oakland University, the University of Michigan–Dearborn, and Madonna University. A community activist, Shichi served on the board of many organizations, including the Japanese American Citizens League, the Japan America Society, CAPA, and the JSD Women's Club. She published a book in Japan in 1988, *Ibunka Syndrome* (Foreign Culture Syndrome), which details some of the factors underlying cultural conflicts between the United States and Japan. Now retired, she lives with her husband, Hitoshi Shichi, a retired professor at Wayne State Medical School, in Bloomfield Township and is active in local senior center programs.

ANNA M. SHIH is a writer whose work has appeared in *Gastronomica: Journal of Food and Culture* and the *Detroit Free Press*. She lives in Royal Oak, Michigan, within walking distance of the farmers' market and too many restaurants to count.

TOSHIKO SHIMOURA was born in California in 1926 and spent her early school years in California public schools. During World War II, she was among 120,000 Japanese and Japanese Americans living in California, Oregon, and Washington who were evacuated and imprisoned in a U.S. government war relocation camp. After graduating from high school in her camp in Topaz, Utah, she moved to Michigan and attended Michigan State University, where she earned a degree in microbiology. She served as director of the Public Health Laboratory in Marysville, California. Her marriage to James N. Shimoura of Detroit brought her back to Michigan. Her interest in the status and welfare of Japanese and Japanese Americans has kept her involved in the Japanese American Citizens League. Her avocation ikebana (Japanese flower arranging) became an important part of her life as a teacher.

SAMIR SINGH was elected in 2012 to the Michigan State House of Representatives for the Sixty-ninth District (D-East Lansing). Singh is the former mayor of the city of East Lansing. He served ten years as president and CEO of the Michigan Nonprofit Association.

RACHEL HYERIM SISCO was adopted from Seoul when she was three months old. She previously served as cofounder and president of the Adopted Koreans Association (AKA) at the University of Michigan and is a cofounder of GIFT, an adoptee-mentoring program in Ann Arbor. Rachel is an attorney in Bloomfield Hills, Michigan, a loving mother and wife, and an avid photographer. Her essay was written during her second undergraduate year in 2005.

MIN HYOUNG SONG is professor of English at Boston College, where he directs both the English MA program and the Asian American Studies Program. He is also the outgoing editor of the *Journal of Asian American Studies*. He received his PhD in English and American literature from Tufts University, and his AB in English and American literature from the University of Michigan at Ann Arbor. Song is the author of two books, *The Children of 1965: On Writing, and Not Writing, as an Asian American* (2013) and *Strange Future: Pessimism and the 1992 Los Angeles Riots* (2005). He is also coeditor of *Asian American Studies: A Reader* (2000).

DYLAN SUGIYAMA is a biracial third-generation Japanese American. He is an immigration attorney who currently lives in North Carolina with his wife and three daughters. Sugiyama previously lived in Lansing, Michigan, where he worked as a civil rights representative with the Michigan Department of Civil Rights.

KYO TAKAHASHI was born in Tokyo in 1929. He studied art and design at the National Art University in Tokyo and the Art Center College of Design in Los Angeles. He worked as an art director with major advertising agencies in New York, Los Angeles, Tokyo, and Detroit. Takahashi earned several design awards. He is the author of *A Passage through Seven Lives—The Pacific War Legacy* (2009), *Japanese of No Return* (revised edition, 2013) (both available from amazon.com), and several other books. Takahashi is a Buddhist-Quaker.

PRATYUSHA TUMMALA-NARRA, PHD, is an associate professor in the Department of Counseling, Developmental and Educational Psychology at Boston College and maintains a private practice in Cambridge, Massachusetts. Dr. Tummala-Narra received her doctoral degree from Michigan State University and completed postdoctoral training in the Victims of Violence Program at the Cambridge Hospital. She founded and directed the Asian Mental Health Clinic at the Cambridge Health Alliance, and was on the faculty at Georgetown University School of Medicine and the Michigan School of Professional Psychology. She has presented nationally and published on the topics of immigration, race, trauma, and psychodynamic psychotherapy.

LYNET UTTAL returned to live in the Midwest after residing in northern California and Memphis, Tennessee. She is a professor in human development and family studies at the University of Wisconsin–Madison and previous director of the Asian American Studies Program. Her social science research focuses on immigrant families, which returns her to thinking about her immigrant mother and her own identity. She regularly discusses the meaning of being mixed-race Asian/Jewish/white with her three sons, who are grappling with this issue in a country where race is currently constructed as black-brown-white or perpetual foreigners.

JEFFREY VANG is a clinical pharmacist at McLaren Macomb Hospital in Mount Clemens, Michigan. He has been a resident of Michigan for twenty-five years after coming to the United States at the age of thirteen as a refugee from Laos. He will continue to be a resident of this Great Lake state for many years to come.

FRANCES KAI-HWA WANG is a second-generation Chinese American from California who divides her time between Michigan and Hawaii. She has worked in the fields of philosophy, anthropology, international development, non-profits, small-business start-ups, and ethnic new media. She team-teaches Asian/Pacific Islander American studies at the University of Michigan. She is a contributor to New America Media, ChicagoIsTheWorld.org, Pacific Citizen, InCultureParent.com, and HuffPostLive. She has published three chapbooks, had work included in several anthologies and art exhibitions, and collaborated with Jyoti Omi Chowdhury on an online multimedia project and traveling art exhibition for the Smithsonian Asian Pacific American Center's Indian American Heritage Project.

SOOK WILKINSON came to the United States at age twenty-two, having just graduated from Ewha Womans University, summa cum laude, with one hundred dollars in her pocket for a three-month job teaching Korean language to Peace Corps trainees in New Jersey. Later, she became a graduate student at Peabody College in Nashville, where she met her future husband, Todd Wilkinson, who was then a Vanderbilt medical student. They moved to the Detroit area to be near his family while they advanced their careers. Wilkinson became a licensed clinical psychologist, author, and a respected community leader. She and her husband are the proud parents of TJ and Gina, and loving grandparents of Graely and Cecilia. In 2005, Governor Granholm appointed her as the chairwoman of the Governor's Advisory Council on Asian Pacific American Affairs, then in 2009, as the chairwoman of the Michigan Asian Pacific American Affairs Commission (MAPAAC), a legislatively mandated state commission. In 2012, Governor Snyder reappointed her as MAPAAC's chairwoman. She successfully secured state appropriations for MAPAAC in 2012. Wilkinson has served as a member of the Board of Trustees at Northern Michigan University since 2009, appointed by Governor Granholm. Several organizations have invited her to serve on their boards—Global Detroit, Asian Pacific Islander American Health Forum (APIAHF), and Korean American Cultural Center of Michigan, to name a few.

LESLIE E. WONG, PHD, was appointed the thirteenth president of San Francisco State University in 2012. Previously, he served eight years as president of Northern Michigan University in Marquette. Dr. Wong's leadership at NMU led to visits by both President George W. Bush and President Barack Obama to recognize trailblazing developments in bringing technology to rural areas. Born in Southern California and raised in Oakland, Dr. Wong earned a BA in psychology at Gonzaga University, an MS in experimental psychology at Eastern Washington University, and a PhD in educational psychology at Washington State University.

FRANK H. WU is chancellor and dean of the University of California's Hastings College of the Law and author of *Yellow: Race in America beyond Black and White*. From 2004 to 2008, he served as dean of the Wayne State University Law School in his hometown of Detroit. Wu also served for a decade on the faculty of Howard University Law School, the nation's leading historically black college/university.

SHEILA XIONG grew up in Okemos, Michigan, and is a graduate of Michigan State University, where she earned a degree in public administration and public policy. She previously served as a legislative aide to former Minnesota state senator Mee Moua. Sheila currently resides in St. Paul, Minnesota, and works in the Government Affairs Department at Target Corporation.

CHELSEA ZUZINDLAK received her law degree, cum laude, and bachelor's degrees in anthropology and Asian studies from Wayne State University in Detroit. In 2009, she pioneered the first public installation of Michigan Chinese American history at the Detroit Historical Museum. The exhibit, Detroit's Chinatown: Works in Progress, is now part of the permanent collection of the Association of Chinese Americans, a Metro Detroit nonprofit organization. Zuzindlak served on the association's board of directors from January 2010 to December 2012.

INDEX

Note: Italicized page numbers indicate tables or illustrations.

Chinatown Revitalization Workgroup, Detroit, 130

Chinese Americans: ABC (American-born Chinese), 190–91; AMVET Post 85, 54; in Ann Arbor, 194; anti-Japanese protesters, 58; Chinese schools for, 189–96; females, 120; at Forest Lawn Mortuary, Detroit, 30; gulf between Japanese Americans and, 123; history of, in Detroit, 64; from Hong Kong, 233; laundries in Detroit, 52–54, 95n41; in Michigan, 131–33, 233–37; move to suburbs following World War II, 132–33; population in Chicago (1880–1900), 66n8; population in Detroit (1963), 25; population in Michigan and Detroit (1900), 66n8; portrayed as "model minorities" by Detroit newspapers, 61; racism against, in 1880s Detroit, 27–28; ratio of women to men, 67n29; role in transforming Detroit, 62–65; second-generation, and inner-city services in Detroit, 56–57; as soldiers in World War II, 58; women in Detroit (1910–1934), 30

Chinese Center, Ann Arbor, 189

Chinese Exclusion Act (1882), 25–28, 32–33, 45–46, 53–54, 56, 58, 66n18

Chinese food and cooking, 180–81, 184

Chinese immigrants, 25–26, 52, 55

Chinese laborer suspension bill (1882), 27

Chinese language, spoken vs. written, 190–91

"Chinese Problem," public perceptions of, 53

Chinese Relief Association, 56

Chinese schools for Chinese Americans, 189–90

Chinese universities, alumni association chapters in Michigan, 133

Chin Tiki nightclub, Detroit, 62

Cho, Brian, 79

Choi, Serena, 83, 86

Choi Kyu Nam, 134

Chow, Rey, 100–101

Choy, Catherine Ceniza, 174

Choy, Christine, 102

Christian issei (first generation), 146

Chrysler Freeway, 128

Chu, Sarah, 76, 79, 89

Chuang, Allen, 79

Chun, Tank, 75

Chung's restaurant, Detroit, 95n41, 132

CIA (Central Intelligence Agency), 199–200

citizenship, 31–32, 40, 58

Civil Liberties Act (1988), 245

civil rights initiative, JACL, 41–42

civil rights movement, in Ann Arbor, 248

civil rights struggles, Asian Indians and, 138–39

Clarke, Hansen, 296, 298

class and identity, 84

Clemens, Paul, 110

Clemente, Ed, 298

Cobo, Albert, 135

Cold War–era Asian and Asian American histories, 36–43

Colonel Billy (CIA agent), 199

Commission on Graduates of Foreign Nursing Schools (CGFNS) examination, 297

Communist reeducation camps, Vietnam, 272

community gardens, Detroit, 127–28

community organizing, 320

Concerned Citizens of East Lansing, 321–22

Consulate General of Japan, Detroit office, 160

consumerism in America, 275

cooking and food, 153, 180–88

Cooley, Keith, 297

Cordova, Fred, 174

Corktown, in Detroit, 54–55

Council of Asian Pacific Americans, 236

crack, and drug economy, 126

Cruz, Maria, 76–77

cultural competency training, 297, 300–301

cultural differences between Japanese and American ways, 158–59

Korean American Cultural Community Center of Michigan, 136
Korean Americans: adoptees, 305; church as center of life for, 136–37; hostility toward, on the playground, 252–56; in Michigan, 134–38, 178; population in Michigan (1970–2014), 136; settlement after 1965 immigration reforms, 72; war heroes, 137; Youngjean, 217
Korean Christian Church, 136–37
Korean immigrants, 136–37
Korean National Association (Dae-Han-Keuk-Min-Hoe), 135
Korean Presbyterian Church of Metro Detroit, 136
Korean Roman Catholic Church, 137
Koreans, Japanese and, 257
Korean War, 135
Korea Relief Committee of Michigan, 135–36
Korematsu, Fred, 243–44, 302
Kue, Ia Yang, 209
Kue, Nou Soua, 210
Kue, WaChong, 209
Kue, WaNeng, 209
Kumar, Anand, 299
Kumar, Anil, 302
Kuo Min Tang, 56
Kuramoto's, 153
Kurashige, Scott, 130
Kuwahara's grocery store, 146
Kyo-Yu-Kai, Detroit, 146
Kyung Joo, meaning of name, 306

labor, imported, 103
landmarks established by Michigan Historical Marker Program, 20, 46
language and languages: Chinese, spoken vs. written, 190–91; civil war in Bangladesh to preserve, 163–64; English, learning, 273–74; Hmong, creation of writing system for, 202; Japanese Japanese vs. Japanese American, 154–55; Tagalog, 218; Vietnamese Americans and, 277

Language Movement Day, Bangladesh, 164
Lansing Sister Cities Commission, 323
Lao People's Democratic Republic (PDR), 198
Laos: CIA's secret war in, 199–200; culture of Hmong people in, 201–3; flight of Hmong to Thailand, 203–5; persecution of Hmong people, 198–201
Laotian population, spatial distribution of, 16
Lawsin, Emily P., 130, 172, 315–17
League of Revolutionary Black Workers, 105
learning about issues and politics as family tradition, 320
Lee, Chi, 78, 80–81, 84
Lee, Tommie, 60–61
Lee Hwa Sook, 134
Lee Won Cheul, 134
legacy keepers, 131–41
Liggett & Myers, 264–65
Lim, David, 305
Lim, Myung Woo, 83
Lim, Ray, 132
Lim Byung Chik (Ben C. Lim), 134
literacy and communication, as problems for Hmong immigrants, 205–6
Little Caesars Pizza Treat, Detroit, 182
Living for Change (Boggs), 104, 129
Lo, Paul, 210
Lopez, Evangeline "Nena," 172–73
Lopez, Joaquin, 173
Los Angeles Times, 118–19
Lotus Bank Corporation, 140
Lu, Guozhen, 299
Lu-how, 52
Lum, Rona, 299
Luzon Indians (Filipinos), 170

MAASU (Midwest Asian American Students Union), 284
Macomb County, Asian American population in, 15
"Made in Japan" label, connotations of, 263
Magellan, Ferdinand, 220–21

16; Michigan, 66n8. *See also names of specific ethnic groups*
poverty, Asian Americans and, 96n57, 287, 289
Poy, George Lim, 131
Poy, Lee, 32
Prasad, Ananda, 299
pregnancy tests, 311–12
Prentiss, Lisa, 253–55
propaganda, racist, 52–53, 103–4
PSG (Philippine Study Group), 173
PSGSA (PSG Student Association), 173
public service, 319–24
Pusan (Busan), Korea, 304

race: categories in Midwest, 248; as category of social organization, analysis, and contestation, 71–72; dialogue in Wisconsin about black and white, 250; dynamics for Asian Americans, 4; representations of, 86–89
race noticing, defined, 247
racial and ethnic diversity of Detroit, 101
racial differences, whites' reaction to, 78
racial/ethnic distribution in the state and southeast Michigan, 15
racial experiences, spatialized, 82
racial formation, as sociohistorical process, 72
racial identity, 79–80, 228–30, 232
racialization of Asian Americans as foreigners in U.S., 77, 81, 247
racialized ethnics, 78, 89–91
racial socialization, and resilience against racism, 249–50
racial spectrum of black to white, 85
racial tensions, between blacks and whites in 1960s, 60
racism: adoptism and, 227–28; against Chinese Americans, 25–28, 52–53; in court system, 129; defeating, 329; in Detroit, 52, 57; exclusion due to "looking different," 251; experienced by Asian Americans, 250; in Hamtramck, 106;

hate crimes against Asian American, 5–6; against Indian Americans, 138–39; and intrusive questions about transracial adoptees, 225, 227; playground bullying, 246, 252–56; as reflex, 328–29; stereotypes and, 325; unequal censure for slurs, 327–28; at University of Michigan, 96n58
railroad days, 51, 53
reading suggestions, 341–44
Reagan, Ronald, 245
"Rebuilding Detroit: An Alternative to Casino Gambling" (Boggs), 126
Regala, Rosalina and Richard, 173
regional identity, 78, 90
regionalism and the Midwest, defining, 74–77
reincarnation, in beliefs of Hmong people, 203
relations among Asian Americans and other minority groups, 84–85
Religious Society of Friends, 270
Republic of Korea, 137
Research Survey of the Hmong Health Needs Assessment (ACJ), 44
residential segregation, 86
responsibility to others, 319–20
Revolution and Evolution in the 20th Century (Boggs and Boggs), 125
RGL (Royal Lao Government), 198
Rhee Choon Jai, 136
rice porridge *(xi-fan)*, 182
Richardson, Ellen, 122
Riley, Lisa, 79
riots: Bellingham, Washington, 138; Twelfth Street neighborhood, Detroit, 104, 114n11, 125, 132
Rivera, Diego, 119, 143
Rizal Day Banquet and Balls, 173–74
RLA (Royal Lao Army), 199
Robinson, Jackie, 116n35
Rochester, Michigan, growing up Asian American in, 216–21
Rog Pim Pab (Mad War), 198